D0821485

Growing Up in France

How did French people write about their own childhood and youth between the 1760s and the 1930s? Colin Heywood argues that this was a critical period in the history of young people, as successive generations moved from the relatively stable and hierarchical society of the Ancien Régime to a more fluid one produced by the industrial and democratic revolutions of the period. The main sources he uses are first-hand accounts of growing up: letters, diaries, childhood reminiscences and autobiographies. The book's first section considers cultural constructions of childhood and adolescence, and representations of growing up. The second considers the process of growing up among family and friends, the third the experience of moving out into the wider world, via education, work, political activity and marriage. This unique account will appeal to historians of childhood and adolescence, as well as social and cultural historians.

COLIN HEYWOOD is Reader in Modern French History at the University of Nottingham. His previous publications include *The Development of the French Economy, 1750–1914* (1995) and *A History of Childhood* (2001).

Growing Up in France

From the Ancien Régime *to the Third Republic*

Colin Heywood

CAMBRIDGE UNIVERSITY PRESS

CAMBRIDGE UNIVERSITY PRESS
Cambridge, New York, Melbourne, Madrid, Cape Town, Singapore, São Paulo

Cambridge University Press
The Edinburgh Building, Cambridge CB2 2RU, UK

Published in the United States of America by Cambridge University Press, New York

www.cambridge.org
Information on this title: www.cambridge.org/9780521868693

© Colin Heywood 2007

First published 2007

Printed in the United Kingdom at the University Press, Cambridge

A catalogue record for this publication is available from the British Library

ISBN-13 978-0-521-86869-3 hardback
ISBN-10 0-521-86869-6 hardback

To Olena

Contents

Contents

Illustrations

Acknowledgements

I would like to thank librarians at the Bibliothèque nationale, and archivists in the various Departmental Archives that I visited, for their efficient and helpful service. I am grateful to Nottingham University for providing the funding to launch this scheme, and to the British Academy for awarding me two Small Research Grants, which allowed me to spend time in France in archives and libraries. I am also pleased to acknowledge the support I received from the Arts and Humanities Research Council, in the form of Research Leave, which allowed me time to write up the project. I would like to make clear the help I received from various colleagues along the way, notably Professor Michelle Perrot for advice on launching the project, Dr Julia Barrow for assistance with medieval history, M. Serge Chassagne for local knowledge in Lyon, and Dr Diane Cunningham for references on attachment theory, not to mention constructive criticism from research seminars at the Universities of Nottingham and Aberystwyth, and at the Institute of Historical Research (the French History seminar). Thanks also to Benoît and Magali van Reeth in Lyon and Jean Jolivet in Plozevet for hospitality while I was 'on the road' as a researcher. Above all, I would like to thank my wife Olena Heywood for reading (and rereading) the manuscript, and for moral support all through.

Introduction

How French people tried to make sense of their childhood and adolescence in past centuries remains something of a mystery. That this should be the case for the medieval and early modern periods is hardly surprising, given that so few contemporaries chose to write about their formative years. For centuries, the majority of clerics maintained a low opinion of the young. St Augustine (354–430) led the way with a dismal image of his own past, his influential *Confessions* lingering on his sins rather than his virtues during the first stages of his life. He at least gave some account of the suffering and humiliation of his boyhood, and the 'surfeit of hell's pleasures' during his teens.[1] Other authorities preferred to ignore entirely those they saw as small creatures wallowing in sinfulness and deficient in both intellectual and moral qualities: the child was 'a poor sighing animal, starting his life in torment', as the twelfth-century monk William of Saint-Thierry put it.[2] They assumed that it was reason that separated mankind from the animal kingdom, and so only took seriously those who had progressed from the early chaotic years to adulthood. A seventeenth-century Jansenist from Port Royal wrote that 'I only wish to count [life] from when one starts to be moved by reason, which normally does not happen before the age of twenty.' The view of the young as deficient was by no means confined to the more austere wings of Christianity. The great Catholic orator and prelate Bossuet (1627–1704) lamented that much of his allotted three-score-and-ten years would count for nothing. Sleep he considered similar to death, childhood merely the life of a beast, and his own adolescence best erased.[3] Similarly, fictional autobiographies written by members of the laity during the seventeenth and

---

[1] Saint Augustine, *Confessions*, transl. R. S. Pine-Coffin (Harmondsworth: Penguin, 1961), books I to IV.

[2] Pierre Riché and Danièle Alexandre-Bidon, *L'Enfance au Moyen Age* (Paris: Editions du Seuil, 1994), p. 22.

[3] *Discours sur les passions de l'amour* (n.d.) and Bossuet, *Méditations sur la brièveté de la vie* (1695), cited in Georges Snyders, *La Pédagogie en France aux XVIIe et XVIIIe siècles* (Paris: Presses Universitaires de France, 1965), pp. 190 and 192 respectively.

eighteenth centuries generally had little to say about the early years of life. The authors of these memoir novels found childhood uninteresting, and indeed 'simply unimportant'. They assumed that one childhood was much like another: a long period when the individual personality was only gradually forming.[4] There was, however, a counter-current in ecclesiastical thinking on childhood that emphasized its purity and innocence. This was a common theme in monastic literature, notably during the period of revival in the twelfth and thirteenth centuries. The author of the *Life of Stephen of Obazine* wrote that the simplicity and pure ignorance of children brought them close to divine knowledge and angelic purity, because they lacked the 'impure wiles' of the worldly.[5] The suggestion from Philippe Ariès that there was a thousand-year silence on childhood after the fall of the Roman Empire now finds few takers. Nonetheless, the claim by Jean-Jacques Rousseau (1712–78) in the mid-eighteenth century that 'childhood is unknown' had some justification.[6]

Come the modern period, childhood and adolescence slowly emerge from the shadows. Leading figures in the Enlightenment, such as John Locke (1632–1704) and Rousseau, found a ready audience for their positive image of the child. By the nineteenth century, some people thought of childhood as the most blessed period of life, and the child as a source of intuitive wisdom lacking in the adult. Poets as diverse as Victor Hugo and Jean Cocteau linked the poetic imagination to childhood. The child hero made a belated but striking entry into French literature in novels such as *Jack* (1876) by Alphonse Daudet and *L'Enfant* (1879) by Jules Vallès.[7] Adolescence in its turn came to fascinate writers like André Gide,

---

[4] Philip Stewart, 'The Child Comes of Age', *Yale French Studies*, 40 (1968), 134–41 (136–7); Adrian P. L. Kempton, 'The Theme of Childhood in French Eighteenth-Century Memoir Novels', *Studies on Voltaire and the Eighteenth Century*, 132 (1975), 205–25.

[5] *Vie d'Etienne d'Aubuzon* cited by Riché and Alexandre-Bidon, *L'Enfance*, p. 25. See also William J. Bouwma, 'Christian Adulthood', *Daedalus* (Spring 1976), 77–92; Shulamith Shahar, *Childhood in the Middle Ages* (London: Routledge, 1990), ch. 1; James A. Schulz, *The Knowledge of Childhood in the German Middle Ages, 1100–1350* (Philadelphia: University of Pennsylvania Press, 1995), pp. 244–51; and David Hunt, *Parents and Children in History: The Psychology of Family Life in Early Modern France* (New York: Harper Torchbooks, 1972).

[6] Philippe Ariès, *Centuries of Childhood* (Harmondsworth: Penguin, 1962); Jean-Jacques Rousseau, *Emile, or On Education* (London: Penguin, 1979 (1762)), p. 33.

[7] Max Primault, Henry Lhong and Jean Malrieu, *Terres de l'enfance: le mythe de l'enfance dans la littérature contemporaine* (Paris: Presses Universitaires de France, 1961), passim; Aimé Dupuy, *Un personnage nouveau du roman français: l'enfant* (Paris: Hachette, 1931), Introduction; Victor Toursch, *L'Enfant français à la fin du XIXe siècle, d'après ses principaux romanciers* (Paris: Les Presses modernes, 1939), passim; Rosemary Lloyd, *The Land of Lost Content: Children and Childhood in Nineteenth-Century French Literature* (Oxford: Clarendon Press, 1992), pp. 3–5; Alphonse Daudet, *Jack* (Paris: Flammarion, 1973 (1876)); Jules Vallès, *L'Enfant* (Paris: Livre de poche, 1985 (1879)).

Jean Cocteau and Colette during the late nineteenth and early twentieth centuries.[8] Rousseau also launched the notion that what happened to the individual during childhood shaped the rest of his or her life. Following the success of his *Confessions* (1781), authors of autobiographies began almost as a matter of routine to include an account of their childhood. Readers now wanted to know about key influences on a personality, about choices made or refused during the early years.[9] In the twentieth century, Sigmund Freud (1856–1939) famously reinforced this line, writing that 'analytic experience has convinced us of the complete truth of the common assertion that the child is psychologically father of the man and that the events of his first years are of paramount importance for his whole subsequent life'.[10] The welfare of the young also became a matter of state, as governments in France became concerned over the threat of 'depopulation' and the 'degeneration of the race'. A whole raft of experts, drawn from the worlds of medicine, education, the Catholic Church and psychology, gave advice supposedly for the benefit of children and adolescents. Finally, reading and writing came to occupy a large amount of people's time. From the late eighteenth century there survives a growing volume of personal diaries, family correspondence, memoirs, autobiographies and reminiscences of childhood. To begin with, the written word was largely the preserve of the nobility and the middle classes: on the eve of the French Revolution, according to the Maggiolo Enquiry, over a half of all bridegrooms and nearly three quarters of all brides were unable to sign their names. However near-universal literacy from the end of the nineteenth century enabled artisans, workers and peasants to begin penetrating the literary circuit.[11]

This outpouring of material has provided the sources for a range of innovative works on issues affecting the young in France. One might cite histories of childbirth, infant welfare, child abandonment, the

---

[8] George Boas, *The Cult of Childhood* (London: Warburg Institute, 1966), pp. 8, 101–2; Marina Bethlenfalvay, *Les Visages de l'enfant dans la littérature française du XIXe siècle: esquisse d'une typologie* (Geneva: Droz, 1979), p. 9; Justin O'Brien, *The Novel of Adolescence in France: The Study of a Literary Theme* (New York: Columbia University Press, 1937), pp. 8–9.

[9] See Gérard Lahouati, 'L'Invention de l'enfance: le statut du souvenir d'enfance dans quelques autobiographies du XVIIIe siècle', and Christine Van Rogger Andreucci, 'Larbaud, Proust, Céline: points et contrepoints pour un mythe de l'enfance', both in Evelyne Berriot-Salvadore and Isabelle Pebay-Clottes (eds.), *Autour de l'enfance* (Biarritz: Atlantica, 1999), pp. 163–90 and 211–35.

[10] S. Freud, *An Outline of Psycho-Analysis* (1949), cited by Ann Clarke and Alan Clarke, *Early Experience and the Life Path* (London: Jessica Kingsley, 2000), p. 12.

[11] The most comprehensive study of the spread of literacy in France remains François Furet and Jacques Ozouf, *Reading and Writing: Literacy in France from Calvin to Jules Ferry* (Cambridge: Cambridge University Press, 1982).

wet-nursing business, child labour reform, education, reformatories for juvenile delinquents, *colonies de vacances*, organized youth movements and concepts of adolescence.[12] However, it is a common complaint that histories of childhood tend to leave out the children. At best the mass of juveniles hover anonymously on the edge of the frame as victims, or suitable cases for treatment. In other words, the existing historiography generally adopts an adult-centred approach, revealing in some depth how adults in the past conceptualized childhood and adolescence, and what they did for (or to) children. Much of it ends up as a history of modern welfare institutions for young people. Where it has hesitated to venture until very recently is towards a more child-centred approach, engaging, for example, with what Richard N. Coe called 'the authentic *small* world of the young child', or the restlessness of youth.[13] Yet every single French man and woman who survived to maturity spent years passing through the successive stages of life ordained by their particular background, experiencing the often searing impact of, among others, relatives, friends, teachers, doctors, priests and employers. Why should there be something of a blind spot in history for first-hand accounts of such an extended period of everyone's life?[14] It surely stems from two sources: a reluctance by most historians to take seriously the concerns of young people, and a general wariness of notoriously 'suspect' sources such as diaries and autobiographies.

[12] From a vast literature, one might cite works such as J. Gélis, M. Laget and M.-F. Morel, *Entrer dans la vie: naissances et enfances dans la France traditionnelle* (Paris: Gallimard/Julliard, 1978); Rachel Fuchs, *Abandoned Children: Foundlings and Child Welfare in Nineteenth-Century France* (Albany: State University of New York Press, 1984); George D. Sussman, *Selling Mother's Milk: The Wet-Nursing Business in France, 1715–1914* (Urbana: University of Illinois Press, 1982); Robert Gildea, *Education in Provincial France, 1800–1914* (Oxford: Oxford University Press, 1983); Catherine Rollet-Echalier, *La Politique à l'égard de la petite enfance sous la Troisième République* (Paris: Presses Universitaires de France, 1990); Lee Shai Weissbach, *Child Labor Reform in Nineteenth-Century France: Assuring the Future Harvest* (Baton Rouge: Louisiana State University Press, 1989); Jean-Noël Luc, *L'Invention du jeune enfant au XIXe siècle: de la salle d'asile à l'école maternelle* (Paris: Belin, 1997); Yves Roumajon, *Enfants perdus, enfants punis: histoire de la jeunesse délinquante en France: huit siècles de controverses* (Paris: Robert Laffont, 1989); Laura Lee Downs, *Childhood in the Promised Land: Working-Class Movements and the Colonies de Vacances in France, 1880–1960* (Durham: Duke University Press, 2002); David M. Pomfret, *Young People and the European City: Age Relations in Nottingham and Saint-Etienne, 1890–1914* (Aldershot: Ashgate, 2004); and Agnès Thiercé, *Histoire de l'adolescence, 1850–1914* (Paris: Belin, 1999).
[13] Richard N. Coe, *When the Grass was Taller: Autobiography and the Experience of Childhood* (New Haven: Yale University Press, 1984), pp. 35–6.
[14] An excellent pioneering survey, which made some use of novels and autobiographies (with some tendency to mix the two), was Maurice Crubellier, *L'Enfance et la jeunesse dans la société française, 1800–1950* (Paris: Armand Colin, 1979). This work is indebted to its comprehensive outline of its subject. A more recent and up-dated survey is Catherine Rollet, *Les Enfants au XIXe siècle* (Paris: Hachette, 2001).

For much of the twentieth century, historians and social scientists simply did not consider young people worth studying on their own terms. They preferred to remain on familiar territory, dominated by the adult male, such as political systems, wars and class structures, rather than the more humdrum domain of women and children. They evidently found it difficult to cope with the inevitably 'trivial' concerns of children in particular, for it is indeed no mean challenge for a writer to convey to the reader 'the supreme significance of the unspeakably, the absurdly trivial'.[15] As far as treatment of the young was concerned, all that mattered was their socialization and development, in preparation for the all-important stage of full adulthood. In other words, children were treated as adults-in-the-making, rather than as children in their own right.[16] Only in the past few years have scholars in history and the social sciences begun to consider this latter approach. Moreover, there were doubts for a long time among historians over whether there was much in the way of source material for any such study. The 'sentiments approach' to the history of the family, and its focus on parent–child relations, has proved vulnerable to the charge that its evidence is too subjective and fragmentary to allow rigorous documentation of change over time in various contexts. Above all, what was happening beyond the literate minority that produced most of the personal records on which such an approach relies has remained obscure. Even a champion of this 'school', during the 1970s, could loftily dismiss history based on literary sources as merely anecdotal, a haphazard collection of 'charming little stories'.[17] For as long as quantitative methods held sway in social history, it was tempting to opt instead for a demographic or a 'household economics' approach, using 'hard' data from sources such as census lists.[18] However, in the late twentieth century, for many historians the sheen began to wear off the statistics, meaning appeared more interesting than function, and cultural history came to the fore. A number of historians have incorporated personal case studies into their work, providing a 'grass-roots' perspective on certain aspects of growing up.[19]

---

[15] Coe, *When the Grass was Taller*, p. xii.

[16] See, for example, Arlene Skolnick, 'Introduction: Rethinking Childhood', in Skolnick (ed.), *Rethinking Childhood: Perspectives on Development and Society* (Boston: Little, Brown and Company, 1976), pp. 1–15 (p. 11); Anne-Marie Ambert, 'Sociology of Childhood: The Place of Children in North American Sociology', *Sociological Studies of Child Development*, 1 (1986), 11–31; Hans Peter Dreitzel (ed.), *Childhood and Socialization* (New York: Macmillan, 1973).

[17] Edward Shorter, *The Making of the Modern Family* (London: Fontana, 1976), p. 18.

[18] See Michael Anderson, *Approaches to the History of the Western Family, 1500–1914* (Cambridge: Cambridge University Press, 1980), ch. 3.

[19] Excellent examples include Mark Motley, *Becoming a French Aristocrat: The Education of the Court Nobility, 1580–1715* (Princeton: Princeton University Press, 1990); Eric

In the background, inspired in part by the pioneering work of the historian Philippe Ariès in his *Centuries of Childhood* (1962), was the emergence of the movement known as the 'new social studies of childhood'. Drawing on the work of anthropologists, sociologists and psychologists as well as historians, it has provided both inspiration and theoretical support for this study.[20] Three of its propositions stand out for our purposes. In the first place, there is the call to give young people a more active role in their own history than has usually been the case. Instead of depicting them simply as passive receptacles of adult teaching, they gain a role as agents in determining their own existence.[21] Research indicates that even infants are capable of manipulating and interacting with adults, despite the fact that the overall power relationship is heavily weighted towards the latter. The sociologist William A. Corsaro set out to show how children 'negotiate, share, and create culture with adults and each other'.[22] The upshot is that in this study the young move close to centre stage than is usual.

Mension-Rigau, *L'Enfance au château: l'éducation familiale des élites françaises au vingtième siècle* (Paris: Rivages, 1990); Denis Bertholet, *Les Français par eux-mêmes, 1815–1885* (Paris: Olivier Orban, 1991); Mary Jo Maynes, *Taking the Hard Road: Life Course in French and German Workers' Autobiographies in the Era of Industrialization* (Chapel Hill: University of North Carolina Press, 1995); Michelle Perrot, 'Roles and Characters', in Philippe Ariès and Georges Duby (eds.), *A History of Private Life*, vol. IV, pp. 167–239; Luc, *L'Invention du jeune enfant au XIXe siècle*; Jean-Louis Lenhof, 'L'Enfant et les mutations du travail industriel en France au XIXe siècle: le regard des contemporains', in Jean-Pierre Bardet, Jean-Noël Luc, Isabelle Robin-Romero and Catherine Rollet (eds.), *Lorsque l'enfant grandit: entre dépendance et autonomie* (Paris: Presses de l'Université de Paris-Sorbonne, 2003), pp. 733–50; and Gabrielle Houbre, *La Discipline de l'amour: l'éducation sentimentale des filles et des garçons à l'âge du romantisme* (Paris: Plon, 1997). For comparative purposes, one might cite Harvey J. Graff, *Conflicting Paths: Growing Up in America* (Cambridge, MA: Harvard University Press, 1995); Anna Davin, *Growing Up Poor: Home, School and Street in London, 1870–1914* (London: Rivers Oram Press, 1996); and Rudolf Dekker, *Children, Memory and Autobiography in Holland: From the Golden Age to Romanticism* (London: Macmillan, 1999.

[20] Alan Prout and Allison James, 'A New Paradigm for the Sociology of Childhood? Provenance, Promise and Problems', in James and Prout (eds.), *Constructing and Reconstructing Childhood: Contemporary Issues in the Sociological Study of Childhood* (London: Falmer Press, 1990), pp. 7–34; and Allison James, Chris Jenks and Alan Prout, *Theorizing Childhood* (Cambridge: Polity, 1998).

[21] This is the theme of recent works in American historiography, such as of Elliott West, *Growing Up with the Country: Childhood on the Far West Frontier* (Albuquerque: University of New Mexico Press, 1989) and Elliott West and Paula Petrick (eds.), *Small Worlds: Children and Adolescents in America, 1850–1950* (Lawrence: University Press of Kansas, 1992).

[22] William A. Corsaro, *The Sociology of Childhood* (Thousand Oaks, CA: Pine Forge Press, 1997), p. 18. See also Prout and James, 'New Paradigm', p. 8; Jens Qvortrup, 'Childhood Matters: An Introduction', in Qvortrup et al. (eds.), *Childhood Matters: Social Theory, Practice and Politics* (Aldershot: Avebury, 1994), pp. 1–23 (pp. 3–5); and Berry Mayall, *Towards a Sociology for Children: Thinking from Children's Lives* (Buckingham: Open University Press, 2002), pp. 20–1.

Secondly, there is the insistence on analysing the age category of child-hood (and of adolescence) according to such variables as gender, social background and religious affiliation.[23] This means that one should be wary of broad generalizations about the experiences of children and ado-lescents in modern France, given the huge disparities in areas such as wealth and education. Indeed, it is the diversity of childhoods in dif-ferent periods and places that stands out in recent scholarship, rather than any universal experience.[24] Hence one needs to bear in mind the particular configuration of French influences on the process of growing up during the eighteenth, nineteenth and twentieth centuries. At vari-ous points, this work will draw attention to a number of these, including the persistence of a large agricultural sector in the economy, the high proportion of married women in the active population (56 per cent of married women worked in France in 1906, compared to 9.6 per cent in England in 1911[25]), the widespread resort to paid wet-nurses by workers and the lower-middle classes in the big cities during the eighteenth and nineteenth centuries, the early resort to birth control within marriage, the concern among ruling elites with 'depopulation', the long battle between Catholics and Republicans for the control of education, and the polar-ization of politics between the Left and the Right in the wake of the 1789 Revolution.

Finally, and relatedly, there is the assertion that childhood and ado-lescence are to be understood as a social construction. That is to say, the search for the 'real' or the 'essential' child and adolescent is con-sidered futile, given the huge variety of definitions we are now aware of in past societies and in other countries today. As William Kessen put it in 1979, anyone adopting a positivist approach now faces the nightmare 'that the child is essentially and eternally a cultural invention and that the variety of the child's definition is not the removable error of an incom-plete science'.[26] Treating the concept of the child or the adolescent as a 'moveable feast', however, raises the problem of avoiding the extremes of

---

[23] Prout and James, 'New Paradigm', p. 8.
[24] The starting point here was Margaret Mead and Martha Wolfenstein (eds.), *Childhood in Contemporary Cultures* (Chicago: Chicago University Press, 1955).
[25] Louise A. Tilly and Joan W. Scott, *Women, Work and Family* (New York and London: Routledge, 1989), p. 196.
[26] William Kessen, 'The American Child and Other Cultural Inventions', *American Psychologist*, 34 (1979), 815–20. See also William Kessen, *The Child* (New York: John Wiley, 1965); Frank S. Kessel and Alexander W. Siegel (eds.), *The Child and Other Cultural Inventions* (New York: Praeger, 1983); C. Philip Hwang, Michael E. Lamb and Irving E. Sigel (eds.), *Images of Childhood* (Mahwah, NJ: Lawrence Erlbaum, 1996); and Robert A. Levine, 'Child Psychology and Anthropology: An Environmental View', in Catherine Panter-Brick (ed.), *Biosocial Perspectives on Children* (Cambridge: Cambridge University Press, 1998), pp. 102–30.

'cultural' and 'biological' determinism. It is quite possible to study these stages of life in evolutionary and biological terms. Thus Barry Bogin defines childhood as 'the period following weaning, when the youngster still depends on older people for feeding and protection', and adolescence as the stage between puberty and the attainment of adult stature. He sees childhood as an evolutionary innovation, unique to *Homo sapiens*, that enabled human parents to raise a higher proportion of their offspring to maturity than any other species. This sociobiological perspective left him open to the criticism that he ignored the social and cultural influences on childhood.[27] Towards the other end of the spectrum, Allison James asserts that childhood is a social and cultural phenomenon: 'biological development must be seen as contextualising, rather than unequivocally determining, children's experience'. This provokes questions on the relationship between the biological base and the child's life. 'What', asked Martin Richards, 'marks out those parts of the child that are biological from those which are social?'[28]

It is not easy to provide an answer, but one can hardly avoid some reference to the biological realities that underpin the adaptability of young people to their cultural environment.[29] One should be aware that child psychology has always suffered from a tendency to make universal claims for its findings when the basis for its empirical observations have come from a narrow, largely American, range of environments. All the same, in the present state of knowledge, there are grounds for thinking that during the first twelve months or so of its life an infant has a 'biological predisposition' to develop a special relationship with a caregiver: usually, but not invariably, the biological mother. According to the psychologist L. Alan Sroufe, the first sign of an attachment relationship, distress at separation, 'shows a strikingly similar course across cultures with a peak onset commonly seen at about 9 months'.[30] Between eighteen and thirty-six months, there is a period when the acquisition of language is at its most rapid. More generally, as the structure of the central nervous system matures during the first twelve years of life, it permits the release of abilities such as walking, talking and self-awareness. Hence every culture

[27] Barry Bogin, 'Evolutionary and Biological Aspects of Childhood', and Martin Richards, 'The Meeting of Nature and Nurture and the Development of Children: Some Conclusions', in Panter-Brick, *Biosocial Perspectives*, pp. 10–44 (pp. 10, 21–3, 30 and 38), and pp. 131–45 (pp. 132–3) respectively.

[28] Allison James, 'From the Child's Point of View: Issues in the Social Construction of Childhood', and Richards, 'The Meeting', in Panter-Brick, *Biosocial Perspectives*, pp. 44–65 (p. 47) and p. 135 respectively.

[29] See below, especially ch. 3.

[30] L. Alan Sroufe, *Emotional Development: The Organization of Emotional Life in the Early Years* (Cambridge: Cambridge University Press, 1996), p. 173.

has some notion of the stages of life, linked more-or-less precisely to age gradations. However, their number and meanings are subject to considerable variation.[31] In the final analysis, one evidently needs to strike a balance between biological and environmental influences on growing up. For a historical study such as this the emphasis is bound to be on the latter. The inclination here is to follow the sociological line that children and adolescents everywhere are immature biologically, but where each society differs in the ways that it interprets and attaches meaning to this immaturity.[32] All this of course takes one back to adult discourses rather than to the young themselves. It remains important as a starting point for this work, given that prevailing conceptions of the child and the adolescent sooner or later had an impact on the way people treated their young in any given society. Robert E. Levine, for example, notes that 'parental practices and the parents' organization of the child's environment are goal-driven, and the goals are largely derived from conceptions of care, infancy and childhood embedded in local cultural ideologies'.[33]

By focusing systematically on what French people had to say about their early years, either at the time in letters and diaries, or retrospectively in autobiographies, childhood reminiscences and oral history projects, this study aims to harness this 'new paradigm' to move on from the existing orientation of the historiography. It gives voice to a sample of young people from all levels of French society, rather than the usual cast of famous reformers, politicians and other adults in positions of authority. It analyses the way the individual child or adolescent reacted to the world around them, rather than the socio-political forces underlying legal and institutional developments. And it takes an interest in the later stages of childhood and adolescence, rather than the intensively studied areas of childbirth and infancy.[34] This is not to deny the importance for the young of the institutional framework in which they grew up. Hence what follows balances the somewhat random testimony of individuals with the

---

[31] This section relies on Levine, 'Child Psychology'; Jerome Kagan, *The Nature of the Child* (New York: Basic Books, 1984); and Josephine Klein, *Our Need for Others and its Roots in Infancy* (London and New York: Tavistock Publications, 1987), ch. 6. It is also influenced by Nicholas Tucker, *What is a Child?* (London: Fontana, 1977); Emily Cahan, Jay Mechling, Brian Sutton-Smith and Sheldon H. White, 'The Elusive Historical Child: Ways of Knowing the Child of History and Psychology', in Glen H. Elder Jr, John Modell and Ross D. Parke (eds.), *Children in Time and Place: Developmental and Historical Insights* (Cambridge: Cambridge University Press, 1993), pp. 192–223; and Chris Jenks, *Childhood* (London: Routledge, 1996).
[32] Prout and James, 'New Paradigm', p. 7.   [33] Levine, 'Child Psychology', p. 113.
[34] On the emphasis in current studies on such topics as the heavy mortality suffered by infants under the *ancien régime*, and the little rituals designed to protect mothers and babies in these difficult circumstances, see Bardet et al., 'Introduction' to *Lorsque l'enfant grandit*, pp. 6–28 (p. 6).

context of changes affecting, say, the family, the school system, child labour legislation and marriage customs in modern France.

In a study of this kind one is bound to ask whether conditions for young people improved or deteriorated over the long term in modern France. The general impression that lingers in the existing historical literature is a positive one of progress from philanthropic and state intervention. Given the numerous dimensions to young people's existence, any comprehensive answer is in fact likely to be complex. A commonsense view would suggest that things have improved considerably for the young from the middle of the eighteenth century. Children and adolescents have taken their share of increased affluence with, on average, better food, clothing and housing, more varied leisure activities, improved medical treatment and more extensive education and training. Their interests have featured prominently in charitable initiatives and the development of the welfare state, from child protection agencies through to universities. The evidence of progress is hard to dispute when one considers such measurable gains as lower infant and child mortality, and rising literacy rates.[35] An opposing tendency in the literature, however, highlights various drawbacks for the young in all this progress. Philippe Ariès betrayed a certain sympathy for medieval practice in suggesting that young people enjoyed a relatively carefree existence before the discipline of the school system began to clamp down on an increasing proportion of them during the sixteenth and seventeenth centuries.[36] The Marxist interpretation of history implies an increasingly 'rational exploitation' of the young in the schools and workshops of capitalist society during the nineteenth century.[37] The persistence of child labour in the twenty-first century and critiques of mass schooling militate against easy optimism on contemporary society.[38] This study veers towards a 'swings and roundabouts' approach, arguing that there was a certain trade-off between the material benefits brought by economic development and the pressures on young people in an increasingly mobile society.

---

[35] Catherine Rollet and Patrice Bordelais, 'Infant Mortality in France, 1750–1950: Evaluation and Perspectives', in Carlo A. Corsini and Pier Paolo Viazzo (eds.), *The Decline of Infant Mortality in Europe, 1800–1950* (Florence: UNICEF, 1993), pp. 51–70; François Furet and Jacques Ozouf, 'The Spread of Literacy in France: A One-Way Ride', in Furet and Ozouf, *Reading and Writing*, pp. 5–57.

[36] Ariès, *Centuries of Childhood*, ch. 10 and p. 397; Adrian Wilson, 'The Infancy of the History of Childhood: An Appraisal of Philippe Ariès', *History and Theory*, 19 (1980), 132–53 (134).

[37] The Marxist critique is forcefully made in Roger Magraw, *A History of the French Working Class*, vol. I, *The Age of Artisan Revolution, 1851–71* (Oxford: Blackwell, 1992), pp. 9–11.

[38] See, for example, Bernard Schlemmer (ed.), *The Exploited Child*, transl. Philip Dresner (London: Zed Books, 2005).

What lay behind such contradictory influences on the process of grow-ing up in France, or, for that matter, in other Western nations?[39] Most in evidence was the changing nature of the demands made on the young as the relatively stable and hierarchical society of the *ancien régime* gradually succumbed to the industrial and democratic revolutions of the modern period. The contention here is that the period running from the mid-dle of the eighteenth century to the middle of the twentieth was critical for this transition in France. To begin with, when most people spent the whole of their lives in the same village or town, their existence revolved around the family, the local community, and various rituals and proscrip-tions arising from their religious beliefs. The status they had in society was largely inherited from their parents, and the authority they acknowledged a matter of obedience to tradition. Childhood was, in effect, an 'appren-ticeship in the conduct of a caste'.[40] Later, a more dynamic, urban-ized type of society encouraged people to move around the country, to identify with 'imagined communities' such as those of class and nation, to think of themselves as individuals rather than as part of a lineage, and to adopt secularized values. This meant that people had to achieve their own status, which might be different from that of their parents or their neighbours, and they were expected to use their own reasoning or conscience to question authority.

The results, this book will suggest, were ambivalent for young people. On the one hand, the new society gradually lifted people above a haz-ardous, near subsistence-level existence, and gave them more opportu-nity for upward social mobility. They could escape the tyrannical grip of a father with property to pass on, the narrow horizons of the popular culture, the stifling atmosphere of a village or small town and the daily grind of life on a farm. In short, childhood and adolescence could be a period of choice and experimentation. On the other hand, there was a downside to these exhilarating possibilities. The school system, for example, might provide a passport to a new life for some, but a reminder to others that they had no hope of escaping from their lowly station in life. The modern period has pressured the young into making a series of critical decisions for their future that were barely in evidence before. Adolescents in particular needed a certain competence, or, to adopt the

---

[39] This paragraph is indebted to Skolnick, 'Rethinking Childhood', p. 11; Coe, *When the Grass was Taller*, p. 274; Jacques Gélis, 'The Child: From Anonymity to Individuality', in Roger Chartier (ed.), *Passions of the Renaissance*, vol. III of Philippe Ariès and Georges Duby, *A History of Private Life* (Cambridge, MA: Harvard University Press, 1989), pp. 309–25.

[40] Jean-Pierre Cuvillier, 'L'Enfant dans la tradition féodale germanique', *Senefiance*, 9 (1980), 45–59 (49).

jargon of the social sciences, 'planful competence'. That is to say, they required 'the ability to think through career choices so as to make more realistic choices in education, occupation and marriage, or – conversely – to refrain from unwise choices in these domains of life'.[41]

This study relies on a varied range of primary sources from libraries and archives. Its core is provided by the first-hand accounts of individual experiences in the 'ego documents', including famous ones such as those from Jean-Jacques Rousseau and Colette, and obscure cases unearthed in local archives. Beyond these, it uses material such as treatises on the child, child rearing and education; novels of childhood and adolescence; folklore studies; and official investigations into organized youth movements. Historians have used the title 'growing up' to cover very different approaches to the subject of childhood and youth.[42] The focus here is on the stages of life between the ages of about seven and twenty-five. The former was the traditional age of reason, and an approximate start to periods that can be recalled in some detail later in life. At the other end, 'civil puberty', defined as the point at which a male is able to love a woman faithfully, support a family and participate in the political order, loomed from the mid-twenties onwards. For women, marriage marked the end of adolescence, or, as the traditional saying went, she might 'coiffer sainte Catherine', with a little ritual marking her arrival at the age of twenty-five without marrying.[43]

The structure of the book, then, is designed to throw light on the historical experience of childhood and adolescence in France between the 1760s and the 1930s. It is divided into three parts. The first part is mainly concerned to establish the foundations for a study of growing up in France. It considers the value of certain types of literary sources for historians, sometimes known as *écritures du moi* ('ego documents'), drawing in particular on the large body of theoretical work on autobiographies. It reveals the growing interest in childhood and adolescence in France from the eighteenth century onwards, in novels, poetry, paintings and philosophical works. It also considers what people thought about turning points in life as they grew up, both from the disinterested perspective of the theorist, and from the personal one of individuals looking back on

---

[41] Luc Goossens, 'Transitions to Adulthood: Developmental Factors', in Martine Corijn and Erik Klijzing (eds.), *Transitions to Adulthood in Europe* (Dordrecht: Kluwer, 2001), pp. 27–42 (p. 34).

[42] One might contrast the approaches in Barbara Hanawalt, *Growing Up in Medieval London: The Experience of Childhood in History* (New York: Oxford University Press, 1993); Davin, *Growing Up Poor*; and Graff, *Conflicting Paths*.

[43] Allan Bloom, 'Introduction' to Jean-Jacques Rousseau, *Emile, or On Education* (London: Penguin, 1991), pp. 3–29 (p. 17); Philippe Lejeune, *Le Moi des demoiselles: enquête sur le journal de jeune fille* (Paris: Seuil, 1993), p. 16.

their own experiences. This section therefore explores theories on the Ages of Man, the folklore model of changes in status through successive *rites de passage*, and the more random impact on individuals of what they perceived as key events in their lives. The second part of the book focuses on the experience of growing up among family and friends. It begins by outlining briefly the demographic context of changing family forms in modern France. It then documents relationships young people enjoyed or endured with their families, servants, neighbours and friends. The final part of the work assembles material on the gradual move towards independence beyond the home and the peer group. It investigates such matters as education and training, the formation of regional, religious and political identities, early sexual experiences and the choice of a marriage partner. The general aim, as indicated already, is to bring out the contrasting experiences of the young according to their various backgrounds, and to grant them some scope for negotiating their own path through life.

Part I

Representations of childhood and adolescence in France

1 'Ego documents' and the French historian in the twenty-first century

When Jean-Jacques Rousseau published the first part of his *Confessions* in 1782, critics were shocked and disappointed by its intimate tone. One of them stated that he was not keen to find out whether Horace and Virgil were beaten at school, had pissed into a cooking pot, stolen apples and other such 'twaddle' that the good citizen of Geneva was determined to recount in his own case. Perhaps, as the historian Catherine Doroszczuk observed, readers as well as authors needed an 'apprenticeship' in this type of material after the long silence on childhood.[1] The nineteenth and twentieth centuries certainly brought a wealth of 'ego documents', that is to say texts in which 'an author writes about his or her own acts, thoughts and feelings'.[2] A study such as this is nonetheless bound to confront the vexed question of whether the sources available will allow the historian to delve very far into the private lives of the young. Letters, diaries and autobiographies have plenty to say about how individuals construed their experiences of childhood and adolescence, but none can be taken as a straightforward 'window on reality'.

One can start by distinguishing those sources produced by the young themselves, and those written by adults reflecting on their early years. On the whole, young people tend to leave few written records, for the obvious reasons that many in the past were unable to write, and the thoughts of those who could were not considered worth preserving. Nonetheless, the historian can pry into diaries and correspondence written by young people in the past. What could be more revealing, as Béatrice Didier put it, than diaries written by adolescents convinced that they were brim full of ideas and feelings that no one was capable of understanding?[3] At the same time, the notion that one can discover the independent and authentic voice of the child or adolescent proves fanciful, not to say absurd, for

---

[1] Catherine Doroszczuk, 'Le Récit impudique: réception du récit d'enfance à la fin du XVIIIe siècle', *Cahiers de sémiotique textuelle*, 12 (1988), 9–20.
[2] Rudolf Dekker, *Childhood, Memory and Autobiography in Holland: From the Golden Age to Romanticism* (London: Macmillan, 2000), p. 12.
[3] Béatrice Didier, *Le Journal intime* (Paris: Presses Universitaires de France 1976), p. 19.

the reality is always an interaction of adult and juvenile worlds.[4] Despite their 'private' character, all forms of *écritures du moi* bear the stamp of changing social and cultural influences.

Personal diaries

The personal diary was particularly associated with femininity, being one of the few forms of written expression available to women in the early nineteenth century. It was also a common form of expression for adolescents. According to a study by Philippe Lejeune, girls from noble and middle-class families first began to write *journaux intimes* during the late eighteenth century. The upheavals of the 1789 Revolution disrupted the practice, but in the nineteenth century he discerns three waves of diaries, influenced in turn by the Romantic movement of the 1830s and 1840s, the 'Moral Order' of the period 1850–80 and finally the democratic and secular values of the Third Republic. To begin with, diaries remained hidden from public view, but during the second half of the nineteenth century a few were published posthumously.

Those written by the younger girls fly in the face of our current conception of the diary as a refuge from family and school life. Rather, it was often the mother who prompted her daughter to write, around the age of ten or twelve, as part of the preparation for first communion. The *Journal de Marguerite* (1858), subtitled 'The Two Preparatory Years for First Communion', provided a template for the girls if they needed one. The aim was to encourage the girl to examine her conscience at the end of each day and to help her with her written composition. Apparently mothers or teachers might routinely read such diaries. The *Journal d'enfant* of Elisabeth Leseur noted in 1877, when she was eleven, 'I will write my diary with plenty of detail so that Mama will be happy and so that my diary will interest her.' Marie Lenéru admitted that she only wrote her diary because her mother forced her to do so, and commented in 1887 that 'Mama read my diary on Thursday; I really regretted it because she made fun of me.'[5] In time, the girls often shifted from initial resentment of maternal pressure to write a diary to a feeling of true ownership. In the early stages, Marie Lenéru complained that her diary bored her enormously. However, two years later in 1888 it helped her to weather

---

[4] Ludmilla Jordanova, 'New Worlds for Children in the Eighteenth Century: Problems of Historical Interpretation', *History of the Human Sciences*, 3 (1990), 69–83 (78–9).

[5] Elisabeth Leseur, *Journal d'enfant* (Paris: J. De Gigord, 1934), entry for Tuesday, 23 October 1877; Marie Lenéru, *Journal, précédé du Journal d'enfance* (Paris: Grasset, 1945), entry for Monday, 28 November 1887.

a difficult period in her life: 'fortunately I have my dear diary to which I can tell everything, being sure that it will never betray me'. By 1893, when she was eighteen, it took on a new importance as deafness made conversation with other people difficult. The diary helped her because, as she put it, 'I feel the need to be mistress of my style.'[6]

Most of the diaries written by slightly older adolescent girls followed in similar vein by taking the form of a spiritual diary. Again, they were somewhat formulaic, with upper-middle-class girls meditating endlessly on their sins and their relationship with God. As Michelle Perrot observes, it is easy today to become impatient with such pious outpourings, and to write off the girls as feeble-minded. Yet she notes that there was a coherent vision of the world underpinning these writings, which provided the basis for the education and indeed the whole existence of girls in this particular milieu.[7] Such diaries in effect give a detailed account of efforts made by the girls to assimilate the Catholic model of femininity. At the other pole, 'profane' diaries written by more worldly young women tended to range quite widely, and give the historian tantalizing hints of their views on family, friends, marriage, careers and the construction of a personal identity. They remained faithful to a strict code of modesty in personal affairs, compelling historians to make do with brief allusions to topics that interest them. The more forthright diary of Marie Bashkirtseff (1858–84), alluding to her interest in young men and her fierce ambition to succeed in life, resounded like an 'anarchist bomb', to quote Philippe Lejeune, when it was published in 1887.[8] During the 1920s, the psychologist Maurice Debesse made enquiries among students at teachers' training colleges, and found that a little over a third said that they had kept a diary at some time. Their motives were threefold: to be able to remember their years of youth so that they could relive them later, to record significant experiences such as falling in love and to have a 'friend' to confide in when under stress.[9] Unfortunately for the historian, as the

[6] Lenéru, *Journal* entries for 8 July, 26 July and 20 August 1887, 26 April 1888 and *année* 1893.
[7] Michelle Perrot, 'Enquête', in Caroline Brame, *Le Journal intime de Caroline B.*, ed. by Michelle Perrot and Georges Ribeill (Paris: Montalba, 1985), pp. 169–213 (p. 199). For details of the education, see Marie-Françoise Lévy, *De mères en filles: l'éducation des françaises, 1850–1880* (Paris: Calmann-Lévy, 1984).
[8] *Journal de Marie Bashkirtseff*, extracts presented by Verena von der Heyden-Rynsch (Paris: Mercure de France, 2000), entry for Wednesday, 19 April 1876. For a recent English translation, there is Marie Bashkirtseff, *I Am the Most Interesting Book of All: The Diary of Marie Bashkirtseff*, vol. I, transl. Phyllis Howard Kernberger with Katherine Kernberger (San Francisco: Chronicle Books, 1997).
[9] Maurice Debesse, *La Crise d'originalité juvénile*, 3rd edn (Paris: Presses Universitaires de France, 1948), pp. 146–8.

journal intime of the adolescent became more intimate, so their authors became more concerned to destroy them before they died.[10]

Family correspondences

The family correspondence has had its history too. During the nineteenth century, members of the upper and middle classes might spend up to three hours a day writing letters to relatives. The aim was arguably not so much to exchange information, for the content was often thin, rather to allow members of a family network to keep in touch with each other. The eminent Parisian doctor Poumiès de la Siboutie (1789–1862) noted in his autobiography that his father insisted that he and his seven siblings maintain a weekly correspondence with the family home in the Périgueux. Besides making up for their long absences, he added, such exchanges preserved him from several *faux pas*.[11] There were certain rituals to go through: to begin with, an acknowledgement of the last letter from the correspondent, or apologies for the delay in replying; then details of the daily round in the household; and finally, the sending of regards to all members of the family. Those who lacked confidence could buy letter-writing manuals to help them. These publications reached a peak of production in the 1850s and 1860s, before mass schooling presumably made them redundant. Some of the manuals were in fact written for children, particularly to help them with such chores as letters to relatives on New Year's Day.[12] With or without the manuals, many young people wrote very stiff and formal missives to their relatives when fulfilling these duties. Alfred de Surian, while attending a *lycée* in Paris in 1815, opened the required New Year's letter to his grandparents with, 'Permit me at the beginning of this new year to reiterate the assurance of my respectful love which does not have sufficient eloquence to express the feelings with which my heart is penetrated.'[13] Others managed to put

---

[10] This paragraph is based on Lejeune, *Le Moi des demoiselles*, passim; Michelle Perrot, 'Journaux intimes: jeunes filles au miroir de l'âme', *Adolescence*, 4 (1986), 29–36; Perrot, 'Enquête'; Didier, *Journal intime*; and Alain Girard, *Le Journal intime* (Paris: Presses Universitaires de France, 1963).

[11] Dr F.-L. Poumiès de la Siboutie, *Souvenirs d'un médecin de Paris* (Paris: Plon, 1910), p. 71.

[12] Cécile Dauphin, 'Letter-Writing Manuals in the Nineteenth Century', in Roger Chartier, Alain Boureau and Cécile Dauphin, *Correspondence: Models of Letter-Writing from the Middle Ages to the Nineteenth Century*, transl. Christopher Woodall (Cambridge: Polity Press, 1997), pp. 112–57.

[13] Archives départementales (hereafter AD) Bouches-du-Rhône, 26 J 7, Fonds des familles Surian, Cadenet-Charleval and Jesse-Charleval, letter from Alfred to his parents, 1 January 1815. See also Rambert George, *Chronique intime d'une famille de notables au XIXe siècle: les Odoard de Mercurol* (Lyon: Presses Universitaires de Lyon, 1989), p. 21.

their own juvenile stamp on the form. A *lycéen* in Paris, keeping his aunt in Provence *au fait* with his life in exile at the beginning of the twentieth century, described a hot summer's day, his studies and his interest in the new science of aviation. He then interrupted himself to announce that it was two o'clock as he wrote, and put in two dots to mark the ringing of the bell.[14]

There were certain taboos on subjects deemed inappropriate for family correspondence. Caroline Chotard-Lioret confessed that she hoped a collection of 11,400 letters, written by her own ancestors between 1868 and 1920, would allow her to 'plunge into the intimacy of the family and discover its passions'. It never did: sex, money and family scandals were simply not discussed. Fortunately, there was a wealth of detail on such topics as children, health and potential marriage partners.[15] As Roger Chartier notes, reading the correspondence of ordinary people from the past gives us the feeling of breaking into a private existence.[16] Occasionally, the underlying emotional tension between the generations comes through, for example when wayward sons mixed with the 'wrong' crowd or daughters resisted parental marriage plans. Some of the published examples of family correspondences do indeed focus on the more sensational side of family life. *Marthe* (1982), for example, documents the harrowing tale of a young woman from the lesser nobility in Normandy who 'fell' pregnant in 1892 and had to spend the next ten years with her mother and sister hiding her shame by wandering from town to town.[17] In the twentieth century, according to Chotard-Lioret, the family correspondence declined along with the cohesion of big family networks.[18]

Autobiographies

A brief history of autobiography

The young rarely published autobiographies, until very recently. Alphonse Daudet wrote *Le Petit Chose: histoire d'un enfant* (*Little What's His Name*, 1868) when he was in his mid-twenties, but he felt that he

---

[14] AD Bouches-du-Rhône, 61 J 13, Fonds Veray, letter from Louis Veray to Mlle Louise Veray, n.d. See also Cécile Dauphin, Pierrette Lebrun-Pézerat and Danièle Poublan, *Ces bonnes lettres: une correspondance familiale au XIXe siècle* (Paris: Albin Michel, 1995), p. 128.
[15] Caroline Chotard-Lioret, 'Correspondre en 1900: le plus public des actes privés ou la manière de gérer un réseau de parenté', *Ethnologie française*, 15 (1985), 63–71 (63).
[16] Roger Chartier, 'Preface' to Dauphin et al., *Ces bonnes lettres*, pp. 11–15 (p. 11).
[17] *Marthe* (Paris: Seuil, 1982).   [18] Chotard-Lioret, 'Correspondre en 1900', 65–6.

would have done better to wait for a longer perspective.[19] The usual approach was to write such a work late in life, when the author had had time to reflect on the significance of his or her experiences. As with other types of ego document, scholars can trace various precursors deep in the past, ranging from the *Confessions* of St Augustine to the *Essays* of Montaigne, but it was not until the nineteenth and twentieth centuries that autobiographical writing flourished. Trawling through the catalogues of the Bibliothèque nationale, to find all surviving examples from the nineteenth century in the collection, the indefatigable Philippe Lejeune noted a growing volume of output as the century wore on. To be precise, before 1815 the corpus was more impressive for its quality than its quantity. A few well-known works from Rousseau, Rétif de la Bretonne and Jamerey-Duval were all that he could unearth. During the Restoration and July Monarchy periods, the obvious market was for works giving a first-hand account of the upheavals of revolution, war and Empire. A cohort of authors stepped forward to oblige with personal memoirs of the 1790s and early 1800s. Finally, after 1848, the genre took off, with an outpouring of autobiographies from famous writers, but also from obscure individuals such as businessmen, militant socialists and criminals.[20] If one considers the sub-genre of autobiographies purely concerned with childhood and youth, the *souvenirs d'enfance et de jeunesse*, a similar evolution is apparent. The obvious starting point in modern France is the publication in 1782 of Rousseau's *Confessions*. This was not strictly a story of childhood, since half of its twelve books covered the adult years of the author. However, to begin with, only the first six books appeared, covering his wanderings in the provinces before reaching Paris at the age of thirty. The name of Rousseau ensured healthy sales, though, as noted at the beginning of this chapter, critics baulked at the revelation of so many intimate details. Other writers hesitated for a while to follow in his footsteps. Hence, the genre did not begin to crystallize until the mid-1830s, with the writing of *The Life of Henry Brulard* by Stendhal (1783–1842). It then flourished in France more than anywhere else, perhaps, in the words of Richard N. Coe, because of a culture that 'tended to combine a passion for the exact analysis of human behaviour with a very high degree of sophistication'.[21]

---

[19] Dupuy, *Un personnage nouveau*, p. 11.
[20] Philippe Lejeune, 'La Cote Ln 27: pour un répertoire des autobiographies écrites en France au XIXe siècle', in Lejeune, *Moi aussi* (Paris: Seuil, 1986), pp. 249–72 (pp. 263–4). See also Georges Gusdorf, 'Conditions and Limits of Autobiography', in James Olney (ed.), *Autobiography: Essays Theoretical and Critical* (Princeton: Princeton University Press, 1980), pp. 28–48.
[21] Coe, *When the Grass was Taller*, p. 40.

Historians have often aired the strengths and weaknesses of autobiographies as primary-source material. On the one hand, there are always concerns that works usually written at an advanced age will forget or even wilfully distort the details of a life. Stendhal, writing in his fifties, repeatedly drew attention to his problems in this area: 'Next to the clearest mental pictures I find *gaps* in this memory, it's like a fresco, large parts of which have fallen away.' Jean Guéhenno (1890–1978) compared his memory to a great artist, forever painting and retouching his portrait in a mysterious workshop. It seemed to work independently of him, though in reality nothing could be more profoundly part of him.[22] Authors of autobiographies have tried a number of techniques to recover childhood memories. Stendhal hoped that the act of writing itself would help him discover the truth about his early years. He had a strategy of writing quickly, as occasional notes in the text make clear, on the assumption that speed helped him dredge up fragments of the truth.[23] Marcel Proust (1871–1922) declared that 'the past is hidden outside the realm of our intelligence and beyond its reach'. He famously relied on the experience of 'involuntary memory' to take him back to his early years: chance physical sensations that brought a surge of memories about the past. The best-known example from *In Search of Lost Time* is the *petite madeleine* dipped in lime-blossom tea that awakened dormant memories of his aunt's house in Combray.[24] However, for all the 'delicious pleasure' involved, the four experiences of involuntary memory he mentioned were hardly enough to sustain a 3,000-page novel.[25] Proust, like all those attempting to recreate childhood, would have to resort to conscious efforts to recall past experience most of the time. Hence the historian is likely to be sceptical about techniques to plumb the depths of what we would now call the unconscious.

A further potential weakness of autobiographies as a source is the unrepresentative nature of the sample provided by their authors compared to the French population as a whole. In the case of the nineteenth

---

[22] Jean Guéhenno, *Changer la vie: mon enfance et ma jeunesse* (Paris: Grasset, 1961), p. 13; and Stendhal, *The Life of Henry Brulard*, transl. John Sturrock (New York: New York Review Books, 2002 (1890)), p. 128.

[23] Richard N. Coe, 'Stendhal, Rousseau and the Search for Self', *Australian Journal of French Studies*, 16 (1979), 27–47 (28–9); John Sturrock, *The Language of Autobiography: Studies in the First Person Singular* (Cambridge: Cambridge University Press, 1993), pp. 185–6.

[24] Marcel Proust, *In Search of Lost Time*, vol. I, *The Way by Swann's*, transl. Lydia Davis (London: Penguin, 2003 (1913)), pp. 47–50.

[25] See Derwent May, *Proust* (Oxford: Oxford University Press, 1983), pp. 55–7; Philip Thody, *Marcel Proust* (Basingstoke: Macmillan, 1987), pp. 1–6; Coe, *When the Grass was Taller*, pp. 87–94.

century, for example, autobiographies written by males were far more in evidence than those from females, and the output of the upper and middle classes heavily outweighed that of the *menu peuple*. Autobiographies written by workers were thus few and far between. A handful of famous ones, such as those by Jacques-Louis Ménétra, Agricol Perdiguier and Norbert Truquin, therefore have to bear a heavy burden as examples of the view 'from below'. The peasantry meanwhile was for a long time notable for its complete absence from the form. As late as the 1890s, the Breton peasant Jean-Marie Déguignet (1834–1905) could complain that although he had read many memoirs written by the rich and famous, he had come across none from poor artisans, workers and labourers. He thought it impossible for such people to write about their lives, since they lacked the necessary time and education – though he depicted himself breaking the mould.[26] Lejeune comments that peasants and workers were barely connected to the 'communication circuit' of the printed word during this period, a circuit monopolized by and operating in the interests of the dominant classes. Their world, where their discourse on memory resided, was the collective one of the village or the *compagnonnage*.[27] Antoine Sylvère (1888–1963) recalled his grandfather, a peasant in the Auvergne, admitting that he could not understand three quarters of the French words in a Sunday newspaper:

> The poor man had a scientific mind and life held him as far from the sources of knowledge as if he had been lost in the polar ice or at the most distant parts of the Amazon forest. He died almost illiterate having sought at all times, the length of his existence, a few scraps of this culture reserved for 'top people' and obstinately refused to those at the bottom by an implacable will and a pre-established classification.[28]

The literary critic John Sturrock surely went to the extreme in asserting that autobiographies were 'the work of resolutely idiosyncratic individuals whose experiences and responses were unlike those of anyone else', but he is right to warn historians about easy assumptions on the typicality of such works.[29] Most people do not write their autobiographies, and one should acknowledge the sheer bravado or exceptional urge to tell a story of those who did so. In the case of childhood reminiscences, Coe drew attention to the fact that 50 to 60 per cent of the 600-odd works he was

---

[26] Jean-Marie Déguignet, *Mémoires d'un paysan bas-breton* (Ar Releg-Kerhuon, Brittany: An Here, 1998), pp. 25–6.

[27] Philippe Lejeune, 'The Autobiography of Those Who Do Not Write', in Lejeune, *On Autobiography* (Minneapolis: University of Minnesota Press, 1989), pp. 185–215.

[28] Antoine Sylvère, *Toinou: le cri d'un enfant auvergnat, pays d'Ambert* (Paris: Plon, 1980), p. 81.

[29] Sturrock, *Language of Autobiography*, p. 12.

studying during the 1980s concerned exceptional children who would grow up to be poets or outstanding masters of prose-style.[30]

On the other hand, many historians consider autobiographies a boon because they can give a direct insight into how people in the past made sense of the world around them. As the British historian David Vincent puts it, 'If we wish to understand the meaning of the past, we must first discover the meaning the past had for those who made it and were made by it.'[31] The partiality or 'subjectivity' of the source then recedes as a problem, since the author reveals how he or she wishes to interpret their experiences. And if the writer makes odd factual errors in their account, as is almost inevitable, this is hardly fatal. What counts is what their experiences meant to them: *his* or *her* truth rather than *the* truth.[32]

Historians have always noted that autobiographers draw on various literary traditions when writing about themselves. Even workers were influenced by models from the past as well as by the social context of their own lives. They might, for example, depict themselves as the hero of a picaresque tale, a bit of a rogue using guile to pull him through a series of adventures. Jacques-Louis Ménétra (b. 1738) is a classic case in point, with his raunchy account of life, first of all on the road as a journeyman doing his *tour de France*, and then in Paris as a young man on the make. Louise Vanderwielen (b. 1906) recounted her life story in the form of a popular romantic novel: the only type of literature she had come across during her long years in Lille and Marseille. Another option was to adapt the Christian conversion narrative to the secular world of the political militant, seeing the light in socialism after early years as a hapless victim of capitalism. One thinks of the young Georges Dumoulin (1877–1963) recalling his sudden awareness at the age of seventeen of exploitation in the Pas-de-Calais during the 1890s, after reading Zola novels and the Marxist literature of the Parti ouvrier français.[33]

---

[30] Coe, *When the Grass was Taller*, pp. 2, 280–1.

[31] David Vincent, *Bread, Knowledge and Freedom: A Study of Nineteenth-Century Working Class Autobiography* (London: Europa, 1981), p. 6. See also John Burnett (ed.), *Destiny Obscure: Autobiographies of Childhood, Education and Family from the 1820s to the 1920s* (Harmondsworth: Penguin, 1984), pp. 10–13; and Maynes, *Taking the Hard Road*, ch. 2.

[32] Coe, *When the Grass was Taller*, pp. 79–80. See also Bertholet, *Les Français par eux-mêmes*, pp. 9–10.

[33] Jacques-Louis Ménétra, *Journal of My Life*, transl. Arthur Goldhammer (New York: Columbia University Press, 1986); Louise Vanderwielen, *Lise du plat pays* (Lille: Presses Universitaires de Lille, 1983), 'Postface' by Françoise Cribier; Georges Dumoulin, *Carnets de route: quarante années de vie militante* (Lille: Editions de 'L'Avenir', 1937). See also Maynes, *Taking the Hard Road*, pp. 34–9; Vincent, *Bread, Knowledge*, ch. 2; Regina Gagnier, *Subjectivities: A History of Self-Representation in Britain, 1832–1920* (New York: Oxford University Press, 1991), ch. 4.

One might go further, and plot the way autobiographies reflect changing literary conventions over the centuries. Richard N. Coe noted in the case of childhood reminiscences that when the custom was to write picaresque novels, then a seventeenth-century author like Tristan l'Hermite would write a picaresque account of his childhood. When Emile Zola was in the ascendant during the late nineteenth century, Jules Vallès followed the fashion with a typically naturalist story of a brutal upbringing. When sexual permissiveness was an issue, André Gide and Jean Cocteau were on hand with accounts of the first stirrings of homosexual feelings, and so it would continue.[34] In the late twentieth century, Lejeune drew attention to a huge public appetite for autobiographical accounts of those 'others' leading a life very different from the ordinary French person. The attraction for the reader was the feeling that these were authentic, eyewitness accounts from those who had experience of, say, resistance during the war, a long prison sentence or the customs of an Indian tribe. More pertinently for the modern historian, there was a flurry of life stories from former peasants or workers, recorded on tape and transcribed by anthropologists or journalists for the benefit of a largely middle-class audience. The emphasis on the 'witness' or the 'lived' experience appeared to avoid the distortion of a literary form. Yet for Lejeune it was simply another case of the form of representation reflecting a particular society.[35] This leads us to questions among theorists on the nature of autobiography.

Autobiography: for and against

Autobiography has always had its detractors as well as its supporters. For the latter, it is an established literary genre that has produced a series of masterpieces from the *Confessions* of St Augustine onwards. For the former, it is mendacious, egotistical and all too easy to write, 'the art of those who are not artists, the novel of those who are not novelists'.[36] One of the most sustained onslaughts started in the 'structuralist'[37] camp late

---

[34] Richard N. Coe, 'Reminiscences of Childhood: An Approach to a Comparative Mythology', *Proceedings of the Leeds Philosophical and Literary Society*, 19 (1984), 285.

[35] Philippe Lejeune, 'Le Document vécu', in *Je est un autre: l'autobiographie de la littérature aux médias* (Paris: Seuil, 1980), pp. 203–28 (pp. 205–11).

[36] Albert Thibaudet, *Gustave Flaubert*, cited by Henri Peyre, *Literature and Sincerity* (New Haven: Yale University Press, 1963), p. 210. Ch. 7, 'Autobiographies and Private Diaries' in the latter work discusses the issue in some detail.

[37] Structuralists seek out the deep structures in texts and cultures in general, thereby denying the concepts of human freedom and choice. Their approach is open to the criticism that it is ahistorical and deterministic. Today poststructuralism is more in vogue, with its emphasis on the ambiguity and instability of meaning in texts.

in the twentieth century.[38] A key issue was the extent to which autobiography should be seen as a referential as opposed to a literary form. The traditional view of autobiography took seriously the claim that it conveyed information on a 'reality' exterior to the text. The structuralists and post-structuralists shifted attention from issues of literary representation to the internal operations of the text itself.[39]

The traditional approach rests on the assumption that there is an autonomous, coherent subject, able to use language to discover an already existing self. Roy Pascal, author of *Design and Truth in Autobiography* (1960), was an influential champion of this view. He asserted that autobiography involved 'the reconstruction of a life, or part of a life, in the actual circumstances in which it was lived'. He added that 'its centre of interest is the self, not the outside world, though of necessity the outside world must appear so that, to give and take with it, the personality finds its peculiar shape'. It followed that an autobiography would fail if its author lacked insight or 'wholeness' of character. From this perspective, the best autobiographies were written by high achievers, who were capable of establishing 'a consistent relationship, a sort of harmony, between outward experience and inward growth or unfolding'.[40] The main French authority in the field was of course Philippe Lejeune. He took a similar line when he began studying the subject in 1971 by defining autobiography as a 'retrospective prose narrative that someone writes, where the focus is his individual life, in particular the story of his personality'.[41] One of his aims at the time was to establish a list of the main autobiographical works written in French, given the general neglect of the genre. He used his definition to distinguish autobiography from related forms such as the memoir, more focused on public events than the private life of the individual, and the personal novel, more fiction than fact. Yet he had to admit that personal novels often imitated autobiographical forms, so that with only the texts to analyse, there was no way for the reader to tell one from the other. He also felt bound to concede that authors of autobiographies created as much as discovered past reality: indeed, as a literary specialist, much of his work concentrated on how they did this.[42]

---

[38] Philippe Lejeune, 'Un siècle de résistance à l'autobiographie', in *Pour l'autobiographie: chroniques* (Paris: Seuil, 1998), pp. 11–25.

[39] Philippe Lejeune, 'The Autobiographical Pact', in Lejeune, *On Autobiography*, pp. 3–30 (p. 22); Leah D. Hewitt, *Autobiographical Tightropes* (Lincoln: University of Nebraska Press, 1990), pp. 1–4.

[40] Roy Pascal, *Design and Truth in Autobiography* (London: Routledge and Kegan Paul, 1960), pp. 9–10 and 186.

[41] Philippe Lejeune, *L'Autobiographie en France* (2nd edn, Paris: Armand Colin, 1998), p. 10.

[42] Paul John Eakin, 'Foreword' to Lejeune, *On Autobiography*, pp. vii–xxviii (p. ix).

He therefore came up with his famous notion of the 'autobiographical pact'. This was a pact between author and reader, in which the latter accepts that the former is making a sincere effort to make sense of his or her life. He went on to suggest that where autobiographies differed from personal novels was in having the author, the narrator and the protagonist share the same name. This resort to the intentions of the author as the defining feature of autobiographical work did not prevent him including a 'referential pact' in his autobiographical one, with the autobiography claiming 'an image of the real'.[43]

Structuralist critics countered by casting doubts on the existence of an autonomous individual, citing various theoretical approaches incompatible with it, including Marxist political economy, Freudian psychoanalysis and cultural anthropology. They also asserted that 'the text now creates the fictions of a "self" rather than the reverse'.[44] Roland Barthes famously pronounced the 'Death of the Author'. That is to say, out went the traditional Author, whose relationship with a book was like that of a father to a child, and in came the modern scriptor. 'The modern scriptor is born simultaneously with the text, is in no way equipped with a being preceding or exceeding the writing, is not the subject with the book as predicate.' He concluded that the death of the author brought the birth of the reader, the focus of the multiple writings, 'the tissue of quotations' that is a text. Such thinking inevitably called into question the 'fathering' of autobiographies by individuals with a distinct personal identity. Michael Sprinker went to the logical conclusion of this line of thinking in his essay 'The End of Autobiography'. In particular he suggested that the concept of subject, self and author as 'independent sovereignties', which underpinned autobiography as a literary genre from the eighteenth century onwards, was no longer tenable. Indeed, post-Freud, he asserted, 'no autobiography can take place except within the boundaries of a writing where concepts of subject, self, and author collapse into the act of producing a text'.[45]

A certain scepticism is in order, since, as Paul John Eakin reminds us, it is a matter of ideology whether or not one believes in the fully constituted

---

[43] Lejeune, *On Autobiography*, passim; Lejeune, 'Le Pacte autobiographique (bis)', in Lejeune, *Moi aussi*, pp. 13–35.

[44] Thomas C. Heller and David E. Wellbery, 'Introduction' to Heller et al. (eds.), *Reconstructing Individualism: Autonomy, Individuality, and the Self in Western Thought* (Stanford: Stanford University Press, 1986), pp. 1–15; Hewitt, *Autobiographical Tightropes*, p. 3.

[45] Roland Barthes, 'The Death of the Author', in Stephen Heath (ed.), *Image Music Text* (London: Fontana, 1977), pp. 142–8; Michael Sprinker, 'Fictions of the Self: The End of Autobiography', in Olney, *Autobiography*, pp. 321–42 (p. 342).

subject.[46] One can sympathize with Lejeune as he struggled to come to terms with structuralist critics during the 1980s:

It is better to get on with the confessions: yes, I have been fooled. I believe that we can promise to tell the truth; I believe in the transparency of language, and in the existence of a complete subject who expresses himself through it; I believe that my own name guarantees my autonomy and my singularity . . . I believe that when I say 'I' it is me who speaks: I believe in the Holy Ghost of the first person. And who doesn't believe in it? But of course it also happens that I believe the contrary, or at least claim to believe it . . . 'In the field of the subject there is no referent . . .' We *indeed know* all this; we are not so dumb, but, once this precaution has been taken, we go on as if we did not know it. Telling the truth about the self, constituting the self as complete subject – it is a fantasy. In spite of the fact that autobiography is impossible, this in no way prevents it from existing.[47]

In 1998 he was more relaxed, feeling that the attacks on autobiography had abated. However, he accepted that new approaches highlighted the 'illusory side of personal mythology': in other words, efforts by the individual to construct an identity were a form of art.[48] The work of Paul Ricoeur, notably his monumental *Time and Narrative* (1984–8), did much to help the cause of autobiography by challenging traditional assumptions about fact and fiction.[49] Ricoeur argued that the claims to the truth of both historical and fictional narratives were based on the human experience of time. Particularly important for autobiography was the idea of the 'narrative identity' of an individual or a community. That is to say, if we ask the question 'who?' the answer will be in the story of a life. He noted various 'points of anchorage' that the narrative can find in the experience of living. In particular he emphasized the 'pre-narrative quality of human experience': life is a story in its nascent state, a story waiting to be told. This identity is by no means stable, given that 'the story of a life continues to be refigured by all the truthful or fictive stories a subject tells about himself or herself'.[50]

[46] Eakin, 'Foreword', p. xiv.
[47] Lejeune, 'The Autobiographical Pact (bis)', in *On Autobiography*, pp. 119–37.
[48] Lejeune, 'Siècle de résistance', p. 23.
[49] Paul Ricoeur, *Time and Narrative*, transl. Kathleen Blamey and David Pellauer (3 vols., Chicago: Chicago University Press, 1984–8). General introductions to his work can be found in Hayden White, 'The Metaphysics of Narrativity: Time and Symbol in Ricoeur's Philosophy of History', in David Wood (ed.), *On Paul Ricoeur: Narrative and Interpretation* (London: Routledge, 1991), pp. 140–59; S. H. Clark, *Paul Ricoeur* (London: Routledge, 1990); and Gaston Pineau and Jean-Louis Le Grand, *Les Histoires de vie*, (3rd edn, Paris: Presses Universitaires de France, 2002), pp. 77–81.
[50] Ricoeur, *Time and Narrative*, I, pp. 1, 54–64; III, p. 246; Ricoeur, 'Life in Quest of Narrative', in Wood, *Ricoeur*, pp. 20–33.

Autobiography and the historian

Where does all this leave the historian at the beginning of the twenty-first century? In the first place, it is worth reiterating the prominence of 'artifice and literary convention' in any autobiography.[51] Such writing can appear deceptively straightforward as a source of information on the life of its author. In reality it is never a 'simple repetition of the past as it was', but then no primary source ever is.[52] The writer has to take a random set of memories from the past and put them into some sort of shape, usually a chronological account. He or she also needs considerable skill to convert visual images into prose, and to arouse the interest of the reader in the private world of the author. Jules Vallès gradually developed a 'blending of two voices' in various works covering his childhood and youth, suggesting both the enunciation of a child, and the insights of an adult narrator.[53] For example, when comparing a family who hesitated to beat their child because they did not like to see him cry with his own, in *L'Enfant* (1879), he wrote:

My mother had more courage. She sacrificed herself, she stifled her weaknesses, she wrung the neck at the first movement to be ready for the second. Instead of kissing me, she pinched me; you think that did not cost her! Sometimes she even broke her fingernails. She beat me for my own good, you see. Her hand hesitated more than once; she had to use her foot.[54]

The creative side of such writing is indeed likely to loom largest in the particular case of childhood reminiscences, given that, as Richard N. Coe has asserted:

The former self-as-child is as alien to the adult writer as to the adult reader. The child sees differently, reasons differently, reacts differently. An *alternative* world has to be created and made convincing.[55]

For this reason, he went on to say, the boundary with the 'autobiographical novel of childhood' is bound to be fuzzy. Indeed, some authors felt freer to explore the 'truth' about childhood in a novel than an autobiography. They enjoyed not being tied down to the details of dates and places, and the possibility of covering gaps in their memory. There is the oft-quoted passage from Anatole France (1844–1924) in *La Vie en fleur* (1922) that in disguising his name and background he felt freer to talk about himself, 'but I am persuaded that no man ever told lies with a deeper concern for the truth'.[56] Coe therefore rejected the strict Lejeune

[51] Sturrock, *Language of Autobiography*, p. 12.
[52] Gusdorf, 'Conditions and Limits', p. 38.
[53] Philippe Lejeune, 'The Ironic Narrative of Childhood: Vallès', in *On Autobiography*, p. 54.
[54] Vallès, *L'Enfant*, p. 90.   [55] Coe, *When the Grass was Taller*, p. 1.
[56] Anatole France, *La Vie en fleur* (Paris: Calmann-Lévy, 1922), p. 345, cited in Coe, *When the Grass was Taller*, pp. 4–5.

criteria for the autobiographical pact, including in his study of childhood reminiscences those novels in which at least 60 per cent of the content was 'precisely detailed autobiographical fact'.[57] This study will follow his lead, and draw autobiographical material from such novels as *Poil de carotte* (1894), by Jules Renard, or *Le Roman d'un enfant* (1890) by Pierre Loti, not to mention the early parts of *In Search of Lost Time*.

In the second place, the traditional focus in an autobiography on the 'inner core' underlying the personality that appears to the world is now difficult to sustain. In the wake of structuralism and poststructuralism, it is advisable to think in terms of the construction of a self through the act of writing an autobiography. Indeed, as Regina Gagnier noted in her work on *Subjectivities* (1991), the whole business of meditating on the self, using writing as a tool for self-exploration, making sense of a life in narrative terms, and a belief in personal creativity, autonomy and freedom for the future, was largely confined to the middle classes during the nineteenth century. Autobiographies coming from such a background are therefore likely to claim an autonomous introspective 'self', while those emerging from other social milieux often made no such claim.[58] It is not hard to see that most studies of autobiography produced in the 1970s and 1980s betrayed their literary background by giving pride of place to virtuoso performers in this narrative of the self. Richard N. Coe, to take a worthy example, assembled a collection of 600 or so works written mainly by 'poets', and peppered his text with quotes from the likes of Rousseau, Gide and Sartre, rather than from 'feebler specimens' and 'failures'.[59]

Critics of proletarian writing have noted that workers often chose to write for other reasons, such as to expose their poverty, to entertain their offspring or to stake out a collective identity. Norbert Truquin, for example, ended his *Mémoires et aventures d'un prolétaire à travers la révolution* (*Memoirs and Adventures of a Proletarian in Times of Revolution*, 1888) with a call for the triumph of socialism. He wrote:

We urgently need all those who work and suffer from the vices of the existing organization of society to rely on themselves alone to escape and to create for themselves a better present and future through solidarity. It is therefore important that they each bring their stone to the common edifice, by publishing their memos, notebooks, their memoirs, in a word all of the documents that can help to destroy the iniquities of the old world and hasten the coming of the social revolution.[60]

Similarly, feminist critics have shown how women writers were generally 'other-regarding' rather than 'self-regarding', looking outwards to their

---

[57] Coe, 'Reminiscences', 225.   [58] Gagnier, *Subjectivities*, pp. 13 and 28.
[59] Coe, *When the Grass was Taller*, pp. 33, 62.
[60] Norbert Truquin, *Mémoires et aventures d'un prolétaire à travers la révolution* (Paris: Maspero, 1977), p. 273.

families and local communities instead of inwards on the self.[61] Significantly, a recent study of life histories has defined autobiography simply as narratives written by the individuals concerned themselves (to exclude biographies), presented as directly referential (to exclude novels) and concerned with the whole life or essence of a life (to exclude reminiscences of childhood and personal diaries).[62] Philippe Lejeune has also adapted readily to changing circumstances, moving on from his original interest in famous literary works to the numerous autobiographies written by ordinary people. He has, for example, written studies of autobiographies by distinctly non-literary types such as businessmen and criminals.[63] Historians can readily adapt to this democratization of autobiographical writing. Works written by those from the 'popular classes' are often anecdotal and disjointed, and of course lacking the flair and willingness to innovate with literary forms of those of, say, a Proust or a Sartre. What they offer the social historian, as already noted, is the opportunity to see how ordinary people made sense of their world.

Finally, part and parcel of the democratization of autobiography is a massive diversification of life stories beyond the traditional literary form.[64] During the twentieth century, in France, there were examples of largely self-taught peasants and workers writing their own autobiographies, such as *Angélina: une fille des champs* by Angélina Bardin or *Travaux* by Georges Navel. These could be set beside the more numerous memoirs by militants from the labour movement such as Jeanne Bouvier or René Michaud.[65] There were also several examples from people who had at least started life in this milieu. The most spectacularly successful of these was *Le Cheval d'orgueil* (*The Horse of Pride*, 1975) by the teacher and broadcaster Pierre-Jakez Hélias, an account of village life in the pays Bigouden of Brittany, which sold no fewer than two million

---

[61] For example, Hewitt, *Autobiographical Tightropes*, passim; and Gagnier, *Subjectivities*, passim.

[62] Pineau and Le Grand, *Histoires de vie*, p. 30.

[63] Philippe Lejeune, 'Autobiography and Social History in the Nineteenth Century', in *On Autobiography*, pp. 163–84; and Philippe Lejeune, 'Crime et testament: les autobiographies de criminels au XIXe siècle', *Cahiers de sémiotique textuelle*, 8–9 (1986), 73–98.

[64] This paragraph relies on Lejeune, 'Those Who Do Not Write'; and Pineau and Le Grand, *Histoires de vie*, pp. 10–18.

[65] Angélina Bardin, *Angélina: une fille des champs* (Paris: André Bonne, 1956); Georges Navel, *Travaux* (Paris: Stock, 1945); Jeanne Bouvier, *Mes mémoires* (Paris: Maspero, 1983); and René Michaud, *J'avais vingt ans: un jeune ouvrier au début du siècle* (Paris: Editions syndicalistes, 1967). See also Michel Ragon, *Histoire de la littérature prolétarienne en France: littérature ouvrière, littérature paysanne, littérature d'expression populaire* (Paris: Albin Michel, 1974), and the useful collection of translations of such works, Mark Traugott (ed.), *The French Worker: Autobiographies from the Early Industrial Era* (Berkeley: University of California Press, 1993).

copies and appeared in eighteen languages.[66] Beyond that there were
numerous innovations: ghostwriters (*nègres*) helping celebrities recount
their experiences;[67] anthropologists starting to investigate case studies
within their own country;[68] journalists and writers collaborating with
retired workers to write their life stories ('the granny school');[69] and
historians beginning to explore the possibilities of oral history.[70] These
developments in the exploration of human experience imply a respect
for the capacity for critical consciousness, initiative and historical action
among ordinary people. Hence one can think in terms of a willingness
of researchers in the social sciences to share their power–knowledge relationship with them.[71] However, such a notion may be unduly unrealistic
if the power relationship between researcher and subject is uneven. There
is the danger that the final work will reflect the preoccupations of the educated interviewer rather than those of the worker. Lejeune cites in some
detail the study of the locksmith Gaston Lucas by the professional writer
Adelaïde Blasquez. Listening to a tape-recording of one her interviews,
he notes a dialogue of the deaf. While Blasquez looked for a political
consciousness and leftist orientation in her anti-hero, Lucas ranted on,
blithely unaware of her concerns, from a populist right-wing perspective. She wanted evidence of worker resistance to the rise of fascism in
1934; he reminisced about the horses of the Garde républicaine and trees
blocking the tramways.[72] None of this tension appeared in the book. The
obvious conclusion is that the quality of these numerous life stories, from
the point of view of the historian, will vary considerably.

[66] Pierre-Jakez Hélias, *Le Cheval d'orgueil: mémoires d'un Breton du pays Bigouden* (Paris:
   Plon, 1975), translated by June Guicharnaud as *The Horse of Pride* (New Haven: Yale
   University Press, 1978).
[67] Even Emilie Carles, who, as a former teacher and ecological activist might have been
   expected to write her own autobiography, resorted to the services of a ghostwriter: Emilie Carles, as told to Robert Destanque, *Une soupe aux herbes sauvages* (Paris: Robert
   Laffont, 1981), transl. Avriel H. Goldberger as *A Wild Herb Soup: The Life of a French
   Countrywoman* (London: Victor Gollancz, 1992).
[68] Notably Jacques Caroux-Destray, *Un couple ouvrier traditionnel: la vieille garde autogestionnaire* (Paris: Anthropos, 1974).
[69] For example, Ephraïm Grenadou and Alain Prévost, *Grenadou: paysan français* (Paris:
   Seuil, 1966); Louis Lengrand and Maria Craipeau, *Louis Lengrand, mineur du Nord*
   (Paris: Seuil, 1974); Serge Grafteaux, *Mémé Santerre, une vie* (Paris: Delarge, 1975);
   Raymonde Anna Rey, *Augustine Rouvière, cévenole* (Paris: Delarge, 1977).
[70] Christiane Germain and Christine de Panafieu, *La Mémoire des femmes: sept témoignages
   de femmes nées avec le siècle* (Paris: Sylvie Messinger, 1982); and Anne Roche and Marie-
   Claude Taranger, *Celles qui n'ont pas écrit: récits de femmes dans la région Marseillaise,
   1914–1945* (Aix-en-Provence: Edisud, 1995).
[71] Pineau and Le Grand, *Histoires de vie*, p. 85.
[72] Philippe Lejeune, 'Ethnologie et littérature: *Gaston Lucas, serrurier*' in *Moi aussi*, pp. 273–
   91; Adelaïde Blasquez, *Gaston Lucas, serrurier: chronique de l'anti-héros* (Paris: Plon,
   1976).

Conclusion

There now exists a steady flow of published 'ego documents', as French publishers seek to meet the demand for glimpses into the fast-disappearing world of the peasant, artisan and coalminer. When added to earlier published primary sources and manuscript material in archives, this means that the historian of childhood and youth can draw on a sizeable pool of first-hand accounts of human experiences in the past in a way that was out of the question even thirty or forty years ago. Such *écritures du moi* can be used in a variety of ways. At one extreme, they can be treated as purely literary texts, without reference to the life of the author. Rosemary Lloyd and Francine Dugast, for example, made no distinction between autobiographies and fiction in their studies of the image of childhood in French literature.[73] At the other extreme, one can accept the 'autobiographical pact' and assume that the author is trying to tell the reader something about his or her experience of life. This book veers towards the latter approach, without ignoring the former.[74] It goes without saying that 'ego documents' need careful scrutiny, like any other primary source, taking into account such considerations as the genre in question, the literary conventions of the period and personal agenda of the author when he or she recorded them. The sample of childhoods is inevitably far from representative, so it makes no sense to try to use it as a database. In other words, it would be rash to assert that a change over time in the percentage of the autobiographies mentioning, say, corporal punishment indicates a similar movement in the population as a whole. The 'ego documents' are better at putting flesh on the bare bones of statistics, and giving an idea of the diversity of experience among different sections of the population. This book will complement them with other material of a more impersonal kind, but they remain its spine. Their very existence is evidence that some of the old certainties of an agrarian society were disappearing, leading to the trials and tribulations of young people in the modern world. Moreover, in the words of Hayden White:

---

[73] Lloyd, *Land of Lost Content*; and Francine Dugast, *L'Image de l'enfance dans la prose littéraire de 1918 à 1930*, 2 vols., Lille: Presses Universitaires de Lille, 1981. Lloyd, it might be noted, does devote a chapter to autobiographical works, 'Remembering Childhood', and talks of the 'cross-fertilization' taking place between fictional writing and memoirs (p. 66).

[74] For a similar conclusion in a recent doctoral thesis on adult–child relations in France, see Darya Vassigh, 'Les Relations adultes–enfants dans la seconde moitié du XIXe siècle (1850–1914): étude discursive des écrits autobiographiques, éducatifs, juridiques et médico-légaux, relatifs à cette question', 2 vols., Thèse de doctorat en histoire, Université de Paris VII, 1996, pp. 13–31.

A scientific (or scientistic) historiography of the sort envisioned by the *Annalistes*, which deals in large-scale, physical and social, anonymous 'forces', is not so much wrong as simply able to tell only a part of the story of human beings at grips with their individual and collective destinies. It produces the historiographical equivalent of a drama that is all scene and no actors, or a novel that is all theme but lacking in character.[75]

[75] White, 'Ricoeur's Philosophy', pp. 145–6.

2 Into the limelight: new conceptions of childhood and adolescence

Eighteenth-century France teemed with children. They could hardly be ignored as they roamed around the fields and the streets in little gangs, helped adults with their work, and pestered relatives and servants for attention. In 1740, according to estimates by French demographers, those aged zero to nineteen accounted for 42 per cent of the population. By the middle of the twentieth century, the 'ageing' of the population associated with modern civilization had reduced this proportion to a still sizeable 30 per cent.[1] Leading figures in the late *ancien régime* were also aware that children embodied the future of their society. It was therefore essential to devote some resources to their health and education. Nonetheless, a low-income, agrarian type of society could hardly afford to allocate much in the way of resources to the welfare of young people. Many children were ephemeral beings who would not survive to adulthood. During the final decades of the *ancien régime* a half of all children died before they reached the age of ten.[2] Most of the rest gradually melted into the adult labour force as they helped around the farms and workshops according to their physical strength and stamina. In these circumstances, it is hardly surprising that the early stages of life did not attract much debate in the written records. However, as already noted above, new currents in the intellectual sphere during the eighteenth century brought increasing attention to childhood and adolescence. Henceforth young people appeared more prominently in paintings, autobiographies, novels and scholarly works.[3] This chapter will explore the key issues raised

[1] Louis Henry and Yves Blayo, 'La Population de la France de 1740 à 1860', *Population*, 30 (1975), 71–122 (100); J. Bourgeois-Pichat, 'The General Development of the Population of France since the Eighteenth Century', in D. V. Glass and D. E. C. Eversley (eds.), *Population in History: Essays in Historical Demography* (London: Edward Arnold, 1965), pp. 474–506.

[2] Yves Blayo, 'La Mortalité en France de 1740 à 1829', *Population*, 30 (1975), 123–42 (133); Jacques Vallin, 'Mortality in Europe from 1720 to 1914: Long-Term Trends and Changes in Patterns by Age and Sex', in R. Schofield, D. Reher and A. Bideau (eds.), *The Decline of Mortality in Europe* (Oxford: Clarendon Press, 1991), pp. 38–67.

[3] See above, pp. 2–3.

by influential adults interested in the young, ranging from high-ranking prelates in the Catholic Church to popular novelists. For the purpose of analysis, it will focus on three topics: the *length* of childhood and adolescence, the *nature* of these stages of life and their *significance* for society at large.[4] The underlying question must be whether the debates helped provide a more hospitable climate for those growing up in modern France.

The length of childhood and adolescence

Brief childhoods

Philippe Ariès probably overplayed a good hand in asserting that medieval society lacked any *sentiment de l'enfance*, any 'awareness of the particular nature of childhood, that particular nature which distinguishes the child from the adult'. He attributed this supposed ignorance of childhood to the social customs of the period. In his view, as soon as children could survive without the care and attention of their mothers, they were launched into the 'great community of men'. This meant that around the age of seven, when they could walk and talk properly, the young joined adults in both their work and their play. On this basis, he argued that medieval society failed to perceive a transition period between infancy and adulthood, considering the young to be simply small adults.[5] Historians have generally remained unconvinced by such sweeping assertions. They have demonstrated a number of ways in which medieval societies revealed some recognition of the 'particular nature' of childhood. Medical texts, for example, usually devoted a section to the care of infants, and in monasteries the regime for children destined for the religious life (the oblates) was slightly less arduous than that for monks.[6] One might follow the philosopher David Archard in arguing that the societies of the medieval period, like all others, had a concept of childhood, allowing people to distinguish between children and adults. But they also had a very different *conception* of it from our own, that is to say, different ways of making the distinction.[7] For Doris Desclais Berkvam what stood out was the 'unstructured and unspecified' character of medieval childhood. It was not so much

---

[4] See David Archard, *Children: Rights and Childhood* (London: Routledge, 1993), p. 27.

[5] Philippe Ariès, *Centuries of Childhood* (Harmondsworth: Penguin, 1962), pp. 125–30, 186, 395–6.

[6] Mayke de Jong, 'Growing Up in a Carolingian Monastery: Magister Hildemar and his Oblates', *Journal of Medieval History*, 9 (1983), 99–128; Jean-Noël Biraben, 'La Médicine et l'enfant au Moyen Age', *Annales de démographie historique* (1973), 73–5; and Luke Demaitre, 'The Idea of Childhood and Child Care in Medical Writings of the Middle Ages', *Journal of Psychohistory*, 4 (1977), 461–90.

[7] Archard, *Children*, pp. 22–4.

ignored as loosely defined, encompassing 'the time and space of youth regardless of where, or how long, this youth takes place'.[8] However, Ariès was surely right to insist that medieval children were gradually inserted into the world of adults from an early age. Hence what we would now call childhood and adolescence merged almost imperceptibly into adulthood. Anthropologists have noted that in many cultures the distance between adult and child behaviour is much less evident than in the West today, and it may well be that great 'civilizing' mission of the Renaissance had the effect of heightening the contrasts.[9] Before the Renaissance, then, one can say that the young in medieval Europe had a 'short' childhood.[10]

'Quarantining' the young

For Ariès, this concept of a brief childhood remained unchallenged until the seventeenth century, when a small group of lawyers, priests and moralists in France and England made some headway in imposing the contrasting concept of a 'long' childhood. Their success rested on the flourishing educational institutions and practices that they supervised. Their perception of the supposed 'special nature of childhood', its innocence and weakness, meant that 'henceforth it was recognized that the child was not ready for life, and that he had to be subjected to a special treatment, a sort of quarantine, before he was allowed to join the adults'. It was, it might be added, boys rather than girls who attended the schools in any numbers at this stage: as he put it, 'boys were the first specialized children', while girls continued to be confused with women. Ariès noted that it was the 'enlightened bourgeoisie' that first embraced this notion of an extended childhood. The lower classes continued in the old ways, avoiding subjection to a long period of influence from the school, until well into the twentieth century.[11]

Whether these 'pedagogues' made such a momentous 'discovery' of childhood in the seventeenth century is doubtful, as is the suggestion that

---

[8] Doris Desclais Berkvam, *Enfance et maternité dans la littérature française des XIIe et XIIIe siècles* (Paris: Honoré Champion, 1981), ch. 5; Doris Desclais Berkvam, 'Nature and Norreture: A Notion of Medieval Childhood and Education', *Mediaevalia*, 9 (1983), 165–80 (169).

[9] Ruth Benedict, 'Continuities and Discontinuities in Cultural Conditioning', in Margaret Mead and Martha Wolfenstein (eds.), *Childhood in Contemporary Cultures* (Chicago: University of Chicago Press, 1955), pp. 21–30 (pp. 21–2); Norbert Elias, *The Civilizing Process*, vol. I, *The History of Manners*, transl. Edmund Jephcott (Oxford: Basil Blackwell, 1978 (1939)).

[10] For a fuller treatment of these issues in the Western context, see Colin Heywood, *A History of Childhood: Children and Childhood in the West from Medieval to Modern Times* (Cambridge: Polity, 2001), part I.

[11] Ariès, *Centuries of Childhood*, pp. 56, 316–23 and 396.

they were conspicuous in asserting the 'innocence' of children. Nonetheless, it was certainly the case in France that, during the sixteenth and seventeenth centuries, the Jesuits and various teaching orders gradually perfected the closed and highly supervised world of the *collège*.[12] The boys in these colleges experienced an early and peculiarly rigorous form of the 'long' childhood now commonplace in the West. In the words of the historian Georges Snyders, the boarding school, its regulations, its very buildings, were designed to defy the adult word, to separate the child from it in a purified, sterilized, 'other world' dedicated to teaching. The college erected a further, spiritual barrier against the outside world by insisting that the pupils spoke only Latin, in the midst of a society that was increasingly won over to French for its speech and its most widely read books. The regime was to be supportive rather than repressive, helping the feeble child resist the ever-present threat of evil. The fear was that once beyond the shelter of the college, the young lad would fall into bad company capable of 'ruining in a few moments of conversation all the fruits of our long labour'.[13] The aim of the teaching programme was to steep the pupils in the culture of classical antiquity. In place of the jumble of ages and abilities characteristic of classes at the beginning of the seventeenth century, the Jesuits led the way in establishing a precise grading of studies. Their *Ratio studiorum* required boys to take three classes in grammar (between the fifth and the third class[14]), one in the humanities (the second) and one in rhetoric (the first). In the larger schools, a sixth class might take the least advanced boys from the fifth level. For those who lasted the whole course, time in the college lasted from around the age of twelve until eighteen. This system took a relatively small number of pupils: on the eve of the 1789 Revolution, less than 5 per cent of the male population of school age attended a *collège*. As will emerge below, it proved remarkably successful, surviving largely intact in the form of state *lycées* and municipal *collèges* until at least the 1880s.[15]

Jean-Jacques Rousseau, as a product of the Enlightenment rather than the Catholic Reformation, was contemptuous of the 'laughable establishments called *collèges*' and their 'barbarous education'. Yet he in his turn supported the notion of segregating children from the world of adults. In

[12] This paragraph is indebted to Snyders, *Pédagogie en France*, especially pp. 35–6, 47 and 68; Roger Chartier, Marie-Madeleine Compère and Dominique Julia, *L'Education en France du XVIe au XVIIIe siècle* (Paris: Société d'édition d'enseignement supérieur, 1976), chs. 5–6; and Marie-Madeleine Compère, *Du collège au lycée (1500–1850): généalogie de l'enseignement français* (Paris: Gallimard/Julliard, 1985), part 1.

[13] P. Charles Porée, *Discours de circonstances*, cited by Snyders, *Pédagogie en France*, p. 42.

[14] French school classes, in contrast to the British ones, start with the high numbers and lead towards a final first.

[15] See below, ch. 11.

Emile, or On Education (1762), his treatise on an education in harmony with nature, he proposed a long period of supervision of Emile by his tutor.[16] Rousseau it was who provided the most provocative and alluring treatise on education during the period, though one should remember that in *Emile* he was trying to establish some general principles rather than write a manual for parents. He insisted that Emile be raised out of harm's way in the country, far from 'the rabble of valets' and from 'the black morals of the cities'.[17] The tutor would allow Emile the illusion of freedom, but in reality manipulate events to a degree that now seems shocking: 'let him always believe he is the master, and let it always be you who are'.[18] No less importantly, Rousseau asserted that children under twelve should enjoy a 'negative education', untroubled by efforts to teach them virtue and truth for which they were not yet ready. He asserted the seemingly obvious proposition, but one radical for its time, that 'nature wants children to be children before being men'. Hence a useful rule for education would be 'not to gain time but to lose it'.[19] He followed this principle through to adolescence, which occurred after the age of fifteen in his schema. He asserted that a young man would end up stronger and more vigorous if this stage of life was retarded rather than accelerated.[20]

All this passed sublimely over the heads of the mass of peasants and workers. They generally remained convinced well into the twentieth century that the young should start earning their keep from an early age. They did consent to allow their children to spend increasing amounts of time in school, but it was a very different school to that of the *notables*. The 'little schools' of the *ancien régime* and the elementary schools of the nineteenth and early twentieth centuries offered only a rudimentary instruction in the three Rs, heavily laced with morality. Members of the 'enlightened bourgeoisie' proved reluctant to encourage education and a 'long' childhood outside their own ranks. Pursuing one line of logic, the *philosophes* of the Enlightenment supported the right of the masses to escape from ignorance and prejudice. Yet they also harboured traditional concerns that education would give peasants and labourers ideas above their station. Thus Voltaire pondered the wisdom of treating nine tenths of the population like 'monkeys', but also argued that most peasants had no need of literacy. In the event the socially conservative approach held sway.[21] Such contradictory impulses continued to

---

[16] Rousseau, *Emile*, pp. 40–1 and 79.   [17] Ibid., p. 95.
[18] Ibid., p. 120.   [19] Ibid., pp. 90–3.   [20] Ibid., p. 216.
[21] Snyders, *Pédagogie en France*, pp. 396–410; James A. Leith, 'Modernisation, Mass Education and Social Mobility in French Thought, 1750–1789', in R. F. Brissenden (ed.), *Studies in the Eighteenth Century*, vol. II (Toronto, 1973), pp. 223–38; Chartier et al., *L'Education*, pp. 38–9; Harvey Chisick, *The Limits of Reform in the Enlightenment:*

influence the spread and diversification of the school system during the nineteenth and early twentieth centuries. Under the liberal regime of the July Monarchy, for example, the *loi Guizot* of 1833 required every commune to provide a school, but allowed parents to decide whether or not to send their children to it. Similarly, the 1841 law on child labour insisted on some schooling for children under twelve, but regulated the conditions of their work rather than banning it entirely. After 1870 the Third Republican elite, influenced by the mildly reformist ideology of Solidarism, went further in imposing a longer childhood on the masses. The *lois Ferry* of the 1880s made schooling compulsory for all children between the ages of six and thirteen, while the 1874 law on child labour, with some exceptions, prohibited the employment of children under twelve. Meanwhile the *loi Camille Sée* of 1880 finally laid the foundations for a proper system of secondary education for girls. This still left intact the divergence between a basic instruction for the people in primary schools and a more elaborate education for the elite in secondary schools.[22]

The 'invention' of adolescence

The combined impact of child labour legislation and measures to promote primary schooling towards the end of the nineteenth century did at least eliminate most children under the age of twelve from full-time work. The attention of reformers therefore began to shift to the welfare of the next age group, paving the way for the so-called 'invention' of adolescence around 1900.[23] For a long time, discussion of adolescence remained in the mould set by thinkers in the seventeenth and eighteenth centuries. Around the 1860s, for example, it still generally touched on the subject

---

Attitudes towards the Education of the Lower Classes in Eighteenth-Century France (Princeton: Princeton University Press, 1981), passim.

[22] These points are covered in Antoine Prost, *Histoire de l'enseignement en France, 1800–1967* (Paris: Colin, 1968); Louis-Henri Parias, *Histoire générale de l'enseignement et de l'éducation en France*, vol. III, *De la Révolution à l'Ecole républicaine*, by François Mayeur (Paris: G. V. Labat, 1981); Weissbach, *Child Labor Reform in Nineteenth-Century France*; Colin Heywood, *Childhood in Nineteenth-Century France* (Cambridge: Cambridge University Press, 1988).

[23] This paragraph relies on Thiercé, *Histoire de l'adolescence*, passim. For comparative purposes, see also John R. Gillis, *Youth and History* (New York: Academic Press, 1974); Rolf E. Muuss, *Theories of Adolescence* (3rd edn, New York: Random House, 1975); Joseph F. Kett, *Rites of Passage: Adolescence in America, 1790 to the Present* (New York: Basic Books, 1977); John Springhall, *Coming of Age: Adolescence in Britain, 1860–1960* (Dublin: Gill and Macmillan, 1986); John Davis, *Youth and the Condition of Britain: Images of Adolescent Conflict* (London: Athlone Press, 1990); Barbara Hanawalt, 'Historical Descriptions and Prescriptions for Adolescence', *Journal of Family History*, 17 (1992), 341–51; and Christine Griffin, *Representations of Youth: The Study of Youth and Adolescence in Britain and America* (Cambridge: Polity Press, 1993).

from an educational or religious perspective, with the familiar figure of the inexperienced and headstrong youth in need of support from the school system. As before, the only section of the population in question was that tiny minority of middle-class males attending a *collège* or a *lycée*. However, from the 1890s onwards, leading lights in the Third Republic began to take an interest in what happened to young workers between the time they left school, around the age of twelve, and call-up for military service at the age of twenty: in other words, during that extended period when they had no supportive framework equivalent to that of the school and the regiment.[24] These thinkers also worried about young women marooned between the school and marriage. Republicans, hotly pursued by their Catholic rivals, experimented with a number of institutions to fill the gap, such as evening classes, clubs (*patronages*) and holiday camps. Meanwhile psychologists in France began to bring their scientific approach to adolescence. They took their lead from the American psychologist G. Stanley Hall, without necessarily agreeing with all of the conclusions in his massive two-volume work, *Adolescence* (1904–5).[25] In 1907 the 'psycho-pédagogue' Pierre Mendousse went as far as to assert that for two-and-a-half thousand years, between a famous page by Aristotle and the 1,300 pages written by Hall, there was 'almost nothing' on the subject.[26] The scientists moved on from the heavily moralistic discourse of their predecessors to include the techniques of observational psychology in their analysis. The upshot was a general acceptance in the twentieth century of adolescence as a stage of life between childhood and youth or adulthood, with its own distinct characteristics, needs and institutions.

The final chapter: 'everyone to school'

During the twentieth century, the call for *tous à l'école* and *une ecole pour tous* ('everyone to school' and 'a school for everyone') became a reality. A series of measures around 1930 made secondary schooling free, and numbers enrolled in this sector began to increase after a long period of stagnation. The unification of various post-primary school institutions into the *collège moderne* under the Vichy regime, the establishment of a technical *baccalauréat* to run beside the academic ones, and plans to raise

---

[24] Agnès Thiercé, 'L'Encadrement de l'adolescence populaire (1894–1914): vers une classe d'âge adolescente', in Bardet et al., *Lorsque l'enfant grandit*, pp. 795–814.

[25] G. Stanley Hall, *Adolescence, its Psychology and its Relations to Physiology, Anthropology, Sociology, Sex, Crime, Religion and Education* (2 vols., New York: Appleton, 1904–5).

[26] Pierre Mendousse, *L'Ame de l'adolescent* (5th edn, Paris: Presses Universitaires de France, 1947), p. ix, preface to the 1st edn.

the school-leaving age to sixteen in 1959 helped further. During the mid-1960s, a quarter of adolescents still left school at fourteen to start an apprenticeship scheme, and by seventeen, less than half were at school. The 'explosion' in the demand for places at school and universities was only beginning at this point. Nonetheless, the progressive segregation of childhood over the centuries was in effect complete.[27] It may well be that the second half of the twentieth century also brought a certain narrowing of the distance that had opened up between adults and children since the seventeenth century, 'a new era of childhood'. The extreme cloistering of children inherited from the past was proving unsustainable. Young people would still remain dependent on adults for a long time as school pupils and students, but with the 'information explosion' already evident at mid-century, with cinema, popular magazines and radio well established, any hopes of protecting 'innocent' children from the outside world began to collapse.[28]

Conclusion

In retrospect, therefore, there was from the perspective of the history of education a certain unity to the period running from the late seventeenth to the middle of the twentieth century. On the one hand, a tiny elite of males, and eventually females, experienced a 'long', sheltered childhood, or adolescence. They acquired a classical or scientific culture in the school system devised by the teaching orders of the Catholic Reformation, with its careful age grading of classes and isolation of the young from the world of adults. On the other hand, the 'popular classes' still had to balance school with work, leading to a 'shorter' childhood. This is not to say that they worked and played with adults from the age of seven, for they spent as much time as they could with their own age group, and often had their own separate jobs, such as shepherding or running errands. There was also a long series of initiatives to boost primary education and vocational training among the people, and to reduce the burdens of child labour. All the same, the long-running concern that an expansion

[27] See Prost, *Histoire de l'enseignement*, parts 5 and 6; Crubellier, *L'Enfance et la jeunesse*, passim; Martine Corijn, 'Transitions to Adulthood in France', in Corijn and Klijzing (eds.), *Transitions to Adulthood in Europe*, pp. 131–51; and Michelle Perrot, 'Sur la ségrégation de l'enfance au XIXe siècle', *Psychiatrie de l'enfance*, 25 (1982), 179–206.

[28] Neil Postman, *The Disappearance of Childhood* (New York: Vintage Books, 1994 (1982)), passim; Hugh Cunningham, *Children and Childhood in Western Society since 1500* (London: Longman, 1995), pp. 179–85; and Shirley R. Steinberg and Joe L. Kincheloe, 'Introduction: No More Secrets – Kinderculture, Information Saturation, and the Postmodern Childhood', in Steinberg and Kincheloe (eds.), *Kinderculture: The Corporate Construction of Childhood* (Boulder, CO: Westview, 1997), pp. 1–30.

of secondary education would produce an excess of educated men, a pool of discontented *déclassés* unable to find work that matched their aspirations, encouraged conservatism in this sphere. In the words of the historian Antoine Prost, during the nineteenth century the 'school of the notables' and the 'school of the people' remained strangers rather than rivals.[29]

By the middle of the twentieth century, the vast majority of French people took it for granted that the young were entitled to a 'proper' childhood, which one way or another would allow them time for play, schooling and a progressive preparation for adulthood.[30] Their entirely reasonable assumption was that this would favour the health, moral welfare and education of rising generations. Yet the success in the West of the campaign to impose an extended childhood should not be allowed to obscure the burdens it imposed on the young. The 'colonization' of childhood by adults, particularly during the nineteenth and twentieth centuries, meant a curbing of the freedom that young people of school age had previously enjoyed with others of their own age.[31] In attempting to distance young people from the worlds of work, sexuality and politics, the new ideal also brought an obvious risk of 'infantilizing' them. A long list of former pupils from the *collèges* and *lycées* railed against the monotony of their existence while cooped up in class for years. Jules Vallès dedicated his autobiographical novel *Le Bachelier* (1881) 'to all those who were fed on Greek and Latin and died of hunger'.[32] The primary-school system resisted efforts by working-class leaders to bring the workshop into the school during the later nineteenth century, and, odd initiatives in bringing manual work to the primary schools during the early Third Republic apart, adhered to a purely academic curriculum well into the twentieth century.[33] In the 1960s, there were complaints that the republican school was out of touch with the surrounding society, having its own set of rules and even a vague notion of recasting the adult world of the future. Writing on the eve of the events of 1968, Antoine Prost confronted the crisis facing education, as adolescence became a general rather than a 'bourgeois' phenomenon, and as adolescents struggled with the inevitable constraints imposed by compulsory secondary schooling. The old escape into work

---

[29] Prost, *Histoire de l'enseignement*, p. 10.
[30] This definition comes from Assef Bequele, 'Emerging Perspectives in the Struggle Against Child Labour', in William E. Myers (ed.), *Protecting Working Children* (London: Zed Books, 1991), pp. 69–86 (p. 77).
[31] Crubellier, *L'Enfance et la jeunesse*, p. 58.
[32] Jules Vallès, *Le Bachelier* (Paris: Gallimard, 1974).
[33] J.-P. Guinot, *Formation professionnelle et travailleurs qualifiées depuis 1789* (Paris: Domat-Montchrestien, 1946), pp. 142–8.

was no longer available, and the 'collective cultural patrimony' promoted by the teaching profession appeared outmoded.[34]

The nature of childhood and adolescence

Some of the first academic studies of representations of childhood in France, written during the 1930s, envisaged using novels as sociological and psychological documents. The aim was to reveal some universal truths about the child.[35] As noted above, the search for the 'essential child' now appears fruitless, given an awareness of the variety of childhoods in different periods and places. A more recent approach in the French and the 'Anglo-Saxon' literature involves treating the images of children in the literature, and even in the scientific works, as social constructions. These constructions would ebb and flow around a few key archetypal images down the centuries, change according to the movement of ideas and social conditions, and compete in various forms at any given time. In the words of the psychologist William Kessen, 'the history of child study is a history of rediscovery. With remarkable regularity, the same themes appear, are elaborated for a while, then fade.'[36] The themes are by no means arbitrary, since they are constructed around salient features of the child, such as its small stature, early dependence on adults and constant growth. They also reveal ambivalent adult attitudes to the young, as theorists struggle to conclude whether children are essentially good or bad, stupid or wise, sexual or asexual, vulnerable or resilient.[37] Similarly, those interested in adolescence usually started with the notion of a 'second birth' around puberty, and constructed on this basis a list of partially contradictory characteristics for the age group.

This section will concentrate on 'pre-sociological' theories, which were concocted from a combination of common sense, philosophy and developmental psychology. As a recent survey written by sociologists put it, they have all been consigned to the 'dustbin of history', though they continue to influence the way people think about the young.[38] Their proponents tended to assume that their particular concept of the child was 'natural' and universal, without reference to prevailing social circumstances. Above all, it will highlight modern French versions of the evil 'Dionysian child' and the sunny and poetic 'Apollonian child': two

---

[34] Crubellier, *L'Enfance et la jeunesse*, pp. 247–9; and Prost, *Histoire de l'enseignement*, pp. 482–6. See also Martin Hoyles, 'History and Politics', in Hoyles (ed.), *Changing Childhood* (London: Writers and Readers Publishing Cooperative, 1979), pp. 1–10.
[35] Notably Dupuy, *Un personnage nouveau*; and Toursch, *L'Enfant français*.
[36] Kessen, *The Child*, p. x.   [37] See Heywood, *Childhood in the West*, ch. 3.
[38] James et al., *Theorizing Childhoods*, ch. 1.

archetypal images that run like a red thread through Western civilization.[39] It will specify where possible the social spheres most likely to be receptive to a particular conception, and the impact it was likely to have on social practice between the eighteenth and the twentieth centuries.

The evil child

Classical and medieval authorities in the West bequeathed to the modern world a mixed view on the nature of childhood, but overall it was an unflattering image that prevailed. The former often had a low opinion of children. Evidence from Greek and Roman times in this area is admittedly thin on the ground, and historians by no means agreed on their conclusions. It may well be, though, that these societies gave children a lowly status, and found little of interest to write about them.[40] Certainly La Bruyère (1645–96), a French writer steeped in the classics, could dismiss children as 'haughty, contemptuous, angry, envious, curious, selfish, idle, fickle, timid, intemperate, mendacious, secretive . . . they do not want to suffer harm at all but like to inflict it'.[41] The medieval Catholic Church in its turn ranged from celebrations of the innocence of children to graphic descriptions of their evil character. The pope, Leo the Great (in office 440–61), might preach that 'Christ loved childhood, mistress of humility, rule of innocence, model of sweetness'. Yet Catholic doctrine always insisted that children were born with the taint of original sin, until the sacrament of baptism washed it away. St Augustine pointed to the envy and jealousy between infants being fed by the same mother or nurse as evidence that there was no such thing as a naturally innocent child. 'If I was born in sin and guilt was with me already when my mother conceived me', he asked rhetorically, 'Lord, where or when was I, your servant, ever innocent?'[42]

---

[39] Jenks, *Childhood*, pp. 70–8.

[40] For syntheses of recent work in this field, see Valerie French, 'Children in Antiquity', in Joseph M. Hawes and N. Ray Hiner (eds.), *Children in Historical and Comparative Perspective: An International Handbook and Research Guide* (New York: Greenwood Press, 1991); Cunningham, *Children and Childhood*, pp. 19–27; Elise P. Garrison, 'Ancient Greece and Rome', in Paula S. Fass (ed.), *Encyclopedia of Children and Childhood in History and Society* (3 vols., New York: Macmillan Reference, 2004), vol. I, pp. 53–7.

[41] Jean de La Bruyère, 'De l'homme', cited by Primault et al., *Terres de l'enfance*, p. 10.

[42] Saint Augustine, *Confessions*, transl. R. S. Pine-Coffin (Harmondsworth: Penguin, 1961), pp. 27–8. See also Richard B. Lyman Jr, 'Barbarism and Religion: Late Roman and Early Medieval Childhood', in Lloyd deMause (ed.), *The History of Childhood* (London: Souvenir Press, 1976), pp. 75–100; Thomas Wiedemann, *Adults and Children in the Roman Empire* (London: Routledge, 1989), ch. 6; Shulamith Shahar, *Childhood in the Middle Ages* (London: Routledge, 1990), ch. 1; Åke Sander, 'Images of the Child and Childhood in Religion', in Hwang et al., *Images of Childhood*, pp. 14–26.

By the sixteenth century, the Catholic Church required that children who had reached the age of reason, traditionally thought to be seven, should attempt to emulate Christian behaviour and confess their sins.[43] Even though children were not thought capable of committing serious sins, this did not prevent some clerics taking an extreme position on the sinfulness of children, particularly among Jansenists and Oratorians during the Catholic Reformation period. It is a little disturbing to hear the founder of the Oratorians, Cardinal de Bérulle (1575–1629), writing off childhood as 'the most vile and abject state of human nature, after that of death'. He perceived children as incapable of thought, affection or a life of grace. All that Catholic theologians like him could say in favour of the child was that, although utterly corrupt, it could achieve a certain innocence since it was too feeble to implement its evil designs.[44] François de Fénelon (1651–1715) took a more liberal view on relations between tutors and the pupils under their care. In his treatise on *The Education of Girls* (1687), most of which was applicable to boys also, he conceded that 'children are naturally but little inclined towards the good'. However, he felt that if at the outset their health was looked after and they were not spoiled, they would turn out well. 'Do not appear shocked or annoyed by their evil tendencies,' he advised, 'on the contrary be sympathetic to their weakness.' He was also prepared 'to follow and to aid nature', taking advantage of their natural curiosity and habit of asking questions.[45]

Modern Catholic thinkers reflected this ambivalent heritage. Bishop Dupanloup (1802–78), for example, was a man who enjoyed a formidable reputation as a teacher and defender of children in the nineteenth century. His book *L'Enfant* (1869) began with a rehearsal of all the qualities Christianity saw in the child. He praised its 'simple and pure heart', its 'innocence and grace'. He noted its divine origins, with the customary line that 'there is in this first age something which comes most recently from heaven, which invokes all the blessings of that divine hand'. And yet, he recalled the stain of original sin, and suggested that if his hair had gone white early, it was because of years in service to children. There were 'depraved instincts' in the child, such as obstinacy, bursts of temper, jealousy, lying, ingratitude and selfishness.[46] He observed that the

---

[43] Richard L. DeMolem, 'Childhood and the Sacraments in the Sixteenth Century', *Archiv für Reformationdeschichte*, 65 (1974), 49–71 (69).

[44] This section relies on Snyders, *Pédagogie en France*, part 2, ch. 4.

[45] Fénelon, 'The Education of Girls', in H. C. Barnard, *Fénelon on Education* (Cambridge: Cambridge University Press, 1966), pp. 1–96 (pp. 9, 11 and 19).

[46] Félix Dupanloup, *L'Enfant* (Paris: Charles Douniol, 1869), ch. 1. For a different reading of this text, see J. Calvet, *L'Enfant dans la littérature française* (2 vols., Paris: Lanore, 1930), vol. I, pp. 202–6; and Theodore Zeldin, *France 1848–1945: Ambition and Love* (Oxford: Oxford University Press, 1979), pp. 322–3.

leanings towards evil in human nature were buried deep in the soul of the child. He devoted over half of his book to sin. In particular, he focused on the 'triple concupiscence' of pride, sensuality and cupidity.

Dupanloup was writing during the Second Empire, under a regime relatively favourable to the Catholic Church. His audience was likely to be middle rather than working class, and female rather than male. As the historian Marie-Françoise Lévy has shown, the period generated a battery of educational works aimed at young girls, which revolved around the figure of the Christian mother encouraging good to triumph over evil. After the 1880s, religious morality steadily disappeared from child-rearing manuals as a more secularized society pinned its faith in domestic science.[47] Even so, the numerous works by Dupanloup on child rearing and education continued to be read well into the twentieth century. The Comtesse de Ségur also kept the traditional Catholic line alive with a series of widely read didactic novels for children. In *Les Malheurs de Sophie* (1864), for example, the four-year-old Sophie emerged as relentlessly disobedient, thoughtless, cruel, coquettish, greedy, mendacious, proud, aggressive, dishonest and lazy. She faced a mother who claimed to know better because she was a grown-up – and was invariably right.[48] Later, in the twentieth century, Georges Bernanos was another Catholic writer who exhibited the same ambiguity in his attitude to children as Dupan-loup. His novel *The Diary of a Country Priest* (1936) depicted the *curé* struggling with the village children during his catechism classes. He had to admit to himself that his most successful pupil was Sylvestre Galuchet, a rather grubby little boy being brought up by a less than sober grand-mother. Even so, 'he is a strangely beautiful child who gives me the almost poignant feeling of innocence, an innocence previous to all sin, the sin-lessness of an innocent beast'. For the rest, children in the novel were consumed by lust and a 'scarcely veiled animality'. One of the girls tor-mented him with her trick of deliberately lifting up her skirt to adjust the shoelace that served as a garter.[49]

The image of the evil or depraved child also had a secularized form in modern culture. It is possible, as the historian Darya Vassigh has argued, that this view was associated with the recapitulation theory of human development fashionable in scientific circles during the late nineteenth century. In this perspective, the child was assimilated to primitive peoples,

[47] Lévy, *De mères en filles*, passim.
[48] Comtesse de Ségur, *Les Malheurs de Sophie* (Paris: Babel, 1997).
[49] Georges Bernanos, *The Diary of a Country Priest*, transl. Pamela Morris (2nd edn, New York: Carroll and Graf, 2002 (1937)), pp. 27–8, 75, 88 and 98; Malcolm Scott, *Bernanos: Journal d'un curé de campagne* (London: Grant and Cutler, 1997).

the adult to civilized ones.[50] In 1882, the psychologist Bernard Pérez insisted that children were innately quick-tempered, jealous and mendacious. The republican educationalist Gabriel Compayré rejected the extremes of the innately innocent or evil child in his *Intellectual and Moral Evolution of the Child* (1893), yet concluded that children had an evil base, a residue of an innate disposition, which could not in any sense be interpreted in a benevolent way.[51] Freudian theory, one might argue, restored some of the carnality of original sin to the child in the form of the id, with the hint of an underlying evil that needs to be repressed.[52] There was already a literary tradition in France of depicting peasant children as close to nature, and hence aware of an earthy sexuality from watching animals or adults copulating around the farms. In *Monsieur Nicolas* (1796), Rétif de la Bretonne commented, 'And they say that innocence is in the villages! Everywhere one finds men and women, there is fermentation and corruption.' His view of childhood was one of perversity and violence.[53] Early in the nineteenth century, the painter Théodore Géricault chipped in at a more rarefied level with his disturbing portrait of the young Louise Vernet. He depicted her as a girl exuding lustfulness. Her dress slides off one shoulder, she has a huge pussy cat on her lap, and she stares knowingly at the viewer (Fig. 1).[54]

Various literary figures followed suit later in the century, providing occasional references to the precocious sexuality or cruelty of children.[55] An early venture along these lines, although not one well known in France until Surrealists took it up during the 1920s, was *Les Chants de Maldoror* (1868–9) by Lautréamont. The author, according to Alex de Jonge, set out to crack the code of French culture, which included revealing the unpalatable truth that humanity was composed of evil with a mere tinge of good.[56] His eponymous hero 'was born wicked', and set out on a series of outrages, notably the infamous assault on an infant girl involving a rape, a bulldog and an American penknife. The Gothic horror was

---

[50] Vassigh, 'Relations adultes–enfants', II, pp. 196–204.
[51] Bernard Pérez, *La Psychologie de l'enfant* (1882), cited in Luc, *L'Invention du jeune enfant au XIXe siècle*, p. 98; Gabriel Compayré, *L'Evolution intellectuelle et morale de l'enfant* (Paris: Hachette, 1893), pp. 314–15, cited in Zeldin, *Ambition and Love*, p. 324.
[52] James et al., *Theorizing Childhood*, p. 20.
[53] Rétif de la Bretonne, *Monsieur Nicolas, ou le cœur humain dévoilé* (Paris: Trianon, 1932), pp. 17 and 33. See also Gérard Lahouati, 'L'Invention de l'enfance: le statut du souvenir d'enfance dans quelques autobiographies du XVIIIe siècle', in Berriot-Salvadore and Pebay-Clottes (eds.), *Autour de l'enfance*, pp. 163–90 (p. 181).
[54] Stefan Germer, 'Pleasurable Fear: Géricault and Uncanny Trends at the Opening of the Nineteenth Century', *Art History*, 22 (1999), 159–83.
[55] Bethlenfalvay, *Les Visages de l'enfant*, ch. 3; Lloyd, *Land of Lost Content*, pp. 93–118.
[56] Alex de Jonge, *Nightmare Culture: Lautréamont and Les Chants de Maldoror* (London: Secker and Warburg, 1973), pp. 47 and 50.

Figure 1. Théodore Géricault, *Louise Vernet, Child, Daughter of the Painter Horace Vernet* (1818–19), Paris, Musée du Louvre, © Photo RMN, © Christian Jean.

at least relieved by a black humour, with little asides such as '*I* have always taken an infamous fancy to the pale youngsters in schools and the sickly mill children.'[57] In 'Le Papa de Simon' (1881), Guy de Maupassant had

---

[57] Lautréamont, *Maldoror*, transl. Alexis Lykiard (London: Allison and Busby, 1970), pp. 2, 93–4 and 158.

a group of village children taunt a boy on his first day at school for not having a father, knock him down, dance round him and shout 'Pas de Papa! Pas de Papa!' Maupassant suggested that these children from the fields were close to beasts, feeling the same 'cruel need' as chickens to finish off one of their number when it is injured. Emile Zola took his realism in *Germinal* (1885) to include the 'love-making' of the ten-year-old Jeanlin and his playmate Lydie, something about which they knew everything, from watching through cracks in doors, but could not do much, because they were too young.[58] In the twentieth century, there was the irrepressible Zazie, eponymous heroine of *Zazie in the Metro* (1959) by Raymond Queneau. Her character embodies all the nightmares of those worried about the 'disappearance' of childhood in the late twentieth century. Aged around eleven or twelve, she is foul-mouthed, desperate for a pair of *bloudjinnzes* (or 'blewgenes') and well versed in the mass media. She revels in the seamy side of life, recounting with some relish tales of attempted rape by her father (before her mother murdered him), and plaguing everyone with questions about whether her uncle is a '*hormosessuel*'.[59]

The logic of those arguing for the depraved nature of childhood was for a strict regime in child rearing. Catholics did not necessarily talk of breaking the will of such perverse creatures, but Dupanloup followed Calvinists before him in arguing that children were like plants needing help to grow straight. He insisted on the need to base education on the twin principles of *authority* and *respect*.[60] Popular responses to juvenile delinquency periodically flushed out such attitudes: during the 1900s, for example, there were calls for *Apaches* in the Parisian street gangs to be flogged or even guillotined.[61] While living in a French village during the years 1950–1, the American Laurence Wylie commented that:

People in Peyrane do not believe that man is naturally good, because it is obvious to them that children are not naturally good. They are more like little animals which must be domesticated at home and in the school. They obey the rules imposed on them because they are forced to obey them, not because they want to.[62]

---

[58] Guy de Maupassant, *La Maison Tellier* (Paris: Albin Michel, 1969), pp. 169–73; Emile Zola, *Germinal*, transl. L. W. Tancock (Harmondsworth: Penguin, 1954), p. 127.

[59] Raymond Queneau, *Zazie in the Metro*, transl. Barbara Wright (London: John Calder, 1982 (1959)); W. D. Redfern, *Queneau: Zazie dans le métro* (London: Grant and Cutler, 1980).

[60] Dupanloup, *L'Enfant*, p. 25.

[61] Michelle Perrot, 'Dans la France de la Belle Epoque, les "Apaches", premières bandes de jeunes', in *Les Marginaux et les exclus dans l'histoire*, special issue of *Les Cahiers Jussieu* (Paris: Union générale d'éditions, 1978), pp. 387–407.

[62] Laurence Wylie, *Village in the Vaucluse* (2nd edn, Cambridge, MA: Harvard University Press, 1964), p. 121.

The innocent child: the child of nature

The thinker who most forcefully rejected the established notion of original sin by proposing in its place the cult of original innocence in the child was assuredly Jean-Jacques Rousseau.[63] His call to 'love childhood; promote its games, its pleasures, its amiable instinct' was a head-on challenge to traditional thinking.[64] Indeed, *Emile, or On Education* (1762) was promptly condemned by both civil and religious authorities in Paris when it first appeared, causing Rousseau to flee the country. This was in spite of the fact that leading Catholics in the past had occasionally made reference to childhood innocence. Moreover, Rousseau had absorbed many ideas about child rearing and education current in mid-eighteenth-century France. His critics went as far as to accuse him of plagiarism: in 1766 the Benedictine Dom Cajot published a 400-page critique, *Les Plagiats de M. J.-J. R. de Genève, sur l'éducation.*[65] In spite of all the uproar, *Emile* struck a chord with the reading public in France and the rest of Europe. It, and the accompanying novel *La Nouvelle Héloïse* (1761), went through numerous editions before 1789, and, in the words of William Kessen, 'were translated, pirated, quoted, imitated, praised, and attacked in sufficiency to suggest that every literate European had read the books'.[66] Besides this breadth of coverage, there is also evidence of depth in its influence, with the example of the Protestant merchant Jean Ranson showing someone who devoured all of the works written by 'l'Ami Jean-Jacques' and tried to model his life on them. His wife breastfed all of their children, he named his second son Emile and for his daughter he hoped that 'by a good education, I can make the most of the goodness of her nature'.[67] The success of *Emile* was hardly surprising, given its lively prose style and its rigorous pursuit of its line on the innocence of childhood.

The opening sentence of *Emile* set the tone for the whole work by proclaiming boldly that 'everything is good as it leaves the hands of the Author of things; everything degenerates in the hands of man'. If there was corruption, it was because prejudice and social institutions had swayed human inclinations. This was Rousseau's version of the Catholic Fall, and context for his concern that the child might lapse into corruption

---

[63] See Roger Mercier, *L'Enfant dans la société du XVIIIe siècle (avant l'Emile)* (Dakar: Université de Dakar, Faculté des lettres et sciences humaines, 1961), pp. 183–8; J. H. Broome, *Rousseau* (London: Edward Arnold, 1963), ch. 5; Peter Coveney, *The Image of Childhood* (Harmondsworth: Penguin, 1967), ch. 1; Maurice Cranston, *The Noble Savage: Jean-Jacques Rousseau 1754–1762* (Chicago: University of Chicago Press, 1991), ch. 7.

[64] Rousseau, *Emile*, p. 79.   [65] Mercier, *L'Enfant*, pp. 7–8.

[66] William Kessen, 'Rousseau's Children', *Daedalus*, 107 (1978), 155–66 (161).

[67] Robert Darnton, 'Readers Respond to Rousseau: The Fabrication of Romantic Sensitivity', in *The Great Cat Massacre and other Episodes in French Cultural History* (Harmondsworth: Penguin, 1985), pp. 209–49.

Figure 2. Jean-Baptiste-Siméon Chardin, *Portrait of the Son of M. Gode-froy, Jeweller, Watching a Top Spin* (1738), Paris, Musée du Louvre, © Photo RMN, © Jean Schormans.

at the least provocation. Rousseau accepted the weakness of children, but distinguished between dependence on things, which is from nature, and dependence on men, which is from society. He wanted to keep the child dependent on things, because this followed the order of nature in the progress of education.[68] He consciously diverged from the earlier approach of John Locke in advising against reasoning with a child during its first twelve years. He argued that reason was a faculty that developed late and with difficulty in man. His famous counterblast to Locke was that 'Childhood has its own ways of seeing, thinking, and feeling which are proper to it. Nothing is less sensible than to substitute ours for theirs.' He set down as an 'incontestable maxim' that 'the first movements of nature are invariably right'. This led to his key point that 'there is no original perversity in the human heart'. If the child were left to respond to nature,

[68] Rousseau, *Emile*, p. 85.

only good would come of it. He accepted that left to his own devices the child might hurt himself or cause some damage, but 'he could do a considerable amount of wrong without wrongdoing' because his intention was not to do harm.[69] With this newfound respect for childhood, it was possible to leave nature to act for a long period before intervening on its behalf.[70]

Besides philosophical treatises like *Some Thoughts* and *Emile*, the odd artistic and literary work provides evidence that ideas of childhood innocence were 'in the air' during the eighteenth century. Chardin (1699–1779) was an early example of a painter who gave a quiet dignity to the world of the child, depicting, for example, *A Girl Toying with her Lunch* (c. 1737) or the absorption of a young boy in his game in the *Portrait of the Son of M. Godefroy, Jeweller, Watching a Top Spin* (1738) (Fig. 2).[71] Greuze (1725–1805) occasionally managed similar gravity, notably in *A Boy with a Lesson Book* (1757) (Fig. 3), but usually his desire to titillate got the better of his urge to preach. His *Innocence* from the 1790s (Fig. 4) was, in the words of Anita Brookner, the head of an adolescent girl 'on the verge of orgasm'.[72] More successful at manipulating the image of the child as innocent was David (1748–1825), with his depiction of a young martyr in the cause of the French Revolution. The unfinished *Death of Joseph Bara* (1794) showed the thirteen-year-old soldier laid out naked and beautiful, in a rather androgynous way, after he was killed by counter-revolutionaries in the Vendée (Fig. 5).[73]

On the literary side, one of the most successful attempts to popularize the myth of childhood innocence came in the form of *Paul and Virginia* (1788) by Bernardin de Saint-Pierre. The novel went through no less than 269 editions between 1789 and 1962. It began as a well-respected literary work, but after 1850 came to be seen as a book for children. School editions and expurgated versions meant that it reached almost every type of audience, even if its didactic nature meant it was often more respected than enjoyed.[74] Bernardin de Saint-Pierre set up two 'children of nature' in the novel by putting them on the exotic Ile-de-France

---

[69] Ibid., pp. 89–93.   [70] Ibid., p. 107.

[71] Pierre Rosenberg, *Chardin, 1699–1779* (Cleveland: Cleveland Museum of Art, 1979), pp. 187–293; and Philip Conisbee, *Chardin* (Oxford: Phaidon, 1986), chs. 6–7.

[72] Anita Brookner, *Greuze: The Rise and Fall of an Eighteenth-Century Phenomenon* (London: Elek, 1972), pp. xvi and 154.

[73] Walter Friedlaender, *David to Delacroix* (Folkestone: Bailey Bros. & Swinfen, 1968), p. 25.

[74] Valérie David, 'Sur l'iconographie de Paul et Virginie', and Jean-Marie Goulemot, 'L'Histoire littéraire en question: l'exemple de Paul et Virginie', in Jean-Michel Racault (ed.), *Etudes sur Paul et Virginie et l'oeuvre de Bernardin de St-Pierre* (Paris: Didier-Erudition, 1986), pp. 238–48 and 203–14 respectively.

Figure 3. Jean-Baptiste Greuze, *A Boy with a Lesson Book* (1757), National Gallery of Scotland, Edinburgh.

(Mauritius). Here, in a quiet valley, they worked small plots of land with their mothers, 'far from the cruel prejudices of Europe'. At the age of twelve, neither could read or write, and they had not been burdened by 'useless sciences' or morality lessons 'superfluous to bosoms unconscious of ill'. They revealed their 'love, innocence, and piety' by helping

Figure 4. Jean-Baptiste Greuze, *Innocence* (date unknown), Reproduced
by permission of the Trustees of the Wallace Collection, London.

a runaway slave and by slowly falling in love. In the end, the author conveniently killed off the two innocents before they reached adulthood. In
a splendidly melodramatic scene, the ship bringing Virginia back from a
visit to France started to break up in a storm. The heroine revealed her
virtue as she refused to save her own life by undressing and jumping into
the sea beside a naked sailor. She prepared for death with one hand on

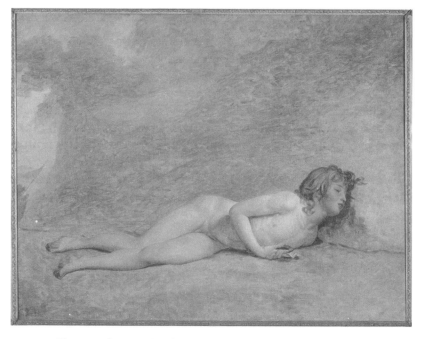

Figure 5. Jacques-Louis David, *Death of Joseph Bara* (1794), Avignon, Musée Calvet, © Photo RMN, © Hervé Lewandowski.

her clothes and the other on her heart; Paul expired from melancholy two months later.[75]

The 'child of nature', and the linking of the innocent child to some Arcadian setting such as an unspoilt village or a luxurious garden, was to remain a popular image throughout the modern period. It was an obvious escape from the harsh realities that preoccupied many people in the wake of the French and the Industrial Revolutions. The child was a neat counterpoint to, say, the new 'barbarians' of the urban slums during the 1830s. Similarly, the countryside of pastoral tradition appeared a haven of tranquillity compared to the turbulent streets of revolutionary Paris or the teeming slums of the new industrial centres. The Romantics latched on to the child of nature with relish. A striking visual example came from the painter Antoine-Jean Gros, whose portrait of *Paulin des Hours* (1793) depicted a small boy on his knees in a field as he captured a goldfinch

[75] J. H. Bernardin de Saint-Pierre, *Paul and Virginia*, transl. Helen Marie Williams (Oxford: Woodstock Books, 1989 (1796)).

Figure 6. Antoine-Jean Gros, *Portrait de Paulin des Hours* (1793), Rennes, Musée des Beaux-Arts, © RENNES, Dist RMN, © Patrick Merret.

(Fig. 6). Set in the grounds of a chateau, the painting revelled in the lively physical presence of its subject and the squawking bird in his hand.[76] Chateaubriand, a fervent admirer of Rousseau, planned his novel *René* (1802) as an 'epic of nature'. As a young man, René looked back fondly to walks in the forest near his father's chateau at the beginning of the eighteenth century. In this remote province of Brittany, he could hear the distant sound of church bells: 'each tremor of the brass bore to my naïve soul the innocence of rustic customs, the calm of solitude, and the delectable melancholy of the memories of my early childhood'.[77] Later, during the 1840s and 1850s, George Sand used her 'rustic novels' to assert the superiority of the primitive life of the peasantry over the 'artificial life' of the towns. She deployed various child figures to good effect for this purpose. In *La Mare au diable* (1846), for example, she presented

[76] Robert Rosenblum, *The Romantic Child: From Runge to Sendak* (London: Thames and Hudson, 1988), pp. 32–3.
[77] Chateaubriand, *René* (Paris: Livre de poche, 1989 (1802)); see also the Introduction by Jean-Claude Berchet.

an idealized view of work in the fields, including a seven-year-old boy, 'beautiful as an angel', leading his father's plough team.[78] Any number of French writers rooted the children of their novels and autobiographies in the countryside during the late nineteenth and twentieth centuries: best known is Marcel Proust (1871–1922) in the villages of Auteuil and Combray (Illiers), but one might also cite Pierre Loti (1850–1923) by the sea near Rochefort, Alain-Fournier (1886–1914) harking back to La Chapelle d'Angillon in the Cher, and Marcel Pagnol (1895–1974) at Aubagne in Provence.[79]

The innocent child: Romantic and realist perspectives

Whereas Rousseau thought that children were different from adults, he did not think that they were better. Far from seeing a little angel in the infant, he feared that their weakness meant that there was a despot waiting to emerge if it was not raised properly.[80] The Romantics of the early nineteenth century, by contrast, asserted that the original innocence of childhood involved a sense of wonder, an intensity of experience and a spiritual wisdom lacking in the adult. During the 1850s, George Sand wrote of childhood that 'There is not one of us who does not recall this golden age as a vanished dream, to which nothing will be comparable afterwards.' Jules Michelet compared human life to a stream, which at its source flowed with clear water, reflecting the sky and the greenery around, but later became clouded with less pure water.[81] Whereas Enlightenment thinkers considered childhood as a time for education, the Romantics saw it as a lost realm that was nonetheless fundamental to the shaping of the adult self. The literary critic Marina Bethlenfalvay suggested that the figure of the Romantic child in France managed to integrate the optimistic vision of humanity espoused by the generation preceding the Revolution of 1789 with the melancholy of the one that followed it.[82] One can agree that the Romantics followed the *philosophes* in rejecting the pessimistic view of human nature adopted

---

[78] George Sand, *François le champi* (Paris: Garnier, 1962 (1850)); and *La Mare au diable* (Paris: Garnier, 1962 (1846)), p. 19. See also *La Petite Fadette* (Paris: Garnier, 1958 (1849)) and *The Master Pipers*, transl. Rosemary Lloyd (Oxford: Oxford University Press, 1994 (1852)).

[79] Proust, *The Way by Swann's*; Loti, *Le Roman d'un enfant*; Alain-Fournier, *Le Grand Meaulnes*, transl. Frank Davison (Oxford: Oxford University Press, 1959 (1913)); Marcel Pagnol, *La Gloire de mon père* (London: Nelson, 1962 (1957)) and *Le Château de ma mère* (Paris: Fallois, 1988).

[80] Broome, *Rousseau*, p. 84.

[81] George Sand, *Histoire de ma vie* (Paris: Livre de poche, 2004 (1854–57)), p. 139; Jules Michelet, *Ma jeunesse* (Paris: Flammarion, 1913), p. 63.

[82] Bethlenfalvay, *Les Visages de l'enfant*, p. 43.

by many medieval churchmen, yet often retreated into nostalgia for a lost paradise. The idea that the child remained in touch with a transcendental world appealed above all to poets.[83] Victor Hugo was one of many to latch on to the traditional image of the child-angel, still close to heaven:

> On devine à ses yeux, pleins d'une pure flamme
> Qu'au Paradis, d'où vient son âme
> Elle a dit un récent adieu.[84]
> (We perceive in her eyes, full of a pure flame
> That in Paradise, from where her soul comes
> She has recently said goodbye.)

Hugo also sometimes deployed the figure of the 'child redeemer' to radiate goodness and love in a murky adult world. The ex-convict Valjean in *Les Misérables* sustains his struggle to choose good over evil in his character with the help of the young vagrant Petit Gervais, and later the orphan Cosette. She it was who 'taught him the meaning of love', and gave him moral support on the path to virtue as he wavered in the face of human malice.[85]

Part of the genius of a poet, it was argued, was to keep some of this mystery of childhood intact during adulthood and communicate it to others. Baudelaire (1821–67), for example, still influenced by Romanticism, sought out the distant 'green paradise of infant love'.[86] He made the most influential exposition of this line on the poetic nature of childhood:

The child sees everything as *new*; it is always *intoxicated*. Nothing is so reminiscent of what is termed inspiration as the joy with which children absorb shape and colour . . . The man of genius has solid nerves; the child's nerves are weak. In the former, reason has assumed a considerable place; in the latter, sensitivity occupies almost the entire individual. But genius is merely *childhood regained* through an act of will, childhood which now, in order to express itself, possesses virile organs and an analytical mind that enables it to impose order on the sum of the material unconsciously amassed.[87]

---

[83] For English parallels, with the argument that the child could become a symbol of Imagination and Sensibility in a harsh machine age, see Coveney, *Image of Childhood*, p. 31.

[84] Victor Hugo, *Odes and Ballades*, V, cited by Bethlenfalvay, *Les Visages de l'enfant*, p. 21. Bethlenfalvay finds no evidence that French poets were aware of the similar sentiments expressed by William Wordsworth in his Immortality Ode. See Barbara Garlitz, 'The Immortality Ode: Its Cultural Progeny', *Studies in English Literature, 1500–1900*, 6 (1966), 639–49. Numerous extracts from the poetry of Hugo feature on the positive side in the anthology collected by Emile Deschanel, *Le Bien et le mal qu'on a dit des enfants* (Paris: Michel Lévy, 1857).

[85] Victor Hugo, *Les Misérables*, transl. Norman Denny (London: Penguin, 1976), pp. 112–18 and 391–4.

[86] Primault et al., *Terres de l'enfance*, p. 11.

[87] Charles Baudelaire, *Oeuvres complètes*, vol. II, p. 690, cited and translated by Lloyd in *Land of Lost Content*, p. 102.

A long succession of French writers followed this line well into the twentieth century. The poet Arthur Rimbaud (1854–91), although only a teenager when writing *Illuminations*, looked back longingly to childhood as a lost paradise. For the critic Nick Osmond, Rimbaud's poem 'L'Enfance' showed how 'the magical world corresponding to the child's sense of the marvellous, gradually fades into solitude and weariness'.[88] In *Les Enfants terribles* (1929), Jean Cocteau allowed only the Breton nurse Mariette, an unlettered peasant, to discern the mysteries of childhood embodied in Paul and Elizabeth:

> But in her perfect simplicity Mariette grasped the inapprehensible. The climate of innocence was one in which she felt herself at home. She had no wish to analyze it. She discerned in the Room a transparency of atmosphere too pure, too vital to harbour any germ of what was base or vile; a spiritual attitude beyond contamination.[89]

Other well-known examples that left their mark on generations of youthful French readers were *Le Grand Mealnes* (1913) of Alain-Fournier, with its pervading sense of nostalgia for the wonders of childhood, and *Le Petit Prince* (1943) by Saint-Exupéry. The latter cheerfully contrasts the deadly dull mentality of adults with the incisive, questioning mind of the young visitor from asteroid B 612.[90]

The second half of the nineteenth century brought a shift towards realism in literature, partly as a reaction against the high-flown excesses of some Romantic works, and with it a corresponding hardening of the edge of childhood figures. As already noted, this produced scenes of cruelty and precocious sexuality among the young, but it also often highlighted the vitality and resilience of a still essentially innocent child. Authors including Jules Vallès, Alphonse Daudet and Eugène Le Roy made a young male the hero of a novel. Alphonse Daudet, for example, used the eponymous hero of *Jack* (1876) to reveal an assortment of malignant forces in French society. This huge 'baggy monster' of a novel depicts Jack as an intelligent, sensitive boy who has the misfortune to be born illegitimate to the flighty and snobbish *demi-mondaine* Ida de Barancy. Jack is an innocent abroad. He laughs at the thought of his mother as a chicken, covered in feathers, when he hears her described as a *cocotte* (a chicken in the language of a child, but also a tart). At the same time, Jack

---

[88] Nick Osmond, 'Introduction' to Arthur Rimbaud, *Illuminations: Coloured Plates* (London: Athlone Press, 1976), p. 17.
[89] Jean Cocteau, *Les Enfants terribles*, transl. Rosamond Lehmann (Harmondsworth: Penguin, 1961 (1929)), p. 48.
[90] Alain-Fournier, *Le Grand Meaulnes*; Antoine de Saint-Exupéry, *Le Petit Prince* (Paris: Gallimard, 1997 (1943)). See also Primault et al., *Terres de l'enfance*, passim; and Bethlenfalvay, *Les Visages de l'enfant*, ch. 1.

illustrates what Daudet calls 'the marvellous resilience of the young, its supple strength to resist'.[91] A very different way of illustrating the liveliness of the child was in a popular genre that recounted amusing scenes in comfortable middle-class households. *Poum* (1897), for example, by Paul and Victor Marguerite, revolved around a mischievous seven-year-old, sly enough to cheat at cards or take advantage of his doddery old grandfather at a puppet show, but also credulous enough to fall for the story from his older cousin of a wild animal out to devour him at the zoo.[92]

The growing influence of Freudian theory during the twentieth century eventually undermined confidence in childhood innocence, or at least in any version involving an asexual childhood. Certainly the image of the innocent child soon palls today: it all too easily descends into sentimentalization, with the little blue-eyed blondes favoured by Victor Hugo, or the tiresomely virtuous peasant girls featured in George Sand's rustic novels. During the 1960s, George Boas mounted a scathing attack on what he perceived to be the pervasive 'cult of childhood' in the modern world, above all because of its anti-intellectual underpinnings. He highlighted the American case, which at that point was certainly different from the French one in terms of relaxing discipline in the schools and tailoring the curriculum to the interests of the child.[93] Nonetheless, French culture was entirely familiar with such notions as the intuitive wisdom of the child, or its greater sensitivity to moral values. With Rousseau, as Boas acknowledges, it even had one of the founding fathers of the 'cult'. Thus the idea of childhood innocence remains an important strand in modern French culture. Doubtless the works of Jean-Jacques, and the great poets from Hugo to Cocteau, always influenced the middle classes more than peasants and workers – though compulsory schooling and mass literacy narrowed the gap during the twentieth century. The logical corollary of the 'child of nature', 'the child from heaven', the poetic child, and so on, was a child-centred education, working with rather than against the grain of the individual. Rousseau and his disciples encouraged educators to think in terms of a careful balance between supervision and liberty in the education system. The assumption of childhood innocence also encouraged measures to protect the young from the realities of the adult world, such as the need to earn a living or have sexual relations. This was all well and good in campaigns against the abuse of child labour and child

---

[91] Daudet. *Jack*, p. 194.
[92] Paul and Victor Marguerite, *Poum, aventures d'un petit garçon* (Paris: Plon, 1948 (1897)), pp. 181–9. See also Primault et al., *Terres de l'enfance*, pp. 11–12; and Bethlenfalvay, *Les Visages de l'enfant*, pp. 119–21.
[93] George Boas, *The Cult of Childhood* (London: The Warburg Institute, 1966).

prostitutes, but in denying children reason, sexuality and inner strength it risked being oppressive sooner or later in their lives.

The adolescent

A whole host of psychologists and novelists homed in on adolescence during the late nineteenth and early twentieth centuries, for reasons already explained above. However, compared to the debate on the nature of childhood, discussion of this stage of life was largely confined to this modern period, and there was more of a consensus among commentators within France. Much of their thinking remains common currency today. The first writer in modern France to take the subject seriously was Jean-Jacques Rousseau, once again well ahead of the pack in the middle of the eighteenth century. Book IV of *Emile* floated many of the themes that would reappear with G. Stanley Hall and other psychologists around 1900. Two points stand out for our purposes. First, Rousseau established a sharp demarcation between childhood and adolescence. He saw adolescence as a 'second birth', starting with puberty around the age of fifteen. The physical changes affecting the two sexes provoked 'a moment of crisis', which was short-lived but of long-lasting influence. 'As the roaring of the sea precedes a tempest from afar, this stormy revolution is proclaimed by the murmur of the nascent passions.' The child became aggressive, agitated and difficult to manage. For Rousseau the passions were natural, and tended to preserve the individual, but, as at all stages of life, there was an ever-present risk of corruption by external influences. He recommended keeping the young man away from 'women and debauchery' in the city in order to preserve childhood innocence for as long as possible. The result would be greater vigour and force in maturity. All the same, adolescence involved the birth of a man, and the end of the 'child's games' organized by the tutor up till then. The second point to note is that Rousseau bequeathed an ambivalent image of this stage of life to subsequent generations. While emphasizing crisis and danger, he also pointed to the 'fire' of adolescence bringing warmth and a generous frankness to the spirit of a young man. He was capable for the first time of the sentiments of friendship and love, and early notions of good and bad.[94] The term 'adolescence' appears from time to time in letters written by members of the elite, though whether this was borrowed from Rousseau it is impossible to tell. During the 1770s the Marquis de Mirabeau complained that his son (later the Comte de Mirabeau) had had a 'monstrous' childhood, an 'impetuous'

[94] Rousseau, *Emile*, pp. 211–32 and 252.

adolescence and was currently experiencing a wayward youth. In 1787, a merchant from Le Havre adopted a more Rousseauistic tone with his son, studying away from home in Hamburg: 'You are at the happy age when one acquires good habits as easily as bad ones; but in a few years, you will not have the same facility and you will be good, mediocre or bad according to whether you acted well or badly during your adolescence.'[95]

During the nineteenth century, people in France thought of adolescence as the *l'âge ingrat* ('the ungrateful age'), a period of physical awkwardness and moral uncertainty, but also one of intellectual awakening and of the affirmation of the self. Pierre Mendousse was one of the first theorists in France to revive an interest in adolescence around 1900, with his influential work *The Soul of the Adolescent*. Like many of his fellow specialists on adolescence in France, Mendousse was a schoolmaster in a *lycée* as well as a psychologist. He contrasted his approach to that of his counterparts in America by proclaiming an interest in the confidences made by the subjects themselves, based on twenty years of observing boys, rather than on an allegedly abusive use of statistics. (He ignored girls completely.) According to the historian Agnès Thiercé, this approach encouraged the French to see adolescence as a process, a matter of 'becoming'. Typically the schema involved minor physical changes in the run-up to puberty, a crisis around puberty itself and a return to equilibrium afterwards. As in *Emile*, the link between the physical changes of a 'second birth' at puberty and the characteristics of this stage of life were highlighted in the literature. Mendousse claimed that the coming of sexuality was the salient influence on the organization of a whole new personality. In so doing he implicitly contrasted an asexual childhood with a sexualized adolescence, impervious, like most of his French colleagues during the early twentieth century, to Freudian psychoanalytical theory. He had a strange tone for a psychologist, often sounding more like a stern moralist than a scientist. He suggested that for a few years the emotional life of the young male centred on sex, with a direct link between the increasing size and elasticity of the scrotum and the mental or nervous state. All this 'psychological excitement', as the 'scrotic reflex' radiated to the thighs and abdomen, risked leading to mental problems 'close to hysteria' even among normal adolescents. The monastic life of the boarding school and the *lycée* was a perfect setting for solitary vices, as noted earlier by Dr Tissot, producing the familiar symptoms of spots,

---

[95] Comte de Mirabeau, *Mémoires biographiques, littéraires et politiques de Mirabeau* (3 vols., Paris: Auffray, 1834), vol. I, letter from Marquis de Mirabeau to the Comtesse de Rochefort, 16 November 1771; AD Seine-Maritime, 188 J, Fonds Delahaye-Le Bouis et Feray, letter from Jean-Baptiste Joseph Delahaye to his son Jean-Baptiste, 8 September 1787.

weakening eyesight, bad breath, a stupid and melancholic look, and general weariness. Mendousse recommended constant activity to distract the adolescent from his sexual obsessions, cold showers and a vegetable-based diet.[96]

A later generation of authorities moved on from Hall and Mendousse by linking the 'crisis' of adolescence to social as well as physical factors. Jules de la Vaissière highlighted pressure on adolescents to prepare for exams around the age of fifteen, and the need to confront choices over a career and religious belief. Maurice Debesse focused on an extended crisis in search of originality, a 'puberty of the mind' not necessarily determined by a 'puberty of the body'. Both sexes in their mid-teens, he suggested, wanted to astonish others with their bizarre dress, ideas and language. They also sought to affirm their individual self, as they discovered the richness of their mental life. Such a process of growing up, Debesse affirmed, was not necessarily the period of storm and stress or catastrophe identified by earlier authorities, merely one of moderate change.[97] Thiercé argues that French psychologists were generally unconvinced by the twelve 'oppositions' in the adolescent character that G. Stanley Hall emphasized, such as egoism/altruism and sociability/solitude. Instead they took an interest in two aspects of adolescence: the 'social birth' that involved altruism and friendships, and the 'interior work' of the introverted and intellectually curious young male. Both involved dangers for the individual, but also a great potential for the future.[98]

As for literature, the novel of adolescence burst on to the scene in France around 1890. The odd writer before that had considered the trials and tribulations of the young, notably Chateaubriand and Flaubert, but in the words of the literary critic Justin O'Brien, it was more what they omitted that mattered.[99] With the novel of adolescence proper, O'Brien could illustrate the principal traits of the adolescent identified by psychologists – not least because psychologists like Mendousse were steeped in the autobiographical novels of the period. Thus O'Brien structured his study of these novels around the physical and intellectual awakening of the young male (still), his sympathetic and egoistic impulses, and finally his spiritual unrest.[100]

The novelists avoided the condescending tone of some of the scientists. They made the most of the supposed restlessness of youth to explore the

---

[96] Mendousse, *L'Ame de l'adolescent*, book 1; Thiercé, *Histoire de l'adolescence*, especially chs. 1 and 8.
[97] Thiercé, *Histoire de l'adolescence*, pp. 230–1; Debesse, *La Crise d'originalité juvénile*, pp. 1–23.
[98] Thiercé, *Histoire de l'adolescence*, pp. 235–43.
[99] O'Brien, *Novel of Adolescence*, p. 4.   [100] Ibid., p. 115.

ideals and discontents of the society around them. Prominent here was André Gide, the youthful characters in his *Les Faux-monnayeurs* (1925) expressing dissatisfaction with the constricting influence of the family, a Protestant education, and the professional bourgeoisie, as each relentlessly probed the development of his own self.[101] Some of the novelists also highlighted the transitionary character of a long-drawn-out adolescence, with adolescents depicted as painfully aware of veering between childlike and adult behaviour. The main characters in *Le Grand Meaulnes* (1913), the narrator Seurel, Augustin Meaulnes and Frantz de Galais, all sought to return to a childhood home, and struggled to come to terms with the realities of adulthood. Frantz de Galais in particular was repeatedly described as a child, despite being engaged to be married, and towards the end the narrator observed, 'At heart no doubt he was more of a child than ever: imperious, whimsical, and suddenly deflated. But it was hard to accept such childishness in a youth already showing signs of age.'[102] Similarly, Raymond Radiguet, outstanding as an author who wrote his *Le Diable au corps* (1923) when he was only seventeen, opened by having the narrator confess that he went through the First World War as a child, yet his adventures would have embarrassed even a man. His 'adventures' involved conducting an affair with a young married woman while still a *lycéen* aged sixteen. The couple eventually came unstuck through inexperience. 'We were children standing on a chair, proud of being a head taller than adults.' They were prepared to risk the opprobrium of an adulterous relationship, but the narrator was too scared to ask for a room in a hotel, thereby undermining his mistress's health with a night spent on the streets.[103]

Conclusion

Åke Sander has observed that one could probably find religious support for almost any conceivable image of childhood.[104] In the French case, the images were many and varied between the eighteenth and the twentieth centuries, drawing on the Catholic heritage, and also those of the Enlightenment, Romanticism, realism and developmental psychology. In the long term, from the late seventeenth century onwards, one can discern a softening of the image of childhood, be it from Catholic thinkers

---

[101] André Gide, *Les Faux-monnayeurs* (Paris: Gallimard, 1925); Michael Tilby, *Gide, les Faux-monnayeurs* (London: Grant and Cutler, 1981); O'Brien, *Novel of Adolescence*, ch. 13.
[102] Alain-Fournier, *Le Grand Meaulnes*, p. 166.
[103] Raymond Radiguet, *Le Diable au corps* (Paris: Grasset, 1923), pp. 7 and 165.
[104] Sander, 'Childhood in Religion', p. 25.

easing up on the traditional figure of the sinful child, or from disciples of Locke and Rousseau arguing for the very different image of the innocent child. All the same, it is easy to lose sight of the persistence of belief in the Fall and original sin, or at least in certain evil tendencies in the child, evident in the work of nineteenth-century writers such as Chateaubriand, Dupanloup and Zola. The 'presociological' theories presented here have bequeathed a number of contradictory images of the child that persist in Western culture to this day, including the child as cruel and savage, as a blank sheet, as innocent or even as angel, and as a source of poetic inspiration. Similarly, in the case of adolescence, various writers relished the positive characteristics they associated with this stage of life, such as its generosity and eccentricity, as well as showing exasperation at its supposed self-centredness and surly behaviour. Underlying this ambivalence towards the young, nonetheless, was a desire to understand their emotions and ways of thinking, and to use this knowledge to orientate them in the right direction for their future development.[105] Of course, few people now think that children are intrinsically evil or innocent. A more sociological approach to childhood thinks in terms of the social construction of childhood, and the 'tribal child', or children as a minority group, as will emerge below.[106]

The significance of childhood and adolescence

In the long term, Western societies like France have considered what happens to their young as a matter of increasing importance. No doubt the contrasts between medieval and modern society can easily be exaggerated. Medieval clerical authorities often thundered over the loathsomeness and insignificance of children, but many of them, as members of teaching orders, were prepared to dedicate large parts of their lives to education. After baptism, children were after all Christian souls to be saved. Conversely, many modern authors of autobiographies have been happy to ignore their own early years when recording their life stories. The fact remains that childhood was often rather brief for many people in an agrarian society, and its course a matter of routine rather than one of choice and experimentation. The influence of the Renaissance, the Protestant and Catholic Reformations, and the beginnings of an urbanized and commercialized society, stimulated a growing role for formal education among the wealthy elites of Europe. More importantly, when Enlightenment thinkers talked of newborn babes as blank sheets, and considered sensory

[105] Thiercé, *Histoire de l'adolescence*, pp. 242–3.
[106] James et al., *Theorizing Childhood*, ch. 2.

experiences the sole source of knowledge, then child rearing and education took on a whole new significance. The wealthier members of French society under the *ancien régime* at least pored over their Locke and their Rousseau for guidance on issues such as diet, clothing, discipline and teaching methods. The Romantic image of childhood, promoted during the nineteenth century by writers such as Chateaubriand, George Sand and Victor Hugo, added a further twist by isolating it as a period of innocence and purity that was worth preserving for as long as possible. These ideas were always contested by a less rosy view of childhood, and presumably passed over the heads of the masses. In the end, though, the intervention of philanthropists and the state led to a certain institutionalization of childhood, in schools, child labour inspectorates and infant welfare services.

The notion of adolescence as a second birth, from the middle of the eighteenth century onwards, extended the span of the formative years considered important. Jean-Jacques informed the fifteen-year-old Emile: 'You are at the critical age when the mind opens to certitude, when the heart receives its form and its character, and when one's whole life, whether for good or for bad, is determined.'[107] However, it was not until the twentieth century that such ideas were taken up on any scale, when pedagogues, psychologists and novelists began to see it as a promising stage to explore and support in the evolution of the individual. Justin O'Brien has suggested that the shift from indifference to intense interest even led to an 'exaggerated exaltation' in this stage of life, a 'cult of adolescence'. He cites a Dr Gilbert-Robin, and the opinion that 'the education system and the society in general made every effort to cure people of their youth, when they ought to be trying to preserve it until death'.[108] This has pointed the way to the modern worship of youth in the West, as a lucrative market, a source of dynamism and a model to emulate into middle age.[109]

Conclusion

There is no disputing the growing volume of material written about childhood and adolescence from the eighteenth century onwards. Scholars have noted various key dates in the French case, such as the publication in 1762 of *Emile*, the emergence of child heroes in the literature from around 1870 and the fascination with adolescence after 1890. Not all of this writing was complimentary to the young, and by no means all of

[107] Rousseau, *Emile*, p. 310.   [108] O'Brien, *Novel of Adolescence*, pp. 46–8.
[109] See the remarks in the Conclusion to Thiercé, *Histoire de l'adolescence*.

the population looked to books for advice on child rearing. One can also make the case, as Philippe Ariès did, that all the extra attention from adults had its drawbacks. There is an element of 'infantilization' inherent in the classically middle-class institution of an extended childhood in the family and the school. Even so, in the seventeenth century the educated male elite was generally indifferent to childhood, and the image of the child was less than flattering. Moreover, children, apprentices and young servants stood at or near the bottom of the pecking order in society. By contrast, the modern period did bring efforts to re-evaluate children and adolescents, noting their charm, creativity and willingness to learn. Linked to these were campaigns to tailor child-rearing and educational practices to the needs of the young. How this worked out in practice we shall see over the rest of this work.

3   Growing up in theory and in practice

Our time on this earth can be represented in the form of a trajectory, passing through phases of growth, maturity and decline. From Antiquity, there has been a tradition of dividing our life span of three-score-and-ten years into a series of 'ages', each with its particular characteristics. Individuals passed through these in their own way, but there was supposedly an underlying natural order of things to which everyone would conform. Cicero (106–43 BC) wrote in *De Senectute*: 'Life's racecourse is fixed; Nature has only a single path and that path is run but once, and to each stage of existence has been allotted its own appropriate quality.' Schema for the 'Ages of Man' have a long and varied history, from, say, the three identified by Aristotle in Ancient Greece to the eight preferred by the Danish-American psychoanalyst Erik Erikson during the 1950s. How much attention they paid to the growing-up phase depended on the complexity of the system. The three ages theory adopted by Aristotle looked no further than a period of *augmentum* running from birth to the age of twenty-five, followed by *status* between twenty-five and forty-five, and *decrementum* at the end. The seven ages of man, familiar from Jaques's speech in Shakespeare's *As You Like It*, was more expansive when considering the early years. Hippocrates allegedly identified successive stages in a man's life in multiples of seven as follows: a little boy, up to the age of shedding his teeth at seven; a boy, until the age of puberty at fourteen; a lad, until his chin grew downy at twenty-one; a young man, until his whole body had grown at twenty-eight; a man, till forty-nine; an elderly man, till fifty-six; and after that an old man.[1] This particular conception of the early years remained influential in the modern period among scholars interested in the young. Various modern French authors, notably

---

[1] See J. A. Burrow, *The Ages of Man: A Study in Medieval Writing and Thought* (Oxford: Clarendon Press, 1986), especially pp. 1, 8, 38 and 93; Elizabeth Sears, *The Ages of Man: Medieval Interpretations of the Life Cycle* (Princeton: Princeton University Press, 1986), passim.

Rousseau, added their theoretical perspective on the Ages of Man, some with a focus on the early phases.

More important for the French population at large were the various *rites de passage*, such as baptism, first communion and marriage, that marked changes in the age and status of each individual. Their forms and significance evolved over time, under such influences as 'dechristianization' and compulsory schooling. Folklore studies in the nineteenth and twentieth centuries collected details of the rituals and beliefs associated with the traditional forms of these transition rites, not least because their authors were aware that the oral tradition of the villages and small towns of the French countryside was dying out or changing its character in modern society.[2] Again, though, the folklorists envisaged everyone passing through a series of quite well-defined stages in life, including childhood and adolescence. The late twentieth century brought some reaction against the rigidities of such an approach. Doubtless this reflected changes in contemporary society, with, for example, the established sequence in life of study, work and retirement being called into question by changes in the labour market. Theorists moved on from the idea of a relatively fixed *life cycle* and began to explore the varied ways in which people went through their individual *life course*.[3]

This chapter and the following one will explore the various ways that philosophers, doctors, folklore specialists, clerics and social scientists have thought about the process of growing up. It will also consider how their theoretical perspectives can help us to understand the experiences of childhood and adolescence in modern France – or the way people construed those experiences. It moves from the general to the particular, that is to say, from stage theories supposedly applicable to the whole of humanity to constructions of the lives of individual French people around key turning points. This chapter falls into two parts, beginning with the Olympian perspective of the stage theorist. Whether based on the study of numbers or scientific observation, schemas for the Ages of Man remain an abstract form of classification. They reveal what intellectuals from various disciplines thought about the process of growing up. Those influential in France had some impact on practical matters affecting the young, such as punishments in schools or paediatric medicine. Nonetheless, individuals

---

[2] See Michael Marrus, 'Folklore as an Ethnographic Source: A "Mise au Point"', in Jacques Beauroy, Marc Bertrand and Edward T. Gargan (eds.), *The Wolf and the Lamb: Popular Culture in France from the Old Regime to the Twentieth Century* (Saratoga, CA: Anima Libri, 1977), pp. 109–25.

[3] Alan Bryman, Bill Bytheway, Patricia Allatt and Teresa Keil (eds.), *Rethinking the Life Cycle* (Houndsmills: Macmillan, 1987), Introduction; and Pineau and Le Grand, *Histoires de vie*, ch. 4.

trying to put some shape on their formative years could hardly adopt this type of framework. The second part of the chapter therefore focuses on the traditional French popular culture, and the way it supported villagers during their childhood and youth. Ethnologists have perceived its various transition rites as part of a coherent system, which took the individual through successive stages of life 'from the cradle to the grave'. Autobiographical material produced by peasants in modern France confirms from a 'bottom-up' perspective that people from this milieu might at least partially structure their lives around the 'universal' turning points identified by the folklore specialists.

The Ages of Man: growing up in stages

In 1950, Erik Erikson marvelled at the way that 'there is in every child at every stage a new miracle of vigorous unfolding, which constitutes a new hope and a new responsibility for all'.[4] Stage theories of life have attracted scholars down the ages. Men of letters in the medieval period relied on such theories to relate human life to the world around them, thus confirming their view that the Ages of Man were part of the natural order. Belief that there were four ages of man was the most widespread in the medieval period, not least because the stages could be linked to the four humours. Childhood was associated with blood, youth with red choler, maturity with black choler, and old age with phlegm. Similarly, those arguing for seven ages of man referred to the seven days of creation, the seven liberal arts or the influence of the seven planets. Classical and medieval authorities on the Ages of Man were not necessarily divorced in their thinking from biological realities, as the comments associated with Hippocrates on the seven ages has already revealed. All the same, the large number of possibilities, ranging from three to twelve ages, indicates that these thinkers were at least as interested in the symmetry and numerology of their classifications as in biological or social turning points in life.[5]

More modern theorists were likely to claim that their 'ages of man' were based on observed facts, and that they would bring practical outcomes such as improvements in child rearing and mental health. Nonetheless, they necessarily rested on theoretical underpinnings, such as the sensationalist theory of a Rousseau or the neo-Freudianism of an Erikson. It perhaps hardly needs emphasizing that their classifications of the life

---

[4] Erik H. Erikson, *Childhood and Society* (Harmondsworth: Penguin, 1965 (1950)), ch. 7 (p. 246).

[5] Burrow, *Ages of Man*, passim; Danièle Alexandre-Bidon, 'Seconde enfance et jeunesse dans la théorie des "âges de la vie" et le vécu familial (XIIIe–début XVIe siècle)', in Bardet et al., *Lorsque l'enfant grandit*, pp. 159–72.

cycle remain an heuristic device. The newfound interest in childhood and adolescence from the eighteenth century onwards inevitably involved thoughts on the process of growing up. Rousseau set himself the task in *Emile* (1762) of studying the stages of development in the young so that he could structure his system of education in an appropriate manner. In particular, as already observed, he wished to delay efforts to teach children to use their reason. He began with a traditional distinction between an *infans*, unable to speak, and a *puer*, who could do so, from around the age of four or five. Between twelve and fifteen he identified a third stage of childhood, approaching adolescence without yet being that of puberty. This was in effect a continuation of the first two stages, for Rousseau still did not consider the child to have reached the age of reason, and so proposed to continue with a 'negative education'. The fourth stage was adolescence, running from the ages of fifteen to twenty. It was only at this late stage that Rousseau saw the young as capable of reasoning like an adult – very different from the traditional age of reason fixed at seven. Emile could at fifteen move on from a preoccupation with himself and the natural world around him, and began to integrate with the society around him. He was at last a moral being, ready to study history, for example, so that he could pass judgement on his fellow men. Finally, a fifth stage started around the age of twenty: originally labelled the 'age of wisdom', it focused on the relationship between Emile and his companion Sophie, and more generally prepared him for his social and civic responsibilities. Rousseau implied that the young woman grew in much the same way as the young man, though he notoriously reserved for her a very different form of education, supposedly suited to her nature. Although the school system in France remained largely impervious to Rousseauistic theory, one can trace his influence in numerous works on the stages of life in later generations of French writers.[6]

In the world of French medicine, well into the nineteenth century, most doctors remained wedded to the Hippocratic tradition of envisaging seven ages of man. This included growing up through infancy or, in French usage, *la première enfance* from birth to seven years of age, childhood or *la seconde enfance* between seven and fourteen, and *l'adolescence* from fourteen to twenty-one. However, the historian Jean-Noël Luc has demonstrated how a growing interest in the health of the very young, spurred initially in the eighteenth century by high infant mortality,

---

[6] Rousseau, *Emile*. See also J. H. Broome, *Rousseau* (London: Edward Arnold, 1963), ch. 5; Peter Jimack, *Rousseau, Emile* (London: Grant and Cutler, 1983); and Maurice Cranston, *The Noble Savage: Jean-Jacques Rousseau, 1754–1762* (Chicago: University of Chicago Press, 1991).

encouraged a more refined definition of the early stages of life. In the second half of the nineteenth century, according to Luc, doctors 'discovered' the early phase of childhood after weaning. That is to say, it was then that 'first' childhood was frequently understood in medical terminology to run from birth to two years, instead of the birth to seven years of the Hippocratic schema. Correspondingly, 'second' childhood often came to mean three to seven, instead of seven to fourteen. Some doctors noted the fragility and limitations of the growing child who had not yet reached the age of reason; others revelled in his or her vigour and experiments with language.[7]

Specialists in adolescence, appearing in France around 1900, took up the baton at this point. Pierre Mendousse felt the years eight to thirteen revealed the first hints of adolescence, suggesting the image of a halt to gather strength before the big effort to come. The child grew in strength but completely lacked an interior life. Following the recapitulation theory current at the time,[8] Mendousse depicted the child enjoying pursuits typical of 'primitive' races that had not yet reached the 'adolescent' stage in their development, such as fishing, hunting, swimming and looting. Adolescence in the individual started with puberty and the 'terrible crisis' of the mind that followed it. However, as observed above, Mendousse restricted his attention to the boys that he had observed as a schoolmaster in a *lycée*.[9] The common assumption in the nineteenth century was that at puberty girls matured physiologically and morally more quickly than boys, so that the transition period between childhood and adulthood was much shorter.[10]

Variations in the onset of puberty attributable to climate, race, hereditary influences and so forth made French as well as other theorists aware that the boundaries between the stages of life were uncertain. However, they tended not to stray far from the benchmark of fourteen to twenty-one established in the traditional seven ages. Gabriel Compayré referred back to the original Latin meaning of *adolescit* as growing up, which indicated the stage of life between puberty and reaching one's maximum height. There were institutional links, such as time spent at a *lycée* by a

---

[7] This paragraph relies on Jean-Noël Luc, '"A trois ans, l'enfant devient intéressant . . .": la découverte médicale de la seconde enfance (1750–1900)', *Revue d'histoire moderne et contemporaine*, 36 (1989), 83–112; and Luc, *L'Invention du jeune enfant au XIXe siècle*, ch. 4. One might note a similar classification for the medieval period in Pierre Riché and Danièle Alexandre-Bidon, *L'Enfance au Moyen Age* (Paris: Seuil, 1994), p. 16.

[8] On ambivalent attitudes in France to recapitulation theory, in which the individual in his or her stages of life recapitulates the development of the human race as a whole, see Thiercé, *Histoire de l'adolescence*, pp. 220–3.

[9] Mendousse, *L'Ame de l'adolescent*, pp. xi, 1–10 and 45.

[10] See Thiercé, *Histoire de l'adolescence*, ch. 4.

middle-class male, or the period between leaving school at thirteen and liability for military service at twenty for those among the 'popular classes'. Somewhere around the age of twenty, then, the *adolescent* or female *adolescente* moved on to join the world of *la jeunesse* (youth).[11]

In sum, scholars have found stage theories useful for describing and explaining human growth. That such theories continue to cast their spell over social scientists in recent times can be seen in the work of twentieth-century child psychologists such as Jean Piaget and Erik Erikson. There is evidently a strong element of continuity in thinking about the human life cycle from classical times down to the present, indicating a deeply rooted belief in Western civilization that human growth follows a predictable pattern. Philosophers, pedagogues, doctors and psychologists, among others, found it useful to draw on such classifications as the starting point for efforts to improve child and adolescent welfare. However, this literature has brought a bewildering array of definitions of the stages of life, so that at all periods of history most people have used such terms to describe the young very loosely. In the 1970s, the historian René Metz revealed that medieval canon law lacked any definition of the various stages of development in the child. The various texts used terms for minors such as *infans, puer, puella, parviculus, iuvenis* and *adolescens*, but without any precision.[12] Even in modern France, casual usage by novelists of words like 'child' and 'adolescent' suggests that, understandably enough, theoretical works on the ages of man did not impinge much on everyday life.[13] Legislation during the nineteenth and twentieth centuries brought some precision in defining children and adolescents. Below the age of eight, the 1841 law on child labour considered children too young to work in a factory. It also imposed tighter restrictions on the employment of children aged eight to twelve compared to those for the age group twelve to sixteen. At the age of twelve, the Assistance publique considered those in its care capable of looking after themselves. Sixteen was an important marker for the end of childhood in the legal system. Up until that age, the penal code of the early nineteenth century allowed the claim that a child acted without cognizance. If found guilty, but recognized to have acted without *discernement*, the child was acquitted and returned to its parents. If it had acted

---

[11] Ibid., Introduction.
[12] René Metz, 'L'Enfant dans le droit canonique mediéval: orientations de recherche', *Recueils de la Société Jean Bodin pour l'histoire comparative des institutions*, vol. XXXVI, *L'Enfant*, part 2, *Europe mediévale et moderne* (Brussels: Librairie encyclopédique, 1976), pp. 9–96. See also Pierre-André Sigal, 'Le Vocabulaire de l'enfance et de l'adolescence dans les recueils de miracles latins des XIe et XIIe siècles', *Senefiance*, 9 (1980), 141–59.
[13] For similar findings in the American case, see Joseph F. Kett, 'The Stages of Life, 1790–1840', in Michael Gordon (ed.), *The American Family in Social-Historical Perspective* (3rd edn, New York: St Martin's Press, 1983), pp. 229–54.

with cognizance, there was a reduced tariff of sentences, which excluded the death penalty, hard labour and deportation.[14] Sixteen was also the age at which the Civil Code ended the liability of young people to imprisonment by fathers under the rights of *puissance paternelle*. Twenty-one was the age of civil majority, and, after the 1848 Revolution, the voting age for males. At twenty-five, young people reached another age of majority in that they were free to marry without parental consent. Twenty-five also brought the right to sit in the Chamber of Deputies. Subsequent legislation raised the minimum age for industrial employment and for criminal responsibility, but lowered the age of citizenship.[15] Not surprisingly, these definitions did not impinge a great deal on the popular vocabulary. More important for the way French people experienced growing up was the series of *rites de passage* that marked the increasing age and status of a young person in society.

From the cradle to the grave: growing up according to the folklore model

The distinguished ethnologist Arnold Van Gennep started his mammoth *Manuel de folklore français contemporain* (1937–58) with two volumes entitled 'From the Cradle to the Grave'. They were devoted to the family ceremonies that took the individual through birth, baptism, childhood, adolescence, betrothal, marriage and burial.[16] This allowed him to highlight his particular contribution to scholarship: the analysis of ceremonies accompanying 'life crises'. He saw the life of an individual in any society as a series of passages from one age or occupation to another, changes that were dangerous or at least disturbing for those involved. Hence society evolved *rites de passage* to help people through the transition period. He identified three phases in all such ceremonies, involving rites of separation, transition rites and rites of incorporation.[17] All members of French society, from farm labourers to nobles, experienced such rites in one form or another, but it was the traditional forms of the oral rather than the literate culture that interested Van Gennep and his fellow folklore specialists. Van Gennep reflected the preoccupations of his time in seeking the *functions* of the various rites, rather than the *meaning* for those involved. The

---

[14] Michelle Perrot, 'Sur la notion d'intérêt de l'enfant et son émergence au XIXe siècle', *Actes: Les Cahiers d'action juridique*, 37 (1982), 40–3.

[15] See Thiercé, *Histoire de l'adolescence*, pp. 20–4.

[16] Arnold Van Gennep, *Manuel de folklore français contemporain* (3 vols., Paris: A. and J. Picard, 1937–58), vols. I.1–I.2, *Du berceau à la tombe*.

[17] Arnold Van Gennep, *The Rites of Passage*, transl. Monika B. Vizedom and Gabrielle L. Caffee (London: Routledge and Kegan Paul, 1960 (1909)), ch. 1.

latter remains difficult for the historian to tease out. All of the French folklore collections put together during the late nineteenth and twentieth centuries by people such as Van Gennep were the work of 'outsiders', living apart from the peasants and artisans they studied. The assorted doctors, teachers and other *érudits* who roamed the villages for material on the traditional customs and beliefs of the peasantry had their own particular prejudices. They had a tendency to associate the popular culture of the villages with a natural spontaneity and naivety, which they felt was sadly absent from its more subversive urban counterpart. Mme Charles d'Abbadie d'Arrast wrote during the 1900s that children in the Basque country benefited from their contact with nature, 'the countryside gives what the town refuses: healthy images to stock the nascent imagination, real and strong things to fashion the intelligence at the beginning'.[18] The folklorists were also inclined to see the oral culture of the villages as a lower form of civilization than their own, and one in terminal decline – which led to a sense of urgency in recording folktales, dances, proverbs and the like before they disappeared.[19] The folklorists can thus provide an outline of the universal turning points in 'traditional' village civilization, as it appeared to them in its final stages.[20] An 'insider's' view is more difficult to grasp, given the almost complete absence of peasants from the ranks of eighteenth- and nineteenth-century autobiographers. The historian is forced to rely on testimony from writers who at least began their lives among the peasantry, or peasants looking back to the dying days of the oral tradition in the early twentieth century.

Modern ethnographers and historians in France have argued that the traditional popular culture of the villages was in effect a system of survival. Before the agricultural and industrial revolutions, peasants saw themselves faced with constant threats such as hunger, epidemics, war and sorcery. With almost no help from Church or State, they turned to a system for explaining the world based on *rites de passage* and a combination of Christian and pagan beliefs. André Varagnac linked different age

---

[18] Mme Charles d'Abbadie d'Arrast, *Causeries sur le pays Basque: la femme et l'enfant* (Paris: Rudeval, 1909), p. 129.

[19] See Michel de Certeau, Dominique Julia and Jacques Revel, 'La Beauté de la mort: le concept de "culture populaire"', *Politique aujourd'hui* (1970), 3–23.

[20] Particularly informative on childhood and adolescence are: A. Desrousseaux, *Moeurs populaires de la Flandre française* (2 vols., Lille: Quarré, 1889); Arnold Van Gennep, *Le Folklore du Dauphiné (Isère)* (Paris: Maisonneuve, 1932); Arnold Van Gennep, *Le Folklore de la Flandre et du Hainaut français (Département du Nord)* (2 vols., Paris: Maisonneuve, 1935–6); Jean Drouillet, *Folklore du Nivernais et du Morvan* (5 vols., La Charité-sur-Loire: Thoreau, 1959); Claude Seignolle, *Le Folklore de la Provence* (Paris: Maisonneuve et Larose, 1963); Pierre Charrié, *Le Folklore du Bas-Vivarais* (Paris: Guénégaud, 1964); Pierre Charrié, *Le Folklore du Haut-Vivarais* (Paris: FERN, 1968); Robert Jalby, *Le Folklore de Languedoc* (Paris: Maisonneuve et Larose, 1971).

groups to particular ceremonies. Children, believed to be newly arrived from another world, had the role of blessing houses, livestock and crops. After puberty, the young helped check family disorders and generally enforce morality as defined by the rights and duties of each age group.[21] This system may have begun to unravel from as early as the sixteenth and seventeenth centuries, under systematic repression from external forces, but parts of it continued into the twentieth century.[22] The *rites de passage* gradually lost what Van Gennep called their 'magico-religious' character.[23]

Birth and baptism

The first of the stages in the life cycle identified by the folklorists revolved around birth and baptism. This stage was beyond recall for the person involved later in life, but of critical importance for the rest of the community, anxious to preserve a fragile new member. The mother and newborn child were considered to be in a vulnerable position from a biological, social and magical point of view. After the Council of Trent (1545–63), the Catholic baptism ceremony took its definitive form, with two sets of stages. The first, at the door of the church, purified the infant, by ridding it of original sin, Satan and demons. This separated it from the world before birth, and eliminated impurities contracted in being born of its ancestors and its mother. The rest of the ceremony, within the church, prepared the infant for incorporation into the Christian world. By the twentieth century, fears of harm from the forces of evil, and hence the need for baptism within a day or two of birth, had receded, though most French families continued to observe the rite. Baptism also brought the child a godfather and a godmother, as a rule its grandparents if it was a first-born. They spoke for their godson or goddaughter during the service, and helped establish him or her as a new member of the local community by distributing nuts, or later sugared almonds, after the service.[24] Pierre-Jakez Hélias gave an account of his own baptism, in 1914 in the Breton pays Bigouden, indicating that the villagers still observed the formalities punctiliously. The women in charge ensured that he wore a white cap, without which there was no valid atonement for original sin. His

---

[21] André Varagnac, *Civilisation traditionnelle et genres de vie* (Paris: Albin Michel, 1948), book 2.

[22] See, for example, Maurice Crubellier, *Histoire culturelle de la France, XIXe–XXe siècles* (Paris: Armand Colin, 1974), ch. 3; and Robert Muchembled, *Culture populaire et culture des élites dans la France moderne, XVe–XVIIIe siècles* (Paris: Flammarion, 1978), passim.

[23] Van Gennep, *Manuel*, I.1, p. 113.

[24] Ibid., pp. 126–47; Jacques Gélis, *History of Childbirth: Fertility, Pregnancy and Birth in Early Modern Europe*, transl. Rosemary Morris (Cambridge: Polity Press, 1991).

wet-nurse led the procession to the parish church, carrying him on her right arm rather than the left, the latter lending itself more to the work of Satan. Finally, priest, godfather and godmother performed their tasks to perfection, and the little group did the rounds of the local bars without mishap.[25]

Infancy (birth to age two)

This stage covered the first two years of life: *première enfance*, or what an English speaker would call infancy. It ended when the child was able to play with others of the same age and escape the constant supervision of the family. In other words, the second stage began when children could walk and run sufficiently well to be able to form a little society of their own within an agrarian or fishing community. At that point they were starting to form personalities of their own and establishing a certain autonomy. In the meantime, important turning points for infants were the appearance of the first tooth, marked by a gift from godparents; the first visit to another house, a contact with what was previously considered dangerous, helped in many provinces by an offer of an egg and salt; and the first steps when they began to walk.

Early childhood (age two to seven years)

The second phase of *première enfance* was a period when children were left free to play around the house and the farmyard. At the age of three, for example, Antoine Sylvère or 'Toinou' (1888–1963) was left for hours to roam his village in the Auvergne, and to poke around in any old rubbish he came across. His mother had far too much on her hands as the wife of an impoverished sharecropper to pay much attention to him. Such freedom, however, was more in evidence for boys than girls. In Upper Brittany, Paul Sébillot specified that little girls stayed at home while boys wandered around in stables, cracked whips and played at being horses.[26] Early childhood was also important for education within the family and the local community. The child learned such things as how to count, how to behave among adults and the basics of religion. Towards the age of seven, an important sign of growing up for a boy was the wearing of the first breeches, in place of the little frock worn by both sexes during infancy. In the Department of the Nièvre, for example, children mocked any boy

---

[25] Hélias, *Horse of Pride*, pp. 33–5.
[26] Sylvère, *Toinou*, pp. 18–19; Paul Sébillot, *Coutumes populaires de la Haut-Bretagne* (Paris: Maisonneuve, 1886), p. 31. See also Olivier Perrin, *Galerie Bretonne, ou vie des Bretons de l'Armorique* (3 vols., Paris: Isidore Pesron, 1835), I, p. 85.

who had to wait too long for his first *culotte* as a 'Jean-Fillette'.[27] Hélias recalled his *fête du pantalonnage* in Brittany immediately after the First World War. From the age of five he chafed at still having to wear a dress like a girl, and the risk of appearing insufficiently toilet-trained to wear trousers. He suggested that mothers often delayed the ceremony because they were reluctant to lose their sons to the world of men. Eventually he was taken to Quimper to buy a set of trousers, cut generously to allow for growth. His family then invited a dozen or so relatives to a special meal and proudly displayed their son in all his glory. Henceforth people might playfully call him 'young man'.[28] This stage gradually meshed into the next around the age of seven, when the child was in a position to start helping its parents in a serious way with household chores or work on the land.

Childhood (age seven to around sixteen)

The 'folklore model' envisaged life becoming more complicated during the next phase, *la deuxième enfance*. The child had to adapt to the demands of various networks around him, principally the family, other children of a similar age and the local community. A modern ethnological study of a Burgundian village, 'Minot', recorded that until around 1960 children of this age group concentrated on study in the primary school during the winter and work looking after cows in the fields during the summer.[29] At this stage the young had to learn the particular code of honour that set children apart from adults, notably from parents and then, later, schoolteachers.[30] They became familiar with rules of ownership and solemn oaths to confirm a deal, for it was unthinkable to appeal to the higher authority of an adult for justice.[31] Boys fought battles with rivals in other parishes of a town or a neighbouring village, as Louis Pergaud described in detail in his *La Guerre des boutons* (1912).[32] Boys and girls became more aware of gender differences at this age. Their games pushed them in different directions, with, for example, marbles reserved for boys, skipping for girls. The education system reinforced these traditional divergences, with separate schools for the two sexes being the norm in both the public and the private sector. The age grading of the

---

[27] Drouillet, *Folklore du Nivernais*, p. 89.   [28] Hélias, *Horse of Pride*, pp. 50–1.

[29] Yvonne Verdier, *Façons de dire, façons de faire: la laveuse, la couturière, la cuisinière* (Paris: Gallimard, 1979), pp. 160–70.

[30] See below, pp. 196–204, for more details.

[31] See Claude Gaignebet, *Le Folklore obscène d'enfants* (Paris: G.-P. Maisonneuve et Larose, 1974); Drouillet, *Folklore du Nivernais*, pp. 88–9.

[32] Louis Pergaud, *La Guerre des boutons* (Paris: Mercure de France, 1963).

schools meant that children felt their status rising as they passed through the various levels.[33] Antoine Sylvère stated that when he moved from the preparatory to the elementary level at his Christian Brothers school, he felt 'rather proud of a change which was for me the recognition of a very advanced intellectual level'.[34]

First communion was an important step in the move from childhood to adolescence. In the eighteenth century, the ceremony might take place at ten or eleven, though twelve to fourteen was a more common age, and fifteen to sixteen not unknown.[35] Protestants took their first communion later rather than earlier. This meant that, from the folklore perspective, as from the perspective of the churches, it was a *social puberty* in the form of an initiation ceremony rather than the onset of physical puberty that often marked the first steps towards adolescence or adulthood.[36] The ceremony of first communion was a comparatively recent innovation for the Catholic Church, starting only in the sixteenth century in France, but by the end of the *ancien régime* it had spread to nearly all parishes. It probably reached its peak as a social event in the nineteenth century, not least because of a growing interest in the child, before dechristianization gradually took its toll. After 1910 the possibility of taking first communion at seven also altered its significance as a turning point in life. The historian Jean Mellot analysed the religious ceremony itself as taking the form of a *rite de passage*.[37] First, the communicants were separated from the rest of the community in their catechism classes. Second, they endured a transition period attending the classes and taking part in a retreat immediately before the great day. This meshed into the incorporation rites of the final preparations for the ceremony, a confession and the first communion day itself. On this day there was a procession of the communicants, with the boys generally wearing blue or black, the girls white, and the former having the right to long trousers for the first time, the latter to a long dress. The group re-formed in their special costumes at Corpus Christi, and the more devout renewed their vows the following year. Although many young people soon gave up attending Mass afterwards, they were officially full members of the parish community.[38]

---

[33] Van Gennep, *Manuel*, I.1, pp. 166–87.   [34] Sylvère, *Toinou*, p. 121.

[35] Odile Robert, 'Fonctionnement et enjeux d'une institution chrétienne au XVIIIe siècle', in Jean Delumeau (ed.), *La Première Communion: quatre siècles d'histoire* (Paris: Desclée de Brouwer, 1987), pp. 77–113 (pp. 93–5).

[36] Van Gennep, *The Rites of Passage*, pp. 65–70; Richard L. DeMolen, 'Childhood and the Sacraments in the Sixteenth Century', *Archiv für Reformationgeschichte*, 65 (1974), 49–71.

[37] Van Gennep asserted that the folklore elements in the ceremony were sparse in France.

[38] Van Gennep, *Manuel*, I.1, pp. 184–7; Jean Mellot, 'Rite de passage et fête familiale: rapprochements', in Delumeau, *Première Communion*, pp. 171–96.

Most of those recalling a village childhood highlighted in one way or another what was supposed to be 'le plus beau jour de la vie' (the most beautiful day in one's life). For some it was the challenge for a barely literate child of coping with the catechism classes that stood out in retrospect. Writing around 1740, Valentin Jamerey-Duval gave a rather too obviously scornful account of his education at the beginning of the eighteenth century, from his adult perspective as a *professeur* at the Academy of Lunéville. He suggested that he was cultivated like a plant rather than a human in his village in what is now the Department of the Yonne. Taught the catechism according to this 'vegetative' approach, he claimed to have had at that stage only a confused knowledge of a God, a Church and some sacraments. During the 1840s, according to the Breton peasant Jean-Marie Déguignet, a number of young people of marriageable age in his village near Quimper remained trapped within the ranks of children because they could not master the catechism to the satisfaction of the village priest. His fellow Breton, Hélias, gave a more positive image from the early twentieth century, with the formidable Sister Bazilize determined to lead the peasant children of Pouldreuzic towards heaven.[39] Other writers remembered the huge feast that followed the religious ceremony, and, if from a poor background, the struggle with all the expenses involved. The parents of Toinou, in the Auvergne around 1900, had to find the considerable sum of 40 francs to dress the boy 'as a *monsieur*', including a black coat, gloves, shoes, a shirt and a missal. Eventually an uncle whose daughter was also taking her first communion helped them out, and they joined forces for a huge meal. Marie-Juliette Barrié (b. 1919) had to rely on the charity of a wealthy *dame patronesse* for her dress, which meant putting up with the letter J sewn on it for the original Jeanne.[40] Finally, there was the memory of first communion as a turning point in life. Typically, Marie-Claire in the autobiographical novel by Marguerite Audoux switched from the classroom to the world of work after her first communion, while the Protestant Augustine Rouvière replaced her mother in a rural silk spinning mill in the Cévennes during the 1890s after her ceremony in the *temple*. Henri Pitaud linked his first communion with the end of his childhood, allowing him to escape school in 1910 for work in the fields.[41]

---

[39] Valentin Jamerey-Duval, *Mémoires: enfance et éducation d'un paysan au XVIIIe siècle* (Paris: Le Sycomore, 1981), Introduction by Jean-Marie Goulemot and p. 112; Déguignet, *Mémoires d'un paysan*, p. 56; Hélias, *Horse of Pride*, pp. 88–90.

[40] Sylvère, *Toinou*, pp. 243–4; and Marie-Juliette Barrié, *Quand les bananes donnent la fièvre* (Paris: La Pensée universelle, 1973), p. 26.

[41] Marguerite Audoux, *Marie-Claire* (Paris: Charpentier, 1910), p. 53; Rey, *Augustine Rouvière*, p. 46; Henri Pitaud, *Le Pain de la terre* (Paris: J.-C. Lattès, 1982), p. 140. See

Other little *rites de passage* among peers completed the gradual shift from childhood to adolescence. Hélias, for example, recorded a series of tests of physical prowess that allowed him to rise a degree in the hierarchy of children in his Breton village of Pouldreuzic. To begin with, he had to crawl on his knees through a dark tunnel that conducted a stream under a road. Then he climbed to the top of an elm tree as it swayed in the wind, trying to bring down a magpie's nest. This saw him through to the highest level of childhood. Before he could consider himself a man, definitively separated from the '*pissouzes*', he needed to wade through the breakers in the sea as far as the ninth wave, and learn to smoke awful cigarettes made with dried catkins. Early experiments with this 'monkey tobacco' brought on nothing but coughing and tears in his eyes, and the realization that this man's pleasure was really a horrible punishment – but one had to appear delighted.[42]

Adolescence (age sixteen to twenty or twenty-five)

Van Gennep settled on the age of sixteen as the real threshold for adolescence in traditional French society. By then nearly everyone had passed through both their first communion and the physical side of puberty. Focusing on the girls in her Burgundian village of 'Minot', Yvonne Verdier preferred fifteen as the turning point, again on the grounds that first communion and two or three years of physical maturation had prepared them for a move from the child's world of the school and *champ-les-vaches* (the cow field). Henceforth males and females in the village went their separate ways, boys to work in the fields or to start an apprenticeship, girls to remain beside their mothers or to leave home for work as a farm servant.[43] Van Gennep envisaged adolescence ending at twenty in the case of a male, with military service, and at twenty-five in the case of a female, with celebration of *la Sainte-Catherine* if she remained unmarried. In *The Rites of Passage* he asserted that with 'social puberty' there was the implicit notion that the young person had moved on from the asexual world of childhood and could mix with the opposite sex at dances and other social occasions. In the villages, as in the towns, he suggested that a sort of 'natural and social law' encouraged young people between childhood and marriage to group together and pursue their own particular interests. That is to say, for centuries the young had struggled against the calls from the state for 'order' to assert what they regarded as their rights: the right

also Batisto Bonnet, *Vido d'enfant*, transl. Alphonse Daudet (Nimes: Tourmagne, 1968), pp. 175–223.
[42] Hélias, *Horse of Pride*, ch. 5.   [43] Verdier, *Façons de dire*, pp. 190–5.

to amuse themselves, to noise, to punish those whose behaviour upset the local community and to various compensatory payments.[44] During the 1950s, Laurence Wylie revealed that the villagers he was studying in the Vaucluse believed that the young had the right to have a good time: 'More than that, they believe it is the *duty* of a young person to have a good time.' Otherwise there was the risk that they harboured 'passions still unexpressed which could burst out'.[45] Peasant memoirs give a hint of brawls to defend the honour of their village, of drinking exploits, of dances and of festivals, at least for those not ground down by poverty and isolation. Ephraïm Grenadou, for example, recalled that his adolescence in the Eure-et-Loire on the eve of World War I included drinking with the men in one of the five local cafés, dances in neighbouring villages, the festival of Mardi gras and wedding celebrations that lasted for two days.[46]

Military service at twenty loomed large over a male in his teens from 1798 onwards, since he could hardly contemplate settling into a career or marriage until he had cleared this obstacle. Before 1872, one could pay for a substitute to perform the service, but the high cost confined this option to an affluent minority. In 1834, a big landowner like Marie-André-Laurent Odoard might be able to afford 900 francs to insure his son against military service, but such a sum exceeded the annual income of a poor household.[47] The Breton writer Adolphe Orain (1834–1918) recalled in an unpublished memoir how he had struggled to find a *remplacement* in 1854, because it was the time of the Crimean War. He eventually had to pay 3,000 francs to secure one, using his contacts in the Prefecture to borrow the money: he was an employee in the Bureau de l'enregistrement (register office). He noted that the poor peasant who took his place in the Crimea never returned.[48] In the novel *The Life of a Simple Man* (1904), written by Emile Guillaumin, and based largely on the experiences of his grandfather, the central character Etienne Bertin ('Tiennon') has to break with his girlfriend when her father insists that he either marry the girl or stop seeing her altogether. Her parents had heard that his family was too poor to be able to afford insurance for a substitute, so that he risked a long absence from the village as a soldier. Similarly, Jean-Baptiste Dumay (b. 1841) lost the fiancée he met while tramping around the country as a metal worker on his Tour de France. Although

[44] Van Gennep, *The Rites of Passage*, p. 67; Van Gennep, *Manuel*, I.1, pp. 196–213.
[45] Wylie, *Village in the Vaucluse*, pp. 103–4.   [46] Grenadou and Prévost, *Grenadou*, ch. 2.
[47] George, *Chronique intime*, p. 22.
[48] AD Ille-et-Vilaine, 105 J 3, Fonds Adolphe Orain, 'Mes souvenirs', unpubl. MS (1905–6).

they promised to be faithful should he be called up, the young woman plumped for the security of marriage to a painting contractor after he had to 'put on red knee breeches'.[49] Before the 1870s a young man was liable to seven years of military service if called up as part of the quota for his canton; after that the system gradually moved towards three years of compulsory service for everyone.

This particular 'life crisis' generated a new folklore of its own – the last innovation before the whole edifice collapsed in the twentieth century. In 1804, and again in 1818, the law established an annual *tirage au sort* (a drawing of lots) for the cohort of twenty-year-olds in each canton. This determined the order in which the young men would be examined by a Conseil de révision to see if they were fit for service. When the canton reached its quota of conscripts, the examinations and hence the recruitment stopped. The point of the rites was to ensure *un bon numéro* (a good number), high enough to make an examination unlikely. After 1889, the number was used to decide which branch of the army the conscript would enter. A low number consigned the young man to the navy or the colonial armies, both dreaded by peasants wary of travelling far from home. The conscripts resorted to various prayers, talismans and pilgrimages to help them secure a good number. On the day of the *tirage*, the conscripts of each village dressed up specially and marched together to the *chef-lieu* of their canton, stopping for drinks along the way. They then enjoyed a day or two of licence to drink and brawl before returning home, full of joy or sorrow. Once he had his number, the conscript had taken a further step towards manhood, in some ways anticipating the traditional end of adolescence upon marriage.[50] Returning to Tiennon of *The Life of a Simple Man*, he struck lucky in the end with the number sixty-three, for the recruitment stopped at fifty-nine. He promptly left home afterwards to work as a farm labourer. Jean-Baptiste Dumay, by contrast, drew number fifty-seven when 320 men were conscripted, 'So there I was, bound in chains for seven years, my life interrupted and almost at a dead end.'[51]

---

[49] Emile Guillaumin, *The Life of a Simple Man*, transl. Margaret Crosland (Hanover, NH: University Press of New England, 1983), p. 53; Jean-Baptiste Dumay, *Mémoires d'un militant ouvrier du Creusot (1841–1905)* (Grenoble: Presses Universitaires de Grenoble, 1976), pp. 95–109, transl. as 'Jean-Baptiste Dumay: Memoirs of a Militant Worker from Le Creusot', in Traugott (ed.), *The French Worker*, pp. 309–35 (p. 325).

[50] Van Gennep, *Manuel*, I.1, pp. 213–23; Michel Bozon, *Les Conscrits* (Paris: Berger-Levrault, 1981), passim; and Odile Roynette, 'L'Age d'homme: les représentations de la masculinité chez les médecins militaires au XIXe siècle', in Bardet et al., *Lorsque l'enfant grandit*, pp. 281–90.

[51] Guillaumin, *Life of a Simple Man*, pp. 63–4; Dumay, 'Memoirs', p. 325.

Betrothal and marriage

Once married, the young man or woman had well and truly grown up, or 'buried his youth' as the saying went for a male. During the eighteenth and nineteenth centuries the average age at first marriage in France hovered around twenty-eight for a male, and twenty-five for a female.[52] Marriage involved leaving the youth group and eventually taking on the responsibilities associated with founding a new household and having children. Moreover, it required one of the marriage partners to move to a new family, and perhaps to a new village also. Augustine Rouvière remembered that a strait-laced Protestant upbringing meant that she was quite unprepared for such changes: marriage came to her rather than the other way around, as she put it, so that she had a great fear of the unknown.[53] The transition rites supported the couple through all of this and involved interested parties such as the families, the young people of the village and the civil and religious authorities. When they became engaged, the couple separated themselves from the adolescents and unmarried of the village, and started on the transition rites. As a very public sign of their new social situation, the engaged couple were not supposed to go out together unless accompanied by a relative or friend, nor were they supposed to sleep under the same roof. In practice, however, the Catholic peasantry took a relaxed attitude if the *fiancée* became pregnant. For those leaving a village, there was a tearful embrace to mark the separation. The marriage celebrations brought a series of incorporation rites, including embracing all of the guests at the wedding, throwing fruit, sweets or money to spectators outside the church, and *la rôtie*: the custom of tracking down the couple to their hiding place on the wedding night and offering them a hot and spicy drink. The community now knew that the couple had fulfilled their 'conjugal duties' and were ready to join the ranks of married couples.[54]

Conclusion

Folklore studies happily waft their readers back to the world of Jacques Bonhomme, the archetypal French peasant. They present the image of a set of 'universal' turning points in life for him and his female counterpart, following a combination of Christian rituals and popular customs in the provinces. For as long as the oral tradition held sway in tight-knit village

---

[52] Louis Henry and Jacques Houdaille, 'Célibat et âge au mariage aux XVIIIe et XIXe siècles en France. II. Age au premier mariage', *Population*, 34 (1979), 403–42.
[53] Rey, *Augustine Rouvière*, p. 86.
[54] Van Gennep, *Manuel*, I.1, section 3 and I.2, section 4.

communities, they suggest, there was a supportive framework for those growing up. Young people could look forward to gradual increases in status as they passed through childhood and adolescence, and became drawn into various activities as Christians, farm workers, organizers of festivals, military conscripts and so on. Most importantly, they had a ritualized expression of their transition from one stage to another: something that the individual often has to bear alone in a modern urban civilization.[55] Given that approximately three quarters of the population still lived in a rural commune in 1851, and that the urban population did not overtake the rural one until the 1920s, this gives a fair insight into the experience of growing up for much of the population in the modern period. Testimony from those with a rural upbringing like Emile Guillaumin and Pierre-Jakez Hélias suggests that 'insiders' in the rural community agreed on the importance of the transition rites identified by the folklorists. However, this 'folklore model' of growing up did gradually lose its hold on the villagers in the modern period, as new ideas and institutions impinged on their daily life. The growing importance of the school system in the nineteenth century, for example, meant that passing (or failing) the *certificat d'études* around the age of thirteen began to rival first communion as a turning point, as did gaining the vote at eighteen in the twentieth century.[56] Moreover, the declining spiritual charge to the rituals in a more secular age weakened the effect. First communion, for example, often became less of a religious experience for young people and more of an opportunity to receive 'unsuitable' presents such as a bicycle.[57]

Conclusion

There was no shortage of ideas and institutions in France to help individuals think about the shape of their lives. Much of the discussion of the life cycle in France was confined to the rarefied atmosphere of philosophical or medical discourse, though ideas on the Ages of Man filtered down to the popular culture through such channels as sermons and child-rearing manuals. More relevant to the lives of ordinary people was the series of *rites de passage* to look forward to as markers of their changing status. These showed that they had moved through a sequence: of complete dependence on their mothers during infancy, the relatively carefree world of the small child, the formative years in school or helping parents, and

---

[55] Luc Goossens, 'Transition to Adulthood: Developmental Factors', in Corijn and Klijzing (eds.), *Transitions to Adulthood in Europe*, pp. 27–42 (p. 29).
[56] Delumeau, *Première Communion*, p. 12.   [57] Mellot, 'Rite de passage', p. 192.

the phase of adolescence and youth. Van Gennep is persuasive in arguing that ceremonies such as baptism and marriage helped villagers support each other through potentially difficult transitions in life. However, this was not the end of the story of growing up. It was also the case that people writing their autobiographies or their personal diaries needed to think in terms of turning points in their lives, even though they may well have crystallized only in retrospect.

This brings us to the perspective of life-course theory.

4   Turning points in a life: the autobiographical model

Expansion of the 'middling' and 'popular' classes in the larger towns and cities during the modern period in France eventually produced a very different social and cultural environment to that of the villages, and many variants on the path through life taken by the peasantry. Moreover, all classes might feel that the 'universal' turning points already outlined were not the only ones in their lives: other more personal ones could intervene also. Reflecting this more urbanized and 'atomized' society of the nineteenth and twentieth centuries, the authors could then tell their unique story of growing up, influenced by the random intervention of fate or their own strategic choices. The classic model for this more personal turning point goes back once again to St Augustine and his fourth-century *Confessions*. In his case it was a religious conversion that changed his life, when he decided in his thirties to renounce his teaching career and marriage prospects for a life of prayer and study. However, it was not until Jean-Jacques Rousseau revived the title for his own autobiography during the eighteenth century, and highlighted the main turning points in his early life, that such ways of thinking became common currency among French people. In the case of Rousseau, the turning points were secular rather than religious in character. The first was the death of his mother while she was giving birth to him. The second was the 'accident', which interrupted his education and 'the consequences of which have influenced the rest of my life', when his father had to flee from Geneva. The third was the notorious 'false turn' in his childhood when he discovered that he rather enjoyed being spanked by Mlle Lambercier, an event which 'would determine my tastes and desires, my passions, my very self for the rest of my life'. The fourth was his first encounter with violence and injustice, when he claimed he was beaten unfairly upon the discovery of a broken comb. This ended the serene phase of his childhood. The fifth turning point was his decision to leave Geneva at sixteen, abandoning the prospect of a 'simple and obscure life' as a tradesman for wider horizons. Soon afterwards he entered what he considered the most decisive stage in his life, reaching his sixth turning point, on meeting Mme de Warens at Annecy. He perceived a further intervention from Providence when in his twenties he passed up the chance of marrying and settling down to a peaceful existence as a music master in Fribourg. Finally, there was the great turning point in his life in 1749 when he read the question set by the Dijon Academy for its annual prize. The question asked whether progress in the arts and sciences had tended to corrupt or improve morals. 'The moment I read this', Rousseau recorded, 'I beheld another universe and became another man.'[1] The figure of Jean-Jacques loomed large over nineteenth-century authors of autobiographies in France. Some reacted against his approach, as in the cases of Chateaubriand and Stendhal. Others, as will emerge below, depicted their lives revolving around one or more decisive turning points. The literary critic Michael Sheringham suggests a further 'turning point in the history of turning points' in France around 1900. At that period the influence of such authorities as Marcel Proust and Sigmund Freud invited people to interpret events from the early part of their life, producing a new turning point in the life of the adult.[2]

This provokes the question of why modern French writers, like their counterparts elsewhere, should wish to frame descriptions of their lives around one or more turning points. The most persuasive answer is that the very act of writing an autobiography encourages people to put a shape on their existence, and even to dramatize it a little. In other words, anyone wishing to go beyond a string of anecdotes in their writing, as most do, is bound retrospectively to create turning points in their lives to give the reader a sense of direction, and to explain why the author turned out the way he or she did. Moreover, as Philippe Lejeune observed, for aesthetic reasons the author can follow in the footsteps of a short-story writer like Maupassant in hinging a life story around a single, fateful decision. In principle, such turning points might help or hinder an individual. They might be passively endured, actively sought out, or at least negotiated.[3] Historians relying on autobiographical material therefore need to be aware of the literary precedents that encouraged authors to frame their lives around one or more turning points. They can also examine some of the more frequently cited turning points, from the endless possibilities available, to throw light on the experiences of people living in a particular

---

[1] Jean-Jacques Rousseau, *The Confessions*, transl. J. M. Cohen (London: Penguin, 1953), p. 327.
[2] Michael Sheringham, 'Le Tournant autobiographique: mort ou vif?', *Recherches interdisciplinaires sur les textes modernes*, 10 (1995), 23–36.
[3] Philippe Lejeune, 'Le Tournant d'une vie', in *Les Brouillons de soi* (Paris: Seuil, 1998), pp. 103–24.

period and place. So what sort of turning points did authors reflecting on their early years in modern France tend to highlight?

Getting started: the first memory

Before they could discuss any turning points, writers of an autobiography needed a beginning for their story. As the literary critic Bruno Vercier pointed out, they immediately faced the dilemma of whether to structure the work around the haphazard series of memories that came to mind later in life, or adopt a chronological organization of material, starting with birth and parental background. Invariably they sacrificed the creativity of free association to the intelligibility of chronology. Stendhal began during the 1830s with a flourish of episodes on the formation of his character but drew up short with 'I am letting myself get carried away, I am digressing, I shall be unintelligible if I don't stick to the order of events, and moreover the circumstances won't come back to me so well.'[4] Hence the first memory is often inserted quite late in the proceedings, after the authors have used documents or what other people have told them to sketch in their origins and infancy. It remains significant as a second birth for them, the start of the life that they are recreating in written form. The poet Francis Jammes (1868–1938) expressed this feeling well, from his infancy in the Hautes-Pyrénées:

I believe I remember my awakening to life, coming out of a big sleep in a bedroom of this lost residence. I was in bed. I opened my eyes. I saw the flame of a hearth and someone moving. It is my extreme memory, the one that reaches the abyss.[5]

The search for origins in autobiographical writing, as French people began to reflect on their early years during the eighteenth and nineteenth centuries, therefore gives the first memory a mythical status. Vercier even suggested that there existed a competition among authors to beat the record for the earliest first memory. He cited George Sand as a prominent contender with her claim in the *Histoire de ma vie* (*History of My Life*, 1854–5) that 'my memories go back to an age when most other individuals can retrieve nothing from their past'. An early investigation into first memories from childhood conducted by French psychologists during the 1890s followed Hippolyte Taine (1828–93) in asserting that these memories involved an intensity of experience, either because they were horrible or delicious, or because they were entirely new, surprising

---

[4] Sand, *Histoire de ma vie*, pp. 139–40; Stendhal, *Henry Brulard*, p. 12; Bruno Vercier, 'Le Mythe du premier souvenir: Pierre Loti, Michel Leiris', *Revue d'histoire littéraire de la France*, 75 (1975), 1029–40.
[5] Francis Jammes, *De l'âge divin à l'âge ingrat: mémoires* (Paris: Plon, 1921), p. 8.

and out of the ordinary. Unsurprisingly, they dredged up memories of strong emotions such as fear, shame or joie de vivre.[6] However, as Georges Gusdorf observed, the psychologists missed the psychology in asking for a description of a memory in space and time. What mattered more was how it was used as part of a 'desperate attempt by the individual to recuperate the totality of his own life'.[7] It follows that although the first memory was something of a literary conceit, it was also an opportunity for authors to start reflecting on the meaning of their lives. It is therefore an obvious starting point for the historian as well as the literary critic.

A common device was to recall an accident during childhood as a first memory.[8] Henri Pitaud (1899–1991), for example, recorded a vivid first memory of nearly drowning in a pond one winter's morning as a way of reinforcing his bleak vision of life as a peasant in the Vendée. He claimed to remember as a one-year-old launching himself in his little carriage from the kitchen doorway and careering out of control into the water. The crux of the story was the struggle of his mother to hold him up in the icy water while she waited for neighbours to fish them both out.[9] Another approach was to use the first memory to give a hint of the future character of the writer. Alphonse de Lamartine (1790–1869) provided a pointer to his future career as a poet through his first memory, in which his father read aloud a poem by the Italian Tasso one winter's evening.[10] Eager to consolidate his reputation as republican educator, Ernest Lavisse (1842–1922) started his memoirs in the appropriate setting of the primary school.[11] His first memory was of being tricked by his grandmother into thinking he was going to join her running an errand, when in fact she was taking him to his first day at school. At the end of the first chapter, he ruminated:

Such are the impressions left in my memory by the schools of my childhood. Why, at the moment when I was giving a hearing to my memories, were these the first ones to come to mind? Is it because my life has been entirely preoccupied with school and education? Or rather for other reasons, such as, for example, an instinctive repugnance for drawing up a biography of my personality starting with

---

[6] Victor and Catherine Henri, 'Enquête sur les premiers souvenirs de l'enfance (1897)', *Cahiers de sémiotique textuelle*, 12 (1988), 237–48 (241–2).

[7] Comment on Vercier, 'Le Mythe', 1041.

[8] See, for example, Sand, *Histoire de ma vie*, p. 140; and Marie Lafarge, *Mémoires de Marie Capelle, veuve Lafarge, écrits par elle-même* (4 vols., Paris: A. René, 1841–2), I, p. 4.

[9] Pitaud, *Le Pain de la terre*, p. 26.

[10] Alphonse de Lamartine, *Les Confidences* (Paris: Hachette, 1879 (1849)), pp. 49–54. See also Rousseau, *Confessions*, p. 19; and Stendhal, *Henry Brulard*, p. 27.

[11] On the self-serving purpose of the *Souvenirs*, see Pierre Nora, 'Ernest Lavisse: son rôle dans la formation du sentiment national', *Revue historique*, 228 (1962), 73–106 (73–4).

'I was born at . . . on the . . .'? I don't know, but I have resolved to follow the order of the pictures offered successively to me during my tranquil meditations.[12]

André Gide (1869–1951) began *Si le grain ne meurt* (1926) with the view from the balcony of the family flat in Paris, and time spent under the dining-room table with the son of the concierge. There they acquired what he later learned to call 'bad habits', not together but side by side. By placing the episode at the very beginning of the novel, he followed Rousseau in highlighting the precocious start to his deep-seated vice, which he felt marked the rest of his life. In this way, he floated one of the major themes of the work, and the one that gave it historical significance, his recognition of his homosexuality.[13] In similar vein, an author might launch childhood reminiscences with the important issue of relations with the family. Jacques Vingtras/Jules Vallès naturally launched his account of a miserable childhood with a spanking from his mother. Antoine Sylvère used his first memory to highlight the distant relations between parents and child in a world dominated by hardship and work on a peasant farm in the Auvergne. He claimed bitter memories of crawling around under a large table and crying for attention:

I had an immense need for consolation and my mother, entirely absorbed by the peeling of vegetables, affected an unpardonable indifference. I considered this attitude as a violation of my rights. I deduced that, if my tears achieved nothing, I had no means of obtaining justice. In the end, because my mother stubbornly persisted in not wishing to console me, I made up my mind to get out of trouble by my own means, to console myself alone, and I formed the opinion that grown-ups were useful things, intervening when it pleased them, but one could not compel them to do things if they dodged their duties.

Henceforth, he asserted in his childhood reminiscences, he resolved at the age of two to run his own life separately from those of his parents as far as was possible.[14]

Alone in the world

The loss of a close relative, looming large for as long as death rates remained high, naturally provoked emotional upheavals for young people at all levels of society. Both Rousseau and Stendhal, the pioneers of childhood reminiscences, attributed the start of their misfortunes to the death

[12] Ernest Lavisse, *Souvenirs* (Paris: Calmann-Lévy, 1988 (1912)), p. 26.
[13] André Gide, *Si le grain ne meurt* (Paris: Gallimard, 1955 (1926)), pp. 9–10; Jean Delay, *The Youth of André Gide*, transl. June Guicharnaud (Chicago: University of Chicago Press, 1963), p. 66.
[14] Vallès, *L'Enfant*, pp. 19–20; and Sylvère, *Toinou*, pp. 6–7.

of their mothers. Rousseau was aware that it was his birth that cost his mother her life. He knew that his father never got over it: 'he seemed to see her again in me, but could never forget that I had robbed him of her'. Stendhal depicted the protagonist in *The Life of Henry Brulard* losing his mother in 1790 when he was seven:

This was the start of my moral life. My aunt Séraphie dared to reproach me for not weeping enough. Judge of my grief and what I felt! But it seemed to me that I would see her again the next day. I didn't understand death. Thus it is forty-five years since I lost what I loved best in the world.

The young Henry suspected that his father subsequently fell in love with the hated aunt Séraphie, which poisoned relations between them and meant that 'all the joys of childhood ended with my mother'.[15] The period covered by this book brought some relief from the high mortality of the 'old demographic regime', and it preceded the soaring divorce rates of the late twentieth century. Even so, in the absence of a welfare state, children and adolescents risked material as well as emotional problems following the death of a close relative. Not surprisingly, those cast adrift without much support rued the day when fate appeared to turn against them. It was surely easy to feel that 'each of us is very much alone', as Marcel Proust put it.[16]

In the seventeenth, eighteenth and even nineteenth centuries, marriages frequently came to an abrupt end through the premature death of a husband or a wife. Death in childbirth, for example, may have occurred less frequently than was once thought, but was far from negligible: one estimate suggests a maternal mortality rate in France of 5 per cent in the eighteenth century.[17] Children often had to contend with the splintering and re-formation of families: at least one marriage in four was a remarriage. The risk of the premature death of a parent declined from the eighteenth century onwards, as in the long term life expectancy increased in modern France. During the 1740s, the expectation of life at birth was 23.8 years for a male and 25.7 years for a female; two centuries later the respective figures were 61.9 and 67.5 years. However, studies of mortality reveal that it maintained most of the traits characteristic of a 'demographic old regime' as late as the 1880s, including substantial fluctuations in the short term, a winter peak and heavy excess mortality in the towns.[18]

---

[15] Rousseau, *Confessions*, p. 19; Stendhal, *Henry Brulard*, pp. 33–5 and 43.

[16] Marcel Proust, *In Search of Lost Time*, vol. III, *The Guermantes Way* (London: Penguin, 2003 (1920–1)), p. 316.

[17] J.-P. Bardet et al., 'La Mortalité maternelle autrefois: une étude comparée (de la France de l'ouest à l'Utah)', *Annales de démographie historique* (1981), 31–48 (40).

[18] André Burguière and François Lebrun, 'The One Hundred and One Families of Europe', in André Burguière et al. (eds.), *A History of the Family*, vol. II, *The Impact of Modernity*,

During the 1860s, the average length of a marriage was 28.5 years, which was probably closer to the eighteenth-century figure than to the 42 years registered in the early 1960s.[19]

Some peasants and workers recorded the death of a parent without suggesting that it made much of a difference to their lives. 'Amédée', a Parisian worker and revolutionary syndicalist interviewed by the ethnographer Jacques Caroux-Destray, mentioned that his father died early in the twentieth century when he was thirteen. He admitted that he did not know his father very well, but this was hardly surprising given the parent's fourteen-hour working days as a stonemason and leisure time spent drinking heavily in the bistro with other workers.[20] Other family members might step in to rescue an orphaned child, as happened to Jacques-Louis Ménétra (b. 1738) in Paris. His father, a glazier, became a widower when Jacques-Louis was two, and it fell to his grandmother to look after him until he was eleven.[21] However, in many cases the loss of a relative caused the child problems sufficient to make it stand out as a turning point in life.

Among the poor, the break-up of a family could see a child thrown on to the streets and struggling on the lowest rungs of the job market. There are a few accounts of the age-old figure of the 'wicked stepmother' or stepfather provoking a crisis in a child's life.[22] The young Valentin Jamerey-Duval (1695–1775) began his existence with a peaceable childhood as the son of a cartwright, but then his family was plunged into the depths of poverty by the death of his father in 1700. His mother's second marriage to an agricultural labourer proved disastrous for him, as the new husband turned out to be a brutal stepfather. Jamerey-Duval ran away from home in 1709, and spent his first year on the road as a vagrant. His casual jobs included looking after sheep and turkeys, assisting a shepherd and working with a miller. He claimed to have had sixteen masters in the space of one year. At least he landed on his feet in the end, the uprooting from a peasant background leading to contacts at the Court of the Duchy of Lorraine and a philosophy degree at a Jesuit university.

transl. Sarah Hanbury Tenison (Cambridge: Polity, 1996), pp. 11–94 (p. 15); Etienne van de Walle, 'France', in W. R. Lee, *European Demography and Economic Growth* (London: Croom Helm, 1979), pp. 123–43; Jacques Dupaquier et al. (eds.), *Histoire de la population française*, vol. III, *De 1789 à 1914* (Paris: Presses Universitaires de France, 1988), ch. 6.

[19] Louis Roussel, *Le Mariage dans la société française*, p. 307, cited by Martine Segalen, *Love and Power in the Peasant Family* (Oxford: Basil Blackwell, 1983), p. 12.

[20] Caroux-Destray, *Un couple ouvrier traditionnel*, pp. 42–5.

[21] Ménétra, *Journal of My Life*, pp. 18–25.

[22] On the common experience of widowhood and remarriage during the seventeenth and eighteenth centuries, and the recognition that it caused problems for the children concerned, see Burguière and Lebrun, 'One Hundred and One Families', p. 15.

Captain Coignet (b. 1776), soldier of the Empire, as the title of his memoirs announced, started life with a not dissimilar background. He too came from a village in the Yonne, and suffered from a remarriage, but in his case it was a stepmother that led him to leave home early. His father's third marriage was to one of his servants, an eighteen-year-old reputed to be a beauty. 'This stepmother ruled everything,' he recounted, 'we poor little orphans were beaten night and day', and complaints to his father only led to harsher treatment. His experience of trying to find casual work at the age of eight led him to a year acting as a 'sheepdog', as he put it, with a shepherdess, and then to three years as a servant with two old farmers. The latter reduced him to the most complete misery, as he lived alone with his cattle, ate the same meal of an omelette with leeks every day, and crawled with vermin picked up from his bed of straw. He was eventually reduced to working, unrecognized, as a stable boy on his half-sister's farm.[23]

Like the death of a male breadwinner, the loss of a mother was potentially disastrous in its own way. Besides providing emotional support, women for long retained significant responsibilities in the economic, educational and welfare spheres. Emilie Carles (1900–79), from a family of small, landowning peasant farmers in the Alps, lost her mother when she was four. 'Her death was a loss beyond telling. Where we lived, the mother was the keystone, holding the structure together. Overnight, my father was cut to half his size.' Her father at least managed to soldier on alone with his farm: the father of Louise Vanderwielen (b. 1906) in a working-class neighbourhood of Lille turned to drink and allowed his family to fall apart when the mother died.[24] Similarly, the young criminal Emile Nouguier, writing as he awaited the guillotine in 1899, rued the death of his mother when he was ten, and the lack of attention from his father that followed. He lost the chance of a scholarship to a *lycée* because his father could not be bothered to produce the documentation required for the final stage. He was bound to wonder whether this was the first cause of his delinquency.[25] The diary of Caroline Brame (1847–92) revealed the near-catastrophic impact for a girl of the loss of a guide and mentor when a mother died. This was a period when the education of a young woman was more likely to depend on time spent with her mother than at school. Caroline had a very comfortable, and very Catholic,

---

[23] Jamerey-Duval, *Mémoires*, passim; Jean-Roch Coignet, *The Narrative of Captain Coignet, Soldier of the Empire, 1776–1850*, transl. Mrs M. Carey (London: Chatto and Windus, 1897), pp. 1–8.

[24] Carles, *Wild Herb Soup*, p. 7; and Vanderwielen, *Lise du plat pays*, pp. 62 and 69.

[25] Philippe Artières (ed.), *Le Livre des vies coupables: autobiographies de criminels (1896–1909)* (Paris: Albin Michel, 2000), p. 91.

background in the Faubourg Saint-Germain. Yet running like red thread through the whole work is a feeling of sadness over the loss of her mother, Paméla de Gardonne, who died when Caroline was fifteen. She later recalled her first ball, full of childish pride, with her mother there as a reassuring presence. After that, there was no one to help her find her way through the formalities of Parisian society. At the age of seventeen she had to act as mistress of the house, entertaining dinner guests and asserting her authority over domestic servants, and appear alone at salons and festivals. She felt certain that her mother was looking down from heaven:

> But her empty place on this earth, Oh! I cannot express the harm she is doing me. I no longer have my mother to love me, console me, guide me, I no longer have my mother at the age when all is danger, I no longer have my mother now that we would be so happy together.

Her father was good to her, but could not understand her feelings, something she found quite natural. Hence she felt isolated and deprived of a confidant.[26]

Other relatives with a prominent role in the life of a child in the past might leave a gap when they died. Pierre-Jakez Hélias considered the death of his grandfather Alain le Goff, the 'Horse of Pride' himself, the end of his Old Testament: 'For me there were very few dates in the history of the world as momentous as that one, precisely because it belongs to me alone.'[27] Marcel Proust provided a more disturbing account of his reaction to the dying days of his beloved grandmother. Following the slight stroke she suffered while they were on a walk together in the gardens of the Champs-Elysées, the Narrator of *In Search of Lost Time* (*The Guermantes Way*, 1920–1) stated, 'She had suddenly restored to my keeping the thoughts, the sorrows, which I had entrusted to her for ever since I was a child. She was not yet dead. But I was already alone.'[28]

It was also possible for a child to fall out with a natural parent, and suffer as the weaker party to the argument. Before the late nineteenth century, the child was in a particularly vulnerable position, as the state had no power to intervene when parents acted in an abusive or negligent fashion.[29] The police in Lyon reported in March 1892 finding a sixteen-year-old lad who had run away from home, and who was so ill from sleeping rough that he could no longer walk. The *gardiens* took him home, but his mother refused to receive him. 'At this', the report ended, 'he was left at the door, as ordered by the Commissaire.'[30] Norbert Truquin (b. 1833) gave a very full account of his switch from a life of opulence

---

[26] Brame, *Journal intime*, passim.   [27] Hélias, *Horse of Pride*, p. 309.
[28] Proust, *The Guermantes Way*, pp. 308–11.   [29] See below, p. 144.
[30] AD Rhône, 4 M 482, Police administrative: fêtes, report of 4–5 March 1892.

during his first five years to a rough existence in industrial Reims. He came to grief at the age of seven when he let slip to a landlady that his father would be unlikely to pay their hotel bill. His hard-pressed father, already bankrupt two years earlier, effectively washed his hands of the boy. The father handed over his son to the tender mercies of a wool comber, and when this employer died in 1843, Truquin found himself a street-urchin, keeping body and soul together by selling mercury scraped from urinals to local pharmacists. Subsequently he struggled to secure a job in the textile mills because of his position as a 'vagabond'. This set the scene for picaresque tales of low-life among prostitutes, Napoleonic War veterans, navvies, hawkers, brick makers and abattoir workers. Exaggerated or not, such accounts reveal how some children had to grow up very fast, taking responsibility for their own livelihood, on account of the random impact of death or a family quarrel.[31]

There were of course various sources of institutionalized support available for orphaned and abandoned children before the coming of the welfare state.[32] Marguerite Audoux provided a relatively benign view of life in an orphanage run by nuns in her autobiographical novel *Marie-Claire* (1910). Entering the institution after the death of her mother and the disappearance of her drunken father, Marie-Claire formed a close relationship with the gentle Sister Marie-Aimée. After her first communion and some basic training in making lingerie, she began a series of placements in local farms and workshops. The position of foundlings was notoriously insecure, as George Sand made clear in *François le champi* (1850).[33] The Audoux novel revealed the orphan moving from one employer to another according to their requirements, one set of farmers proving very helpful to her, another barely speaking to her much of the time. At the age of eighteen she chose to return to work in the kitchens of her orphanage for a while.[34] Charlotte Poulet conveyed to her interviewer a more conventional view of life in an orphanage in Paris before the First World War. This was forced on her by poverty at the age of seven when her father died of tuberculosis. She resented being given the number fifteen instead of a name by the sisters at the Orphelins d'Auteuil (near Paris). She also alleged a heartless regime, with no supper if she received a bad report from school and a fierce response when she wet herself during prayers: 'little wretch! Do you not recall then the gutter which I pulled you from!' In similar vein, Julien Blanc recalled the shock of entering

[31] Truquin, *Mémoires et aventures*, chs. 1–4.
[32] See in particular Fuchs, *Abandoned Children*.
[33] See also the story of 'Rose' in Sylvère, *Toinou*, pp. 222–32.
[34] Audoux, *Marie-Claire*, passim.

an orphanage near Angers run by the Sisters of Saint-Vincent de Paul
at the same period. The nuns shaved his head, put him into a uniform
and later left him alone to cry for his dead mother. His reminiscences
dwelt on memories of not having enough to eat and frequent corporal
punishments.[35]

A study by the historian Christophe Escuriol of the fate of orphaned
and abandoned children who grew up in and around Bordeaux during the
middle of the nineteenth century tends to confirm this nuanced picture.
Taking a sample from the registers of the Hôpital de la Manufacture
de Bordeaux of those born between 1840 and 1844, he revealed them
having some success in integrating with the society around them, but
on generally unfavourable terms. Looked at in their twenties, the young
men were generally illiterate, consigned to unskilled work and more likely
than most to be too short or too feeble for military service. At the same
time, they worked in similar sectors of the economy to those around
them, above all agriculture and certain artisan trades, and they had a fair
chance of marrying a bride from the local population. The young women
fared less well, being even more illiterate than the males, employed almost
exclusively as servants, and older than most women when they married.[36]

Seeing the light

The classic religious conversion that had inspired so many autobiographies in the past was comparatively rare in modern France. If St Augustine
abandoned teaching for the Church, Ernest Renan (1823–92) was more
typical of his age in moving the other way, going down the steps of
the Saint-Sulpice Seminary on 6 October 1845, 'never to go up them
again in a soutane'.[37] The chequered history of the Catholic faith and
Catholic practice in modern France, in the wake of the Enlightenment
and 1789, meant that young people were more likely to boast of free-
ing themselves from the clutches of a religious education than of finding
God. There were of course devout Catholics proud to assert their spiritual progress through life. Chateaubriand (1768–1848) gave a dramatic
account of how first communion around the age of twelve made him
a virtuous *honnête homme*. While at his college, his ardent Catholic faith
could not prevent him remaining uncommunicative at confession. On the

---

[35] 'Charlotte Poulet', in Germain and de Panafieu, *Mémoire des femmes*, pp. 184–5; and
Julien Blanc, *Seul, la vie: 1, Confusion des peines* (Paris: Editions du Pré-aux-Clercs,
1943), pp. 37–42.
[36] Christophe Escuriol, 'Les Enfants de l'hôpital survivants', in Bardet et al., *Lorsque l'enfant
grandit*, pp. 69–92.
[37] Ernest Renan, *Souvenirs d'enfance et de jeunesse* (Paris: Gallimard, 1983 (1883)), p. 184.

day of his first communion he adopted the usual reticent tone with his confessor, and was about to receive absolution, but then 'a thunderbolt thrown from heaven could not have caused me less terror, and I cried out: "I have not said everything"'. With his confessor in tears, he unburdened himself, and 'if someone had taken the weight of a mountain off me, I could not have been more relieved'.[38] Marie-Françoise-Thérèse Martin (1873–97), the future St Thérèse de Lisieux, described a religious conversion in 1886 that led to entry into a convent at the age of fifteen, an early death from tuberculosis, and canonization in 1925. The turning point followed a spectacular recovery from serious illness:

God had to perform a miracle on a small scale to make me grow up; grow up all in a moment. And the occasion he chose for it was Christmas, that night of illumination which somehow lights up for us the inner life of the Blessed Trinity. Our Lord, newly born, turned this darkness of mine into a flood of light; born to share my human weakness, he brought me the strength and courage I needed. He armed me so well, that holy night, that I never looked back; I was like a soldier, winning one vantage point after another, like a 'great runner who sees the track before him'.[39]

At the other extreme was the scepticism of the apprentice glazier Jacques-Louis Ménétra, in the middle of the eighteenth century, with his doubts at his first communion that 'the son of God allowed himself to be fed to men just like that' and his railings against the 'fanaticism and superstition' of priests. Much later, during the 1890s, the poet Catherine Pozzi recorded the details of her loss of faith at the age of fourteen. Although from a devout background, she experienced a crisis after reading Nietzsche and perceiving 'the stupidity of all religions'. After that she took the difficult path for a young woman during that period of attempting a literary career.[40]

What tended to replace a religious conversion in the life of a young person during the nineteenth and twentieth centuries was a political one as, say, a socialist or a feminist. René Belin, secretary of the Confédération générale du travail during the 1930s, sketched a model life story for the

---

[38] Chateaubriand, Viconte de, *Mémoires d'outre-tombe* (Paris: Flammarion, 1948 (1849–50)), pp. 87–8. On the ups and downs of the Church in modern France, see Ralph Gibson, *A Social History of French Catholicism, 1789–1914* (London: Routledge, 1989), passim.

[39] *Autobiography of St Thérèse of Lisieux* (1957), extract transl. in Erna Olafson Hellerstein, Leslie Parker Hume and Karen M. Offen (eds.), *Victorian Women* (Stanford: Stanford University Press, 1981), pp. 107–10.

[40] Ménétra, *Journal of My Life*, pp. 19 and 22; and Catherine Pozzi, *Journal de jeunesse, 1893–1906*, cited in Françoise Simonet-Tenant, '*Agnès* de Catherine Pozzi: une réécriture fusionnelle', in Philippe Lejeune and Catherine Viollet (eds.), *Genèses du 'Je': manuscrits et autobiographie* (Paris: CNRS, 2000), pp. 157–68 (p. 158).

men and women who led the trade union movement. They would begin with a childhood in the emptiness of a home 'without light, without coal, without bread and above all without hope'. Surrounded by hunger and premature death, they worked hard to improve their minds, and became aware of the injustices of the capitalist regime. Out of this hard school of life there emerged hard but also proud men, inspired by an idea: socialism. Georges Dumoulin (1877–1963) was the original militant Belin had in mind. Dumoulin started life in the Pas-de-Calais, with miserable lodgings consisting of two rooms for a family of eight. The seasonal nature of his father's job as a labourer meant that winters were often difficult for the Dumoulin family, while his mother worked night and day for pitiful wages as a home worker in textile manufacturing. He flourished at school, but struggled to keep up with his better-off classmates because he lost time working in the fields each year from March to November. His lot in the end was work in a sugar refinery and then a coalmine. However, salvation was at hand. At the age of seventeen he became aware of his exploitation by the system after reading novels by Emile Zola and literature from the Marxist Parti ouvrier français. His life as a militant in the syndicalist movement had begun. Similarly, René Michaud endured extreme poverty with his widowed mother in the tough Thirteenth Arrondissement Paris on the eve of the First World War. His teacher considered him a good pupil, but in the end he failed his primary school certificate and started work at thirteen in a shoe factory. He too talked in terms of a growing consciousness of capitalist exploitation, influenced by a couple of militant uncles in the Paris building trade, strikes taking place around him in 1917 and his reading of the socialist newspaper *L'Humanité*. He became an anarchist with the leather workers federation. He particularly recalled his first strike in the shoe-manufacturing industry in 1917, 'a date which stands out in the life of a militant!'[41] Jeanne Bouvier was an early example of a female taking this path. Born in 1865 in the Isère, she endured the ruin of her father as a cooper during the phylloxera crisis, work in a silk-throwing mill at the age of eleven, bailiffs seizing furniture for unpaid rent while her father was unemployed and gruelling tasks as a domestic servant in Paris. Eventually she became a skilled seamstress, and had her conversion to syndicalism. Later, during the interwar period, she established herself as a feminist author.[42]

---

[41] Dumoulin, *Carnets de route* Introduction by René Belin, secretary of the CGT, and pp. 15–34; and Michaud, *J'avais vingt ans*, pp. 71–9.

[42] Bouvier, *Mes mémoires*, passim. Excerpts from the memoirs by Dumoulin and Bouvier, and also from those by Suzanne Voilquin and Jean-Baptiste Dumay, appear in Traugott (ed.), *The French Worker*. See also Maynes, *Taking the Hard Road*.

Grown up?

Life-stage theories suggest an orderly progress to growing up, a steady and even congenial process of maturation. This was not the way everyone experienced it. The determination of Jean-Jacques Rousseau to 'make my soul transparent to the reader's eye' in his *Confessions*, during the mid-eighteenth century, produced an early challenge to any such notion. He began by asserting: 'Mine was no true childhood; I always thought and felt like a man. Only as I grew up did I become my true age, which I had not been at my birth.' His evidence for such a startling claim was that no other child was attracted to novels at the age of six, let alone moved to tears by them. Later he presented a very different view:

These long details of my early youth may well seem extremely childish, and I am sorry for it. Although in certain respects I have been a man since birth, I was for a long time, and still am, a child in many others. I never promised to present the public with a great personage.[43]

The idea that some people have to grow up fast while others never grow up at all remains common currency today. Before the near-universal imposition of a 'long' childhood during the twentieth century, and the framework provided by the school system, such uncertainty over boundaries may have been more in evidence. Among the poor, premature deaths of parents or long working hours often required girls to take responsibility for the care of younger siblings at a tender age. Before the age of ten, for example, Jeanne Bouvier (1865–1935) took over from her parents on days they went to market, feeding and changing her six-month-old brother and preparing meals for three farm workers. Soon after starting work in a silk mill at the age of eleven, she found herself the major breadwinner for a spell when her father was partially unemployed. This meant putting in a thirteen-hour day at the mill, supplemented by crochet work at home in the evening.[44] At the upper levels of society, the premature death of her mother abruptly propelled Caroline Brame from the sheltered existence of a girl in the Faubourg Saint-Germain to running a household. During the spring of 1865, she cheerfully described herself in her diary as being a rather giddy child when with her friends, but her eighteenth birthday in May of that year brought a more sombre tone. 'Childhood,' she wrote, 'ah! despite the years, childhood has long disappeared; despite myself, I was almost a young woman at fifteen . . . and now, I know how this life is that the poets sing about; among the flowers, alas, there are many thorns and despite my eighteen years, how many loved ones are no more!' She at least presented the end of her youth in strictly conventional terms,

[43] Rousseau, *Confessions*, pp. 67 and 169.   [44] Bouvier, *Mes mémoires*, pp. 49 and 58–9.

writing that she had put down her diary as a *jeune fille* (young woman) on 19 April 1866, and, following her marriage, was picking it up again a month later as a *dame* (lady).[45]

Conclusion

One could readily cite other turning points outside these categories that blighted or lit up individual lives. On 1 June 1905, for example, there was the famous scene on the steps of the Grand Palais in Paris when Henri Fournier spotted a beautiful but unattainable young woman: he was the son of a village schoolteacher, she turned out to be Yvonne de Quiévrecourt, the daughter of an aristocratic naval officer. His passion for her was the inspiration for *Le Grand Meaulnes*.[46] The point is that all of these individual experiences were a counterpoint to the universal turning points marking French childhood and adolescence during the modern period. They introduced a random element into the rigid framework of the *rites de passage*, and make it clear that ultimately everyone had their own particular life course. They were also, one way or another, the product of historical circumstances in France, given that the young in the period covered here were still vulnerable to, say, the premature death of a parent or the lure of anarchism. The various turning points often reveal children at the mercy of impersonal forces such as the death of a parent, poverty and military conscription, or more personal ones such as conflict within a family. Yet there was also evidence of young people taking the initiative themselves, be it rescuing themselves when abandoned by parents, or eagerly embracing such faiths as Catholicism and socialism. Bruno Vercier argued that eventually an ideal life story emerged, a sort of template that all writers of childhood reminiscences used to tell their own particular tale. It took the following form: my birth, my father and my mother, the house, the rest of the family, my first memory, language, the external world, animals, death, books, a vocation, sex, the end of childhood.[47] It remains in the rest of this work to flesh out and extend the detail of this framework.

---

[45] Brame, *Journal intime*, entries for 14 March, 14 April and 5 May 1865, and 24 May 1866.

[46] Robert Gibson, *Alain-Fournier: Le Grand Meaulnes* (London: Grant and Cutler, 1986), pp. 10–12.

[47] Vercier, 'Le Mythe', 1033.

Part II

Growing up among family and friends

.

5   The demographic context: family forms in modern France

Early in 1798, peasants in the village of Lacaune (Tarn) spotted a naked boy running wild in the woods. The next day they observed him foraging for acorns and roots. Occasional contacts with people in the region over the following months revealed the boy to be a feral child of around twelve years of age, who loped along at great speed, fed himself on roots and bulbs, and emitted the occasional shrill cry. When he was eventually captured, the 'Wild Boy of Aveyron' created a huge stir in French society. Apart from his attraction as a freak-show type of figure, he appeared a promising subject for *savants* interested in the age-old question of what was innate in human nature, and what was acquired from civilization. They hoped to discover whether he had an innate idea of God, and how he developed sensations, thoughts and ideas. In the event, the persistent mutism of the young 'Victor' made him a disappointing case study. The well-known efforts to educate him by Dr Itard, from the National Institute for Deaf-Mutes in Paris, were largely in vain. 'Victor' gained some understanding of language spoken by others but never managed to produce speech himself; he remained entirely self-centred; and he could not overcome his sexual inhibitions. Once returned to civilization, the 'child of nature' soon appeared a sad figure, seared by the experience of early abandonment by his family. A scar across his throat that could only have been made by a knife told its own story: that of a failed attempt at infanticide by 'a hand more disposed than adapted to acts of cruelty', as Itard put it. Some contemporaries thought the wild boy an incurable 'idiot', abandoned by long-suffering parents. It may well be that 'Victor' was the first documented case of autism in history. Yet it is also conceivable that it was his long period of isolation in the wild during early childhood that led to his retarded condition, in the form of irreversible muteness and an inability to interact with other people.[1]

---

[1] This section relies on Harlan Lane, *The Wild Boy of Aveyron* (London: George Allen and Unwin, 1977); Roger Shattuck, *The Forbidden Experiment: The Story of the Wild Boy of Aveyron* (New York: Kodansha International, 1994); Nancy Youssef, 'Savage or

These rare cases reveal the potentially disastrous consequences of denying a child contact with its parents or other caregivers. Modern studies in child psychology reveal that infants form part of a complex social world from the very beginning of their lives. As indicated above, attachment theory proposes that an infant has an instinctive urge (or rather some sort of biological proclivity) to seek out an attachment figure during the early part of its life. This figure is usually the mother, but it has a 'small hierarchy' or network of such figures, which might include the father, grandparents, siblings, and other friends and relatives. The theory asserts that emotions are 'wired in' and act as behavioural signals to the caregiver. They provide evidence of physical distress or a psychological experience of loss. If the parents or other caregivers act in a sensitive and responsive manner, the infant is likely to form a secure attachment. Should they prove insensitive, the risk is of an insecurely attached child. Evidence on the long-term effects of early attachment relations is ambivalent. Some studies find a strong element of continuity between, say, secure attachment in infancy and stable relationships in adulthood; others do not. There is an element of contingency, whereby a new context may cause a fundamental change of behaviour. Even so, the model does insist that early experiences act as a constraint on later development.[2] Certainly, campaigns by social reformers to substitute for the family environment, or even improve on it, with long-term care by experts in institutions such as foundling homes and reformatories, have invariably foundered on the detached nature of the relationships involved.[3]

The 'natural' environment created by parents, it might be added, proves on closer inspection to be anything but natural. Anthropologists have long emphasized the importance of cultural influences on child-rearing practices, affecting the way different societies socialize their young into biological events such as first menstruation. Hence one finds

Solitary? The Wild Child and Rousseau's Man of Nature', *Journal of the History of Ideas*, 62 (2001), 245–63; and Michael Newton, *Savage Girls and Wild Boys: A History of Feral Children* (London: Faber and Faber, 2002), ch. 4. There is also an excellent website, FeralChildren.com, edited by Andrew Ward, consulted on 10 August 2004.

[2] This section relies on Klein, *Our Need for Others*, ch. 6; Peter Fonagy, Miriam Steele, Howard Steele, George S. Moran and Anna C. Higgit, 'The Capacity for Understanding Mental States: The Reflective Self in Parent and Child and its Significance for Security of Attachment', *Infant Mental Health Journal*, 12 (1991), 201–18; Jeremy Holmes, *John Bowlby and Attachment Theory* (Hove: Brunner-Routledge, 1993), ch. 3; Sroufe, *Emotional Development*, ch. 10; Robert E. Levine, 'Child Psychology and Anthropology: An Environmental View', in Panter-Brick (ed.), *Biosocial Perspectives*, pp. 102–30; and Peter Fonagy, *Attachment Theory and Psychoanalysis* (New York: Other Press, 2001), passim.

[3] See, for example, Martine Segalen, *Historical Anthropology of the Family*, transl. J. C. Whitehouse and Sarah Matthews (Cambridge: Cambridge University Press, 1986), p. 189.

variations in child-rearing practices across periods in history, not to mention different social groups within the same society.[4] All this provokes an important preliminary question: what type of family were French children likely to grow up in during the past three centuries? Would it have been large or small, simple or complex in structure? To answer it, one needs to resort to the largely quantitative evidence of demography.

The historical debate

Demographic historians have had good sport in disabusing us of our received notions on family life in the past.[5] For much of the twentieth century, it was generally assumed by scholars that industrialization in the West had brought the substitution of small, nuclear families for the large, extended ones of the past. It was tempting to envisage children in medieval and early modern times growing up among a huge array of parents, siblings, servants, grandparents, aunts and uncles, cousins and neighbours from the local community. By contrast, in the modern city the child supposedly spent most of his or her time in a restricted circle comprising mother, father and their offspring only. Some observers considered this a matter of progress, with the nuclear family being well adapted to the demands of a highly mobile urban and industrial society. Others lamented the disappearance of the extended family, fondly imagining that its large numbers provided a stimulating and supportive environment for the young.

In the French case, the most influential champion of the latter approach was the economist and engineer Frédéric Le Play (1806–82). As a staunchly conservative defender of the family, religion and property,

---

[4] Margaret Mead, 'Adolescence in Primitive and in Modern Society', in *Readings in Social Psychology* (New York: Henry Holt, 1952), pp. 531–9; Segalen, *Historical Anthropology*, pp. 173–4. See also Geneviève Delaisi de Parseval and Suzanne Lallemand, *L'Art d'accommoder les bébés: 100 ans de recettes françaises de puériculture* (Paris: Seuil, 1980), pp. 13–18.

[5] Key texts include Peter Laslett and Richard Wall (eds.), *Household and Family in Past Time* (Cambridge: Cambridge University Press, 1972); Jean-Louis Flandrin, *Families in Former Times: Kinship, Household and Sexuality*, transl. Richard Southern (Cambridge: Cambridge University Press, 1979); Robert Wheaton and Tamara K. Hareven (eds.), *Family and Sexuality in French History* (Philadelphia: University of Pennsylvania Press, 1980); Michael Mitterauer and Reinhard Sieder, *The European Family: Patriarchy to Partnership from the Middle Ages to the Present*, transl. Karla Oosterveen and Manfred Hörzinger (Oxford: Blackwell, 1982); Richard Wall, Jean Robin and Peter Laslett (eds.), *Family Forms in Historic Europe* (Cambridge: Cambridge University Press, 1983); Segalen, *Historical Anthropology*; Beatrice Gottlieb, *The Family in the Western World: From the Black Death to the Industrial Age* (New York: Oxford University Press, 1993); Burguière et al. (eds.), *A History of the Family*, vol. II; and Jack Goody, *The European Family: An Historico-Anthropological Essay* (Oxford: Blackwell, 2000).

he argued that the reforms introduced by the revolutionaries of 1789, notably the insistence on partible inheritance, were undermining the stability of French society. For him it was paternal authority that guaranteed the social order. The ancient *patriarchal family*, in which all the sons married and remained in the paternal household, supported paternal authority admirably, as children picked up the customs and ideas of their ancestors from an early age. By contrast, in the eyes of Le Play, the predominant family form in the post-revolutionary era, the nuclear or *unstable* family, failed miserably. Children left home as soon as they could survive on their own, and were inspired above all by a spirit of independence. The intermediary form he plumped for as a source of both stability and enterprise was his famous *famille-souche* (stem family). Here one child alone married and lived with the parents, to ensure the continuity of the family tradition. The other children could either remain as celibate members of the original family, or leave for an independent existence elsewhere. From his own researches in the Pyrenees during the 1850s, he provided an example of a stem family, with its characteristic three generations living under the same roof. It had fifteen members: the widowed master of the house; his oldest daughter (the designated heiress) and her husband; the daughter's seven children; an unmarried aunt and an unmarried uncle of the daughter; two of her brothers; and a shepherd-cum-servant. Le Play enthused over the way children in this family basked in the care and amusements provided by a sizeable community. He suggested that they were used to seeing everyone obey the head of household in all circumstances, encouraging a respect for social superiors, while at the same time family affection lightened the burden of authority.[6]

The findings of recent research

Painstaking work by historical demographers in reconstituting families from parish registers and in analysing household structures from census registers demolished much of this established thinking. First, the researchers revealed that families in the past were much smaller than was once thought. They showed how a relatively late age for marriage, extended breastfeeding and high mortality combined to limit family size.

---

[6] Frédéric Le Play, *Les Ouvriers des deux mondes* (5 vols., Paris: Société internationale des études pratiques d'économie sociale, 1857–85), I, 'Paysans en communauté du Lavedan (Hautes-Pyrénées)', pp. 107–60; Frédéric Le Play, *L'Organisation de la famille* (Tours: Alfred Mame et fils, 1884), passim. See also Laslett, 'Introduction: the history of the family', in Laslett and Wall (eds.), *Household and Family*, pp. 1–85 (pp. 16–23); Flandrin, *Families*, pp. 50–3; Mitterauer and Sieder, *The European Family*, pp. 24–6.

A sample of 100 English parishes produced a remarkably constant figure of 4.75 for mean household size between the late sixteenth and the early twentieth centuries. Nowhere in Europe, Serbia apart, did the monographs assembled for an influential Cambridge conference in 1969 indicate a mean of more than five or six people per household. The French example of Longuenesse (Pas-de-Calais) in 1778 emerged with a mean of 5.05.[7] This does not mean that there were no large households in the past: big and small household groups, 'castles and thatched cottages',[8] coexisted in the same community. On the one hand, the mass of farm labourers and small peasants could not afford to maintain either grandparents or older children, and so they tended to live in small, simple households. On the other, the upper classes could display their wealth by assembling servants and dependent relatives in more complex household structures. Well-to-do farmers could also manage larger households, in their case as a function of their productive power, as farm servants and relatives helped work the land.[9] Best known is the household of Edme Rétif, lovingly described by Rétif de la Bretonne in his *La Vie de mon père* (*The Life of My Father*, 1779). As a prosperous farmer in Burgundy, he regularly had twenty-two people sitting at his table each evening, including his wife, his sons and daughters from two marriages, the ploughman and the vine-grower, the cowherd and the shepherd, and, at the bottom of the hierarchy, two female servants. A study of three Limousin villages by Jean-Claude Peyronnet noted that at the 1836 census the mean household size (excluding farm servants) for sharecroppers was twice that for day labourers and *bordiers*: 8.47 persons as opposed to 4.37. Here it was not so much a matter of wealth, more one of sharecroppers with a sufficiently large area of land to cultivate doing so by assembling a large family group.[10]

Second, it is possible to argue that almost everywhere in the past 'the nuclear family predominates'. Certainly, the evidence is compelling for such an assertion in the north-western part of Europe, which includes northern France. Complex families accounted for less than 20 per cent of households, and often for less than 10 per cent, in the Cambridge

[7] Peter Laslett, 'Mean Household Size in England since the Sixteenth Century', in Laslett and Wall (eds.), *Household and Family*, pp. 125–58 (p. 126); Laslett, 'Introduction', table 1.3.

[8] Flandrin, *Families*, p. 65.

[9] Ibid., ch. 2; Gottlieb, *The Family*, ch. 1; André Burguière and François Lebrun, 'The One Hundred and One Families of Europe', in Burguière et al. (eds.), *A History of the Family*, vol. II, pp. 32–3.

[10] Rétif de la Bretonne, *La Vie de mon père* (Paris: Garnier, 1970 (1779)); and Jean-Claude Peyronnet, 'Famille élargie ou famille nucléaire? L'exemple du Limousin au début du XIXe siècle', *Revue d'histoire moderne et contemporaine*, 22 (1975), 568–82 (581).

international sample. The figure for Longuenesse was 17 per cent.[11] However, in the centre and south of France, more complex family structures might have been the dominant or preferred model. The extreme rarity of early census material in France, compared to England, hampered researches in this area. However, during the 1970s the historian Alain Collomp used notarial archives to demonstrate that in a sample of villages in Haute-Provence during the early eighteenth century, nearly half (47 per cent) of all marriage contracts concerned extended families. Likewise, a few years later Peyronnet found that in his sample of three Limousin villages 41 to 42 per cent of all households were of a complex type during the 1830s, harbouring over half of the population in each case. Moreover, other historians concluded that a high proportion of simple households in a parish did not necessarily mean that they were the dominant family form. Agnès Fine-Souriac used the example of four villages in the Pyrenean villages to argue that, although complex households comprised only between 25 and 34 per cent of the total in 1836, the stem family was the rule. This was because of the evolutionary cycle that affected each household. She cited the example of the household of Joseph Marion in the village of Bessède. At the 1846 census it appeared as a typical stem family, with three generations living together. It remained that way until 1866, when the death of the two grandparents produced a nuclear family. Given that the family consisted of apparently well-off millers it would in all likelihood return to stem family form when a new married couple came on the scene. Similarly, Nicole Lemaitre insisted on the primacy of complex families in her study of Ussel, in the Bas-Limousin, again, *pace* Le Play, because of the very *instability* of the stem family form. This was particularly the case in rural parts of the commune, where stem families and *frérèches*[12] accounted for around a third of households in 1806, and 43.1 per cent of the population. Such complex households made possible a large labour force for the labour-intensive agriculture, and avoided the break-up of the domain under partible inheritance.[13]

Finally, extended families do not emerge as havens of stability and harmony in the way that Le Play suggested.[14] As already shown, high

---

[11] Laslett, 'Introduction', pp. 9, 59–61 and table 1.15.

[12] This term means a group of married brothers living together to exploit an asset.

[13] Alain Collomp, 'Famille nucléaire et famille élargie en Haute Provence au XVIIIe siècle (1703–1734)', *Annales ESC*, 27 (1972), 969–75; Peyronnet, 'Famille élargie', passim; Agnès Fine-Souriac, 'La Famille-souche pyrénéenne au XIXe siècle: quelques réflexions de méthode', *Annales ESC*, 32 (1977), 478–87. See also Flandrin, *Families*, ch. 2; Alain Collomp, 'Ménage et famille: études comparatives sur la dimension et la structure du groupe domestique', *Annales ESC*, 29 (1976), 777–86; Segalen, *Historical Anthropology*, ch. 1; and Burguière and Lebrun, 'One Hundred and One Families', pp. 19–56.

[14] Burguière and Lebrun, 'One Hundred and One Families', pp. 50–2.

levels of mortality meant that it was not always possible to maintain continuity with three generations residing together: the master or mistress of the house often died before their grandchildren were born. Moreover, the need to sacrifice the interests of individual family members to secure the transmission of property could generate resentment. A study of relationships among kin in the Gevaudan between the seventeenth and the nineteenth century noted a mixture of 'socialization and oppression' for the peasantry. The mingling of all ages did create bonds of interdependence, and even of affection, as family members worked together and stood firm against all outsiders. In general, paternal authority remained unchallenged. The young were submissive to the old, as women were to men, if only for the want of an alternative. Nonetheless, the custom that required parents to choose a single heir sometimes led to family tensions and even outright violence. Daughters, for example, might feel that they had received an inadequate dowry; sons might become impatient with an ageing father unwilling to relinquish his authority.[15] Similarly, in Haute-Provence during the seventeenth and eighteenth centuries, the historian Alain Collomp concluded that there was a spectrum of households where there was a 'community' between two couples in successive generations. At one end were those households where members loved and supported each other through their joys and their sorrows. At the other, were those seething with discontent, with ill feeling between the generations or among siblings. The weight of patriarchal authority generally kept the lid on any such tensions, though occasionally they were so intolerable that the household agreed to break the agreement. This happened in 30 out of the 500 contracts in his sample.[16]

Conclusion

In short, it would be unwise to think too much in terms of a 'contraction' of the family in modern times, given the relatively modest size of most households in the past, and the predominance of small, simple households in much of Europe, perhaps from as early as medieval times. In the French case, one is bound to draw attention to the varied structures persisting into the modern period, with stem families and 'communitarian' forms such as the *frérèche* persisting in central and southern France. These structures had considerable influence on the experience of growing up. Nuclear

[15] Elizabeth Claverie and Pierre Lamaison, *L'Impossible Mariage: violence et parenté en Gevaudan, 17e, 18e et 19e siècles* (Paris: Hachette, 1982), chs. 3–4. See also Yves Castan, *Honnêteté et relations sociales en Languedoc, 1715–1780* (Paris: Plon, 1974), pp. 230–2.

[16] Alain Collomp, *La Maison du père: famille et village en Haute-Provence aux XVIIe et XVIIIe siècle* (Paris: Presses Universitaires de France, 1983), passim.

families among the 'popular classes' in northern France, for example, routinely sent off their adolescent children to gain experience as servants in other households, while complex ones in the south preferred to keep them at home until marriage.[17] Of course, a declining birth rate has in the long term led to smaller families, more rapidly in France than elsewhere. Whereas mothers in the eighteenth century might normally have five or six children, by the late twentieth century it was more likely to be one or two. From the 1930s onwards, as Martine Segalen notes, women in particular took full control of their fertility through modern contraceptive methods, instead of accepting what 'nature' or the unreliable withdrawal method foisted on them. The decline in co-residence of married couples, as people left the land, and the rise in the numbers living alone also contributed to a fall in mean household size: according to a French census, in 1982 it stood at 2.57. The family also lost some of its earlier functions from the eighteenth century onwards, or at least shared them with professionals, such as health care, looking after the old and education, not to mention acting as a unit of production. Its main purpose was reduced to raising children and satisfying the emotional and sexual needs of the husband and wife. All the same, it would be misleading to suggest that the recent trend was towards an isolated and impoverished emotional existence for French children. Studies by sociologists, starting in the 1970s, confirmed what historians had established for the nineteenth: that young people had contacts with kin networks stretching well beyond the nuclear family, for example when parents were absent or when they were looking for a job. The family may have narrowed its functions, but French people evidently continue to value it as a 'haven in a heartless world'.[18]

[17] J. Hajnal, 'Two Kinds of Pre-Industrial Household Formation System', in Wall et al., (eds). *Family Forms*, pp. 65–104.
[18] This paragraph relies on Segalan, *Historical Anthropology*, passim; and Martine Segalen and Françoise Zonabend, 'Families in France', in Burguière et al., (eds.) *A History of the Family*, pp. 502–30.

6   Of mothers and motherhood

'My mother says that one should not spoil children, and she beats me every morning; when she does not have time in the morning, it is at noon, rarely after four o'clock.' A number of 'bad mothers' stand out among modern French childhood reminiscences. Besides the brutal Mme Vingtras described here by Jules Vallès in *L'Enfant* (*The Child*, 1879), one might cite the heartless Mme Lepic, immortalized by Jules Renard in *Poil de carotte* (*Ginger*, 1894); the 'glacial' and jealous Mme Lambert depicted by Juliette Adam in *Le Roman de mon enfance* (*The Novel of My Childhood*, 1902); and the scheming Mme Rezeau from *Vipère au poing* (*Viper in the Hand*, 1948) by Hervé Bazin.[1] These negative images appear to fly in the face of an influential school of thought among historians that the modern period brought a warmer and more sensitive family environment for children in the West. During the 1970s, Edward Shorter famously asserted that 'good mothering is an invention of modernization'. Before the eighteenth century, he argued, mothers remained indifferent to the happiness and development of their infants; in 'modern society', nothing was more important. He rested his case for the traditional indifference of mothers in the 'popular classes' on a series of child-rearing practices that certainly appear callous or negligent to the modern mind. There was, for example, their willingness to leave infants alone for long periods of time, the lack of play and affection, and the resort to 'mercenary' wet-nurses. He argued that both the urban mothers who dispatched their offspring to the countryside, and the peasant nurses who endangered their own babies' lives by sharing out their milk, failed his 'sacrifice' test: that is to say, they did not put the life and happiness of the infant above all else.[2] The French author Elisabeth Badinter, writing a popular polemic rather than a work of academic history, went as far as to argue

---

[1] Vallès, *L'Enfant*, p. 19; Jules Renard, *Poil de carotte* (Paris: Garnier-Flammarion, 1965); Juliette Adam, *Le Roman de mon enfance* (Paris: Alphonse Lemerre, 1902); and Hervé Bazin, *Vipère au poing* (Paris: Livre de poche, 1976). See also Coe, *When the Grass was Taller*, p. 147.

[2] Shorter, *Modern Family*, ch. 5.

that maternal love was a feeling that ebbed and flowed down the centuries according to social custom. She asserted that it was largely absent in the seventeenth and early eighteenth centuries, and resurgent from the late eighteenth century onwards.[3] But was there such a sweeping shift from indifference to loving care in France during the eighteenth and nineteenth centuries? Were various child-rearing practices that are now abhorrent to us a matter of indifference, or of poverty and a very different system of beliefs? Were there not examples of 'bad mothers' in modern as well as 'traditional' society? And, a question not usually confronted but important for this work, how did children cope with varying approaches to motherhood?

The child–mother relationship

It may be that autobiographies give a misleading impression of mothers. Wicked mothers do after all make better copy than virtuous ones. The former provoke a morbid fascination in the reader as they think up new ways to torment their young. The latter, as Richard N. Coe observed, risk sliding into sentimentalization and a statement of the obvious.[4] However, on both theoretical and empirical grounds, one might approach the 'good mothering' line taken by Shorter and Badinter with a certain scepticism. In the first place, the tendency to focus on the importance of the mother for human development, at the expense of other possible caregivers, now appears peculiarly characteristic of Western thought during the nineteenth and twentieth centuries.[5] A prominent figure here was the British psychologist John Bowlby, the inspiration behind attachment theory. In 1951 he wrote that 'the quality of the parental care which a child receives in his earliest years is of vital importance for his future mental health . . . it is this complex, rich, and rewarding relationship with the mother in the early years, varied in countless ways by relations with the father and with siblings, that child psychiatrists and many others now believe to underline the development of character and of mental health'.[6]

[3] Elisabeth Badinter, *The Myth of Motherhood: An Historical View of the Maternal 'Instinct'*, transl. Roger DeGaris (London: Souvenir Press, 1981), passim. See also Philippe Ariès, *Centuries of Childhood* (Harmondsworth: Penguin, 1962), part III; Lloyd B. DeMause, 'The Evolution of Childhood', in DeMause (ed.), *The History of Childhood* (London: Souvenir Press, 1976), pp. 1–73; and Michael Anderson, *Approaches to the History of the Western Family, 1500–1914* (Cambridge: Cambridge University Press, 1995), p. 34.
[4] Coe, *When the Grass was Taller*, p. 156.
[5] See, for example, Denise Riley, *War in the Nursery: Theories of the Child and Mother* (London: Virago, 1983), passim.
[6] John Bowlby, *Maternal Care and Mental Health* (1951), cited by Clarke and Clarke, *Early Experience*, p. 13. See also John Bowlby, *Attachment and Loss*, vol. 1, *Attachment* (London: Hogarth Press, 1970).

The inclination of Bowlby and other psychologists to concentrate on the child–mother attachment was perhaps understandable at a period when few mothers with young children in Britain and America worked regularly outside the home. By the late twentieth century, however, the growing importance of two-income families among the well-off as well as the poor has meant that more than one caregiver now cares for most children in these countries.[7] Moreover, a number of cross-cultural studies have encouraged scholars to look beyond the mother–child dyad. In African societies, for example, nonparental care has emerged as either the norm or a common practice. Although most societies assign care of infants to the biological mother, she may delegate the responsibility to others, or hand it over permanently.[8] Attachment theorists have responded by investigating the way children form multiple attachment relationships, both within the family and beyond it. It is also the case that attachment theorists have moved on from some of the dire predictions associated with 'Bowlbyism' on the impact of separation from the mother during the first three years of life. They still assume that children with secure attachment relations are more likely to be emotionally independent later in life. However, as noted above, they accept that anxious attachment in infancy does necessarily lead to emotional dependency. What matters then is the quality of care available at later stages and the resilience of the individual. Indeed, it is arguable that children have more psychological resilience than Bowlby originally allowed for, giving them a chance of recovering from all but the most extreme cases of maternal deprivation.[9] Such considerations help us to avoid some of the ethnocentrism of earlier generations of historians of motherhood, and to assess more sympathetically certain child-rearing practices that today would be unacceptable.

In the second place, historians have doubted that the evidence will support any notion of contrasts between 'good' and 'bad' mothering at various periods in the past. Above all, they have criticized Shorter for asserting that mothers in 'pre-modern' Europe were indifferent to the fate of their offspring. Historians have questioned, for example, whether mothers in *ancien-régime* France could go through a sequence of births

---

[7] Carollee Holmes, 'Attachment Relationships in the Context of Multiple Caregivers', in Jude Cassidy and Phillip R. Shaver (eds.), *Handbook of Attachment: Theory, Research, and Clinical Applications* (New York and London: Guilford Press, 1999), pp. 671–87 (pp. 671 and 683–4).

[8] Marinus H. Van Ijzendoorn and Abraham Sagi, 'Cross-Cultural Patterns of Attachment: Universal and Contextual Dimensions', in Cassidy and Shaver, *Handbook of Attachment*, pp. 713–34 (p. 715); Robert A. Levine, 'Child Psychology and Anthropology: An Environmental View', in Panter-Brick (ed.), *Biosocial Perspectives*, pp. 102–30 (p. 114).

[9] Sroufe, *Emotional Development*, pp. 189–91; Clarke and Clarke, *Early Experience*, pp. 15–16 and 84; Holmes, *John Bowlby*, ch. 3.

followed all too often by an infant death without some form of trauma. They have noted that the willingness of mothers among the nobility to delegate primary responsibility for child rearing to servants did not mean indifference to the health and moral development of their offspring. The historian Mark Motley cites evidence of mothers in seventeenth-century French aristocratic families paying close attention to such problems as feeding, teething and illness during infancy.[10] Critics also point to the anachronistic tone to much of the writing by Shorter and Badinter when accusing mothers of negligence. They note the difficulties with hygiene in a poor household, and the efforts made by peasants to keep their children alive, however bizarre various charms, amulets and rituals might seem to us now. If aristocratic parents held back in showing affection for their children, this was because of the expectation that from an early stage the young noble would develop a wider network of personal relations, including kin, servants and clients.[11] It would also be possible to counter the assertions of Shorter and Badinter on 'good mothering' by providing evidence that 'bad mothers' are likely to exist in any society, including modern and contemporary France. Yet their work has the advantage of giving motherhood a history, showing change in practice according to social and cultural circumstances. It usefully highlights a propaganda campaign in favour of better care for infants during the late eighteenth century, and indicates areas where there were undoubtedly improvements during the modern period. That said, it is not immediately obvious whether a Mme Vingtras was an isolated case of a bad mother, and considered as such by her contemporaries, or a pointer to a grim child-rearing regime for many children in the past.

The obvious way to proceed is to discard any simplistic assumptions about wholesale 'good' or 'bad' mothering and explore the different approaches to child rearing in various social milieux. The 'ego documents' particularly support the argument that there were a number of 'models' for parenting in modern France. Michelle Perrot, for example, contrasted the aristocratic, the bourgeois and the popular family in the nineteenth century. The aristocratic model gave priority to the training of a young man for public life, looking back to life at court, and so encouraged him to go to become a *gentilhomme* by attending a *collège*, learning

---

[10] Segalen, *Historical Anthropology*, p. 174; and Motley, *Becoming a French Aristocrat*, pp. 23 and 28.

[11] Stephen Wilson, 'The Myth of Motherhood a Myth: The Historical View of European Child-Rearing', *Social History*, 9 (1984), 181–98; Gélis et al., *Entrer dans la vie*; and Motley, *Becoming a French Aristocrat*, pp. 23–4. See also Jay Mechling, 'Advice to Historians on Advice to Mothers', *Journal of Social History*, 9 (1975), 44–63.

foreign languages and hunting and playing sports. The bourgeois family was more focused on the home. The child was at its centre, and was
the object of considerable investment of time and affection. Finally the
popular family survived industrialization and urbanization by develop-
ing networks of solidarity, and looking outwards on to the street and
the neighbourhood rather than the home. Relationships with children
were often strained, though not without affection in their own way.[12]
This chapter will therefore begin by analysing in more detail the various
approaches to motherhood at different levels of French society. Second,
it will consider how these worked out in practice for children, including
any support they received when mothers acted in deviant fashion. Finally,
one must keep in mind the question of how far there was change over
time in this sphere in the French case.[13]

Exalting motherhood

Advice for mothers

If there was a 'revolution in mothering'[14] in Europe during the eighteenth
century, then Jean-Jacques Rousseau was its most prominent advocate.
He began with the character of Julie in *La Nouvelle Héloïse* (1761), a
young woman who, after a shaky start in the form of an affair with her
tutor, becomes a model of maternal love. The second half of the novel
describes her fidelity to the husband she agrees to marry in place of the
tutor, and her devotion to the education of her three children. Rousseau's
educational treatise *Emile* (1762) carried the same message, with its call
for mothers to take seriously their responsibilities for the health and education of young children. It attacked common practices such as kneading
the head of a newborn baby, swaddling and 'mercenary' wet-nursing.
'Let mothers deign to nurse their children,' Rousseau argued, 'morals
will reform themselves, nature's sentiments will be awakened in every
heart, the state will be repeopled.' What was missing with a wet-nurse
was the tenderness of a mother, which vastly reduced the likelihood of
the infant perishing.[15] Various artists proclaimed the same message in the
late eighteenth century, painting scenes of domestic bliss or of contented
mothers and infants breastfeeding. Greuze, for example, created a stir at

---

[12] Perrot, 'Sur la ségrégation de l'enfance', 179–81.
[13] This analysis draws on Wilson, 'Myth of Motherhood', 185–6.
[14] Shorter, *Modern Family*, p. 202.
[15] Jean-Jacques Rousseau, *Julie, ou la Nouvelle Héloïse* (Paris: Flammarion, 1967 (1761)),
and *Emile*, book I.

the Salon of 1765 with *The Beloved Mother*, a depiction of a farmer's wife happily surrounded by her six children.[16] A combination of eighteenth-century concerns about the regeneration of society through education, the fear of 'depopulation' from a high infant mortality rate and the role of women in a more democratic society post-1789 gave a particular sense of urgency in France to this interest among the elite in the functions of the mother.[17]

Nineteenth-century French observers went even further in their enthusiasm for maternity, producing what the historians Yvonne Knibiehler and Catherine Fouquet described as a veritable cult of motherhood. 'Fall at the feet of this sex to which you owe your mother!' intoned a much-quoted line from the poet Gabriel Legouvé and his *Le Mérite des femmes* (*The Merit of Women*, 1802).[18] Doctors laid down detailed instructions for mothers on hygiene, diet and exercise for the young children in their care. Manuals on child rearing emphasized the importance of the moral and religious instruction given by the mother, though they differed on whether she should follow Rousseau in his 'negative' education or start early on their intellectual education. The history teacher Henri Duval took the latter line in 1840 in his advice book for mothers with children under the age of seven. He suggested that children start to learn to read and cipher around the age of four, and from five take up writing, spelling and music. He was thoroughly 'modern' in advising mothers to tell stories to amuse as well as instruct children; to avoid instilling false fears with tales of ghosts, werewolves, bogeymen and other such 'foolishness'; and to avoid harsh punishments such as beatings, deprivation of food and spells locked in a darkened room.[19]

Circumstances in nineteenth-century French society, as elsewhere in the West, favoured this cult of motherhood. It was the period when the birth rate steadily declined. Mothers could therefore devote more attention to the upbringing of each child. Moreover, the notion of 'separate spheres' for the two sexes encouraged a gradual withdrawal of married women from the active population – though this phenomenon was far less in evidence in France than in England, owing to the continued importance of peasant farms and small, family businesses. Where it did occur,

[16] Carol Duncan, 'Happy Mothers and Other New Ideas in French Art', *Art Bulletin*, 55 (1973), 570–83.
[17] Yvonne Knibiehler and Catherine Fouquet, *L'Histoire des mères du moyen âge à nos jours* (Paris: Editions Montalba, 1980), pp. 138–73.
[18] Ibid., p. 174.
[19] Henri Duval, *Conseils aux mères de familles ou manière de soigner et d'élever ses enfants jusqu'à l'âge de sept ans* (Paris: Alexandre Johanneau, 1840), passim.

it left women free (or trapped) for full-time mothering. Among the bourgeoisie of the Nord, for example, the increasing scale and technological
complexity of businesses served as a backdrop for the gradual exclusion
of wives from the running of textile mills. Towards the end of the century,
organized labour began to demand a 'family wage', sufficient to allow men
to support their families without the need for their wives and children to
work. Delegates to the workers' congress at Marseille in 1879 voted in
favour of a motion that 'a woman's true place is not in the workshop or
the factory, but in the home, within the family'.[20] Finally, in the wake
of military defeat at the hands of the Prussians in 1870, there was once
again the peculiarly French concern with 'depopulation' and its impact
on the military strength of the country. Hence there was a long campaign
to improve maternal and infant welfare.[21]

All this attention paid to mothering was not without its drawbacks
for women, it might be added. The 'folk wisdom' that mothers passed
down the generations, and their own intuition, was devalued as childhood
became increasingly 'medicalized'. Towards the end of the nineteenth
century this process gained momentum, as doctors became increasingly
confident of their expertise in '*puériculture*'. The tone of child-rearing
manuals shifted from giving advice to establishing rules. Doctors convinced themselves that child rearing was too important a matter to be
left exclusively in the hands of women.[22] The sociologist Luc Boltanski argued in 1969 that the campaign to diffuse scientific methods of
child rearing was linked to a more sinister project: imposing order on
an anarchic working class. He cited *La Jeune Ménagère* (1904) by Mme
Sevrette, a manual for young housewives, which set up a 'good' and a 'bad'
working-class mother. Louise Raimbaud took it as her mission to teach

[20] Bonnie Smith, *Ladies of the Leisure Class: The Bourgeoises of Northern France in the Nineteenth* Century (Princeton: Princeton University Press, 1981), passim; Michelle Perrot, 'L'Eloge de la ménagère dans le discours des ouvriers français au XIXe siècle',
in *Mythes et représentations de la femme au dix-neuvième siècle* (Paris: Campion, 1976),
p. 110. See also Ariès and Duby (eds.), *History of Private Life*, vol. IV, passim;
Rollet-Echalier, *La Politique*, ch. X; Luc, *L'Invention du jeune enfant au XIXe siècle*,
ch. 4.

[21] See Alisa Klaus, *Every Child a Lion: The Origins of Maternal and Infant Health Policy in
the United States and France, 1890–1920* (Ithaca, NY: Cornell University Press, 1993);
Seth Koven and Sonya Michel (eds.), *Mothers of a New World: Maternalist Politics and the
Origins of Welfare States* (New York: Routledge, 1993); and Elinor A. Accampo, Rachel
G. Fuchs and Mary Lynn Stewart (eds.), *Gender and the Politics of Social Reform in France,
1870–1914* (Baltimore: Johns Hopkins University Press, 1995).

[22] Marie-France Morel, 'The Care of Children: The Influence of Medical Innovation and
Medical Institutions on Infant Mortality, 1750–1914', in R. Schofield et al., *The Decline
of Mortality in Europe* (Oxford: Clarendon Press, 1991), pp. 196–219 (p. 210).

'*la puériculture moderne*' to Mme Perrin, the 'wild' worker who needed to be domesticated:

Mme Perrin gave soup to her nursling to make him stronger, Louise taught her that babies should only drink milk during their first year. Mme Perrin fears removing the scabs that ring the head of her child, Louise teaches her how to wash them away.

Reformers, according to Boltanski, sought to infiltrate the working-class household, and penetrate the minds of workers, in order to substitute rational authority based on knowledge for the traditional authority of the family. Working-class girls were therefore compelled to take lessons on child rearing, hygiene and housekeeping in the state primary schools. Only in the 1960s did the medical profession ease up on this bid to create a new morality.[23]

The social dimension

It follows that the first families to react against traditional child-rearing methods and exalt the mother figure were in the educated and relatively affluent middle classes of Paris and the cities. They were the ones whom Rousseau and other reformers had in mind as they wrote.[24] They could spare their womenfolk time to devote to their children, and, no less importantly, they could afford servants to help with the new demands being made on the mother. The late eighteenth century spawned a few devoted disciples of Jean-Jacques among intellectual women in the upper reaches of society, such as Louise d'Epinay (1726–83) and later Mme Roland (1754–93). However, most of those who dedicated themselves to mothering were drawn from the professional and commercial middle classes. One might cite the example of Madame de Maraise, who was from 1767 to 1789 the wife of an obscure associate of the cotton printer Oberkampf. She took an active part in looking after the accounts of the business, but also revealed herself a faithful '*rousseauiste*', insisting on breastfeeding her eight children (six of whom survived).[25] This is not to deny that many mothers in the aristocracy, and even the *bonne bourgeoisie*, continued to delegate child rearing to other women. Although they might follow the progress of their children attentively, they also felt free to lead an active

---

[23] Luc Boltanski, *Prime éducation et morale de classe* (Paris: Mouton, 1969), passim; and Gélis et al., *Entrer dans la vie*, ch. 5.

[24] See Mercier, *L'Enfant*, p. 41.

[25] Serge Chassagne, *Une Femme d'affaires au XVIIIe siècle: la correspondance de Madame de Maraise, collaboratrice d'Oberkampf* (Toulouse: Privat, 1981), pp. 24–30.

social life without much thought or fear of censure.[26] According to the historian Anne Martin-Fugier, it required a long evolution over the course of the eighteenth and nineteenth centuries for the traditional aristocratic model to be 'besieged and colonized' by a newer bourgeois model. By the late nineteenth century, to avoid being castigated as idle and frivolous, the *mondaine* would have to take her household duties a little more seriously than in the past.[27]

At the opposite end of the spectrum were women in peasant families. Most of them remained firmly committed to the traditional customs and beliefs of the popular culture until the nineteenth or early twentieth century, depending on their region. Although their methods of child rearing only gradually yielded to the authority of medical science and 'enlightened' urban opinion, they hardly deserve the accusations of 'brutal indifference'[28] to the interests of their offspring. At the very least, they did the best they could for their children in difficult circumstances. Even Antoine Sylvère, whose relations with his peasant mother in the Auvergne were generally strained, grasped that she and other poor women like her had little time to spare for their children. The struggle to keep body and soul together as poor sharecroppers, he wrote, poisoned the existence of his parents until the day they died.[29]

Attachment during infancy

Much of the campaigning in France for improved child-rearing methods during the eighteenth and nineteenth centuries concerned infant welfare. As noted above, modern psychologists subscribing to attachment theory consider the first three years of life important for the child in its efforts to form a secure attachment with the mother, or a mother-substitute, and other caregivers. This was a period which people reflecting on their childhood could hardly be expected to recall with any confidence. However, some writers 'extended' their memoirs to this early stage of life, by recounting what their relatives told them, and others provided evidence from later years that gave a hint of the strength of such an attachment. In so doing, many resurrected powerful emotions of either love or hatred for a mother figure. They also revealed the contrasting attitudes to mothering in different sections of French society.

---

[26] See Knibiehler and Fouquet, *Histoire des mères*, part 2; Badinter, *Myth of Motherhood*, ch. 5; Luc, *L'Invention du jeune enfant au XIXe siècle*, part 2.

[27] Anne Martin-Fugier, *La Bourgeoise: femme au temps de Paul Bourget* (Paris: Bernard Grasset, 1983), pp. 13–14.

[28] Francine Du Plessis Gray, 'Foreword' to Badinter, *Myth of Motherhood*, p. xi.

[29] Sylvère, *Toinou*, pp. 12 and 18.

Mothering at a distance: the aristocracy

The Comtesse de Boigne depicted her mother as a resolute follower of Jean-Jacques while at court in Versailles towards the end of the *ancien régime*. The mother did not follow the usual practice of swaddling, instead dressing her daughter loosely *à l'anglaise*, and she breastfed her at court.[30] But such a mother was of course the exception rather than the rule in aristocratic circles. The evidence of a handful of well-known memoirs from eighteenth-century nobles confirms that the resort to servants meant that mothers in this milieu did not attempt to establish affectionate relations with their offspring during infancy.[31] Charles Maurice de Talleyrand (1754–1838) was surely an extreme case in claiming that at the age of eight, as he was whisked off to the Collège d'Harcourt in Paris, 'the eyes of my parents had not yet rested on me'. Chateaubriand (1768–1848) suffered his 'first exile' to a wet-nurse as soon as he was born, and did not return home for three years. He was then readily abandoned to the hands of others: 'My mother besides, full of spirit and virtue, was pre-occupied with the cares of society and the duties of religion . . . she liked politics, bustle, people.' Similarly, Madame de Genlis (1756–1830) recorded that during her childhood her mother had never looked after her, being distracted by her own affairs and continual visits from neighbours. She gathered that she had had a live-in wet-nurse at her chateau, but the woman managed to conceal a pregnancy and fed her a mixture of wine, water and rye breadcrumbs instead of milk.

The reactions to this lack of contact with a mother varied. Mme de Genlis emphasized a happy childhood during the first six years of her life, in the congenial surroundings of various chateaux. Talleyrand, by contrast, lamented his miserable early childhood on the outskirts of Paris. At the age of four, the anonymous 'woman' looking after him failed to report a dislocated foot after he accidentally fell from a cupboard. This left him lame for life and, worse still, provoked his father to transfer his right of succession as the first-born to a younger brother. Talleyrand explained that what he called 'paternal care' had not come into fashion when he was a child, rather the reverse. 'For, in great families', as he put it, 'the *family* was far more cared for than its members individually, especially than those young members who were still unknown.'

---

[30] *Récits d'une tante: mémoires de la comtesse de Boigne, née d'Osmond* (Paris: Emile-Paul, 1921), p. 25. See also Françoise Wagener, *La Comtesse de Boigne (1781–1866)* (Paris: Flammarion, 1997), ch. 2. For English parallels, there is Randolph Trumbach, *The Rise of the Egalitarian Family: Aristocratic Kinship and Domestic Relations in Eighteenth-Century England* (New York: Academic Press, 1978), ch. 5.

[31] Cf. Motley, *Becoming a French Aristocrat*, p. 28, suggesting an affectionate relationship, from the mother's point of view.

The way out for these young aristocrats was to seek affection from another relative or member of the household. Talleyrand doted on his grandmother, Madame de Chalais, the first member of his family to show any signs of affection towards him. 'Many a time have I bitterly understood how priceless is the sincere affection of some member of one's own family,' he wrote wistfully in later life. At the same period Chateaubriand recalled attaching himself to *la Villeneuve*, a sort of housekeeper who carried him around and affectionately attended to his needs.[32] If aristocratic mothers in the nineteenth century gradually shifted the balance between their worldly and their domestic roles in favour of the latter, the figure of the day-nurse nonetheless continued to loom large in the life of their infants. Most desirable for a noble family during the Third Republic was an English nurse, fully imbued with the mores of the highly stratified Victorian society. Pauline de Broglie (b. 1888) for long spoke English more fluently than French on account of the constant presence from infancy of her '*nurse anglaise*'.[33]

Mothering in the countryside

The occasional peasant autobiography from the late nineteenth- and early twentieth-century period gives a hint of the experience of another form of 'traditional' childhood, in Shorter's sense, even as it began to disappear. There is some evidence to support the view from the historians Gélis, Laget and Morel that people in the countryside had a lively and spontaneous way of loving their children.[34] Frédéric Mistral (1830–1914), famous for his Provençal poetry, looked back on a warm relationship with his mother in a well-off family of landowning peasants. This included being wrapped up in swaddling bands for the first six months of his life on the advice of his grandmother, who feared that otherwise he would be knock-kneed or bandy-legged.[35] Batisto Bonnet gave a suspiciously bright and breezy account of his childhood in a peasant family between Arles and Nîmes, on the frontier between Provence and Languedoc. He depicted an impoverished family with seven children, blessed by a loving

[32] *Memoirs of the Prince de Talleyrand*, transl. Raphaël Ledos de Beaufort, 2 vols. (London: Griffith Farran Okeden and Welsh, 1891), I, pp. 4–13; Chateaubriand, *Mémoires d'outre-tombe*, I, 'Petite enfance'; Comtesse de Genlis, *Mémoires inédits sur le XVIIIe siècle et la Révolution française depuis 1756 jusqu'à nos jours* (Paris: Ladvocat, 1825), pp. 34–52.

[33] Mension-Rigau, *L'Enfance au château*, ch. 5; and Comtesse Jean de Pange, *Comment j'ai vu 1900* (2 vols., Paris: Grasset, 1962), II, pp. 34 and 45.

[34] Gélis et al., *Entrer dans la vie*, p. 44.

[35] Frédéric Mistral, *Memoirs*, transl. George Wickes (Paris: Alyscamps Press, 1994 (1906)), p. 6.

father and a mother who spoiled him with caresses.[36] Pierre-Jakez Hélias
in his turn wrote a very positive account of his infancy in Brittany around
the time of the First World War. He mentioned that he was tightly bound
in swaddling clothes, and that he spent hours alone each day in his cradle.[37] Yet, like the overwhelming majority of peasant mothers in Europe,
his mother breastfed him herself. Although in her case wartime conditions
meant that she had to shoulder extra farm work, she managed to feed him
in the morning before she went off to work in the fields, during her midday
break and at around five o'clock when she finally returned home. After
weaning him at eighteen months, she carried him around everywhere,
taking him to mass, to visit relatives and to the fields. Hélias evidently
had no problem in his relationship with his 'wonderful mother'. What he
remembered above all from his early years was her jovial disposition: 'I
have the impression that I heard her laugh without stop ever since I was
born.'[38] The carpenter Agricol Perdiguier (1805–75) also wrote in glow-
ing terms of his mother as a 'good and valiant woman', as he described
another 'traditional' upbringing in a small town near Avignon.[39]

Other testimony sounds a more sombre note, with poverty and an endless work routine blighting relations in some households. It ties in with
the contradictory notion that, until the late nineteenth century, the 'popular classes' in France considered a newborn child as a burden rather
than a source of pleasure.[40] Antoine Sylvère regretted his mother's decision to profit from her condition by temporarily residing in Lyon as a
wet-nurse.[41] He remained in the Auvergne with his grandmother, and
attributed his rude health to milk from her cow 'la Jasse'. He recognized
that she and her father loved him as best they could, but any tenderness
quickly evaporated under the strain of constant hardship. Well before his
'breeching' his parents gave up kissing him, not because he no longer
desired it, but because they told him that he was too big. Fortunately, his
'need to love' found a ready outlet through his grandmother, and then
the young lad who worked as a farm servant beside his father.[42]

---

[36] Bonnet, *Vie d'enfant*, p. 47.
[37] For echoes of these customs in a village in the Vaucluse around 1950, see Wylie, *Village in the Vaucluse*, pp. 37–9.
[38] Hélias, *Horse of Pride*, pp. 38–42.
[39] Agricol Perdiguier, *Mémoires d'un compagnon* (Paris: Maspero, 1977 (1854–5)), p. 41.
[40] Bernard Schnapper, 'Le Temps des poupards (le bébé au XIXe siècle)', in *Voies nouvelles en histoire du droit: la justice, la famille, la répression pénale (XVIe–XXe siècles)* (Paris: Presses Universitaires de France, 1991), pp. 509–22 (pp. 510–11).
[41] See also, for this 'supply-side' perspective, André Armengaud, 'Les Nourrices du Mor-van au XIXe siècle', *Etudes et chroniques de démographie historique* (1964), 131–9; and James R. Lehning, 'Family Life and Wetnursing in a French Village', *Journal of Interdis-ciplinary History*, 12 (1982), 645–56.
[42] Sylvère, *Toinou*, ch. 1.

Mothering in the popular neighbourhoods of the towns

Members of the 'popular classes' in the towns tended to suggest that their relationship with their mother was strained by a rude existence. Often this was part of the desire by political activists to demonstrate the corrosive effects of industrial capitalism on working-class family life. René Michaud is a case in point, as the son of working-class parents in Paris at the beginning of the twentieth century. Life for him became particularly difficult after his father committed suicide, leaving a young widow and three children. Long hours ironing the fine clothes of the rich took their toll on his mother. Michaud remembered her as constantly harassed by some pressing task, with the result that she had lost the ability to express her emotions. She was rarely effusive, sparing with her caresses and inclined to hide her feelings behind an abrupt manner. Under it all, though, he did not doubt her tireless devotion to him.[43] Jeanne Bouvier, born in 1865 to the daughter of a railway worker, could only say that her mother beat her frequently and never gave her the caresses she craved. The miner Louis Lengrand recalled a fearsome mother, perhaps embittered by her difficult circumstances under German occupation during the First World War, who laid into sons and daughters alike with a poker. Oral testimony from Madeleine Dissais, born around 1912 to a 'modest family' near Bordeaux, noted that her mother was ahead of her time in showing affection to her children. She was probably right to suggest that most parents from her background at that period remained hard on their children, in that they avoided caressing them and only kissed them on New Year's Day.[44]

The wet-nursing business

A potential obstacle to the attachment of a child to its mother, and one far more in evidence in France than in neighbouring countries, was indeed the custom of paying a wet-nurse to suckle one's child. Mothers in the villages of pre-industrial Europe normally breastfed their children, even if only because they could not afford to do otherwise.[45] However, what stood out in the French case was the widespread resort to paid wet-nurses by the 'lower orders' as well as the upper ranks of society in the big cities. It is worth lingering on the scale of this wet-nursing business during

---

[43] Michaud, *J'avais vingt ans*, pp. 9–12.

[44] Bouvier, *Mes mémoires*, p. 52; Lengrand and Craipeau, *Louis Lengrand*, p. 28; Madeleine Dissais, in Germain and de Panafieu, *Mémoire des femmes*, p. 14. See also Eugen Weber, Introduction to Guillaumin, *Life of a Simple Man*, p. xiii.

[45] Valerie A. Fildes, *Breasts, Bottles and Babies* (Edinburgh: Edinburgh University Press, 1986), ch. 3; and Olwen Hufton, *The Prospect Before Her: A History of Women in Western Europe*, vol. I, *1500–1800* (London: Fontana, 1997), pp. 193–9.

the eighteenth and nineteenth centuries. At a time when it was dying out among its traditional clients among the upper classes in most European countries, it attracted custom from shopkeepers, artisans and even domestic servants in urban France. According to the historian George Sussman, at the end of the *ancien régime* families in cities such as Paris and Lyon sent almost all of their newborn children to *nourrices* in outlying suburbs or villages. In 1780, for example, the Lieutenant-General of Police in Paris estimated that less than 5 per cent of infants in the city were breastfed by their mothers. His colleague in Lyon reported infants from the city being dispersed into the Vivarais, Velay, Forez, Beaujolais, Bugey and even Savoy in the search for nurses.[46] During the nineteenth century, the campaigns of Rousseau and fellow reformers finally made some headway among the masses: by 1869, an estimated 59 per cent of mothers in Paris were breastfeeding their children. However, the process of urbanization caused the absolute numbers of infants sent out to a wet-nurse to increase during the first three quarters of the century.[47]

The result was that, in contrast to other European nations, a significant proportion of French infants faced an extended period of separation from their mother. It was common practice to send a child into the countryside a few days after its birth, and it might remain there with its nurse for one or two years, or more – assuming it survived that long. Conditions for the nurslings varied according to their family background. During the nineteenth century, the wealthy increasingly turned to live-in nurses, whom they could more easily supervise than those in the villages. The burden of separation from the mother then fell on the peasant family of the nurse.[48] A study of the small Burgundian town of Thoissey-en-Dombes during the late eighteenth century revealed that families often placed their infants with relatives in the countryside, such as an uncle or a cousin, and in a narrow band of villages within 7 kilometres of the town.[49] In the big cities, only the better-off families could afford to place their children nearby; the poor and above all the Assistance publique had to look further afield, helped in the nineteenth century by the development of the road and railway systems. An impoverished region like the Morvan, 300 kilometres away from the capital, could therefore take placings from Paris.[50]

---

[46] George D. Sussman, 'The Wet-Nursing Business in Nineteenth-Century France', *French Historical Studies*, 9 (1975), 304–28; Sussman, *Selling Mother's Milk*, ch. 2; and Maurice Garden, *Lyon et les Lyonnais au XVIIIe siècle* (Paris: Les Belles-Lettres, 1970), p. 120.

[47] Sussman, 'The Wet-Nursing Business', passim.   [48] Lehning, 'Family Life', passim.

[49] Alain Bideau, 'L'Envoi des jeunes enfants en nourrice: l'exemple d'une petite ville: Thoissey-en-Dombes, 1740–1840', in *Hommage à Marcel Reinhard: sur la population française au XVIIIe et au XIXe siècles* (Paris: Société de démographie historique, 1973), pp. 49–58.

[50] Armengaud, 'Les Nourrices du Morvan'.

A long line of critics accused mothers of irresponsibility in paying more attention to the frivolities of their social life than to the welfare of their children. In the late nineteenth century, medical opinion was making a link between the widespread resort to wet-nursing in France, compared to neighbours such as Belgium, England and Germany, and her exceptionally high levels of infant mortality.[51] Undoubtedly, many mothers in aristocratic and *haute bourgeoisie* circles considered breastfeeding below their dignity. For those lower down the social scale, involved in the running of a family business, wet-nursing was doubtless 'a necessity, but not a very attractive one', as Sussman put it.[52] The high death rate among the infants stands as a cruel indictment of the whole system. The journey to the countryside, premature weaning and negligence on the part of the wet-nurses all took their toll. It is impossible to calculate mortality rates for the little *nourrissons*. A doctor from Lyon estimated in the late eighteenth century that a quarter of children in the region died with their mothers or a good nurse, two thirds with a bad nurse. Sussman proposed an infant mortality rate for those born in eighteenth-century cities of 180 to 200 per 1,000 among babies nursed by their mothers, 250 to 400 among those sent to a rural wet-nurse and a catastrophic 650 to 900 among foundlings placed in the countryside by charitable institutions.[53]

The psychological effects on those that survived are harder to gauge, though one might assume that the quality of care with the nurse would have an influence. Rétif de la Bretonne, in *Monsieur Nicolas* (1796), followed a common belief in asserting that he acquired certain character traits from his wet-nurse, 'the most temperamental in the canton'. Premature weaning at six months, under pressure from her husband, did not help either, but he did not hold it against her: 'she always loved me so tenderly that I would be ungrateful if I lacked the respect owing to my second mother'. D'Alembert (1717–83) was a famous example of someone who maintained an affection for his wet-nurse, Mme Rousseau, throughout his life. Manon Phlipon (later Mme Roland) provides a further benign example from eighteenth-century Paris. Her father was a master engraver, therefore half artisan and half artist. She spent two years with a 'good' wet-nurse near Arpajon, chosen by her aunt. Afterwards, she kept in contact with her nurse, and at the same time established a comfortable

---

[51] Nancy Senior, 'Aspects of Infant Feeding in Eighteenth-Century France', *Eighteenth–Century Studies*, 16 (1983), 367–88; and Fanny Fay-Sallois, *Les Nourrices à Paris au XIXe siècle* (Paris: Payot, 1980), ch. 3.

[52] George D. Sussman, 'Parisian Infants and Norman Wet Nurses in the Early Nineteenth Century: A Statistical Study', *Journal of Interdisciplinary History*, 7 (1977), 637–53 (652).

[53] Garden, *Lyon au XVIIIe siècle*, p. 139; and Sussman, *Selling Mother's Milk*, p. 67.

relationship with her mother. Jacques-Louis Ménétra, son of a Parisian glazier, survived the experience apparently unscathed during the 1730s. Although he was found begging in a church when his relatives came to collect him, he lived happily with a loving grandmother during his childhood. During the nineteenth century, Jean Guéhenno began life with his nurse, who was also his great-aunt,[54] a few miles from his native town of Fougères (Ile-et-Vilaine). He described his time with her as paradise lost, spending his holidays with her until he was around twelve: 'according to my memory, it was always sunny in this part of the universe where I grew up. Time did not pass by and life was without problems. It was like an eternal July.'[55]

Mrs Robert Henry, born in Montmartre in 1906, wrote of what must have been a common experience for mothers visiting their babies in the countryside: 'I was then eleven months old, and when my mother saw me she was jealous because I treated her as a stranger, calling out "Mama!" to the women she paid to look after me.' This did not prevent mother and daughter enjoying a close relationship when Madeleine returned to Paris around 1907.[56] Emilie Carles (b. 1900) was more damning in her verdict, when discussing the case of her younger sister Marie-Rose. The real problem was doubtless the sudden death of the mother from a lightning strike when the baby was only four months old:

Overnight she had been torn from the maternal breast to go off among strangers. For almost two years she lived outside the warmth of family life. A wet-nurse is no substitute for a mother; some of them are certainly good, but that was not the case here, for while Marie-Rose was housed and fed, she was deprived of what was fundamental.

This meant that the infant was very backward for her age, being unable to walk or talk at two. Fortunately she learned fast when back among brothers and sisters.[57] In any case, the entire 'wet-nursing business' gradually disappeared in France during the early twentieth century, as sterilized milk and feeding bottles finally brought a safe alternative to breastfeeding, and as small family businesses declined in importance in the economy.[58]

---

[54] After raising her own children, she nursed cohorts of around twenty infants with feeding bottles, while their mothers worked in the local boot and shoe industry.

[55] Rétif de la Bretonne, *Monsieur Nicolas*, pp. 10–11; Mercier, *L'Enfant*, p. 51 (on d'Alembert); Jeanne-Marie Roland de la Platière, *Mémoires de Madame Roland*, ed. Paul de Roux (Paris: Mercure de France, 1986), pp. 204–5; Ménétra, *Journal of My Life*, pp. 18–19; and Guéhenno, *Changer la vie*, pp. 20–43 (p. 22).

[56] Mrs Robert Henry, *The Little Madeleine* (London: Dent, 1951), p. 28.

[57] Carles, *Wild Herb Soup*, p. 33.

[58] Sussman, 'The Wet-Nursing Business', ch. 7; and Anne Martin-Fugier, 'La Fin des nourrices', *Le Mouvement social*, 105 (1978), 11–32.

Mothering among the middle classes

Families among the middle classes appeared to provide exception-ally favourable material and cultural conditions for a close attachment between mother and child, along the lines envisaged by Rousseau. In the event, as noted above, such a textbook bond rarely appears in the remi-niscences, perhaps because it would be too banal. Instead, the extremes grab the attention of the reader, running from males enjoying a some-what overheated relationship with their mother to people recalling feelings of outright hostility. All this suggests at least some caution in assum-ing a smooth passage towards 'good mothering' in the midst of bour-geois domesticity. The famous passage from Stendhal on his feelings for his mother still leaps from the page for the smug post-Freudian reader:

I wanted to cover my mother in kisses and for there not to be any clothes. She loved me passionately and kissed me often, I returned her kisses with such ardour she was as if compelled to move away. I loathed my father when he came and interrupted our kissing. I always wanted to give her them on her bosom.

He at least gave a hint of what was going on in his mind by asking the reader to 'kindly condescend to remember that I lost her in childbirth when I was scarcely seven years old'.[59] Pierre Loti wrote around 1890 that his mother was for him 'the natural refuge, the shelter from all of the fears of the unknown, from all the black sorrows, which have no definite cause'. Marcel Proust of course endured his 'drame du coucher' in *In Search of Lost Time*, when the presence of the outsider Swann at dinner deprived him of his usual 'precious and fragile kiss' last thing at night from his mother. Although he managed a 'victory' of sorts, in that his father allowed his mother to sleep in the same room as him, and 'my mother's lovely face still shone with youth that evening when she so gently held my hands and tried to stop my tears', he later reflected that it had exposed key traits in his character: his nervous sensitivity and 'weak will'.[60]

At the other extreme were the plaintive opening lines from Jules Vallès in *L'Enfant*:

Have I been fed by my mother? Was it a peasant woman who gave me her milk? I do not know. Whichever breast I latched on to, I do not recall a caress from the time I was very small; I have not been pampered, patted, smothered in kisses; I have been beaten a lot.

[59] Stendhal, *Henry Brulard*, p. 33.
[60] Loti, *Le Roman d'un enfant*, pp. 46–7, 55; and Proust, *The Way by Swann's*, pp. 26–42. See also Jammes, *De l'âge divin*, p. 137.

The mother figure in *L'Enfant* was the wife of a schoolteacher. Neighbours and colleagues of her husband did regard her as strange. A neighbour tried to help young Jacques by deceiving his mother into thinking that she had taken over the job of beating him, and a new *proviseur* in his father's school made clear his hostility to corporal punishment. Nonetheless, for the most part his mother was left to treat him as she saw fit.[61] She at least tried to love her son in her own peculiar way. Juliette Adam (1836–1936), by contrast, depicted her mother as a cold fish, who had agreed to marry her father at the behest of her parents with the observation that: 'Since you want it, since you are committed to the point where it would be difficult to break off, I will resign myself to it; where you tie the goat, it will graze.' She breastfed Juliette, but with her usual sour temper and recriminations, provoking the grandmother to spirit Juliette away and raise her herself.[62] The widespread resort to servants meant that many children from 'bourgeois' families became attached to them as well as to their mother. Simone de Beauvoir, for example, mentioned her feeling of 'unalterable security' from the presence of her maid Louise as well as the tender feelings she had for her 'more distant and capricious' mother.[63]

Conclusion

That some children failed to develop a secure attachment to their mother in modern France is hardly surprising: cross-cultural studies indicate that this happens to a minority of children in a variety of contexts.[64] In some cases this was a matter of circumstances current in the eighteenth and nineteenth centuries, such as the resort to domestic servants for childrearing activities in wealthy families. In others it appeared a matter of a temperament unsuited to 'good mothering' that might appear at any period. Several writers conveyed their belief that parent–child relations had become closer over the course of their lifetime, be that in the eighteenth, nineteenth or twentieth century.

Mothers as teachers

Mothers in the villages traditionally started the education of their children by singing them songs, teasing them with riddles, playing little games with

---

[61] Vallès, *L'Enfant*, p. 19.   [62] Adam, *Mon Enfance*, pp. 43 and 52.

[63] Simone de Beauvoir, *Memoirs of a Dutiful Daughter*, transl. James Kirkup (Harmondsworth: Penguin, 1963), pp. 5–6. See also Olga Varni and Suzanne Lehmann Lefranc, in Germain and de Panafieu, *Mémoire des femmes*, pp. 46–7, 142–4.

[64] Van Ijzendoorn and Sagi, 'Cross-Cultural Patterns of Attachment', passim.

words and numbers, telling them stories and passing on the religious and moral values of the family. Aristocratic families also expected mothers to begin the long process of acquainting the child with the 'art of living' from a tender age.[65] Etiquette manuals for the 'middle classes' in the nineteenth century followed suit with their advice to the 'mother-teacher'. They recommended that she introduce them to these same religious and moral values, and prepare them for primary school with instruction in the three Rs.[66] In the wake of the systematic policy of 'dechristianization' during the Terror of the French Revolution, and the consequent weakening of the clergy, it fell to mothers and other women to play a prominent role in the defence of the Christian faith during the nineteenth century.[67]

Folklore studies give an idea of the content of this educational dimension to the popular culture among the peasantry, even as it began to retreat in the early twentieth century. For example, each region had its *comptines* and *formulettes* to help the child with language and numbers, working through its fingers, face, the days of the week, months of the year and so on. A common formula combined numbers with the catechism, including 'One, is God the Father . . . Four, are the four Evangelists . . . Ten, are the Ten Commandments.' In Provence, mothers or nurses relied on the rhymes and rhythms of words (lost in the translation) such as these to stimulate the child:

> Quand passo la becasso
>   aquéu la casso
>   acquéu la fricasso
>   acquéu la boulis
>   acquéu la roustis
> Riéu piéu-piéu!
> Rèsto rèn per iéu
> (When the woodcock passes
>   This one hunts it [the thumb]
>   This one makes it laugh [the index]
>   This one boils it [the second finger]
>   This one roasts it [the third finger]
> Riéu piéu-piéu!
> There is nothing for me the little finger)[68]

---

[65] Mension-Rigau, *L'Enfance au château*, p. 75.

[66] James F. McMillan, *France and Women, 1789–1914: Gender, Society and Politics* (London: Routledge, 2000), p. 50.

[67] Geneviève Gabbois, '"Vous êtes presque la seule consolation de l'église": la foi des femmes face à la déchristianisation de 1789 à 1880', in Jean Delumeau (ed.), *La Religion de ma mère: le rôle des femmes dans la transmission de la foi* (Paris: Cerf, 1992), pp. 301–25.

[68] Van Gennep, *Manuel*, I, p. 163; and Claude Seignolle, *Folklore de la Provence* (Paris: Maisonneuve, 1963), p. 69.

As one might expect from a leading figure in the defence of Provençal culture, Frédéric Mistral presented a pleasing picture of his mother steeping him in the stories, legends and beliefs of the region during his infancy during the 1830s. Pierre-Jakez Hélias recorded some Breton versions of such games, in his case learned on his grandfather's knee, and songs sung to him by his mother. His family had drifted away from their religious faith, but, as was often the case, his mother remained a good Catholic. She presented him with a copy of a Breton hymnbook, which she knew by heart, and made sure that he did so too. They conveyed Christian morality, mingled with threats to hardened sinners, including a diatribe against drunkenness. The militant worker Joseph Benoit also looked back to a religious education from his mother, acknowledging in a rather formulaic manner his peasant background in the Jura mountains early in the nineteenth century: 'My first years passed like those from my background, divided between care from a gentle, good and pious mother, as they are in the countryside, or were then, with a naïve and resigned faith, plus games and jobs done by young rural folk.' He claimed to have absorbed from this early education a love for his fellow creatures, 'and above all the poor whom I learned to consider as outcast brothers, as gifts from God'.[69]

Working-class mothers in the towns might well follow a similar path, though the atmosphere was less favourable to organized religion. Xavier-Edouard Lejeune admitted that his mother only arranged for him to attend catechism classes in his Parisian parish during the 1850s because it was the custom: she never went to church herself. Similarly, Georges Dumoulin attended catechism classes regularly at the behest of his mother in the Pas-de-Calais during the 1880s – though he added that she only sent him to Mass when she expected a handout of bread or a meat voucher from the priest.[70] And not all mothers in the 'popular classes' had the time or the inclination to foster the moral and intellectual development of their children. The mother of Antoine Sylvère, for example, working from dawn till dusk, left his early education to others.

Aristocratic and upper-middle-class mothers might well take an interest in the early education of their offspring, but they tended to leave much of the teaching to a governess or private tutor. Relations between the child and these outsiders might be close, as each party sought affection missing from elsewhere, but there was always a risk of tension. Clara

---

[69] Mistral, *Memoirs*, p. 30; Hélias, *Horse of Pride*, pp. 38–40; and Joseph Benoit, *Confessions d'un prolétaire* (Lyon, 1871; Paris: Editions sociates, 1968), p. 35.

[70] Xavier-Edouard Lejeune, *Calicot: enquête de Michel et Philippe Lejeune* (Paris: Montalba, 1984), p. 105; Dumoulin, *Carnets de route*, p. 17. See also Caroux-Destray, *Un couple ouvrier traditionnel*, pp. 48–9.

Malraux, for example, claimed that during the early twentieth century a Czech governess 'poisoned' her childhood with her harshness, injustice and even stupidity.[71] There was also a notion within these circles that children might experience a 'first education' mingling with cultivated adults at court or within the family. The child could then quietly absorb the speech and *etiquette* of *le monde* (fashionable society).[72] Childhood reminiscences from those involved suggest that this approach was treated lightly, though this may reflect an awareness of increasing disapproval of the distant, supervisory role taken by mothers. Talleyrand wrote that his education 'was rather left to take care of itself'. He thought himself typical of aristocratic children at court in Versailles during the 1750s.[73] During the nineteenth century, this aristocratic tradition proved remarkably tenacious. Well-to-do French families, unlike their English counterparts, often preferred children to mingle with adults rather than live their own separate existence in a nursery. An English observer was persuasive in suggesting during the early twentieth century that this experience of adult life and conversation caused French children to be extraordinarily precocious. At the same time, he felt it deprived them of simplicity and spontaneity: the atmosphere of reason and good sense in which they lived allegedly overlaid the imagination with a sediment of logic.[74]

The group most inclined to ensure that their children had a flying start early in life was the broad swathe of 'middle classes', part and parcel of their receptiveness to new ideas on education and a 'long' childhood from the seventeenth and eighteenth centuries onwards. They were the ones most eager for their children to 'get on' in life, which required discipline and success at school.[75] Jules Vallès treated his readers to a grotesque caricature of the whole process in *L'Enfant*. The underlying problem for Mme Vingtras, that made her so obnoxious to her son, was her desire for him to become a model 'bourgeois', 'un *Monsieur*', as she tried to lay the ghost of her own peasant origins. The futility of her efforts came to light when the young Jacques was given dinner by one of his father's colleagues:

[71] Mension-Rigau, *L'Enfance au château*, p. 109; and Clara Malraux, *Apprendre à vivre* (Paris: Bernard Grasset, 1963), pp. 16–18.

[72] Lucien Bély, 'L'Elève et le monde: essai sur l'éducation des lumières d'après les mémoires autobiographiques du temps', *Revue d'histoire moderne et contemporaine*, 28 (1981), 3–35 (15).

[73] Talleyrand, *Memoirs*, p. 4.

[74] Cloudesley Brereton, 'L'Enfant français dans la famille et à l'école', *Revue pédagogique*, 22 (1918), 237–49 (a translation from the *Contemporary Review*); Wagener, *Comtesse de Boigne*, pp. 32–3.

[75] See Vassigh, 'Les Relations adultes–enfants', I, pp. 45–86.

'You are hungry?'
'Yes, *M'sieu!*'
'You want to eat?'
'No, *M'sieu!*'
I believed it more polite to say *no*: my mother had advised me not to accept straightaway, that is not done in polite society.[76]

There were many more successful mothers among the middle classes. Suzanne Voilquin (b. c. 1798), the daughter of a reasonably prosperous small businessman in Paris, remembered the devoutly Catholic upbringing provided by her 'beloved mother'. The family letters of Eugénie Desnoyers, second wife of the Alsatian industrialist Charles Mertzdorff during the 1870s, revealed a devoted mother and teacher. As she wrote, she described the little ones around her, playing with their dolls, painting, playing the piano, reading, writing letters or doing their homework.[77] Other mothers revealed a steely determination to give their daughters a head start in life. Mme Necker taught her daughter Minette (Mme de Staël, 1766–1817) to read from the Bible and gave her a grounding in a range of academic subjects. From the petty bourgeoisie of pre-revolutionary Paris, Manon Phlipon learned to read by the age of four and started her catechism classes around the age of seven with the help of her mother.[78] Aurore Dupin (later George Sand, 1804–76) had an aristocratic father but a mother with a background in petty trading. The latter taught the young Aurore to read, recite various prayers and reel off a number of La Fontaine fables – though later in life George Sand admitted that at the time she could not understand the content of either the prayers or the fables that she had learned by heart.[79] During the early twentieth century, in Paris, the mother of Simone de Beauvoir learned English and Latin herself to help her daughter with her studies, besides ensuring that they both attended Mass on Sundays.[80]

Mothers and sons

Elisabeth Badinter followed eighteenth-century reformers in accusing mothers of 'selective love', of a kind difficult to accept in the twentieth century, as they favoured boys over girls and the eldest son over his

---

[76] Vallès, *L'Enfant*, pp. 157–60.
[77] Suzanne Voilquin, 'Recollections of a Daughter of the People', in Traugott, *The French Worker*, pp. 92–115 (p. 93); and Dauphin et al., *Ces bonnes lettres*, pp. 126–8.
[78] Renée Winegarten, *Mme de Staël* (Leamington Spa: Berg, 1985), ch. 2; Roland, *Mémoires de Madame Roland*, p. 205.
[79] Sand, *Histoire de ma vie*, pp. 141–2.
[80] De Beauvoir, *Memoirs of a Dutiful Daughter*, p. 38.

younger brothers.[81] This is hard to dispute in some ways, but it is not clear that it should go under the heading of maternal 'indifference' to children. Parents and children alike could hardly fail to be influenced by prevailing social and cultural influences, such as the value placed on boys in agrarian society, and the importance of securing a male heir in aristocratic and landowning circles. Mark Motley drew attention to the special treatment of male heirs in seventeenth-century families of the court nobility, and the need for younger brothers and sisters to 'work harder for attention from parents and kin'.[82] Chateaubriand stood out as a perfect example of a younger brother complaining that his mother concentrated all her affections on her first-born son. It was not a case of failing to love her other children, he emphasized, but he did accuse her of a 'blind preference' for the young Comte de Combourg. While scolding him, she eulogized his brother as a Cato, a hero. He in his turn admitted to having some privileges over his four sisters as a boy, and as the last-born.[83] Further down the social scale, as the son of a master tailor from the Limousin, the *philosophe* and dramatist Jean-François Marmontel (1723–99) proclaimed that his mother had a weakness for him, the oldest of her seven children. He was the only one she breastfed, he noted. The imposition of partible inheritance from the 1790s militated against such favours. It may be that they continued during the nineteenth century among peasant families in southern France attempting to keep their landholdings intact by designating a single heir. However, there is no first-hand account to prove the point.

Looked at from the child's point of view, one should also bear in mind the evolution of feelings as the child grew up, from the uncritical admiration of the early years to the more measured views of the adolescent, and particularly the adult writing in later years.[84] The desire that sons work towards a successful career, as opposed to simply following in their father's footsteps, was a potential source of conflict. One can see the first traces of the pressures on the young among the swelling 'middle classes' to do well at school and discipline themselves. A mother from a family of well-off farmers in Anjou wrote to her cousin in 1906 that she was furious with her son because of a lack of application to his studies: 'what a pain these boys are!' she exclaimed.[85] Some young males continued to look to their mothers for support and affection as they grew up, without

---

[81] Badinter, *Myth of Motherhood*, pp. 64–6.
[82] Motley, *Becoming a French Aristocrat*, p. 30.   [83] Chateaubriand, *Mémoires*, p. 46.
[84] Coe, *When the Grass was Taller*, p. 156.
[85] Letter from Berthe to Marie, 24 June 1906, cited in Caroline Chotard-Lioret, 'La Société familiale en province: une correspondance privée entre 1870 et 1920', Thèse pour le doctorat, 3e cycle, Université de Paris V, 1983, p. 168.

any complaints. An orthodox view came from Gustave-Emmanuel Roy (b. 1823) when he wrote his life story as a successful businessman for the edification of his children and grandchildren. He emphasized the support from his mother, a cultivated woman who took care of his early education and supported him in difficult times: 'if I reached the position I did, I owe it to her'.[86] However, many other such accounts were more nuanced. Charles Nicolle (1866–1936), a Professor of Medicine at the Collège de France, wrote a thoughtful (and unpublished) account of his relationship with his mother during his upbringing in Normandy. On the one hand, he admitted that her strictness as a 'rigid goddess' brought little joy to his childhood: 'for a long time I misunderstood you. Your dignity constricted my tenderness. All of your acts and thoughts seemed to be a matter of duty.' However, the death of his father when Nicolle was eighteen brought him closer to her, and in the end he acknowledged that he owed to her the best of his achievements.[87] The writer André Gide (1869–1951) in his turn reflected on a difficult relationship with his austere, Calvinist mother. He conceded that she played her maternal role conscientiously, and indeed gave him all of her love once his father had died. However, he also suffered from what his biographer called her 'authoritarianism and narrow-mindedness'. He confessed that she had worn him down by bombarding him with advice, and generally trying to subdue him: 'she had a way of loving that sometimes made me hate her and put my nerves on edge'.[88]

Further along the spectrum, *L'Enfant* (1879) by Jules Vallès was historically significant as the first novel in France to try to dent the revered public image of motherhood and the family. Its hostile reception from the critics indicated a reluctance to accept such head-on criticism during the late nineteenth century.[89] Over the course of this autobiographical work he deftly revealed the increasing disillusionment of the young Jacques Vingtras with his violently abusive mother. To start with, he suggested that she was right to beat her wayward son. Recalling his infancy, he wrote that 'I am persuaded that she is a good mother and that I am an ungrateful child.'[90] However, once in school, he wondered why he was not allowed to join the other children in their playground games, or keep the little presents given to him by his father's colleagues. The irony of the

---

[86] Gustave-Emmanuel Roy, *Souvenirs, 1823–1906* (Nancy: Berger-Levrault, 1906), pp. 12–14.
[87] AD Seine-Maritime, 146 J 13, Fonds Charles Nicolle, 'Mémoires et souvenirs de Charles Nicolle', MS dictated 1935–6 in Tunis, p. 8.
[88] Gide, *Si le grain ne meurt*, pp. 91 and 361–2; Delay, *André Gide*, ch. 3.
[89] See Zeldin, *Ambition and Love*, pp. 335–9.   [90] Vallès, *L'Enfant*, p. 25.

adult narrator came into play. Having lost his toy trumpet and drum, he transferred his attention to his sweets and started to lick them. 'But my mother did not want me to have the ways of a courtesan: "you start by licking the belly of a sweet, you finish by licking . . .".'[91] The boy started to grasp the jealous and shameful character of his mother, when, as the wife of a schoolmaster in a *collège*, she forbade him to mix with the son of a shoemaker while he recovered from a broken arm. Hervé Bazin also depicted his mother in his *Vipère au poing* (1948) as a faintly ridiculous as well as sinister figure. Again, the mother acted without interference from outside, but the author made it clear that she was anything but 'normal'. The Bazin character, Jean Rezeau, contrasted her heartless regime with that of his paternal grandmother, enjoyed for four years as a young child when his mother was abroad. Mme Rezeau, 'who had missed her vocation as a warden in a women's prison',[92] enforced a strict timetable for each minute of the day, suppressed the heating in their rooms, removed pillows and eiderdowns, and shaved their heads. She also dismissed the governess for protesting over the changes she introduced. As the boys reached their teens, the mother resorted to devious methods to keep the upper hand, including trying to plant a stolen purse in Jean's room. In the end Jean claimed that his mother's influence had blighted his existence, with what one would now call evidence of an insecurely attached child: 'All faith seems to me a deception, all authority a scourge, all tenderness a matter of calculation. The most sincere friendships, good will, tenderness to come, I am going to be suspicious, discourage them, deny them. Man must live alone.'[93]

Mothers and daughters

The bond between mothers and daughters is usually described as a close and enduring one throughout the modern period in France. While boys were expected to join the world of men after the age of seven or eight, girls usually remained beside their mothers, learning their future role as wife and mother. The mother–daughter relationship might start awkwardly in a traditional family, as mothers came to terms with their 'failure' to produce a boy. However, most soon saw a way around this problem. During the eighteenth century, the Comtesse de Boigne recorded that she was 'pardoned' for being a girl, because of the joy surrounding her arrival after a stillbirth. Later on, Marie-Catherine Gardez, the daughter

---

[91] Ibid., p. 67.   [92] Bazin, *Vipère au poing*, p. 33.
[93] Ibid., p. 185. See also Holmes, *Attachment Theory*, pp. 78–9.

of a handloom weaver in the Pas-de-Calais, stated that her mother cried when she found she had had yet another daughter in 1891. However, she was comforted with the thought that Marie-Catherine would be her support in old age.[94] The diaries kept by young, middle-class girls provide evidence of daughters constantly seeking approval from their mothers. In adolescence, at the age of eighteen, the young Lucile Duplessis mingled tender thoughts on her suitor Camille Desmoulins with others on her mother. In March 1788 she wrote in the declamatory style typical of the period about a walk in the woods with her mother: 'What a delicious walk: overcast weather, both melancholy, both on the same subject of our troubles . . . Ô Maman.'[95]

To some extent daughters struggled to develop an affectionate relationship with their mother, as improved education and career prospects for girls had the potential to create a generation gap. Mathilde Shaw was put off in the middle of the nineteenth century by the 'blind bigotry' and the narrowness of the religious ideas of her mother, the product of ten years in a convent in Bordeaux. She acknowledged the 'pure diamond heart' of her mother, but sneered at the 'mixture of childish and idiotic literature' in her bedroom. Similarly, the forthright Marie Bashkirtseff in the 1880s summed up her mother from the perspective of a 'modern', career-orientated daughter: 'Mama has plenty of wit, little education, no knowledge of the world, no tact, and her mind is rusty and mouldy from talking about nothing but servants, my health and dogs.'[96] Yet, with the weakening of the hold of fathers over their sons, it is arguable that the mother–daughter nexus became the backbone of the modern family. After reading the huge family correspondence written by her forebears during the period 1868 to 1920, Caroline Chotard-Lioret remarked that while mothers often criticized the idleness and poor school results of their sons, they never had a bad word to say about the conduct of their daughters. In similar vein, Madeleine Dissais informed her interviewer during the 1980s that she loved her children in various ways, talking freely to her daughters but never considering taking her sons into her confidence.[97] As already noted in the case of Caroline Brame, girls whose mothers

---

[94] Boigne, *Mémoires*, p. 25; and Grafteaux, *Mémé Santerre*, p. 11. See also Dauphin et al., *Ces bonnes lettres*, p. 50.

[95] Lucile Desmoulins, *Journal, 1788–1793*, ed. Philippe Lejeune (Paris: Cendres, 1995), entry for 9 July 1788.

[96] Mathilde Shaw, *Illustres et inconnus: souvenirs de ma vie* (Paris: Charpentier, 1906), pp. 13 and 29; *Journal de Marie Bashkirtseff*, ed. Verena von der Heyden-Rynsch (Paris: Mercure de France, 2000), entry for 2 July 1876.

[97] Chotard-Lioret, 'Correspondre en 1900', 67; Madeleine Dissais, in Germain and de Panafieu, *Mémoire des femmes*, p. 25.

had died young might feel deprived of their most important source of emotional support.[98]

Conclusion

The idea of a mother figure prepared to sacrifice all for the welfare of her children is best seen as an impossible ideal, perhaps even a ludicrous one, a product of the peculiar circumstances that produced the 'domestic ideology' for women in the nineteenth and early twentieth centuries. Inevitably, mothers had other functions to fulfil, varying according to their circumstances. Of Mme Necker, mother of the future Mme de Staël, the historian Renée Winegarten wrote, 'Her watchword was duty, and she carefully divided her day into her duty to God, her husband, her child, her friends, the poor, the household, her toilette.'[99] Certainly there were various 'external' indicators from the mid-eighteenth century onwards to suggest the emergence of a warmer relationship between mother and child, such as the propaganda campaign calling for this to happen by Rousseau and many others, the decline of mercenary wet-nursing and the long-term shift towards smaller families. There was also first-hand evidence from sons and daughters at all levels of society to show 'good' mothering, in the form of a close attachment from an early stage, plus time and effort devoted to the first stages of education. This is not to deny the existence of bastions of the older ways, where it was good form for mothers to maintain their distance from their sons and daughters, notably the aristocracy, or difficult for them to do so because of the pressures of poverty and long working hours, as in some peasant and working-class families. Overall, though, the impression is of children managing to form a loving relationship with their mothers in varying circumstances, both 'traditional' and 'modern', accepting in retrospect at least the obstacles faced by mothers, and where necessary resorting to substitutes for support and affection.

Chateaubriand confronted the question of whether the hard upbringing he went through caused him to detest those who brought him into this world. His answer was emphatic: 'Not at all; the memory of their rigour is almost agreeable to me: I esteem and honour their great qualities.' The future author of Le Génie du christianisme (1802) acknowledged that it was from his mother that he owed his religion, learning the truth

---

[98] See above, pp. 96–7. See also Dissais, in Germain and de Panafieu, Mémoire des femmes, p. 15.
[99] Winegarten, Mme de Staël, p. 19.

of Christianity from her. He also doubted whether launching him into his studies earlier in life would have helped develop his intelligence. He reflected that the time spent alone with the elements on the beach at Saint-Malo might have suited his native disposition.[100] Examples of violently abusive mothers allowed free rein by those around them are not hard to find in modern France, not least because they lend themselves to revenge on the printed page later in life. All the same, given that they contravene the various norms prevailing at different levels of society, one might assume that they will exist as exceptional cases in any society. Overall, then, from the 'bottom-up' perspective of the child, the adaptability and resilience of many young people in the family stand out, and a greater element of continuity than the eighteenth-century 'revolution' posited by Shorter will allow for.

[100] Chateaubriand, *Mémoires*, pp. 60–1.

7   Of fathers, fatherhood, kin and discipline

Fathers and fatherhood

Historians on fatherhood

'Fatherhood has a very long history, but virtually no historians,' observed John Demos in 1983.[1] However, during the late twentieth century, a growing awareness of the insecurity of fathers, and a questioning of their future even, has paved the way for an interest in the history of fatherhood.[2] A very full study of the French case, published by a team of historians in 1990, traced a long identity crisis for fathers from the middle of the eighteenth century onwards.[3] The historian Jean Delumeau highlighted the seventeenth century as the 'golden age of the paternal monarchy' in France, when fathers were associated with the figure of God the Father. They dominated wives and children, unchallenged as the person who engendered, fed and educated the family. Most importantly, they acted as guardians of the family patrimony, handing it on to the next generation as they saw fit.[4] Indeed, the divine monarchy of the father in his little domain served to guarantee the authority of the state. Among the court nobility, parents expected elaborate signs of respect from their children, including silence in their presence, lowered eyes when speaking and the raising of hats.[5] The eighteenth-century Enlightenment began the process of questioning this 'despotic' vision of *la puissance paternelle* (paternal authority), and the Revolution of 1789 abolished it entirely, in principle at least, in the name of individual liberty. The revolutionaries undermined the authority

---

[1] John Demos, 'The Changing Faces of Fatherhood: A New Exploration in Family History', in Kessel and Siegel (eds.), *The Child*, pp. 158–81 (p. 160).

[2] French examples include Geneviève Delaisi de Parseval and Françoise Hurstel, 'La Paternité "à la française"', *Les Temps modernes*, 42 (1986), 51–93; Yvonne Knibiehler, *Les Pères aussi ont une histoire* (Paris: Hachette, 1987); and Gérard Guicheteau and Gisèle Namur, *Mémoires des pères* (Paris: Editions de la Martinière, 1993), an anthology of memoirs.

[3] Jean Delumeau and Daniel Roche (eds.), *Histoire des pères et de la paternité* (Paris: Larousse, 1990).

[4] Knibiehler, *Les Pères*, part I.   [5] Motley, *Becoming a French Aristocrat*, p. 36.

of fathers in a number of ways. They executed the supreme father figure of the king in 1793. They abolished the ban on marriage without
parental authorization. And, through the system of partible inheritance,
they denied the father the right to favour one child over another in his
will.[6] The Civil Code of 1804 formally re-established paternal authority,
and both the Catholic Church on the political right and the republicans
on the left did all they could to reinforce it during the nineteenth century. The Code also maintained the right of fathers to 'chastise' children,
which included having children under sixteen imprisoned for a month.
This was a continuation, in modified form, of the notorious *lettres de cachet*
of the *ancien régime*. The historian Bernard Schnapper pointed out that
this gave fathers in France more rights over their children than any other
country in Europe before 1914, except Sardinia.[7]

Yet the long 'humiliation' of fathers continued apace, with the state
gradually encroaching on their powers and various forces strengthening
the position of wives and children. In an increasingly urban and industrial society, fathers lost their power to pass on an inheritance, and, as
we have seen, mothers exercised the role of educating the young in the
home. The legal right to divorce, introduced for a short period during the
revolutionary and Napoleonic eras, and established definitively in 1884,
represented a triumph for wives over husbands. A law of 1889 brought
an important turning point in removing paternal authority from fathers
who committed crimes against their children or encouraged minors into
vice. It also condemned parents whose habitual drunkenness, scandalous
behaviour or harsh treatment risked compromising the health, security or
morality of children, making provisions for the mother or the Assistance
publique to take responsibility. A further law of 1898 aimed to protect
children under fifteen from injuries inflicted by fathers and mothers, and
from efforts to sell their services to street acrobats, charlatans and travelling circuses.[8] The huge loss of male life in the First World War forced

---

[6] Olivier Faron, 'Le Père face à ses enfants: quelques jalons sur l'évolution de l'autorité
paternelle (XIXe–XXe siècles)', in Bardet et al., *Lorsque l'enfant grandit*, pp. 349–61
(p. 351).

[7] Michelle Perrot, 'Roles and Characters', in Ariès and Duby (eds.), *History of Private Life*,
vol. IV, pp. 167–260 (p. 167); Arlette Farge and Michel Foucault (eds.), *Le Désordre des
familles: lettres de cachet des Archives de la Bastille* (Paris: Gallimard/Julliard, 1982); and
Bernard Schnapper, 'La Correction paternelle et le mouvement des idées au dix-neuvième
siècle (1789–1935)', *Revue historique*, 263 (1980), 319–49 (319).

[8] *Bulletin des lois*, 'loi sur la protection des enfants maltraités ou moralement abandonnés
du 24 juillet 1889'; and 'loi sur la répression des violences, voies de fait, actes de cruauté
et attentats commis envers les enfants du 19 avril 1898'. See also Jacques Donzelot, *The
Policing of Families*, transl. Robert Hurley (Baltimore: The Johns Hopkins University Press,
1979), passim; Rachel Ginnis Fuchs, 'Crimes Against Children in Nineteenth-Century
France', *Law and Human Behaviour*, 6 (1982), 237–59; Rollet-Echalier, *La Politique*,
ch. IV; and Bernard Schnapper, 'Le Père, le procureur et l'enfant: le mythe des enfants

further change, by encouraging measures to support the women who were required to survive on their own. In 1935 fathers lost the right of 'correction paternelle', though it was a dead letter well before that.[9] The final decline of the traditional Christian father figure occurred with such events as May 1968, which proclaimed the death of the father, and the substitution of parental for paternal authority in 1972.[10]

The patriarch

The traditional patriarch, characteristic of the seventeenth-century model, maintained his God-given authority by keeping a certain distance from his children. As the historian Alain Collomp noted, this type of respect for the father rested on a combination of fear and love.[11] Besides formalities such as *voussoiement*, the father asserted himself by remaining aloof from the humdrum business of child rearing, particularly during their early years. Such fathers restricted themselves to intervening only in important issues of discipline, education and the choice of a marriage partner. A much-quoted example was Edme Rétif, a well-off farmer ruling the roost in his Burgundian village during the eighteenth century. His son Rétif de la Bretonne depicted him as 'severe, without being hard', on sons and daughters alike, dispensing impartial justice and teaching good principles in a corrupt world. Unfortunately, *La Vie de mon père* (1779) now appears something of a 'hagiography', which has easily lent itself to the reactionary legend of the rural patriarchal family and the family of the good old days.[12] By the eighteenth century, the model was becoming less easy to enforce. Even so, it remained influential during the nineteenth century among aristocratic and wealthy 'bourgeois' families, among the peasantry and among the new working classes of the towns. Frédéric Mistral in his *Mémoires* (1912) recalled 'the austere manners of the ancient *pater* familias' when thinking of his father.[13]

'New fathers'

If in retrospect one can discern a long decline in paternal authority, there were always various currents of opinion seeking to provide new horizons

---

martyrs au XIXe siècle', in *Voies nouvelles en histoire du droit* (Paris: Presses Universitaires de France, 1991), pp. 509–22.

[9] Schnapper, 'Correction paternelle', 345–9; and Faron, 'Autorité', pp. 358–9.

[10] Jean Delumeau, 'Preface' to Delumeau and Roche, *Histoire des pères*, pp. 9–16.

[11] Collomp, *Maison du père*, p. 181.

[12] Rétif de la Bretonne, *Vie de mon père*, pp. 142–6; Georges Benrekassa, 'Le Typique et le fabuleux: histoire et roman dans la *Vie de mon père*', *Revue des sciences humaines*, 172 (1978), 31–56 (54).

[13] Mistral, *Memoirs*, p. 6.

for fathers, besides those eager to bolster the traditional form. During the eighteenth century, the *philosophes* of the Enlightenment promoted a new image of the father as a peaceable, family-orientated figure, to replace the tyrannical, 'gothic' father they associated with the *ancien régime*. Once again, it was a literate minority in the towns that proved most receptive to this message, drawn from members of the wealthy aristocratic and bourgeois elite, and also from commercial and artisan groups. In 1787, for example, the Le Havre-based merchant Jean-Baptiste Joseph Delahaye wrote a twenty-four-page letter to his son, studying in Hamburg, very much in this vein. He addressed him as 'my good friend', emphasized that he was giving advice rather than orders, and claimed to be acting through 'paternal friendship'.[14] After the utopian schemes of the Revolution for the reform of the family came to grief, the Civil Code restored the traditional authority of the father in the legal system. Article 373 proclaimed that 'the father alone exercises this authority during marriage'.[15] However, throughout the nineteenth century, a series of influential figures declared that affection was replacing a combination of respect and fear in relations between fathers and their children. Republicans during the second half of the century blended in a political dimension. They felt that authoritarian child-rearing methods could produce only authoritarian characters. To breed a new generation of citizens, families would have to rely on tenderness and affection.[16] Thus Gustave Droz, journalist and author of the hugely successful *Monsieur, madame et bébé* (1866), advised fathers to become friends with their children, and to develop a deep and reciprocal affection with them. The writer Ernest Legouvé thought that this was already happening, noting that in the past people used the informal *tu* with servants and the formal *vous* with children, but that now it was the other way round. The *vous* marked the equality of servants, and the *tutoiement* between parents and children the new habits of affection in the family. Only a few aristocratic families now expected children to address their parents in a formal manner. Early in the twentieth century, Marcel Braunschvig asserted that love and equality had replaced severe authority and immutable hierarchy, and that a warm intimacy had taken over from a ceremonious and cold etiquette. The child now reigned as the master of the household.[17] This vision of the father and child basking in cosy

---

[14] AD Seine-Maritime, 188 J I, letter from Jean-Baptiste Joseph Delahaye to Jean-Baptiste Delahaye, 8 September 1787.

[15] Delumeau and Roche, *Histoire des pères*, part III.

[16] Philip Nord, *The Republican Moment: Struggles for Democracy in Nineteenth-Century France* (Cambridge, MA: Harvard University Press, 1995), pp. 232–7.

[17] Gustave Droz, *Monsieur, madame et bébé* (116th edn, Paris: Victor-Havard, 1882); and Gustave Droz, *L'Enfant* (Paris: Victor-Havard, 1885), p. 50; Ernest Legouvé, *Les Pères*

domesticity originated in solidly 'bourgeois' circles, and flew in the face of both traditional views on paternal authority and the harsh realities of life in most households. During the 1890s, for example, the writer Alfred Franklin denounced contemporary family life in no uncertain terms:

> Under the reign of Louis XVI, paternal authority was reduced even more. Since that period, the rigidity, the sometimes exaggerated severity that presided over family life in the past has been replaced, in all classes of society, by an unpardonable indulgence, a weakness without limits, a most exaggerated familiarity also, which makes the child the equal of his father, turns him into a companion, a playmate, so that it becomes very difficult to make him accept a reprimand or to give orders.[18]

Hence one might expect a range of father figures to appear in 'ego documents' between the middle of the eighteenth and the middle of the twentieth century, both distant and affectionate, as well as 'good' and 'bad'. In some respects the ideal of the affectionate father of this period would mutate into the sensitive 'new father' (or New Man, in Anglo-Saxon terminology) of the late twentieth century, marking its victory over the older image of the patriarch. However, it would be more accurate to think in terms of a crisis of identity for fathers coming to a head at this late stage.[19]

Fathers and daughters

If Rétif de la Bretonne presented the patriarchal father as an ideal type, others in the eighteenth century were less impressed with the results of such an approach to parenting. Madame de Genlis gave a qualified appreciation of her father during the late *ancien régime*. He was an aristocrat who spent most of his time hunting with dogs or conducting scientific experiments. His interest in her education was confined to one point: ensuring that she was a strong woman. For him this meant a willingness to handle spiders and toads. Such was his ascendancy over her that she recalled never daring to disobey his 'terrible commands'. In retrospect, she conceded that the experience of picking up toads gave her tremendous self-control, but the '*violences*' involved made her nervy and only served to increase her antipathies.[20] A daughter who did dare to disobey a heavy-handed father at the same period was Manon Phlipon. She claimed to

---

et les enfants au XIXe siècle: enfance et adolescence (new edn, Paris: Hetzel, 1907), p. 5; Marcel Braunschvig, 'L'Enfant au XIXe siècle', *Pages libres*, 139 (1903), 169–84 (170–2). See also Zeldin, *Ambition and Love*, pp. 328–9; Delumeau and Roche, *Histoire des pères*, part IV.

[18] Alfred Franklin, *La Vie privée d'autrefois: l'enfant* (Paris: Plon, 1896), pp. 224–5.

[19] Delumeau and Roche, *Histoire des pères*, pp. 323–4.

[20] Comtesse de Genlis, *Mémoires*, I, pp. 55–6.

have 'become a lion' when he beat her as a young girl, biting his thigh and putting up a stubborn resistance when he tried to force her to take some medicine with threats of repeated beating. 'I feel as I write', in a revolutionary gaol under threat of the guillotine as it happened, 'the sort of revolution and the development of strength that I was experiencing then.' Her father never laid a hand on her again after the incident with the medicine, or even reprimanded her. Instead, he caressed her a great deal, taught her to draw and took her for walks, putting the relationship on a whole new footing.[21] Among the peasantry and the new working classes, the authoritarian father was a stock figure well into the twentieth century. Emilie Carles (1900–79), for example, described her family in an Alpine village as a patriarchy, with her father maintaining his discretionary powers, not speaking much and expecting a respectful attitude. Louise Vanderwielen, born into a working-class family in Lille in 1906, wrote that her father was a 'hard man' who expected to be obeyed without hesitation.[22]

Affectionate relations between fathers and daughters at various ages were common well before the twentieth century. Daughters were perhaps less turbulent than sons and a potential companion in old age.[23] The historian Yvonne Knibiehler went as far as to suggest a 'sort of idyll' between fathers and daughters during the late eighteenth and nineteenth centuries. She reasoned that education for daughters was still relatively straightforward, as girls had yet to aspire to higher education. All the father had to worry about was preserving his daughter's virginity and securing a good marriage for her.[24] The father of the future Comtesse de Boigne was exceptional in eighteenth-century aristocratic circles, but not necessarily to be ignored, in educating his young daughter to be a 'little prodigy'. She claimed that he had taught her to read by the age of three, so that she could manage the tragedies of Racine. The aristocratic father of George Sand liked to spend hours playing with his daughter when home on leave from the army during the 1800s, and was even happy to carry her through the streets when dressed in full uniform. Mathilde Shaw also benefited from having a scholarly father, a specialist in Oriental languages, who was both affectionate and willing to introduce

---

[21] Roland, *Mémoires de Madame Roland*, pp. 209–10.
[22] Carles, *Wild Herb Soup*, p. 14; and Vanderwielen, *Lise du plat pays*, pp. 51 and 57. See also Aline Lucas in Germain and de Panafieu, *Mémoire des femmes*, p. 223.
[23] Motley, *Becoming a French Aristocrat*, p. 31, n. 25. Randolph Trumbach asserts the contradictory view that aristocratic fathers in England 'never managed to associate very closely with their daughters at any age'; *The Rise of the Egalitarian Family: Aristocratic Kinship and Domestic Relations in Eighteenth-Century England* (New York: Academic Press, 1978), p. 238.
[24] Knibiehler, *Les Pères*, p. 200.

her to the worlds of astronomy and literature. This pleasant interlude in her life, it might be added, conveniently provided a dramatic contrast to the impending catastrophe of her parents' separation.[25] The age-old task of defending the virtue of their daughters was a potential source of tension for fathers.[26] Among the handloom weavers of northern France, for example, Marie-Catherine Gardez (b. 1891) provoked the wrath of her father by talking a little too freely about her feelings for the son of a neighbour and subcontractor for their finished goods. She realized that she had gone too far in allowing herself to be complimented by a boy without her father's authorization. When he calmed down, he explained that he disliked being exploited by the father, and in any case thought the lad too short and feeble to be able to produce fine children. She yielded to her father's experience, and normal relations resumed.[27]

A slightly different image of fathers often emerges in the letters and diaries written by young girls from the middle classes: of a peripheral figure, spending much of his time at work, who veered between bouts of exasperated shouting at his offspring and efforts to take them out for treats at weekends. In 1877 Elisabeth Leseur referred to her 'dear good father', a Parisian lawyer, but evidently did not see much of him. Jeanne G. complained in a letter to her mother, away from home on a cure, that life was not pleasant without her, as her father had scolded her on her birthday. Yet a year later, in 1899, her efforts to make him laugh while he was alone at home in Marseille suggest an easy-going relationship. Her letter from the spa-town of Vals (Ardèche) teased him with the suggestion that she had gone gambling in the casino, while describing days traipsing between churches, baths and parks.[28] Caroline Brame, in similar vein, sometimes wrote tenderly of her father, noting the bouquet of flowers he gave her on her eighteenth birthday or the ice creams he bought her on the Parisian boulevards, at others struggling to make him smile or to put up with his colleagues: '18 engineers in the salon. All they do is talk about machines; nothing could be more boring.'[29] The childhood

---

[25] Comtesse de Boigne, *Mémoires*, p. 70; George Sand, *Histoire de ma vie*, p. 152; and Shaw, *Souvenirs*, ch. IX.

[26] See below, pp. 269–76.   [27] Grafteaux, *Mémé Santerre*, pp. 55–8.

[28] Leseur, *Journal d'enfant*, entries for 2 and 14 November 1877; and Jeanne G., *Journal et correspondance de Jeanne G., recueillis et publiés après sa mort* (Marseille: Verdot, 1906), letters to mother of 28 August 1898 and to father of 12 July 1898. See also Desmoulins, *Journal*, entries for 12 and 27 July 1788; and Perrot, 'Enquête', in Brame, *Journal intime*, pp. 175–6, 185–6, and entries for 5 May, 4 and 10 June 1865.

[29] Brame, *Journal intime*, entries for 7 December 1864, 5 May, 4 June and 10 June 1865. See also Desmoulins, *Journal*, passim; and Dauphin et al., *Ces bonnes lettres*, which includes affectionate letters to the Alsatian industrialist Charles Mertzdorff during the 1870s, while he was marooned in Alsace and they were living in Paris.

reminiscences of Simone de Beauvoir suggest a more tender relationship, though again she recorded that during her early years she saw very little of him, as he was away at the law courts all day. 'I found him amusing, and I was pleased whenever he made a fuss of me', she wrote, 'but he didn't play a very well-defined role in my life.' Only when she started going to school, and he could engage with her mind, did he take a closer interest in her, though a 'distance' still lay between them.[30] Finally, there were the absent fathers, who had little influence over their daughters. Besides those who spent their time away at work or drinking with their friends in a café, there was the more modern phenomenon of fathers conscripted into the army for war service. Madeleine Henry (b. 1906) recalled her mother's relief when her father was called up in 1914. Mother and daughter settled into a 'holiday' phase, spared the expense of wine, spirits and tobacco by his absence, relieved of rent payments by the state, and free to run their lives as they pleased.[31]

Fathers and sons

The traditional relationship between a father and his son was influenced, for better or for worse, by the expectation of inheriting land or a business in some circles, or at least the skills necessary for a trade. There was in addition for those of noble birth the need to preserve the lineage from father to son. This latter obligation proved increasingly difficult in French society after 1789. Chateaubriand (b. 1768) sketched in his ancestry, including its two sets of links to the English royal family, 'Geoffroy IV de Chateaubriand having married as his second wife Agnès de Laval, grand-daughter of the Comte d'Anjou and of Mathilde, daughter of Henry I; Marguerite de Lusignan, widow of the King of England and grand-daughter of Louis-le-gros, marrying Geoffroy V, twelfth Baron de Chateaubriand'. He then apologized for such 'puerile recitations', pointing out that they were necessary to convey the abiding passion of his father. This passion he placed at the heart of the drama afflicting his youth and determining the nature of his education. His father was obsessed with the family name. Given the trials and tribulations of the nobility towards the end of the *ancien régime*, the older Chateaubriand developed 'one of the most gloomy characters ever'. The son claimed neither to glorify the old society nor complain of the new, preferring the name François de Chateaubriand to the title Vicomte de Chateaubriand.[32] Stendhal

---

[30] De Beauvoir, *Memoirs of a Dutiful Daughter*, pp. 6, 25 and 36.
[31] Henry, *Little Madeleine*, pp. 98–103.
[32] Chateaubriand, *Mémoires d'outre-tombe*, pp. 34–9. See above, pp. 141–2.

(b. 1783), also looking back on the eighteenth century from the perspective of the nineteenth, reckoned that his father wanted to bequeath a position as *consistorial* in the Parlement, a 'noble distinction' among the lawyers there. He concluded that his father did not love him as an individual, 'but as a son who would carry on his family'.[33]

More tangible inheritances proved easier to manage. The merchant Gustave-Emmanuel Roy (b. 1823) admitted that he was always afraid of displeasing his father, a severe and methodical character, but he could hardly fail to respect such a personage for leaving him and his sister 1.2 million francs at his death.[34] Agricol Perdiguier (1805–75), raised near Avignon as the son of a joiner and smallholder, enthused over the way his father had him and his two brothers working in the fields and in the workshop so that they could learn how to farm and work with wood. In this way he started on his life as a joiner, though he made it clear that his father was too hard on him to make a good teacher. Higher up the social scale, Constant Lepage (b. 1825) left school early to follow his father's wish that he take up an apprenticeship as an *ajusteur mécanicien* (fitter). He thus received a practical training to prepare him for work in the family foundry and machine shop in Le Havre, helped by lessons from his father in technical drawing. In the twentieth century, Ephraïm Grenadou also followed in his father's footsteps, to become a peasant farmer near Chartres. From the age of three or four his father took him out to the fields to watch him work, and when he was ten his father bought him 100 geese. In his teens he learned to be a ploughman by taking over the reins of the horses and labouring beside his father.[35] During the 1950s, a village lad in the Vaucluse presented a pleasing image of continuity in his family of tenant farmers:

My great-grandparents were farmers. My grandparents were farmers. My parents are farmers. My father decided to be a farmer because he liked it and because he didn't know how to do anything else. He learned to farm by working in the fields with his father. I shall be a farmer, too, because I like it. I am learning to be a farmer by helping my father in the fields.[36]

Over the course of the nineteenth and twentieth centuries, however, these links weakened, as the Civil Code made it difficult for fathers to designate an heir, and as, in a more urban and industrial society, sons were less

---

[33] Stendhal, *Henry Brulard*, p. 78.   [34] Roy, *Souvenirs*, p. 11.

[35] Agricol Perdiguier, *Mémoires d'un compagnon* (Paris: Denoel, 1943), pp. 3–16 and 52; and Grenadou and Prévost, *Grenadou*, chs. I–II; Constant Lepage, *Soixante ans de la vie d'un prolétaire* (Paris: L. Vanier, 1900), pp. 15–16.

[36] Wylie, *Village in the Vaucluse*, p. 99.

likely to pursue the same career as their fathers.[37] What counted for the middling classes in particular was academic success, and here fathers had less control, causing anxiety all round.[38] Like their spouses, they did all they could to encourage their sons, but sometimes felt let down. Already, at the end of the *ancien régime*, the lawyer and administrator Jean-Baptiste Carpentier was berating his three sons for their idleness and poor results at their *collèges*. In one of his numerous letters he informed one that his brother was an 'imbecile' who knew nothing, and 'never left the kitchen, his bed and the dining room during his holidays'. As the historian Philippe Marchand observed, Carpentier was in a position to secure his sons a comfortable position in life, but only on condition that they worked for it. During the 1830s and 1840s, a family correspondence reveals the landowner Marie-André-Laurent Odoard seeing his hopes for the future of his eldest son completely dashed. The young Auguste only passed his *baccalauréat* with the supposed 'moral authority' of a family friend who was a member of the Académie behind him, and he eventually gave up his studies for a law degree in Grenoble following some sort of breakdown, a *crise de folie furieuse*. The stricken youth complained to relatives that his parents were making him study a subject that was beyond him.[39]

Attempts by middle-class fathers to form a friendly relationship with sons, as recommended in *Monsieur, madame et bébé*, did not always succeed in reducing the distance between them. As with daughters, sons often found fathers too preoccupied with their work to have much time for them. Jules Michelet (b. 1798) acknowledged that he had a gentle upbringing, but felt that he had perhaps spent too much time with his mother, since his father was nearly always away on business for his printing works. André Gide emphasized the extreme gentleness of his father, but he also wrote:

Preoccupied with the preparation of his course at the Faculty of Law, my father hardly paid any attention to me. He spent the greatest part of the day shut away in a vast, rather dark study, to which I had no access unless invited to enter.

Similarly, Charles Nicolle (b. 1866) described his father as a 'slave to his profession'. As a doctor, a long round of visits, consultations and talks to pharmacists monopolized his day, leaving little time for the young

---

[37] 'La Fin des patriarches', in Delumeau and Roche, *Histoire des pères*, pp. 323–48.
[38] Knibiehler, *Les Pères*, p. 174.
[39] Philippe Marchand, '"Vos importunités, mon fils, m'ennuient": un père et ses enfants au XVIIIe siècle', in Bardet et al., *Lorsque l'enfant grandit*, pp. 437–55; and George, *Chronique intime*, pp. 21–5. See also Catherine Pellissier, 'Loisirs et sociabilités juvéniles au sein du patriciat lyonnais (1848–1914)', in Bardet et al., *Lorsque l'enfant grandit*, pp. 471–86.

Charles. He died young, worn down by his job.[40] Conversely, the tough, masculine world of peasants, artisans and workers in heavy industry did not necessarily exclude tender feelings between fathers and sons. Batisto Bonnet maintained the lyrical tone of his description of a peasant upbringing in the Rhône valley by recording that he idolized his father, despite regular spankings. Georges Navel contrasted the tense relations between his brothers and his father, a foundry worker at Pont-à-Mousson, with his own. As the youngest in the family, he remembered in *Travaux* (1945) little presents of fruit, and time spent dancing on his father's stomach while he lay in bed on a Sunday.[41]

Fathers all too easily lent themselves to depiction as the villains of the piece, in contrast to a virtuous mother, as they neglected or abandoned their families, tyrannized those around them or drank themselves into oblivion. Talleyrand of course stands out as the extreme example of a victim of paternal indifference. He wrote in his memoirs that 'I am, perhaps, the only man of distinguished birth and belonging to a numerous and esteemed family, who did not, for one week in his life, enjoy the sweetness of being under his father's roof.' Such a 'sad and cheerless childhood', he reflected, may at least have strengthened his thinking powers, and prepared him for the misfortunes and disappointments of life.[42] The Comte de Mirabeau (1749–91) was another member of the *ancien-régime* nobility who had a difficult relationship with his father, though in this case it was a matter of excessive severity. The despotic character of the father, a product of his military background and ancient lineage, made him impossible to please. An uncle, replying in 1770 to a long line of letters from the father in which he described his son as a 'wretch', a 'maniac' and a 'sewer', wrote:

For the rest, your son fears you, respects you and loves you, but I believe I have discovered his way of thinking, in showing him affection. I think that, without losing paternal gravity and authority, you should show kindness and an interest in this young man.[43]

Jacques-Louis Ménétra (b. 1738) framed his whole *Journal of My Life* around a tempestuous relationship with his father. The historian Daniel Roche described the work as an attempt to fashion 'a new myth of a motherless Oedipus', following the death of Ménétra's mother when he was two, with the drama entirely played out between father and son. By blackening the character of his father, Jacques-Louis comes out all the

---

[40] Michelet, *Ma jeunesse*, p. 19; Gide, *Si le grain ne meurt*, p. 15; Delay, *André Gide*, ch. 2; and Nicolle, 'Mémoires', pp. 18–20.
[41] Bonnet, *Vie d'enfant*, p. 117; Navel, *Travaux*, ch. 1.
[42] Talleyrand, *Memoirs*, pp. 11–13.   [43] Mirabeau, *Mémoires*, I, p. 350.

better by contrast.[44] Hence he described his father regularly drinking too much, falling into violent, uncontrollable rages, and kicking him out on to the street. Although he followed his father into the glazing trade, he retained his independence by buying his own workshop, instead of following the obvious route of inheriting that of his father.[45] Interviews in Paris during the 1970s with the worker Amedée brought to light another classic boozer. Born in 1865, the father worked at various labouring jobs in Paris, putting in a sixteen-hour day and then going off to the *bistrot* to drink with his workmates. Amedée calculated that his father consumed two to three litres of wine a day, and was drunk five days out of seven. He did not see him as a bad father, feeling loved, but 'the only fault he had, was that he had a hole under his nose, which cost us dear'. Not surprisingly, the father died when Amedée was only thirteen.[46]

Fathers might also appear ineffectual in their paternal role, especially when trying to run a business or cope with an abusive wife and mother. Alphonse Daudet in *Le Petit Chose* (1868) portrayed his father becoming increasingly irascible as the family textile business gradually slid under in the wake of the 1848 Revolution, to the extent that his children crept in fear around him. Eventually members of the family went their separate ways to survive as best they could on their own. Adolphe Orain (b. 1834) described his father as a dreamer who was not cut out for business. While the father sighed night and day over the accounts of his failing tannery in the Breton town of Bain, it fell to his energetic mother to work, raise the family and pay off the debts. Hervé Bazin gave his father short shrift in his account of his long battle with his mother. Near the beginning, Rezeau senior is introduced as head of the family, 'and so unworthy of this title'. He later reflects that his father had for years passively acquiesced in his 'martyrization', and says 'Excuse me for being frank, *papa*. But you are revealing yourself very jealous of an authority that you scarcely exercise.'[47]

Conclusion

By the late eighteenth century, various obstacles were beginning to appear that hindered fathers acting in their traditional role as patriarchs, yet the alternative ideal of the friendly but still authoritative figure was not easy to achieve either. Doubtless it is easy to read history backwards in this area,

[44] Daniel Roche, 'Jacques-Louis Ménétra: An Eighteenth-Century Way of Life', in Ménétra, *Journal of My Life*, pp. 243–358 (pp. 244–5).
[45] Ménétra, *Journal of My Life*, pp. 24–5, 31, 88–9, 155 and 168–9.
[46] Caroux-Destray, *Un couple ouvrier traditionnel*, pp. 42–7.
[47] Daudet, *Petit Chose*, ch. 1; AD Ille-et-Vilaine, 105 J 3, Fonds Adolphe Orain, 'Mes souvenirs', unpubl. MS (1905–6), pp. 6–7; Bazin, *Vipère au poing*, pp. 23 and 145.

and overemphasize early signs of a crisis in paternal identities. During the 1870s, Marie Bashkirtseff might write in the most dismissive terms about her father. She described him as 'dry, bruised, and flattened by the terrible general, his father'. She even boasted of an argument with him during her late teens in which she told him to hold his tongue, and called him impertinent and badly brought-up.[48] However, such a forthright attitude typified the exceptional nature of the Bashkirtseff diary. The historian Michelle Perrot is surely right to assert that 'the father figure dominates the history of private life in the nineteenth century', buttressed by the law, philosophy and politics.[49] One should evidently avoid the simple stereotype of the formidable paterfamilias, given the wide range of feelings aroused by fathers. Nonetheless, the evidence does suggest that most French children continued to view their father as a somewhat remote figure, however loving, either because of an unbending sense of discipline or because of the large amount of time he spent away from home. No less than with mothers, it also reveals children able to form an attachment with fathers in varying contexts, be it the rather fierce approach of, say, many peasants or coalminers, the chaotic and potentially violent stance commonly associated with the very poor, or the gentler but often episodic interventions common among the middle classes. Chateaubriand, writing about an *ancien-régime* upbringing from a nineteenth-century perspective, wondered whether 'children love their parents more today when they *tutoient* them and no longer fear them'. He doubted it, pointing to the fact that while he was treated severely and his friend Gesril was spoiled by his parents, both turned out to be tender and respectful sons.[50]

Relationships with kin

The role of kin in modern society

It must by now be apparent that children in France, as elsewhere in Europe, had a potentially large number of relatives, as well as servants and neighbours, to act as assistants to or even substitutes for parents. Although co-resident kin were rarer than was once thought, this does not mean that social contact with an extended family was missing in the modern period. Kin relations were stronger in the countryside than in the towns, more important for aristocratic families and peasants than for

---

[48] Bashkirtseff, *Journal*, entry for 22 August 1876.
[49] Perrot, 'Roles and Characters', p. 167.
[50] Chateaubriand, *Mémoires d'outre-tombe*, p. 61.

the urban middle classes. In the case of the aristocracy and the upper bourgeoisie, for example, a study by Eric Mension-Rigau has revealed the intense sociability within an exclusive family network of those raised during the Third Republic. At the same time, extended families provided material and emotional support for their members across the social spectrum.[51] This continues to be the case down to the present, though to some extent the welfare state has encroached on their role during the late twentieth century. During the nineteenth century, grandparents took on a new importance for children, shaking off their distant, venerable status in favour of a more approachable image.[52] They often spent time with young children when parents were hard pressed by other tasks, or took over completely in difficult circumstances. Older siblings might take on a parental role, aunts and uncles provided support in various ways, and cousins were often good friends. Uncles, for example, kept cropping up in autobiographies to tell war stories. During the eighteenth century, Chateaubriand had his uncle the Comte de Bedée to boast of his part in the battle of Fontenoy in 1745. Henri Pitaud (b. 1899) could rely on his great-uncle Henri to spin yarns on his time with the Zouaves in Algeria and in the Crimean War: at weddings, the cry would go up, 'Come on! Come on! Uncle Henri, tell us the story of the siege of Sebastopol and the taking of Malakoff.' Antoine Sylvère had his *tontons* Lassalle and Liaude, two men who seemed to him unlikely killers, recounting gory stories of fighting Prussians in 1870.[53] Beyond kin, servants and neighbours could also provide a reassuring human contact.[54] Most 'ego documents' give at least a hint of these networks, and the emotional warmth felt by the child.

Not all was sweetness and light with kin, though this does not alter the underlying importance of these links. Relationships with brothers and sisters were sometimes fraught with tension, as might be expected in any period of history. Emilie Carles, for example, remembered being afraid of her older brother 'playing the heavy' as the son-and-heir, and detesting her foul-tempered older sister.[55] Marcel Proust had a younger brother, Robert, but made no mention of him in *In Search of Lost Time* (1913). Some critics have speculated that this silence revealed a latent jealousy over the affections of his mother, but it seems more likely a matter of aesthetics: according to Jean-Yves Tadié, 'a brother, a contemporary but neither an artist nor a mover in fashionable society, would not have had

[51] Mension-Rigau, *L'Enfance au château*, ch. 4.
[52] Rollet, *Les Enfants au XIXe siècle*, p. 85.
[53] Ibid., p. 50; Pitaud, *Le Pain de la terre*, pp. 31–2; and Sylvère, *Toinou*, pp. 83–4.
[54] Perrot, 'Roles and Characters', pp. 223–39; and Segalen, *Historical Anthropology*, part 1.
[55] Carles, *Wild Herb Soup*, p. 35.

any role to play in this action'.[56] Children also had favourite grandparents, aunts, uncles and cousins, as well as those they disliked or hardly knew. The Breton folklorist Adolphe Orain loved his maternal grandmother, but recalled that his other one reminded him of the fairy Carabosse, on account of her permanent bad temper. He also described his maternal grandfather as a violent and authoritarian character who expected him to read out chapters from a twelve-volume history of the Napoleonic Wars. Orain admitted that he hated Napoleon for the rest of his life.[57] Access to the networks also varied. Marie-Catherine Gardez spent her childhood in Flanders 'with no other joy than the company of my parents', for all of her sisters had left home, and had neither time nor money for visits. Françoise H. spoke in an oral history project of being raised in a 'desert', an isolated hamlet bordering the Beauce and Normandy early in the twentieth century. Her brothers and sisters were too old to be companions, and she had no friends around her. Yet even she had a grandmother to move in with when her parents separated, and a neighbour to rescue her valuables when her house was burned down.[58]

Growing up with kin

Jacques-Louis Ménétra provided an eighteenth-century example of the large and varied network of kin available to help a boy from an artisanal background in Paris. After the death of his mother, when he was two, his maternal grandmother or 'good mother' raised him until he was eleven. She had already revealed her love for him by rescuing him from a nurse whose milk had gone bad, curing him and finding a 'pretty good woman' to continue the nursing. She emerged in his *Journal* as a formidable matriarch, keeping him on the straight-and-narrow with good advice and smoothing relations with his father. She even managed to buy him his master's certificate, as she had done for her four sons, giving him the chance of an independent career as a glazier. Ménétra also benefited from contacts with his four uncles, as they helped him to learn his trade by taking him out on jobs or setting him up with work. The youngest of his uncles, for example, took him off for six weeks while fulfilling a contract at the abbey of Saint-Denis. Two further uncles appeared on his father's side of the family, the country house built by one of them providing a gathering place for the clan. These various uncles spawned cousins,

---

[56] George D. Painter, *Marcel Proust: A Biography* (London: Chatto & Windus, 1959), pp. 5–6; and Jean-Yves Tadié, *Marcel Proust: biographie* (Paris: Gallimard, 1996), pp. 57–61.
[57] Orain, 'Souvenirs', pp. 10–19.
[58] Grafteaux, *Mémé Santerre*, p. 23; and Françoise H., in Germain and de Panafieu, *Mémoire des femmes*, pp. 123–4.

and later nephews and nieces for Ménétra, a basis for further adventures and even sexual conquests in his picaresque account. Chateaubriand gave a rather different account of family contacts in the eighteenth century, from the comfortable vantage point of a Breton noble. During the 1770s, when he was around the age of seven, he and his mother visited his grandmother's house at Plancouët and the nearby chateau belonging to his uncle, the Comte de Bedée. He asserted that going from the family home at Comberg to the chateau at Monchoix was like passing from the desert into society, from a medieval donjon to the villa of a Roman prince. He and numerous cousins made music, danced, hunted and generally enjoyed themselves from morning to night. The only shadow over the festivities was his aunt, Madame de Bedée, justly annoyed that his uncle was insouciantly burning up his wealth. But then she was not without eccentricities of her own, as she always sat with a fierce hunting dog on her lap, and wandered the chateau with her own wild boar.[59]

Peasant memoirs from the nineteenth century sometimes make reference to support from a network of local kin. Antoine Sylvère, as noted already, started his life in the Auvergne during the 1880s with his grandparents, and learned 'a thousand things each more amusing than the other' from a thirteen-year-old farm servant employed by the family. Given his distant relations with his parents, his grandparents were the main focus of his affections during his early childhood:

The visits of le Grand and la Grande stand out at this period; they mark the good days. When they came to the house, the world changed its appearance, life lost its harshness, all the light around became different. Beyond them, I found neither hope nor joy in life.

When an accident with a boiler scalded his leg, aunts and uncles rallied round during his convalescence, bringing him cakes and telling him stories. Yet it was his grandparents who remained the predominant influence on his development. Time spent with them as a young boy learning how to be a farmer was 'incomparable'. His grandfather, he wrote, treated him like a man, explaining his own point of view and his experiences, while listening sympathetically to his grandson's wildest hypotheses. Above all, the grandfather fired him up with a thirst for knowledge of the outside world that he himself conspicuously lacked.[60] Pierre-Jakez Hélias (b. 1914) also gave pride of place to his grandfather, Alain le Goff, in his childhood reminiscences of Brittany. Hélias enjoyed easy relations with both of his parents, yet it was the old 'Horse of Pride' who took charge

---

[59] Chateaubriand, *Mémoires d'outre-tombe*, pp. 48–51.
[60] Sylvère, *Toinou*, pp. 2, 4–5, 20–4, 78–81.

of the education of his grandson before school. His grandfather taught him all the little Breton rhymes, riddles and finger games he needed to master his language, and later plied him with practical advice on village life. Hélias reflected that grandfathers made excellent teachers for their grandsons, since they had few responsibilities, and they advised rather than commanded. Hence he observed that parents were content to leave the two together for a few years until the father felt it was time to take his son in hand: the end of paradise.[61]

However, the extreme mobility in search of work of some workers, or the need to uproot from the land, might make contact with relatives difficult. The father of Jeanne Bouvier worked for the railways when she was born in 1865; switched to another post with the PLM company sixteen months later; returned to his native village to take over a family farm in 1869; and moved again during the mid-seventies when this failed. Kin did not make much of an appearance in her story. The situation of Louise Vanderwielen (b. 1906) in Lille is another case in point. Her mother started life in the care of the Assistance sociale, while her father had run away from his 'bourgeois' family in Brussels to marry beneath himself, thereby severing all ties with his family. The only relatives to intrude into her childhood were an aunt and her family who looked after her in Belgium during an extended period during her adolescence.[62] Conversely, kin might help members of a family to settle when they migrated, with contacts for lodgings and jobs. Martin Nadaud (1815–98) wrote a famous account of an early form of such links, supporting the migrant stonemasons who shuttled between Paris and the Creuse Department. Arriving in Paris for the first time with his father at the age of fourteen, he immediately started work with an uncle and lodged in his house. 'The day after my arrival, I might have thought that I was still in La Martinèche. There I was, at my uncle's home and in the company of his children, two of whom had been born in my father's house, so there was no question of being bored.'[63]

Among the poor, siblings of both sexes often took over childminding duties to release mothers for other duties. Antoine Sylvère recorded the birth of his younger brother as a 'catastrophic event'. At the age of six, he had to spend his evenings after school and the whole of 'interminable Sundays' by the cradle of the baby Damien, 'a most demanding little monster'. To make matters worse, he also had to take on a second infant

---

[61] Hélias, *Horse of Pride*, ch. 2.
[62] Bouvier, *Mes mémoires*, ch. 1; and Vanderwielen, *Lise du plat pays*, pp. 18, 32 and 57–62.
[63] Martin Nadaud, *Léonard, maçon de la Creuse* (Paris: François Maspero, 1977), cited in Traugott, *The French Worker*, p. 197.

that his mother was wet-nursing for a local wholesaler.[64] Others, such as Georges Dumoulin and Jeanne Bouvier, took such tasks more in their stride. The latter recalled that on days when her parents went off to market, during the 1870s in the Isère, she fed and changed her baby brother, as well as providing meals for three farm workers.[65]

For the urban middle classes, kin might have appeared on the surface less important, compared to friends, contacts from work and voluntary associations. Yet a close look reveals the continued importance of extensive family relationships in this milieu. The personal diary of Caroline Brame gives a good indication of the varied social life of an upper-middle-class adolescent during the 1860s. The daughter of an engineer and high-ranking administrator, she described a full round of dinners, balls and excursions with family and friends. At the same time, in her particular case, frequent references to her deceased mother brought an underlying note of sadness to the writing. In Paris, she had her great-uncle Edouard Gatteaux to turn to as a representative of her mother's family: he was 'tender and affectionate'. On her father's side, there was an aunt Céline, who made some attempt to substitute for her mother, and cousin Marie, a good companion even as Caroline felt her slipping away towards marriage. She also looked back with fondness to the chateau at Fontaine, near Lille, where she was reunited with her family each year.[66] One can hardly fail to mention Pierre Loti and his *Le Roman d'un enfant* (1890) in this context. He conveyed a pleasing image of himself as the only child in a household full of grandmothers, aunts and great-aunts, not to mention a much older sister always ready to spoil him.[67] Aristocratic and middle-class families were also likely to keep in touch with kin by a regular exchange of letters. Sometimes they used these to seek favours. Around 1790, Deu de Montigny wrote to his aunt and uncle, Deu de Marsan, from the military school at Brienne asking for help with his military career. He pleaded with them, 'with tears in his eyes', to write to the minister for a place in a regiment. He confessed 'that in the sadness into which I am plunged there are times when I am no longer master of myself and especially when I think that I am the oldest, the most senior, and the biggest in the whole school (*toute lecolle*)'.[68] Other letters to relatives were purely to keep in touch. Louis Veray maintained a long correspondence

---

[64] Sylvère, *Toinou*, pp. 82–8.
[65] Dumoulin, *Carnets de route*, p. 16; and Bouvier, *Mes mémoires*, p. 49.
[66] Perrot, 'Enquête', in Brame, *Journal intime*, pp. 187–9, and especially entries for 25 November 1864, 25 March 1865 and 16 October 1867.
[67] Loti, *Le Roman d'un enfant*, pp. 63–4.
[68] AD Marne, 1 E 140, Deu de Marson, Deu de Montigny to Deu de Marsan, 12 November (c. 1790–1).

with his aunt in Marseille, starting during his time as a *lycéen* in Paris in 1907. He described routine matters such as his train journey back to school, his academic progress and his visits to the theatre. He also at one point 'opened his heart to her', because of her pious readings, confessing his pessimistic view of life, and his strategies for survival in the wider world.[69]

Conclusion

In sum, whatever the ups and downs of relations with parents, French children at all levels of society were likely to have other relatives to help support them. It may well be that in an agrarian society the knowledge and experiences that young people could acquire from older members of their family were more useful to them than they would be today, helping them as peasant farmers, say, and heirs to an oral rather than a literate culture. All the same, for children raised in the towns, the network of kin usually featured prominently in their life story. Relatives might provide useful contacts for a career, but no less important for both upper and lower classes was the emotional warmth of family gatherings. On the other side of the coin, children orphaned or abandoned at an early stage in their lives had to make do with the substitutes for a family provided by charities or the state. As described in a previous chapter, institutional care and placements with families gave such children a chance of making their way in society, though with a definite handicap.[70]

Discipline and control

Some underlying assumptions

'Spare the rod, and spoil the child': this was the fear that had haunted many parents for centuries, exemplified in the story of the condemned man who bit off his father's nose during his final moments on the scaffold for failing to drive out the 'old Adam' during his childhood. However, once people began to doubt the natural perversity of children, as the emphasis on the taint of original sin eased from the eighteenth century onwards, a gentler approach began to make sense.[71] During the 1760s Rousseau worked on the principle that 'as long as children find resistance only in things and never in wills, they will become neither rebellious nor

---

[69] AD Bouches-du-Rhône, 61 J 13, Fonds Veray, letters from Louis Veray to Louise Veray, 1907–30.
[70] See above, pp. 98–9.   [71] See above, pp. 46–51.

irascible'. He wanted them to feel the 'heavy yoke of necessity under which every finite being must bend'. It followed that the parent should never punish children, but rather ensure that they felt the consequences of a bad action. If they broke a window, they would have to sleep in a draught. If they told a lie, they risked not being believed when they told the truth.[72] The spiritual heirs of Rousseau in the nineteenth and twentieth centuries were not necessarily opposed to punishments *per se*, given their practical concerns as teachers and parents, but they criticized traditional efforts to terrify the child into submission. What these educators sought above all was a rationality to any system of punishment, to ensure that it achieved its aim of preventing offences. Félix Hément used his experience in the Parisian school system to write a *Petit traité des punitions et des récompenses* (*Little Treatise on Punishments and Rewards*, 1890). He cited Jean-Jacques to buttress his argument that education should counter bad tendencies in the child and encourage good ones. He wanted children to grasp what was allowed and what was forbidden, acting through a moral sense rather than fear. He opposed hitting children, and only accepted spanking of the very young. He asserted the importance of explaining to children the gravity and consequences of their offences.[73] Jules Vallès mounted a more visceral attack on the corporal punishment of children in *L'Enfant* (1879). He particularly singled out a colleague of his father for his systematic beating of his sons. Terrible cries emerged from his house from time to time, he wrote. Local people pointed out the Villa Bergougnard:

'That is where the philosopher lives, they said stretching their arms towards the villa, that is where M. Bergougnard is writing *On Reason among the Greeks* . . . It is the home of the sage'.

All of a sudden his sons appeared at the window writhing like monkeys and howling like jackals.[74]

Worse, Vallès claimed nothing had made him sadder in his whole life than the vicious beatings of the helpless daughter Louisette. 'She died of sorrow at the age of ten.'

Parental practice

Old habits died hard in France, as elsewhere in Europe and North America, when parents confronted their unruly offspring.[75] Fathers

---

[72] Rousseau, *Emile*, pp, 66, 91 and 101. See above, pp. 52–4.

[73] Félix Hément, *Petit traité des punitions et des récompenses à l'usage des maîtres et des parents* (Paris: Georges Carré, 1890), passim.

[74] Vallès, *L'Enfant*, p. 219.

[75] See, for example, Linda A. Pollock, *Forgotten Children: Parent–Child Relations from 1500 to 1900* (Cambridge: Cambridge University Press, 1983), ch. 5; and Elizabeth Pleck,

tended to see discipline as their responsibility, but inevitably mothers and, to a lesser extent, other relatives were also involved. The traditional patriarch tended to enforce his authority with the rod – though they were not necessarily as harsh as they first sounded, since contemporaries frequently used the word *fouetter* (to whip) to mean spank or beat with a switch.[76] The Marquis de Mirabeau insisted that his son's teachers punish him regularly, inviting the notoriously tough Abbé Choquard to deal out extra punishments in the younger Mirabeau's case. The Abbé claimed to have 'broken him in and more than half reined him back'. Rétif de Bretonne described another grim eighteenth-century regime, whereby his father announced the sentence of a beating for his children a week in advance, and then spared them, applied a moderate chastisement or a 'rigorous' one according to their behaviour in between. Rétif added that his father reserved the 'whip' for serious offences, and that he had only endured it twice himself.[77] More common, notably in peasant and working-class circles, was testimony from both men and women that their parents had routinely enforced discipline by slapping and beating them. Doubtless this was more often threatened than carried out, and considered normal by everyone concerned. All the same, it was part and parcel of a relationship in which children were expected to submit without question to the parental will through a mixture of fear and love. Ephraïm Grenadou (b. 1897) recalled that after school:

If I forgot to do my work around the house, my father measured me up when he came home. He said to me:
   'Go and get the nettles.'
   I collected some nettles from behind the barn, I put them on the table and I waited.
   'Take down your trousers.'
   I was not really afraid. He gave the orders, and then he struck. My buttocks remained red for a week. My mother did not dare say anything, she only looked to see if I was harmed. This happened two or three times a year.

Emilie Carles described a similar regime in her Alpine village, with the slightest fault met with a slap on both cheeks or a spanking with nettles. Françoise H. informed her interviewer that she had wanted to give up her work as a dressmaker during her early teens, a little before the First World War, but dared not oppose the will of her mother. 'My mother said to me, "If you do that, you will have a spanking and then drink only

---

Domestic Tyranny: The Making of Social Policy against Family Violence from Colonial Times to the Present (New York: Oxford University Press, 1987), passim.

[76] The same usage applied in English: see Pollock, *Forgotten Children*, pp. 200–1.

[77] Mirabeau, *Mémoires*, pp. 247–9 and 276–7; and Rétif de la Bretonne, *Vie de mon père*, pp. 144–5.

water."'[78] At the extreme, Emile Nouguier (b. 1878) wrote of the way his father invariably punished him by making him kneel bare-kneed on sharp triangles of wood, knives or even burning coals. 'When he saw me weaken a wicked smile played on his lips and I thought I understood that he took pleasure in my sufferings.' Not surprisingly, he began to hate this sadistic father, a clerk in the Prefecture in Lyon.[79]

Other parents, whether by conviction or temperament, were less inclined to resort to corporal punishment. Marie-Catherine Gardez (b. 1891) spoke of a loving relationship with her father, a handloom weaver, without the least *beigne* (blow). 'He earned our respect by his austere habits which alas not all of the family heads in our group of houses had.'[80] Georges Navel remembered his father as a rather terrifying figure, wheezing heavily and reeking of dust from the foundry at Pont-à-Mousson, but he gave no recollection in his novel *Travaux* (1945) of ever being beaten at home. By the nineteenth century, middle-class parents were more inclined to use reason and close supervision of their children than corporal punishment.[81] Charles Nicolle, for example, wrote as the son of a doctor in Rouen that his mother never slapped him and that his father had only spanked him once, when he made a nuisance of himself while his brother was ill.[82]

Childhood reminiscences suggest a general attitude of resignation to corporal punishment, where it existed. But when the authors felt that a parent had abused their authority, as in the case of a Jules Vallès or a Hervé Bazin, they made clear their indignation. Where they wished to convey an almost idyllic view of their childhood, they glossed over it easily enough. Batisto Bonnet (b. 1844) claimed his fair share of beatings with a switch and kicks up the backside, but he cited the old French adage that 'he who loves well chastises well'. Similarly, Marie-Juliette Barrié (b. 1919) described her childhood in southern France as a series of mischievous escapades invariably followed by a spanking. Pierre-Jakez Hélias observed that none of the children around him held a grudge against parents or schoolteachers who chastised them for their faults: 'we paid the price and that was that'.[83] There was the occasional hint of

---

[78] Grenadou and Prévost, *Grenadou*, p. 15; Carles, *Wild Herb Soup*, p. 35; and Françoise H., in Germain and de Panafieu, *Mémoire des femmes*, p. 124. See also Wylie, *Village in the Vaucluse*, p. 53.

[79] Philippe Artières (ed.), *Livre des vies coupables*, p. 88.

[80] Grafteaux, *Mémé Santerre*, p. 14.

[81] Navel, *Travaux*, pp. 29 and 33; Crubellier, *L'Enfance et la jeunesse*, pp. 52–3.

[82] Nicolle, 'Mémoires', pp. 41–2.

[83] Bonnet, *Vie d'enfant*, p. 117; Barrié, *Quand les bananes*, passim; and Hélias, *Horse of Pride*, p. 143.

rebellion. The brother of Poil de Carotte, for example, saw off his mother when she tried to beat him by arming himself with a broomstick. Georges Navel, in *Travaux* (1945), depicted the family helping his brother escape from the house when his father tried to attack the thirteen-year-old lad with a pickaxe handle for running off with a circus. André Chamson boasted in *Le Chiffre de nos jours* (1954) that he would continue to hit his own face when his mother hesitated to slap him further. If he were forbidden dessert, he would refuse to eat for two days. 'I had grasped that in pushing a punishment to absurd levels, you made it monstrous.'[84] Otherwise, twentieth-century writers could hardly fail to be aware that public opinion was hardening against the harsh punishments that they had experienced early in life. Emilie Carles pronounced herself against physical violence, but she wrote of her father, 'He was not cruel, but we were entitled to it [punishment] like everyone else. That was the rule; children were beaten much more than they are today.'[85]

'Fear and irony'

Besides physical threats, parents traditionally resorted to a series of bogey-men and sarcastic comments to keep young children in order. Curiously, historians have regularly followed the ethnologist Arnold Van Gennep in asserting that the resort to fear and irony were peculiarly French procedures. Evidence from elsewhere suggests that this was a curiously insular view from Van Gennep, for such stratagems were common currency among populations still wedded to an oral culture.[86] He based this judgement on very thin evidence: a single quotation from one Mme Vernay, an Austrian woman married to a Breton.[87] All the same, folklorists did bring to light a splendid array of fairies, goblins, *croque-mitaines* (bogeymen), *loups-garous* (werewolves), *lumerottes* (will-o'-the-wisp) and other supernatural beings, deployed to keep children away from dangerous places such as rivers and woods. In the Breton Department of the Morbihan, children were discouraged from going out at night with threats of the *bugul-noz*, or werewolf; in the Ardèche disobedient children were faced

---

[84] Jules Renard, *Poil de carotte* (Paris: Garnier-Flammarion, 1965), p. 122; Navel, *Travaux*, p. 21; and André Chamson, *Le Chiffre de nos jours: roman* (Paris: Gallimard, 1954), pp. 86–7.

[85] Carles, *Wild Herb Soup*, p. 35.

[86] See, for example, Peter N. Stearns and Timothy Haggerty, 'The Role of Fear: Transitions in American Emotional Standards for Children, 1850–1950', *American Historical Review*, 96 (1991), 63–94; and Rudolf M. Dekker, *Childhood, Memory and Autobiography in Holland* (Basingstoke: Macmillan, 2000), ch. 10.

[87] Van Gennep, *Manuel*, I, pp. 156–7.

with *lou potoro*, a bogeyman; a female version, *Kludde*, presided over parts of the Nord.[88] Parents also relished rather cruel and humiliating responses to children in distress: to a child who was bleeding, 'that will make a good black pudding!' for example, or to a girl who had pricked her finger while sewing, 'be careful, your guts will come out there!'[89] Educated opinion bristled at such attempts to play on the imaginary fears of children. How the supposed 'victims' reacted is impossible to say. They must have felt the sting of parental disapproval, but at the same time, they had a fascination with the supernatural – and with blood and gore. Pierre-Jakez Hélias happily recounted tales of the Man with Carrot Fingers, a tall figure in a cloak and hat who liked to play tricks on travellers caught on their own at night.[90] But then by the early twentieth century the whole popular culture on which such beliefs rested was beginning to fade. The menace had gone.

Conclusion

What stands out when one looks closely at the experience of growing up in a family in modern France is the variety of 'paths' taken by the different social 'classes'. These ranged from the model of the aloof and all-powerful patriarch, characteristic of landowning families, the similarly authoritarian and inflexible father figure common among workers, and the more amiable 'new father' produced by the Enlightenment. There was always a risk that fathers would abuse their authority and their physical strength to tyrannize the young. However, there was some protection from mothers and other relatives, and eventually in the late nineteenth century the state began to lend its weight with a series of laws protecting children. As in the case of mothers, children proved adaptable, finding security in relationships with an assortment of domestic tyrants, rough diamonds and dedicated careerists, as well as more easy-going characters. At the same time, they drew lines to separate out parents and relatives who went beyond reasonable limits in their relationships. There was much discussion of the trend towards informality and affection in family relations, linked to a more benign view of the 'innocent' child. In a modern egalitarian society, most people would consider this an improvement. A 'long' childhood implied a commitment by parents to investing in the future of

---

[88] J. Frison, 'Les Etres fantastiques du Morbihan', series on 'Mythologie et folklore de l'enfance', *Revue des traditions populaires*, 22 (1907), 247–8; Pierre Charrié, *Le Folklore du Haut-Vivarais* (Paris: FERN, 1968), p. 194; and Arnold Van Gennep, *Le Folklore de la Flandre et du Hainaut français* (2 vols., Paris: Maisonneuve, 1935–6), I, p. 671.

[89] Van Gennep, *Manuel*, I, pp. 159–60.   [90] Hélias, *Horse of Pride*, pp. 6–7.

their child, though there was always a risk of tensions over whether sons in particular were making the most of their educational opportunities. At the same time, the forces of inertia were strong in the area of child rearing, with a hard edge to the relationship still evident in many families during the early twentieth century. At least children usually had an array of kin, neighbours and in some cases servants to turn to for support when they felt they needed it.

8   'Small memories' from childhood[1]

On his first sighting of the sea, early in his childhood, Pierre Loti (1850–1923) claimed that he had 'an elusive foreboding that one day it would take me, despite all my hesitations, despite the will that tried to hold me back'. Running like a red thread through his *Le Roman d'un enfant* (1890) were dreams of distant, sun-baked lands, the troubling and magic associations of the word 'colonies', the 'latent' desire to join the groups of sailors that went past his house on the Ile d'Oleron. One hardly needs reminding that these were the childhood reminiscences of a naval officer.[2] Writers of an autobiography inevitably know the end of their story. Our task in this chapter and the next is to follow in their footsteps in an effort to recreate a sense of the unfolding of the world during the early years. Childhood starts in the home, but it soon extends into the neighbourhood and the local *pays*. The family gradually yields ground to the society of other children and youth. Dependence becomes mingled with elements of independence, reassuring memories of loved ones run into more disturbing ones such as those of death and solitude. In the longer term, as will emerge in Part III of this work, children would have to cope with the peculiar world of the school system, and the need to earn a living. They might already live on a farm or in a mining community, and be half-immersed in its routines, or they might dream of escape to the big city and beyond. One can start to see the outline of various strategies open to writers of autobiographies, as they depict themselves as, say, victims of a harsh childhood on the way to political militancy, ambitious 'men on the make' or bookish middle-class youths retreating into the world of the intellect.

Living in a material world

The small world of the child in the first instance centred on basic desires for food and warmth. Many children of the 'popular classes' struggled

---

[1] Stendhal, *Henry Brulard*, p. 47.
[2] Loti, *Le Roman d'un enfant*, pp. 51, 54, 85–7 and 117.

to keep body and soul together, even in the early twentieth century. Those looking back on a childhood among, say, small sharecroppers or unskilled labourers, provided vivid testimony on a harsh, poverty-stricken world that the modern reader was unlikely to have encountered. This was a world of poor housing, sparse meals and hand-me-down clothing. Richard N. Coe perceptively noted the correlation between the poverty of a childhood and the intensity of detailed observation appearing in the reminiscences of an adult. In his own words, 'the wealthier child who is surrounded by a multitude of frequently changed objects, and who travels comfortably and regularly, tends to be less deeply, less "existentially," aware of the tiny but significant details of his surrounding world than is the child of the slum or the subsistence-level village'.[3] Economic development from the eighteenth century onwards brought gradual improvements to the standard of living of the French population. However, these ebbed and flowed over time and were far from evenly distributed across the various socio-economic groups in society. Hence there were massive disparities between accounts from poor children of begging food and from the rich of being forced on principle to eat dishes they disliked.

Housing

The grim housing conditions endured by many among the 'popular classes' proved particularly difficult to overcome until the middle of the twentieth century. In the villages, there was a huge diversity in the style and quality of houses according to region and social background. The nineteenth century did bring some advances, notably from the 1860s onwards. In the Mantois, for example, the folklorist Eugène Bougeâtre gave an idea of the limited progress involved, mentioning extra sleeping space, covered latrines and dung-heaps sited away from doorways.[4] Henri Pitaud (b. 1899), a future pioneer of peasant syndicalism, emphasized the contrast between the pleasing image of a 'Belle Epoque' during his childhood, and the continuing misery of the agricultural labourer. His 'trou de maison' in the Vendée, a 'hole' to live in, was a hovel consisting of a kitchen and a 'belle chambre' (bedroom) with a stable, a garden and a chicken run attached. Ephraïm Grenadou (b. 1897) recalled his upbringing in a similar house in the Beauce, with a tiny bedroom and a

---

[3] Coe, *When the Grass was Taller*, p. 206.
[4] Eugène Bougeâtre, *La Vie rurale dans le Mantois et le Vexin au XIXe siècle* (Meudon: Collection de travaux et de documents pour servir à l'histoire du Mantois et du Vexin, 1971), p. 23. See also Georges Duby and Armand Wallon (eds.), *Histoire de la France rurale*, vol. III, *Apogée et crise de la civilisation paysanne, 1789–1914* (Paris: Seuil, 1976), pp. 318–23.

main room known as 'la maison'. Pressure on space meant that for most of his childhood and adolescence he slept in a stable. Keeping warm in these circumstances was difficult. The extreme conditions of an Alpine village exacerbated this problem: during the 1900s families like those of Emilie Carles closed off the colder rooms in their house and crowded for warmth into the kitchens and stables. Such primitive surroundings were not entirely uncongenial. Pierre-Jakez Hélias (b. 1914) pointed out that the beaten-earth floor of his Breton house was cold for a child learning to walk, especially if you sat down with a bare bottom, but easy to look after. If he peed on it, a handful of sawdust and a few sweeps of a brush were the end of the matter.[5]

The towns also struggled with a housing crisis during the first half of the twentieth century, as the 'rural exodus' gained momentum.[6] People with urban working-class backgrounds recalled cramped quarters, plus the peculiar smells swirling around their houses. René Michaud banged the drum of the militant in describing the squalid living conditions in the Thirteenth Arrondissement, in the south of Paris, at the beginning of the twentieth century. Many of the inhabitants were migrants from the countryside like himself. His family of four lived in a small lodging with a kitchen and a bedroom in the rue Charles Berthau. He lingered on the disgusting latrines in his building, one set for sixty people, with their flaking paint, dirty finger marks, graffiti and repulsive fumes. He even waxed lyrical over the joys of stepping into the backyard in the countryside:

For ordinary folk like us, transplanted peasants (*culs-terreux*), shaped by rustic habits that required you to 'go' outside, in the midst of nature, on a pile of manure or sometimes, among the most advanced, in a *cabane* at the end of the garden, with the buzzing of huge bluebottles, more than the discomfort, it was the concentrated stench that oppressed us.

The smells from the '*wécé*' engulfed the surrounding lodgings, mingling with others left over from cooking, clothes washing, coal fires and urine in the corridors. At least it was never boring. The neighbours entertained each other with a 'cinéma vérité' of drunken arguments, clowning from kids and banter with young women.[7] 'Sixty years of combat and solidarity' in the mining industry had not dimmed memories of conditions in the terraced housing of Liéven for Augustin Visieux (b. 1909). He

[5] Pitaud, *Le Pain de la terre*, pp. 14–17; Grenadou and Prévost, *Grenadou*, pp. 11–12; Carles, *Wild Herb Soup*, p. 17; and Hélias, *Horse of Pride*, pp. 48–9. See also Lejeune, *Calicot*, pp. 19–22.

[6] Georges Duby (ed.), *Histoire de la France urbaine*, vol. IV, *La Ville de l'âge industriel: le cycle haussmannien* (Paris: Seuil, 1983), pp. 314–37.

[7] Michaud, *J'avais vingt ans*, pp. 12–20.

recalled houses in the *corons* reeking of a potent mixture of fried onions, garlic, the '*purlage*' or liquid manure spread over the soil, and on Mondays and Tuesdays, the lingering smell of washing. Fortunately for the young Visieux, he was brought up in a separate house provided by the mining company, because his father was a skilled and respectable family man.[8]

The occasional writer takes the reader back to the more luxurious surroundings of a middle-class childhood. Pierre Loti fondly recalled Sunday evenings with his parents, when he spent time with them instead of having to do homework:

> The *salon* for these evenings, as I knew it then, was large and appeared to me immense. It was very simple, but had a certain good taste in the arrangement: the walls and the wood of the doors were brown with fine threads of matt gold; the furniture had red velvet, which must have dated from the time of Louis-Philippe; there were family portraits, in austere black and gold frames; on the fireplace, there were serious-looking bronzes; and in the middle of the table, in a place of honour, a big sixteenth-century Bible, a venerable relic from our Huguenot ancestors persecuted for their faith; and flowers, always baskets and vases of flowers, at a time when the fashion for them was not as widespread as it is today.

The stage was set for little games in the family circle: 'everything had a good atmosphere of peace and comfort'.[9] André Gide (b. 1869) found the study of his father, a professor in the Faculty of Law in Paris, more intimidating. He entered it reverentially like a temple, remembering the thick carpet that deadened his footsteps; a lectern near one of the windows, and an enormous table covered in books and papers. In this case, the setting led inexorably to readings from uplifting books.[10] True to the spirit of childhood, a Professor of Medicine at the Collège de France gave a brief review of the varied latrines in his homes during his childhood in Normandy. Charles Nicolle (b. 1866) made no mention of overpowering fumes, coming from the well-heeled family of a doctor. However, he remembered his first as one that was too dark to read in, another papered floor to ceiling in illustrated newspapers, and one that had such a huge opening that it required careful manoeuvring to avoid falling into the ancient drains underneath. He also liked the twin ones in a friend's

---

[8] Augustin Visieux, *Mineur de fond: fosses de Lens: soixante ans de combat et de solidarité* (Paris: Plon, 1991), pp. 13–15 and 30. See also Navel, *Travaux*, p. 41, for a similar description of slums in Lyon during the First World War.

[9] Loti, *Le Roman d'un enfant*, pp. 112–14. See also Roy, *Souvenirs*, pp. 17–18, for a description of his grandparents' house in the Marais district of Paris.

[10] Gide, *Si le grain ne meurt*, pp. 14–16.

house: a locked one for Madame, and another for the husband, the servants and visitors.[11]

Childhood reminiscences did not spend much time on washing and personal hygiene. For a poor villager like Antoine Sylvère, looking back to the *fin-de-siècle* Auvergne, the question of cleaning up only arose on a Sunday. On that day a large bowl was cleared of the food scraps it usually held, and all members of the family washed themselves in the warmth of the cowshed. At the same time his mother would wash his hair and smear on a grey ointment in an uphill battle against lice. Baths and toothbrushes were unknown to him. As a doctor, and son of a doctor, Charles Nicolle could write of the same period that it was still a stranger to hygiene. He at least, when a child, had had a washbasin, sponge, comb, hairbrush and toothbrush, plus a monthly visit to the Corneille Baths. As for the high aristocracy, it wallowed in a form of luxurious living that did not involve much washing. In 1900 the family of Pauline de Broglie was put on the spot when her doctor recommended taking a bath to help her recover from a bout of measles. No one in her family ever bathed. The only solution was to hire a portable tin bath. She noted that when her family restored their chateau in Anjou, they installed the latest 'modern comforts, but that meant a 'WC à l'anglaise' and a hot-water system, not a bathroom.[12]

Food

As far as getting enough to eat was concerned, all the quantitative evidence points to steady progress in the long term for the French population. Improvements in the organization of the market during the eighteenth century smoothed the jagged peaks in the mortality rate caused by subsistence crises.[13] The coming of the railways and new agricultural techniques at home and abroad ensured a regular grain supply from the 1850s onwards. The upshot was that the average intake of calories of the French population reached a 'desirable' level in the 1880s.[14] Yet the popular diet for long remained heavily dependent on carbohydrates and fats,

---

[11] Nicolle, 'Mémoires', p. 80.

[12] Sylvère, *Toinou*, pp. 101 and 155; Nicolle, 'Mémoires', pp. 52–3; Pange, *1900*, I, pp. 195–6.

[13] See Jacques Dupâquier et al. (eds.), *Histoire de la population française*, vol. II, *De la Renaissance de 1789* (Paris: Presses Universitaires de France, 1988), passim; and Jacques Dupâquier, 'Demographic Crises and Subsistence Crises in France, 1650–1725', in John Walter and Roger Schofield (eds.), *Famine, Disease and the Social Order in Early Modern Society* (Cambridge: Cambridge University Press, 1989), pp. 189–99.

[14] J.-C. Toutain, *La Consommation alimentaire en France de 1789 à 1964* (Geneva: Droz, 1970), passim; Bartolomé Bennassar and Joseph Guy, 'Consommation alimentaire

with insufficient milk, lean meat and fresh fruit and vegetables. Children in particular suffered from these imbalances in the diet.

On the one hand, then, it is not surprising to find Georges Navel in *Travaux* (1945) depicting the son of a labourer in the Pont-à-Mousson ironworks proclaiming that as a child during the 1900s he never went hungry. The boy was aware that his mother sometimes struggled to pay the rent and the grocer's bill, but he asserted that there was plenty of food around, helped by the fact that the family kept a pig, plus some chickens and rabbits. By the early twentieth century, sons of miners in the northern coalfields lived on a substantial diet that prepared them for their turn in the pits. Augustin Visieux described a typical lunch of stew made from hunks of bacon with cabbage, turnips, celery, carrots, haricot beans and potatoes, supplemented with bread. In the evening there might be a supper of red herrings with potatoes and onions, or a salad with hard-boiled eggs or cheese, followed by a rhubarb tart.[15] As for the children of the middle and upper classes, they might occasionally fret over being forced to eat dishes they hated, but they could take their meals for granted. The historian Michelle Perrot noted that the diary of Caroline Brame treated dinners as a time to meet the family and visitors rather than to eat food. At the very top of the social hierarchy, the Comtesse Jean de Pange (born Pauline de Broglie) recalled an *haute cuisine* from the 1900s that has long disappeared. At both midday and evening meals there were always seven or eight dishes on offer, including an *entrée*, a serving of meat with potatoes, roast game, a plate of vegetables and assorted *entremets* such as enormous puddings, sorbets, *soufflés*, *charlottes*, *bavaroises*, ices and cakes. As a child, she was free to eat what she liked, though she was excluded from the animated conversation of the adults around her.[16]

On the other hand, it is equally unsurprising to hear the children of the poor complaining of not having enough to eat. Both Jean-Marie Déguignet and Henri Pitaud wrote of children having to go around their villages begging food from neighbours. The former, around 1840, doubt-less cut a pitiful figure in his Breton village, aged six but 'no taller than a riding boot'. 'Every day then I went to the local farmers asking for a dinner, and often, having filled my belly with gruel, they gave me some more pieces of black bread and mouldy crêpes to take home.'[17]

(XIVe–XIXe siècle)', *Annales ESC*, 30 (1975), 402–30; Duby and Wallon (eds.), *Histoire de la France rurale*, pp. 327–33.

[15] Navel, *Travaux*, pp. 29–30; Visieux, *Mineur de fond*, p. 30; Lengrand and Craipeau, *Louis Lengrand*, p. 15.

[16] Vallès, *L'Enfant*, p. 108; Brame, *Journal intime*, p. 178; and Pange, *1900*, I, pp. 27–9.

[17] Déguignet, *Mémoires d'un paysan*, pp. 27–8. See also Pitaud, *Le Pain de la terre*, p. 18, referring to the children of the very poor rather than himself.

Pierre-Jakez Hélias reported that even though families in the pays Bigouden of Brittany were smaller after the First World War, the returning soldiers still found themselves struggling with poverty: *la chienne du monde*. 'Give us each day our daily bread' was a prayer that came from the heart among the poor. Children soon learned that bread was Paradise on Earth, a food to be eaten slowly and carefully savoured. To supplement their meagre rations, Hélias added, the children of the poor scoured the countryside for fruit and edible plants. They drank the 'sugared milk' of honeysuckle, treated the seeds of pine cones as a dessert, ate any wild peas they came across, added salt to cowslip, and gathered sorrel, medlar fruit, bilberries, beech-nuts and blackberries.[18] If the poorest diets were largely to be found among the poorer peasantry, the urban working classes were not necessarily much better off. Louise Vanderwielen (b. 1906) wrote that on Saturday evenings the inhabitants of her *courette* in Lille clustered round a fire to boil potatoes, supplemented with little smoked herrings and lemonade bought from the local publican. That was her best supper of the week.[19]

Clothing

Finally, clothing emerges in childhood reminiscences as partly a matter of keeping dry and warm, partly one of not looking outlandish. Before that, though, there was the important transition for boys from a simple robe to trousers, and the need to master dressing and undressing alone. Antoine Sylvère had painful memories of struggling with breeches that were cut generously to allow for his growth, to the extent that he could not reach the buttons to the braces on his back. Caught short at school during an attack of diarrhoea, the nuns humiliated him by inviting his classmates to parade in front of him one by one to sniff his 'infamy'.[20] Children of the poor had to make do with eminently practical clothing, made of sturdy material and passed down from older to younger siblings. Emilie Carles had painful memories of the big, hobnailed boots she had to wear all the time. 'I was condemned to wear boots passed down from my elder brothers and sisters, shapeless old clodhoppers that battered my feet. It was inevitable; I was the fifth in the family and those shoes were so sturdy, in such good condition, that there was always a pair to finish off.' The boys in her village wore trousers made from thick corduroy or blue duck, and heavy shirts. Girls went around in dresses made from thick serge material, plain and almost indestructible, covered by a

---

[18] Hélias, *Horse of Pride*, pp. 226–30.   [19] Vanderwielen, *Lise du plat pays*, pp. 22.
[20] Hélias, *Horse of Pride*, pp. 50–1; and Sylvère, *Toinou*, pp. 54–6. See above, pp. 79–80.

smock.[21] This was not necessarily comfortable, but the children were inconspicuous among their own. Problems arose at school if they found themselves surrounded by wealthier and more smartly dressed peers. At primary level, this was not a problem, since all French schoolchildren wore a black alpaca apron from the neck to the knees.[22] However, Alphonse Daudet had the protagonist in *Le Petit Chose* (1868) acquire his nickname ('little thingammy') when he emerged as the only boy in his *collège* wearing a smock, the uniform of a street child in Lyon. At the other extreme were the fiendish devices to mould the bodies of young girls from the upper classes. At the age of six, the future Comtesse de Genlis was wearing a whalebone corset that pressed too tightly, shoes that pinched her feet, huge numbers of curling papers in her hair, an iron necklace so that she would not look provincial, and spectacles to correct a squint. Looking back from the 1820s, she still had vivid memories of these 'tortures'.[23]

If the poor risked looking uniformly drab, middle-class children might feel conspicuous when parental tastes were imposed on them. Jules Vallès took revenge on his mother by depicting himself as a victim of her lethal combination of penny-pinching and a bizarre dress sense. An absurd scene in *L'Enfant* (1879) had the protagonist turning up to the annual prize-giving dressed in a top hat, a frock-coat with special green buttons that she had sewn on, shaped like gherkins, and white trousers with straps under the shoes. When one of these latter snapped and his trousers rode up his leg, the order went out, 'remove the child with the gherkins'.[24] André Gide (b. 1869) admitted that he was sensitive about what he wore, suffering badly if he was hideously dressed, which may mean that he was another extreme case. Nonetheless, it is hard to imagine a boy taking to the garments chosen for him by his mother:

I therefore wore small tight jackets, short trousers, tight at the knees and striped socks; excessively short socks that looked like a tulip and hung down sadly or went back into the shoes to hide. I have saved the most horrible part for the end: it was the starched shirt.

Understandably, he bemoaned having to wear a starched shirt, like a white breastplate, every day of the year, whether he was studying or playing. On top of that there was a stiff, detachable collar, usually the wrong size for the shirt and so doubly uncomfortable, and a 'ridiculous little bowler hat'.[25] At the same period, Colette (1873–1954) revealed the delight of

[21] Carles, *Wild Herb Soup*, pp. 36–7.
[22] Julian Green, *Memories of Happy Days* (New York: Harper, 1942), p. 103.
[23] Genlis, *Mémoires*, I, pp. 40–1.   [24] Vallès, *L'Enfant*, pp. 47–52 and 137–8.
[25] Gide, *Si le grain ne meurt*, pp. 84–5.

an adolescent in the newly available fashionable clothing, girls of thirteen or fourteen with their hair up in a chignon, a leather belt buckled to the last hole, painful shoes and cropped hair. She even staged a family row, with her mother warning of the moral dangers of overdressing. When 'Minet-Chéri' wanted a chignon, high heels and a mohair blouse, like one of her friends at school, her mother argued that all this would lead inexorably to secret letters, lovers reeking of cheap wine and cigars, and later an illicit, puny child.[26]

Illness and death

Premature death

The various 'ego documents' concerning children in France provide compelling evidence of the fragility of life, particularly among the poor, up until the early twentieth century. Writers frequently recorded the number of their brothers and sisters who died young. Among the peasantry and rural artisans, for example, Agricol Perdiguier (b. 1805) mentioned two out of his mother's nine children failing to survive, Jean-Marie Déguignet (b. 1834) two out of five, Jeanne Bouvier (b. 1865) one out of three, and Marie-Juliette Barrié (b. 1919), two out of eight.[27] Sometimes they also mentioned the grief brought on by such deaths. Measles carried off the little brother of Jeanne Bouvier when he was sixteen months old:

I sensed that something strange was happening. The curtains of the little bed were drawn, a candle burned on a table covered with white linen, a branch of boxwood was soaking in a saucer full of holy water. The women of the neighbourhood came to visit my mother. They would spread the curtains of the little bed, say a prayer, and sprinkle a few drops of holy water. Then they would speak a few words of consolation to my mother and her sobs would redouble.

Madeleine Henry managed to survive being very ill with diphtheria, in Paris a little before the First World War, but her little brother did not. For entire afternoons, she wrote, her mother 'would howl with pain, like a she-wolf barking, or again, her head in her hands, her whole frail body

---

[26] Colette, *La Maison de Claudine*, in *Oeuvres complètes*, vol. VII (Paris: Le Fleuron, 1949 (1922)), pp. 90 and 108. See also Guillaumin, *Life of a Simple Man*, p. 128. The 'new code of appearances' for young women under the Third Republic, as regional dress gave way to Paris-based fashions, is discussed in Anne-Marie Sohn, *Chrysalides: femmes dans la vie privée (XIXe–XXe siècles)* (2 vols., Paris: Publications de la Sorbonne, 1996), I, pp. 486–93.

[27] Agricol Perdiguier, *Mémoires d'un compagnon* (Paris: Denoel, 1943 (1854)), p. 3; Déguignet, *Mémoires d'un paysan*, p. 27; Bouvier, *Mes mémoires*, p. 36; and Barrié, *Quand les bananes*, p. 7.

would shake with heaving sobs'. Pierre Loti, from a relatively affluent background, described the death of his young friend Lucette as 'one of the first real sorrows of a small boy'.[28] Writers of autobiographies had to survive into adulthood, but not all of the diarists did so. Jeanne G., the daughter of a naval officer in Marseille, died of typhoid fever at the age of fifteen in 1900. This allowed Catholic priests to promote her as a 'celestial child' able to speak to the souls of children. Marie Bashkirtseff recorded her own descent into tuberculosis during her late teens and twenties, before succumbing to the disease in 1884. In 1883 she wrote with a despondent air:

Dying? I am very afraid of it. And I do not want it. It would be dreadful. I do not know what contented people do; but I find plenty to complain of since expecting nothing from God. When this supreme refuge is missing, there is nothing for it but to die. Without God, there can be no poetry, no tenderness, no genius, no love, no ambition.[29]

The context for these accounts was a long-term decline in mortality among children and adolescents from the middle of the eighteenth century onwards, to be set against persistent social inequalities in death rates, and high infant mortality lasting through until the early twentieth century. The infant mortality rate in France began at around 300 infant deaths per 1,000 live births in the middle of the eighteenth century. The period 1795 to 1825 brought a slight decline in the rate, but it levelled off for much of the nineteenth century, and even increased slightly between 1850 and 1880. This rise also occurred in England and Wales, and is probably attributable to the impact of early industrialization and urbanization. The infant mortality rate only achieved a sustained decline from the 1880s onwards, though it remained a little higher than countries such as England and Sweden. The male infant mortality rate in France stood at around 185 per 1,000 live births in 1895; by the 1970s it was down to 13 per 1,000.[30] Children aged five to fifteen fared better, in that their mortality rate declined in the nineteenth as well as in the late eighteenth century, indeed outstripping all other age groups. By 1913, the age group five to ten years had recorded the largest fall in the risk of dying, with

---

[28] Bouvier, *Mes mémoires*, pp. 36–7, as transl. in Traugott, *The French Worker*, p. 338; Henry, *Little Madeleine*, p. 45; Loti, *Le Roman d'un enfant*, p. 52. See also Visieux, *Mineur de fond*, p. 37.

[29] Jeanne G., *Journal*, Preface by J. A., priest; and Bashkirtseff, *Journal*, entry for Sunday, 29 August 1883.

[30] Catherine Rollet and Patrice Bourdelais, 'Infant Mortality in France, 1750–1950: Evaluation and Perspectives', in Carlo A. Corsini and Pier Paolo Viazzo (eds.), *The Decline of Infant Mortality in Europe, 1800–1950: Four National Case Studies* (Florence: UNICEF, 1993), pp. 51–70.

a probability of only 15 per cent of the value recorded in 1740–9. This fall of 85 per cent was a little ahead of that achieved by the next age group, ten to fifteen years, of 75 per cent. Otherwise, among the under-fives and adolescents aged fifteen to twenty-five, mortality in the early twentieth century was still considerably higher than at present, and the fall in their rates more impressive after 1913 than before.[31] The reasons for this improvement in the mortality of the younger age groups now appear more complex than was once thought, with the older emphasis on single influences such as medical advances now discredited. There were long-term influences from an improved standard of living, such as better nutrition and housing. But there was also significant intervention from politicians, administrators, philanthropists and doctors to combat diseases among children.[32] The historian Marie-France Morel concedes there was no medical breakthrough to account for the decline in infant mortality after 1790, but she argues that 'medical men took a new and increasingly passionate interest in saving children's lives'. With Rousseau and others in the elite stimulating an interest in childhood, the campaigns to encourage maternal breastfeeding and better midwifery made an impact. There was a further flurry of activity during the late nineteenth and early twentieth centuries, fuelled in France by concerns over depopulation and military weakness in the wake of the Franco-Prussian War of 1870. Important developments included the promotion of mass education, public health measures affecting sewage and the water supply, the Pasteurian revolution and, a French speciality, institutions such as the 'Gouttes de lait' (milk depots) to support feeding and hygiene among mothers and babies.[33]

[31] Jacques Vallin, 'Mortality in Europe from 1720 to 1914: Long-Term Trends and Changes in Patterns by Age and Sex', in R. Schofield, D. Reher and A. Bideau (eds.), *The Decline of Mortality in Europe* (Oxford: Clarendon Press, 1991), pp. 39–67 (pp. 52–5). For another comparative study of age-specific mortality, see Michel Poulain and Dominique Tabutin, 'La Mortalité aux jeunes âges en Europe et en Amérique du Nord du XIXe à nos jours', in Paul Marie Boulanger and Dominique Tabutin (eds.), *La Mortalité des enfants dans l'histoire* (Liège: Ordina Editions, 1980), pp. 119–57.

[32] Roger Schofield and David Reher, 'The Decline of Mortality in Europe', in Schofield et al., *Decline of Mortality*, pp. 1–17.

[33] Marie-France Morel, 'The Care of Children: The Influence of Medical Innovation and Medical Institutions on Infant Mortality, 1750–1914', in ibid., pp. 196–219 (p. 197); Rollet-Echalier, *La Politique*, passim. The comparative literature in this area is illuminating. See, for example, Jane Jenson, 'Representations of Gender: Policies to "Protect" Women Workers and Infants in France and the United States before 1914', in Linda Gordon (ed.), *Women, the State, and Welfare* (Madison: University of Wisconsin Press, 1990), pp. 152–77; Rachel G. Fuchs, 'France in a Comparative Perspective', in Elinor A. Accampo, Rachel G. Fuchs and Mary Lynn Stewart (eds.), *Gender and the Politics of Social Reform in France, 1870–1914* (Baltimore: Johns Hopkins University Press, 1995), pp. 157–87; Seth Koven and Sonya Michel (eds.), *Mothers of a New World: Maternalist*

For all this movement towards lower mortality among the young, the evidence suggesting that the poor were more vulnerable to a premature death than the rich rather tarnished the record. The historian Edmonde Vedrenne-Villeneuve examined various studies by contemporaries of social inequalities in the death rate during the first half of the nineteenth century. She found that their work was often innovative, and their findings influential at the time, but their statistical techniques were by modern standards far from rigorous. The difficulties of measuring differential death rates according to occupation or wealth remain formidable. For what it is worth, the social reformer Dr Louis Villermé produced figures during the 1820s to show higher mortality in a sample of poor Departments than in a sample of rich ones, especially around the ages of ten and twenty. In 1840 he sought to demonstrate that the child of a manufacturer or merchant in Mulhouse had a far longer life expectancy at birth than the child of a local weaver or worker in a spinning mill. In similar fashion, Guépin and Bonamy attempted to prove a considerably higher death toll among the young in poor streets than in rich ones during the 1830s, as did Brion and Paillart in Abbeville. Working from Parisian data, Vedrenne-Villeneuve concluded that the period when the greatest inequalities in the death rate occurred was the second half of the nineteenth century.[34] The literary evidence from the '*écritures du moi*' is compatible with these findings. It also indicates differences in health and access to medical support according to the social background of the young.

Illness in childhood

Some writers tended to ignore the state of their health, while others devoted considerable attention to it. Some boasted of their good health and boundless energy in childhood,[35] others dwelt more on their afflictions. Childhood diseases and minor illnesses naturally affected young people from all backgrounds. Mirabeau and Madame de Genlis were two children from noble families who went down with smallpox, the former left scarred and 'ugly' by the experience.[36] The diary of Caroline Brame revealed an upper-middle-class Parisian girl in her teens preoccupied

Politics and the Origins of Welfare States (New York: Routledge, 1993); and Alisa Klaus, *Every Child a Lion: The Origins of Maternal and Infant Health Policy in the United States and France, 1890–1920* (Ithaca, NY: Cornell University Press, 1993).

[34] Edmonde Vedrenne-Villeneuve, 'L'Inégalité sociale devant la mort dans la première moitié du XIXe siècle', *Population*, 16 (1961), 665–98.

[35] For example, Chamson, *Chiffre de nos jours*, p. 86.

[36] Mirabeau, *Mémoires*, I, p. 241; and Genlis, *Mémoires*, I, p. 82.

during the 1860s with a succession of coughs, colds and stomach upsets, in addition to insomnia and occasional breathing difficulties. That of Elisabeth Leseur, also from the Parisian bourgeoisie, mentioned a bout of measles in 1881, and recorded that it was 'not amusing at all'. Jeanne G. adopted a lighter tone, admitting in 1895 that she was quite happy to have a moderate case of scarlet fever, since it allowed her to amuse herself for two or three days. She thanked God for making her better – and also for making her a little bit ill. The novelist André Chamson went as far as to claim that as a boy he had coped with real diseases, but struggled with the imaginary ones he awarded himself after reading an old medical dictionary: tetanus, meningitis, anthrax and tuberculosis. André Gide admitted faking attacks of nerves after a bout of smallpox to stay away from school.[37] Among the poor, the misery caused by such illnesses might be compounded by harsh living conditions. Valentin Jamerey-Duval provided one such example after he ran away from home and survived as best he could as a farm labourer. He recorded that during the exceptionally cold winter of 1709 he suffered an attack of smallpox. All the impoverished farmer who employed him could do was to put him in the sheepfold for warmth and wrap him in straw and manure. He existed on thin soup and water for two weeks, until rescued by a priest.[38] Antoine Sylvère also provided a vivid insight into the sheer misery of feeling unwell among the peasantry of the Auvergne during the 1890s. First, he had an unsympathetic mother. If he told her first thing in the morning that he felt ill, her response was to grab him from his bed and stand him on his feet. A couple of boxes to the ears rounded off this rude awakening. Second, he made an enemy of his teacher at the Christian Brothers school, and claimed that his 'executioner' refused him time to leave class when he had periodic bouts of diarrhoea. He therefore had to walk around with damp trousers after rinsing them in a stream. Third, problems with his adenoids flattened his nostrils and caused a permanent runny nose every winter. He claimed that his family coughed its way through the night in much the same way that it sweated in the summer: there was nothing to be done about it. He remembered being close to despair at this point: he saw himself as a pitiful character, dirty and ugly at the age of eight.[39]

Child medicine: the scientific and the popular

Until the twentieth century, medical science did not have much to offer sick children. As in the case of adults, much of its repertoire still followed

---

[37] Brame, *Journal intime*, pp. 208–9; Leseur, *Journal d'enfant*, entry for 31 March 1881; Jeanne G., *Journal*, entry for 29 November 1895; Chamson, *Chiffre de nos jours*, p. 80; and Gide, *Si le grain ne meurt*, pp. 111–12.
[38] Jamerey-Duval, *Mémoires*, pp. 161–3.   [39] Sylvère, *Toinou*, pp. 100–1 and 157–8.

the Hippocratic tradition of neutralizing noxious humours by bleeding, purging and administering emetics to the patient. The peasant Pierre Prion expressed little confidence in the two 'health officers' in his village in the Languedoc, operating in the middle of the eighteenth century. Their skill lay in lancing their patients, but their success was less than brilliant. During the late nineteenth century, according to the folklorist Eugène Bougeâtre, the peasants still only turned to the doctor as a last resort.[40] From a child's perspective, the young Francis Jammes took a dislike to the local pharmacist, M. Fourcade, following his first experience of leeching during the 1870s. To begin with, Fourcade spread milk over his stomach, and then he applied the black, slug-like creatures. Their suction, comparable to a burn, made Jammes howl. Caroline Duméril, a young woman drawn from the intellectual elite in Paris, revealed the debilitating effects of such treatment even at the age of twenty-one. In a letter to a friend written in 1857 she wrote that a bad sore throat was being treated with innumerable poultices and mustard plasters, leeches, gargles and fasting. A month later she was still enduring three bleedings a day, with the result that she felt weak and was trying 'courageously to put up with the anxieties that the good Lord sends me'.[41] To support this type of regime, according to the correspondence of a bourgeois family in Anjou, purchases from the local pharmacy around 1900 included disinfectants, sedatives, laxatives, diuretics and ingredients for poultices.[42] However it was not all misery, since doctors recommended rest and special diets. Antoine Sylvère commented: 'Illness seemed to me an infinitely desirable condition. The essential treatment consisted of a long stay in bed, doing nothing, without worrying about the consequences, drinking strongly sugared herb teas if, by chance, one was lucky enough to have the doctor involved.' Unfortunately for him, he found it almost impossible to achieve this pampered condition: peasants could hardly afford time off for illness. The anonymous family in Anjou revealed in its letters that, besides bleeding, purging and so forth, milk was regarded as something of a panacea, used to treat such conditions as anaemia and measles. A mother concerned about the lack of appetite in her two-year-old son countered the condition, hard though it is to believe, with brains to go with his chops, three egg yolks and three glasses of milk.[43]

Popular medicine had for centuries filled the breach for those unable to afford the services of a doctor. Even the father of Chateaubriand, a

[40] E.-G. Léonard, *Mon village sous Louis XV, d'après les mémoires d'un paysan* (Paris: Presses Universitaires de France, 1941), p. 108; and Bougeâtre, *Vie rurale dans le Mantois*, p. 123.
[41] Jammes, *De l'âge divin*, pp. 14–17; and Dauphin et al., *Ces bonnes lettres*, letter from Caroline Duméril to Isabelle Latham, 25 November and 24 December 1857.
[42] Chotard-Lioret, 'Société familiale, p. 92.
[43] Ibid., pp. 87–9; and Sylvère, *Toinou*, p. 100.

member of the nobility, believed in charlatans and not regular doctors. Around 1780 he hired one such to cure a fever caught by his son. The *'empirique'* certainly looked the part, if one can imagine someone wearing a green costume braided with gold, a large powdered wig, big cuffs of a dirty muslin, fake diamonds on his fingers, breeches of worn black satin, silk stockings of a blueish white and shoes with enormous buckles. Chateaubriand *père* approved the suggested remedy of caramel to purge his son, on the grounds that all illnesses were caused by indigestion. However, he changed his tune when his son began to vomit uncontrollably, threatening to throw the terrified charlatan through the window.[44] Doctors remained rare in the countryside before 1914. In the mountainous parts of the Haut-Vivarais, the folklorist Pierre Charrié discovered that the resort to magic lingered on until the Second World War, though more through habit than conviction.[45] A veterinary surgeon in the Cambrésis observed in 1880 that 'Illnesses for country folk are always a strange phenomenon, which they surround with an aura of fear and mystery. It is therefore entirely natural that certain villagers believe that to cure them it is necessary to employ equally strange methods.'[46] Popular medicine did indeed appear to the outsider as a combination of the magical and the empirical. Jean Drouillet suggested from his knowledge of the Nivernais and the Morvan that the villagers started with traditional 'remèdes de bonne femme', plant-based remedies passed down within families, and prayers. If these failed, they turned to an assortment of healers and bonesetters, and, in the last resort, sorcerers. Similarly, Alain le Goff (the 'Horse of Pride') declared in the early twentieth century that the cure for all bodily ailments was readily available in the plants growing nearby. Their Breton names revealed the disease they could cure or the saint who gave protection. He believed in the powers of healing saints, thought the incantations of 'old crones' and quacks were a matter of superstition and sorcery, and was confident that bonesetters knew their trade. If you were seriously ill, and had some money, there was always the doctor.[47] Children in the countryside soon became acquainted with this popular medicine. Their mothers used various herb concoctions, poultices and ointments on them: an infusion of black alder as a laxative, and of red poppy leaves for whooping cough, for example. There were also animal-based medicines, including syrups from snails or slugs for a chest

[44] Chateaubriand, *Mémoires d'outre-tombe*, vol. I, p. 80.

[45] Pierre Charrié, *Le Folklore du Haut-Vivarais* (Paris: FERN, 1968), p. 177.

[46] Jacquemart, 'Erreurs, préjugés, coutumes et légendes du Cambrésis' (1880), cited by Arnold Van Gennep, *Le Folklore de la Flandre et du Hainaut français (Département du Nord)* (2 vols., Paris: Maisonneuve, 1935–6), I, p. 639.

[47] Drouillet, *Folklore du Nivernais*, IV, pp. 165–6; and Hélias, *Horse of Pride*, p. 85.

illness, fried rats for bed-wetters and fresh cowpats for a burn. Mothers took sick or feeble children to local chapels or springs to seek the intercession of saints, and had a repertoire of more mystical remedies.[48] In Languedoc, for example, serious cases of worms required a visit to a healer, who would make the child wear a necklace with a tiny bag containing a magic formula – illegible of course.[49] Pierre-Jakez Hélias provided a rare 'insider's' view of these practices in Brittany. While a baby, his mother made him drink water from a nearby chapel to cure his stomach problems. He knew that if he cut his foot on a nail while out barefoot he was to let the wound bleed then soak it in urine. After that a slug or a snail would provide the slime to seal it. When one of his friends fell out of a tree and broke a bone in his shoulder, the boy dared not tell his parents. Eventually another lad took him to a *rebouteur*, most of whom in his locality were millers, accustomed to dealing with breaks and sprains of their own.[50]

The doctors, schoolteachers and other members of the educated elite could hardly refrain from a certain scepticism about the effectiveness of many folk remedies, and often used such terms as 'charlatanism', 'sorcery' and 'superstition'.[51] Nonetheless, they recognized the obstacles facing peasants wishing to consult a doctor, and sometimes acknowledged the skill of the bonesetters: people with little knowledge but much know-how, as Félix Chapiseau put it in 1902.[52] In the meantime, physicians made strenuous efforts to enhance their professional status, and became more effective with such discoveries as a vaccine for smallpox and a serum for diphtheria. André Chamson gave an early indication of what was to come for children in the twentieth century. Raised in Alès (Gard) during the early twentieth century, and son of a businessman, he had a similar experience to the wretched Antoine Sylvère of persistent colds and coughs. In his case, though, his parents could afford a consultation with an ear, nose and throat specialist. First, Chamson went through the ritual of

---

[48] All of the folklore collections have a section on popular medicine. See, for example, C. Fraysse, *Le Folk-lore du Baugeois* (Baugé, Maine-et-Loire: R. Dangin, 1906), pp. 111–23; Arnold Van Gennep, *Le Folklore du Dauphiné (Isère)* (2 vols., Paris: Maisonneuve, 1932), I, p. 58; Van Gennep, *Folklore de la Flandre*, I, pp. 60–1; Drouillet, *Folklore du Nivernais*, I, pp. 80–3 and IV, pp. 159–92; Pierre Charrié, *Le Folklore du Bas-Vivarais* (Paris: Guénégaud, 1964); Bougeâtre, *Vie rurale dans le Mantois*, pp. 127–32; Georges Rocal, *Le Vieux Périgord* (Périgueux: Pierre Fanlac, 1980 (1927)), pp. 61–8.
[49] Robert Jalby, *Le Folklore du Languedoc (Ariège-Aude-Lauraguais- Tarn)* (Paris: Maisonneuve et Larose, 1971), pp. 207–9.
[50] Hélias, *Horse of Pride*, pp. 77–85.
[51] See, for example, Albert Dauzat, *Le Village et le paysan de France* (12th edn, Paris: Gallimard, 1941), p. 154.
[52] Félix Chapiseau, *Le Folk-lore de la Beauce et du Perche* (2 vols., Paris: Maisonneuve, 1902), I, p. 161.

examination by the terrible figure of Dr Mourier. While a nurse held him tight on her knees, and a spatula stifled his cries, the terrified child gasped an 'A' for the doctor. Next came an operation to remove his adenoids, in his own home. His mother asserted that with the most modern methods, all would be well. With sheets spread around the room and the apartment fumigated, the boy recalled counting to thirty-eight before falling asleep under the anaesthetic. Next, he awoke to a room looking like 'an ambulance in the Crimean War', with a bucket full of blood and bloodstains all over the sheets. Finally, six days in bed and plenty of ice-cream ('vanilla, strawberry, lemon, and for the first time in my life, pistachio') allowed him to recover.[53] 'Modern' medical methods were not always so painless. As with the doctors, the dentistry of Chamson's cousin Armand seemed to have reached 'a point of perfection beyond which no progress was possible'. Unfortunately this included extracting teeth without anaesthetic, a form of liberation from suffering through an 'abominable torture'. One might also cite the experience of the young Madeleine Henry during the First World War in Paris. Suffering from tonsillitis, a 'picturesque old Alsatian doctor' referred her to the Gouin Hospital.

I arrived with my mother in a dark room where a doctor took me on his knees and proceeded, without an anaesthetic or any sort of drug, savagely to hack at my throat. I howled with pain and scratched. A nurse scolded me. I kept on seeing this brutal wretch, a lamp attached to his forehead, thrusting curved scissors into my throat and then withdrawing them. At last, mastering me, he got to work properly. I could hear, though mad with pain, the snipping of tissues cut. This unbelievable torture lasted a matter of minutes or seconds. A nurse tied a towel round my neck and tipped me over a basin as if I had been a bundle of dirty washing. The blood gushed out. When they were tired of watching it flow they put a piece of ice in my mouth, and giving me back to my mother told us to go home.

When her mother confronted the old Alsatian doctor with his cruelty in sending her to such a place, he replied that an anaesthetic cost money and that she could never have paid for it.[54]

Private pleasures

Among children of peasants and workers

'Can one speak of leisure for the peasant woman?' the folklorist Jean Drouillet wondered.[55] Any free time she might have was readily absorbed

---

[53] Chamson, *Chiffre de nos jours*, pp. 43–6.

[54] Henry, *Little Madeleine*, pp. 112–13. See also Maurice Genevoix, *Trente mille jours* (Paris: Seuil, 1980), pp. 37–8, for a gruesome contraption applied by his uncle in 1894 to cure a potentially lethal attack of croup.

[55] Drouillet, *Folklore du Nivernais*, III, p. 69.

by the endless possibilities of sewing and knitting for her family. Antoine Sylvère noted that the only relaxation his mother allowed herself in the week was a reading from him or his father from the serial in her weekly newspaper, the *Moniteur du dimanche*.[56] Children in their turn were soon drawn into the punishing routine of work on a small farm, from the age of five or six onwards. When asked in the 1970s about their childhood games, a group of old people in a Burgundian village invariably replied to the effect that 'we didn't play'. On coming home from school, they recounted, girls fed the poultry and helped their mothers prepare dinner, boys mopped up various little tasks around the farm.[57] Everywhere girls in particular helped their mothers around the home and the farmyard. Jeanne Bouvier revealed that as a young girl during the 1870s in her southern French village she worked beside her mother morning and afternoon. While in the pastures looking after cows she could play games with other children, but first had to fulfil a task such as knitting a certain number of rows.[58] She was not alone in putting the emphasis on poverty and work rather than play in her childhood. Besides having little time for leisure, children of the poorer peasants also had few toys or books to amuse them before the twentieth century, and limited opportunities for family outings in the villages, beyond visits to relatives. The schoolteacher and folklore collector Eugène Bougeâtre wrote of village life in the Mantois as 'monotonous', with only the visit of a peddler, the departure of the chatelaine, or births, marriages and deaths worth talking about. Antoine Sylvère gave the impression of deadly dull evenings passed in his household, with his exhausted father quietly leafing through a serialized version of *Les Misérables*, and his mother and the servant Anna preoccupied with sewing: 'we would have provided the sitters for an excellent engraving illustrating happiness in mediocrity'.[59]

However, Sunday was a day set aside for rest, as far as was possible in a farming community, and children had a few early years of freedom. It was easy to keep them happy with the simplest of playthings, such as little rag dolls, clay marbles and windmills made from bits of wood and feathers, or for children to improvise themselves with sticks, pebbles and pieces of cloth.[60] Pierre-Jakez Hélias loved the sound of his 'pine pig' trailing behind him (a pine cone on a piece of string), and described in detail the balls, teetotums, spinning tops, marbles, catapults, water pistols and musical instruments he and his friends cobbled together in

---

[56] Sylvère, *Toinou*, p. 41.
[57] P. Dibie, 'Techniques et jeux traditionnels en Bourgogne', in P. N. Denieul et al., *Jeux et jouets* (Paris: Aubier, 1979), pp. 109–25 (p. 110).
[58] Bouvier, *Mes mémoires*, p. 341.
[59] Bougeâtre, *Vie rural dans le Mantois*, p. 225; and Sylvère, *Toinou*, pp. 20–1.
[60] See, for example, Jalby, *Folklore de Languedoc*, pp. 53–4.

the Breton countryside. Boys, and to a lesser extent girls, were free to explore the farms and the countryside around them. Antoine Sylvère remembered disappearing for hours from home to wander as he pleased without anyone worrying.[61] Most importantly, children in the villages and popular quarters of the towns formed their own little society, with the streets as their territory. When they played games, they did so collectively. This might involve a toy such as a spinning top, made by a local artisan, which they played with in teams or in competition with each other. Pierre-Jakez Hélias mentioned that one of his friends was given a rubber ball by a relative, but they had no use for it since it was not as suitable as a rag one for their rustic games.[62] It was only when these *sociétés enfantines* gradually disappeared in the nineteenth and twentieth centuries that children began to play more on their own, and manufactured toys proliferated in a mass market.

As for books for the child to read, there were often a few in the peasant household, albeit mainly almanacs and religious works.[63] Rétif de la Bretonne, in *Monsieur Nicolas* (1796) learned to read using the Bible, a life of the saints and another of Jesus Christ. He also fell wholeheartedly for his father's ploy of trying to interest him in literature by reading out passages from the *Bibliothèque bleue*: little chap books recounting ancient legends, fairy stories and adventures.[64] An oral history project investigating popular reading habits among those born at the end of the nineteenth century invariably provoked a response along the lines of 'we didn't read anything, we didn't have the time, we were always working'. Further probing revealed that ordinary people in town and countryside regarded reading as something of an indulgence, an 'illicit leisure': the daughter of a baker in Privas (Ardèche) said that her mother did not like her reading as she thought it encouraged idleness. Nonetheless, the school system made an impact, with the prizes of books it distributed liberally under the Third Republic. The daughter of a peasant in the Ardèche recalled reading books borrowed from her schoolteacher while minding cows in the fields. For Henri Pitaud (b. 1899), the son of a peasant in the Vendée and later the Garonne, a taste for the 'enchanted world of books' began with loans from his school library, including works by the Comtesse de Ségur, Mark Twain, Mayne Reid and Jules Verne.[65] Publishers also tapped the market

---

[61] Sylvère, *Toinou*, pp. 18–19; see also Aline Lucas, in Germain and de Panafieu, *Mémoire des femmes*, p. 223.

[62] Pierre-Jakéz Hélias, *Le Cheval d'orgueil* (Paris: Plon, 1975), p. 271 (this passage was omitted from the English translation).

[63] Martyn Lyons, *Readers and Society in Nineteenth-Century France: Workers, Women, Peasants* (London: Palgrave, 2001), ch. 6.

[64] Rétif de la Bretonne, *Monsieur Nicolas*, pp. 57–8.

[65] Pitaud, *Le Pain de la terre*, pp. 84–105.

for undemanding but pleasurable reading matter, churning out popular novels in instalments for families on a modest budget.[66]

Some peasant families were less taciturn than others, and the custom of the *veillée*, passing the time with other families in a stable or a barn during a winter evening, brought some sociability. Emilie Carles remembered that her mother livened up such gatherings with her stories and her singing. At the same period, early in the twentieth century, Pierre-Jakez Hélias remembered his paternal grandfather as a gifted storyteller at the *veillées*. The old man used to practise on his own children, and any others who cared to listen, carrying a little audience with such stories as 'How a Breton became King of England'.[67] Commercial leisure activities were not entirely absent from the villages. Hélias described children in his village aping the circus acts that passed through once a year, risking life and limb as acrobats or trying to get farm animals to jump through flaming hoops. He also described film shows during the 1920s, projected on to a sheet in the garage of the cycle repairman. A noisy and excitable audience tried to follow the stories, helped by those who could read the captions.[68] Working-class children in the towns were also thrown back on their own devices, with little money for toys or outings, compensated for by games with other children on the streets. There were more *spectacles* for children in the towns than in the countryside. In Lille, during the 1880s, Desrousseaux found makeshift theatres putting on amateur productions of plays for workers and their families, and puppet theatres for the local *gamins* and *gamines* (street children) with subjects such as the temptation of St Anthony and Ali Baba and the Forty Thieves.[69] Later there was the cinema: Louis Lengrand mentioned raucous cinema audiences, similar to those in Brittany, watching silent films in a northern mining village. He remembered war films accompanied by a fireman on a bugle, not always in time with the action, and others with everyone shouting and throwing peanuts at the pianist, Mlle Rose.[70]

Among the children of the 'classes aisées'

While women from the 'popular classes' struggled with work and domestic chores, those wishing to live as a 'bourgeois' in the nineteenth century

---

[66] Anne-Marie Thiesse, 'Mutations et permanences de la culture populaire: la lecture à la Belle Epoque', *Annales ESC*, 39 (1984), 70–91; and Anne-Marie Thiesse, *Le Roman du quotidien: lecteurs et lectures populaires à la Belle Epoque* (Paris: Le Chemin Vert, 1984), passim.

[67] Carles, *Wild Herb Soup*, p. 9; Hélias, *Horse of Pride*, pp. 73–4.

[68] Hélias, *Horse of Pride*, pp. 162–3.

[69] Desrousseaux, *Moeurs populaires de la Flandre française* (2 vols., Lille: Quarré, 1889), I, pp. 131–3 and 167–8.

[70] Lengrand and Craipeau, *Louis Lengrand*, pp. 23–4.

had to lead a leisured existence. This did not mean a life of idleness, but rather one of devotion to the family, to its social relations and to philanthropic activities.[71] The ideal of the 'angel in the home' meant that mothers often featured prominently in the 'small world' of middle-class children. One can discern a pattern in many autobiographies written by males from this milieu: of the clever boy who struggled to mix with his peers, turned inwards to a life revolving around books and the imagination, and then moved on to a literary or professional career. Jean-Jacques Rousseau set the ball rolling in his *Confessions* (1781) by boasting that he and his cousin were 'not tempted to mix with the riff-raff of our own age'. Stendhal (b. 1783) complained that his father followed the aristocracy in not allowing him to mix with the common children. Jules Michelet (b. 1798), by contrast, admitted to being too gauche to mix with other children, so that he spent time in early childhood learning to read and write beside his mother. The future poet Francis Jammes scorned his coarse schoolfellows in Tournay (Hautes-Pyrénées) during the 1870s, while Jean-Paul Sartre in Paris was himself scorned by other children playing in the Luxembourg Gardens.[72] Those from the provinces might for good measure scoff at the dreary atmosphere of life outside the metropolis. Stendhal wrote that 'whatever is mean and commonplace reminds me of Grenoble'. Charles Nicolle, a Professor of Medicine in Paris, looked back to the dreadful boredom of Rouen in the 1870s. Although beautiful, industrial and wealthy, he described the town as a desert, a tomb, with its 'dull streets and dull people'. He lingered on Sunday walks with his parents, passing shops that were closed, exchanging polite remarks with worried lads and submissive daughters, and putting up with the 'conversation of tired people who never moved outside their professional circle'. And if Rouen seemed dull, his mother's hometown of Bayeux appeared dead.[73] Hence these characters retreated into the private pleasures of the home. Francis Jammes wrote of his solitary life as a child, beside his mother and father, starting with a delight in a set of *images d'Epinal* (brightly coloured pictures) bought by his father and a pearl-handled knife from his mother. André Gide (b. 1869) also recalled 'playing with his friend Pierre', his mother's way of telling him to amuse himself alone, in the absence of any friends. He described various solitary occupations, such as playing with marbles, a kaleidoscope, transfers, puzzles and a building set.[74]

---

[71] Martin-Fugier, *La Bourgeoise*, pp. 11–16.
[72] Rousseau, *Confessions*, p. 34; Stendhal, *Henry Brulard*, p. 91; Michelet, *Ma jeunesse*, p. 19; Jammes, *De l'âge divin*, p. 21; and Jean-Paul Sartre, *Les Mots* (Paris: Gallimard, 1964), p. 111.
[73] Stendhal, *Henry Brulard*, pp. 101–2; and Nicolle 'Mémoires', pp. 21–4.
[74] Jammes, *De l'âge divin*, pp. 16–17 and 39; and Gide, *Si le grain ne meurt*, pp. 11–14.

These literary men naturally dwelt on the books they read in childhood. These were a combination of ancient and modern classics, adventure stories, sallies into the illustrated Grand Larousse dictionary and miscellaneous lighter works. *Robinson Crusoe* (1719) also cropped up regularly, which would have pleased Rousseau: as the 'most felicitous treatise on natural education', it was the only book he allowed the young 'Emile' to read.[75] Those raised in the eighteenth century had a limited choice of reading matter. There were few books specifically written for children until the 1780s, and those that were now appear heavily didactic.[76] (Madame de Genlis, whose lively set of memoirs we have quoted from often, wrote numerous examples of these.)[77] The future poet Alphonse de Lamartine (1790–1869) mentioned a programme of reading closely controlled by his mother, including the fables of La Fontaine, which he hated, works by Madame de Genlis, Berquin, Fénelon and Bernardin de Saint-Pierre.[78] Children therefore often turned to certain works written for adults. Stendhal, for example, cited a French version of *Don Quixote* as a delightful escape from the 'awful joylessness' of his aristocratic and religious education. The comedies of Molière inspired him to become a writer himself, while a collection of cheap novels from around 1780 heightened this resolve during his adolescence. The effect of reading one entitled *Félicia, ou mes fredaines* appeared to confirm all the strictures of Catholic moralists on novel reading. 'I went absolutely berserk; the possession of a real-life mistress, then the object of all my desires, wouldn't have plunged me into such a torrent of voluptuousness.'[79]

Children raised in the nineteenth and twentieth centuries could draw on this ancient repertoire, plus the growing volume of books written for children – including works translated from English.[80] Sartre (b. 1905) structured the whole of his childhood reminiscences around the themes

---

[75] Rousseau, *Emile*, pp. 184–5. See also Daudet, *Petit Chose*, pp. 15–19; Vallès, *L'Enfant*, p. 103.

[76] Jean Glénisson, 'Le Livre pour la jeunesse', in *Histoire de l'édition française*, vol. III, *Le Temps des éditeurs* (Paris: Promodis, 1985), pp. 417–43 (p. 417); Didier Masseau, 'La Littérature enfantine et la Révolution: rupture ou continuité?', in Marie-Françoise Lévy (ed.), *L'Enfant, la famille et la Révolution française* (Paris: Olivier Orban, 1990), pp. 263–73.

[77] Bettina Hürlimann, *Three Centuries of Children's Books in Europe*, transl. Brian Alderson (London: Oxford University Press, 1967), Introduction; 'Genlis, comtesse de', in Marc Soriano, *Guide de littérature pour la jeunesse* (Paris: Flammarion, 1975).

[78] Lamartine, *Les Confidences*, p. 74.   [79] Stendhal, *Henry Brulard*, pp. 99 and 184–5.

[80] Glénisson, 'Livre pour la jeunesse'; Laura Noesser, 'Le Livre pour enfants', in *Histoire de l'édition française*, vol. IV, *Le Livre concurrencé, 1900–1950* (Paris: Promodis, 1986), pp. 457–67; and Francis Marcoin, 'La Fiction pour enfants au XIXe siècle', in Jean Glénisson and Ségolène Le Men (eds.), *Le Livre d'enfance et de jeunesse en France* (Bordeaux: Société des bibliophiles de Guyenne, 1994), pp. 127–44.

of reading and writing. As an only child without any friends, books were his sole companions. Alone among adults, he observed, he read adult works, yet remained a child. Thus his grandfather steeped him in the classics, but he did not necessarily understand them. Reading works by Corneille, he struggled with the word 'lover': 'lovers kissed and promised to sleep in the same bed (strange custom: why not sleep in twin beds like my mother and I did?)'. Meanwhile his mother indulged his leanings towards works for children, such as the weekly serial of *Le Tour du monde en aeroplane* (*Around the World in an Aeroplane*) by Arnould Galopin, and, later, translations of *The Last of the Mohicans* and *Nicholas Nickleby*. (He admitted that, as he wrote in 1963, he still preferred reading detective stories to Wittgenstein.) The First World War forced him to change tack, as his favourite authors gave up on the heroic exploits of adolescents in the colonies, and wrote instead war stories full of young sailors, Alsatians and orphans. He detested these newcomers and the 'epics of mediocrity' about the war. He therefore scoured the second-hand bookstalls along the Seine for copies of American westerns and detective stories, the world of Nick Carter, Buffalo Bill and Sitting Bull.[81] The future scientist Charles Nicolle also had a 'hunger to read', working his way through the works of Jules Verne, fairy stories, and books on history and travel.[82] Finally, some of the would-be writers started to practise their craft early. While still at primary school, Francis Jammes became aware of his gift for poetry. As he put it, poetically enough, 'I had just received from heaven a reed that was both intense and dull, humble and sublime, sad and joyful, sharper than the dart of a savage, and sweeter than honey.' Sartre in his turn prepared himself for 'the most irremediable bourgeois solitude: that of the creator'. He began by revamping well-known fairy tales and then moved on to adventure stories – though for a long time he never reread what he wrote, and was embarrassed when he first did so.[83]

The path taken by women who, one way or another, became writers was necessarily different before the twentieth century, since no one expected them to develop their talents seriously. Madame de Genlis provides a random example from the aristocracy in the middle of the eighteenth century. She was evidently a forthright character, acting the schoolteacher with local village boys by passing on to them all she knew about music and literature (shades of a later vocation). She learned to play the harpsichord, sang quite well, took a part in her mother's amateur comic opera production and spent hours dreaming of 'castles in Spain'. She and her young tutor found the Père Bouffier's concise history boring, so gave it

---

[81] Sartre, *Les Mots*, pp. 43–65 and 171–6.   [82] Nicolle, 'Mémoires', p. 54.
[83] Jammes, *De l'âge divin*, p. 117; Sartre, *Les Mots*, pp. 94–8.

up. She concentrated on reading works fashionable in polite society such as *Clélie* by Mlle Scudéry, plays by Mlle Barbier and, a work she read and reread, an early historical romance on the Queen of Navarre by Mlle de la Force. She noted that she had to teach herself to write: 'it is rather odd that someone who has written so much, never learnt to write; but it is a fact'.[84] At the same period, Manon Phlipon also had to take the initiative in enhancing her literary education. Her background as the daughter of an engraver in Paris produced a typical small collection of books for her to read, including the Bible, the Lives of the Saints, and odd memoirs and novels. Fortunately for her, one of her father's young employees had a hiding place for his books, from which she and her mother 'borrowed'. They were generally 'good' books, such as *Télémarque* by Fénelon and Voltaire's *Candide*.[85]

Aurore Dupin (George Sand) detailed her literary progress in the early nineteenth century, following her own whims for much of the time. She began with fairy stories and an abbreviated version of Greek mythology, rather liked the novels of Mme de Genlis and the magic of the *Grand Albert* and the *Petit Albert*, and then moved on to the poetry of Homer and Tasso. She started writing during her teens with poems for the uncritical audience of friends in her convent, and a religiously inspired novel.[86] Simone de Beauvoir (b. 1908) presented herself as an exemplary product of middle-class culture, reading only children's books carefully chosen by her parents:

Lying on the Turkey carpet, I used to read Madame de Ségur, Zenaïde Fleuriot, Perrault's fairy-tales, Grimm, Madame d'Aulney, the Bavarian author of children's tales, Canon Schmid, the books of Töpffer and Bécassine, the adventures of the Fenouillard family and those of Sapper Camember, *Sans famille*, Jules Verne, Paul d'Ivoi, André Laurie, and the series of little pink books, the 'Livres Roses' published by Larousse, which contained legends and folk tales from every country in the world, and which during the war included stories of the great heroes.

Despite the 'conventionality' of such works, they launched her on the path to writing, beginning with pastiches of her reading: *La Famille Fenouillard* became *La Famille Cornichon*.[87]

The eighteenth and nineteenth centuries brought the first flowering of a market for toys, board games, jigsaw puzzles and the like.[88] Richard

---

[84] Genlis, *Mémoires*, I, pp. 56–61, 67–8, 77 and 85.
[85] Roland, *Mémoires de Madame Roland*, pp. 211–12.
[86] Sand, *Histoire de ma vie*, pp. 202, 210, 262, 318 and 387–8.
[87] De Beauvoir, *Memoirs of a Dutiful Daughter*, pp. 50–2.
[88] Denieul, *Jeux et jouets*, passim. See also the pioneering article in this field, J. H. Plumb, 'The New World of Children in Eighteenth-Century England', *Past and Present*, 67 (1975), 64–95.

N. Coe was surely right to argue that the 'child-poets' he studied paid little attention to such playthings, being interested either in the world of immediate reality or of the imagination. Toys did highlight differences between rich and poor, the former having too many, the latter none, but either way, the upshot was almost total silence on the subject. Those that did feature, such as the marbles and kaleidoscope mentioned by André Gide, were anything but 'cuddly', and required some skill to obtain full satisfaction. Simone de Beauvoir recalled her preference for the optical illusions produced by such toys as magic lanterns and shadow theatres, since they were the product of her own eyes, 'like the mirages which haunt the traveller in the desert'.[89] Others, besides famous literary figures, were little different: the future merchant Gustave-Emmanuel Roy (b. 1823) mentioned in passing a wooden horse running on wheels, Xavier-Edouard Lejeune, later a shop assistant, a kite that he and his friends made themselves.[90] In principle, middle-class children could improve themselves with the help of their parents by visiting the museums and galleries that sprang up in the nineteenth century. However, children appeared unimpressed: most made no mention of them. André Gide gave a notably jaundiced view of the weekly visits organized by his school to cultural high spots in Paris, such as the Sainte-Chapelle, Notre-Dame, the Musée des arts et métiers ('drearily boring' for the most part) and the Louvre. He was most dismissive of something called the *Géorama universel* in the Parc Montsouris. He described a miserable little garden that the owner, a big trickster dressed in alpaca, had turned into a map. Mountains appeared as a rockery; the lakes were dry and made of cement; in the Mediterranean a few red fish showed up the small size of the Italian boot. The owner outlined frontiers, named towns, proclaimed masses of hazy and absurd points, and exalted his own work.[91] The theatre was more to children's taste, not to mention the cinema. Sartre confessed that on rainy days, he and his mother weighed up going to the circus, the Châtelet theatre, *La Maison electrique* (the Electric House) and the Grévin Museum. At the last minute, with calculated insouciance, they always went to the cinema. He likened the Parisian theatre to an Old Regime court, with its gold and purple furnishings and elegant ladies on display during the intervals. He claimed to be more at home in the cinema, the art of the common people, and one only a little older than him. He recalled the grainy silent films, where it was always raining, even when the sun was shining, even in the apartments, and where the occasional

[89] Coe, *When the Grass was Taller*, pp. 135 and 208–10; de Beauvoir, *Memoirs of a Dutiful Daughter*, p. 23.
[90] Roy, *Souvenirs*, p. 28; Lejeune, *Calicot*, p. 51.   [91] Gide, *Si le grain ne meurt*, pp. 80–1.

flaming asteroid crossed the *salon* of a Baroness without her appearing to notice. He liked the feeling of being in a crowd in his local fleapit, mixing with soldiers, servants from the neighbourhood, a bony old man, and bareheaded women workers who laughed loudly.[92]

Finally, children from affluent backgrounds had a fair chance of travelling and experiencing a world beyond their particular *pays*. At the very least they might shuttle between their parental home and holidays with relatives elsewhere in France, or, in the time-honoured aristocratic fashion, a 'seasonal *transhumance*' between a town house in Paris and a chateau in the provinces.[93] Thus Pierre Loti moved between Rochefort, on the Atlantic coast, and his uncle's house at Bretenoux (Lot); Caroline Brame between Paris and her deceased mother's family in the Nord; Charles Nicolle between home in Rouen and kin in Bayeux; André Chamson between Alès and the mountains of the Cévennes; Marcel Proust between Paris and Combray. Travel did not necessarily broaden the mind of the young, as the patronizing attitude of Caroline Brame to Lille and Charles Nicolle to Bayeux made clear, but it did offer the opportunity to do so. Pierre Loti presented himself as a child of both the Saintonge and the Midi, marvelling at the novelty of mountains, the style of the houses and the strange *patois* of the latter: 'my whole intellect was stretched, vibrant, dangerously charmed by this first revelation of foreign and unknown sights'.[94] Jeanne G., on holiday in July 1899 when she was aged fifteen, evidently had a sharp eye for what was going on around her. She wrote to her father from a holiday villa in Vals giving thumbnail sketches of the other guests:

There is a M. and Mme X . . . whom I have nicknamed 'the human bones'. A mother-in-law who really looks like one! A small boy who bites everyone, I call him 'l'Enragé'. A gentleman and his lady who argue all the time; I think that they even fight in their bedroom. A fine lady, who looks like a gendarme, speaks loudly, eats with solemnity and moves majestically.[95]

There was too the sheer pleasure of travelling. One thinks of the young protagonist in *Le Petit Chose* (1868) sitting for three days in the bow of the steamboat taking him up the Rhône to Lyon, imagining the river as a sea and little islands along the way as desert islands.[96]

---

[92] Sartre, *Les Mots*, pp. 98–102.
[93] Mension-Rigau, *L'Enfance au château*, p. 23 and ch. 3.
[94] Loti, *Le Roman d'un enfant*, pp. 165–7.
[95] Jeanne G., *Journal*, letter to father of 12 July 1898. See also Desmoulins, *Journal*, entries for 12 and 27 July 1788; and Perrot, 'Enquête', in Brame, *Journal intime*, pp. 175–6, 185–6, and entries for 5 May, 4 and 10 June 1865.
[96] Daudet, *Le Petit Chose*, pp. 20–2.

Conclusion

It is probably in the nature of the autobiographical sources used here to emphasize light and shade: the extremes of poverty and wealth, of good times and bad. Hence one veers between shocking accounts of cold and hunger and reminiscences of cosy bourgeois domesticity, or between the freedom to wander the fields and stifling confinement to a respectable home. Underlying it all was the narrow horizon to these childhood preoccupations. The 'small world' of the child, and to some extent the adolescent, revolved around a few local streets and fields, satisfying the basic necessities of life, and keeping oneself amused. There were hints of a wider world, from books or from travel, but the young needed to move beyond the confines of home and family to experience it further.

9   The society of children and youth

Evidence from the French 'ego documents' studied here includes a good deal of attention to relations with mothers, fathers and siblings, but it also reveals the influence of wider circles of relatives, servants and, as will now emerge, other young people in the local community. Under the *ancien régime*, according to the historian François Lebrun, parents played 'quite a thin' role in the socialization of children. More important influences came from relatives, friends, neighbours and other children. Moreover, with first communion at around the age of twelve to fourteen, boys and girls began to detach themselves from their families. At that point they came into the orbit of such institutions as the *collège*, the apprenticeships of the guild system or the youth group.[1] Studies by sociologists and psychologists indicate that young people in the West have continued to learn how to behave in the wider world from social groups, and notably those formed by their peers during childhood and adolescence, as well as from their parents.[2]

There is material available from historians on the organization of youth into *abbés de jeunesse* or their equivalent in early modern and modern France, and on the role these organizations played in the social and cultural life of a community. As Lebrun noted, the institutionalization of youth in the villages left little doubt that this was a separate age group, whose members were to some degree independent of parental influence. As we shall see, these institutions only died slowly in some parts of France during the nineteenth and even twentieth centuries. There is also a wealth of evidence from French folklore specialists on the language and lore of childhood during the late nineteenth and early twentieth centuries. Returning to a theoretical perspective, one might think in terms here of a 'tribal child'. This approach recognizes that there is a community of

---

[1] François Lebrun, *La Vie conjugale sous l'ancien régime* (Paris: Armand Colin, 1975), p. 138.
[2] See, for example, William A. Corsaro, *The Sociology of Childhood* (Thousand Oaks, CA: Pine Forge Press, 1997), ch. 8; and Judith Rich Harris, 'Where is the Child's Environment? A Group Socialization Theory of Development', *Psychological Review*, 102 (1995), 458–89.

children, aged, say, between around seven and thirteen, enjoying partial autonomy from the world of adults. It takes seriously the point of view of the child: what might be called a children's childhood.[3] This chapter will explore the experience of mixing with other young people in the light of changing social and cultural conditions in modern France. It concentrates on contexts where young people mingled in their leisure time, leaving aside for the moment other contexts such as schools and workplaces.

La société enfantine

The findings of the folklorists

The informal groups of children that continued to flourish within the traditional popular culture during the nineteenth and twentieth centuries provide an excellent example of the 'tribal child'. Folklorists collected examples of the rules, the games and the ritualized battles of children in different regions at this period. With parents in peasant and artisan households preoccupied with their work routines, and children left to amuse themselves for much of the time, a relative autonomy from adults was possible well before adolescence. The folklore collections had little to say about the composition of the gangs, though historians tend to assume that they were dominated by boys. Girls, as already noted, were expected to help more around the home than their brothers, and may have preferred to mix in smaller groups of two or three. However, the two sexes might play games together, particularly when their numbers were small.[4] Within the little groupings or gangs, the children were under pressure to conform, learning what to say and how to act from those around them.

Folklore collections made a spirited attempt to penetrate this secretive world of children. It was after all based on an unwritten lore, passed down by generations of young people, and soon scorned as they grew up. The folklorists recorded the firm rules on property, such as the 'finder's keeper's' principle ('if I say it three times, this will be mine'), the warnings to thieves thinking of stealing one's belongings, and the possibilities for trading or swapping. The gang punished anyone who sulked, refused to join in games or sneaked to adults, by refusing to speak to them.[5] The folklore specialists solemnly wrote down the 'rhymed code' by which

[3] James et al., *Theorizing Childhood*, pp. 28–30.
[4] Crubellier, *L'Enfance et la jeunesse*, pp. 60–1; Alain Faure, 'Enfance ouvrière, enfance coupable', *Les Révoltes logiques*, 13 (1981), 13–35 (19).
[5] Van Gennep, *Manuel*, I, pp. 167–9.

children sealed transactions or made promises. The usual way to take an oath was to spit on the back of their left hand, cut a cross in the spit with the edge of the right hand, and say:

> *Boul' de feu, boul' de fer*
> *Si j'dis pas vrai, j'vas en enfer*
> (Cross my heart
> If I lie, I'll go to hell.)

Should someone fail to keep such a solemn oath in the Nivernais, they were excluded from the group with:

> *Compagnie des loups,*
> *Vins pas avec nous!*
> *Compagnie des chiens,*
> *Va toi t'en plus loin.*
> (Company of wolves,
> Don't come with us!
> Company of dogs,
> Go further away.)[6]

Folklorists made long lists of the games played by children on the streets or in the fields. Many of these are familiar today, for, as Iona and Peter Opie noted in the British context, the conservatism of children meant that many games played in the modern schoolyard were inherited from past centuries.[7]

The schoolteacher and folklorist Eugène Bougeâtre described a typical Sunday afternoon during the summer in the villages of the Mantois at the end of the nineteenth century. Boys met on the village square and played games such as quoits and *boules*, or went further afield to play various ball games, tag and *saute-mouton* (leapfrog). When they reached adolescence, they preferred fishing and raiding birds' nests. Girls meanwhile skipped, collected flowers and met the boys, or, if they were younger, played at hopscotch and knucklebones, and organized interminable dances in a ring (Bougeâtre, one might recall, found it all very monotonous). Where girls and boys played together, they had games such as *colin-maillard* (blind man's buff) and *furet* (hunt-the-slipper) to divert them.[8] In the Bas-Vivarais, Pierre Charrié found games ranging from the traditional to the modern: from hide-and-seek to *lou couqui et lou gendarmo* (cops-and-robbers, or 'thief and gendarme' in the local *patois*).[9] Everywhere

---

[6] Drouillet, *Folklore du Nivernais*, I, p. 88.
[7] Iona and Peter Opie, *Children's Games in Street and Playground* (Oxford: Clarendon Press, 1969), Introduction.
[8] Bougeâtre, *Vie rurale dans le Mantois*, pp. 223–5.
[9] Pierre Charrié, *Le Folklore du Bas-Vivarais* (Paris: Guénégaud, 1964), pp. 27–9.

there was a huge volume of material on songs for skipping and dancing, *formulettes* that decided who would be 'it' in a game, *comptines* for numbers, and riddles. In Languedoc, for example, children started with *'Qu'es aco? Qu'es aco?'* ('what is this?'):

> *Cap sense cirbèlho*
> *Col sense gargamèlho*
> *Bentre sense tripos*
> *Tiul sense trauc*
> (Head without brains
> Neck without gullet
> Belly without guts
> Bottom without a hole.
> [A bottle])

> *Madamo la Negro*
> *Mounto au carrosso;*
> *Moussu le Rouge*
> *La pico pel tiul.*
> (Madame Black
> Climbs into the carriage;
> Monsieur Red
> Pinches her bottom.
> [The cooking-pot over the fire])[10]

Finally, the folklorists mentioned references to those battles between children of different parishes that still continued in the nineteenth and twentieth centuries. They suggested that these territorial struggles were highly ritualized. They took place on certain fields only; they were restricted to a few days of the year; and they were preceded by exchanges of insults. Desrousseaux asserted that in Lille such fighting still went on every Thursday in summer during the 1840s. The various parishes had their war cries, and ways of provoking the opposition, before engaging with stones and catapults. Attempts to revive the battles around 1870 were stamped on by the police. In the Dauphiné, Van Gennep described fights between the children of Allevard and those of Saint-Pierre, which took place on certain Sundays by a particular stream. After the *crapautais* and *randolias* (toads and frogs) had warmed up the proceedings with mutual insults, they moved on to the stone-throwing, sometimes cheering fights between leaders of the two sides.[11]

---

[10] Robert Jalby, *Le Folklore de Languedoc* (Paris: Maisonneuve et Larose, 1971), p. 52.

[11] Desrousseaux, *Moeurs populaires de la Flandre françaises* (2 vols., Lille: Quarré, 1889), II, pp. 245–8; Van Gennep, *Manuel*, I, pp. 169–72; and Arnold Van Gennep, *Le Folklore du Dauphiné (Isére)* (2 vols., Paris: Maisonneuve, 1932), I, p. 61.

The view from below

Accounts from peasants and workers themselves of this dimension to the world of children are few and far between. The number of autobiographies available from these milieux is very restricted, and some of these chose not to mention it. Political militants in particular preferred to concentrate on the grim features of their working-class existence, such as poverty, limited educational opportunities and child labour, rather than the apparently frivolous subject of games. The isolation of many children was also an influence. Those living in dispersed villages and hamlets, or from families that moved from one job to another without putting down roots anywhere, risked finding themselves alone much of the time. Antoine Sylvère noted that one year the five families in the hamlet of Montsimon were, quite exceptionally, living harmoniously. Only in those circumstances could the boys and girls of these families play games together.[12] Fortunately, from time to time authors did make an effort to recreate the arcane world of the 'tribal child' in France. One might mention as an early example the image of Jacques-Louis Ménétra and his friends running relatively freely in the popular neighbourhoods of central Paris during the 1740s, playing games and annoying adults with various tricks. He refers to hide-and-seek and swimming, and little japes such as slipping firecrackers under the chairs of market traders.[13] There was also the very full description of games played by young shepherds of both sexes in Burgundy from Rétif de la Bretonne. In *Monsieur Nicolas* (1796), he revealed that come July, when the pastures were ready for horses to graze, the young people watching over them came together to amuse themselves. Although not a shepherd himself, the young Monsieur Nicolas was attracted by the shouts and laughter he heard at dusk. Some of the games were very simple. '*La chèvre*' was a gentler version of an old game whereby youths threw staves at a goat from a distance of fifty paces, the winner being the one who delivered the mortal blow. The later version required the players simply to knock over a stick. Some were potentially lewd, when played by adolescents. '*Le loup*' (the wolf), always played in the dark, allowed a blindfolded male tied to a post to grab the other players. If it was a boy, he beat him; if it was a girl, he 'ate' her, that is to say, he 'foraged freely'. Other games were more elaborate, but in their own way presumably opened the eyes of the young on to a new world. '*La pucelle*' (the young woman) started with a girl lying down and all the

---

[12] Sylvère, *Toinou*, pp. 114–15. See also Françoise H., in Germain and de Panafieu, *Mémoire des femmes*, p. 124.
[13] Ménétra, *Journal of My Life*, pp. 22–5.

players covering her with a piece of their clothing. The girls then formed a ring to defend this pyramid, while the boys tried to snatch the garments. Eventually the girls delivered her to the boys, despite her supplications:

> – *Oh! m'abandonnerez-vous?*
>   *Et suis-je livrée?*
> – *C'est votre destinée*:
> *Il faut suivre l'époux*;
> *Mais vous serez pleurée*
> *Toute l'année*,
> *En entendant les coups*
> (– Oh! Are you going to abandon me?
> And am I handed over?
> It is your destiny:
> You must follow the husband;
> But we will weep for you
> All year,
> As we hear the blows.)

The girl finally offered her hand to the boy that pleased her most, her 'husband'. Rétif felt that by the time he was writing, in the 1790s, these games had disappeared from the countryside.[14]

One has to wait until the interwar period of the twentieth century for a full 'inside' account of the traditional *société enfantine*, though it too was written by a male and by someone who looked back from the perspective of an educated man. Pierre-Jakez Hélias was nonetheless plausible in conveying the codes of the society as part of a lived experience in an agrarian society, as opposed to the set of rules and rather quaint recitations recorded by the folklorists. Thus the leaders of his little gang in Pouldreuzic (Finistère) assisted his rise up the hierarchy from child to 'man' (at ten). The rules were eminently practical. They eased tensions by, for example, enforcing the right of the boy who first spotted a bird's nest to claim its eggs later. During battles between the upper and lower *bourgs*, the combatants were careful to use only smooth stones, to avoid cutting their opponents:

'If you hurt my son, I'll kill you,' all fathers used to say. And since the culprit would be killed a second time by his own father, or so the father had given him to believe, it was only sensible to obey the laws of our own warfare insofar as possible.

The boys learned to approach girls with caution: a boy who spent too much time with them was open to insult, the girls knew how to cause trouble by crying loudly, but they gave little presents to those they admired.

[14] Rétif de la Bretonne, *Monsieur Nicolas*, pp. 34–8.

The battles between children reinforced the tendency for the populations of the upper and lower halves of the village to mix in separate circles. The various games involved a certain defiance of adults: Hélias cited a girl punished by nuns for whistling like a boy in her convent school, retribution from farmers for those who dared fire a catapult at their ducks or geese, and trouble with parents for lost buttons, wet clothes and injuries: 'if you ever come home drowned, you can settle the matter with your father'. At the same time, Hélias emphasized that the adults of the village watched at a discreet distance the progress of the children, to see who was argumentative or too clever for their own good, and who was worthy of respect. Above all, he depicted the activities of the gang as part of an apprenticeship for a peasant. His education, he felt, began with learning how to use all the resources of the countryside: the trees, the plants, the water, the stones, the birds and the wind. The process of knowing how to make the most of one's environment started early, as members of the 'tribe' of children roamed the fields, made little watermills and knocked together useful items such as tops, catapults, slings, stilts, popguns and whistles:

Now in those days, to live in the country and to work the land meant that you had to learn a number of bodily gestures which were a means of saving your energy and which had to be acquired early on so that you wouldn't tire yourself out to no purpose. Moreover, a certain manual dexterity was essential to a peasant, since he had to be prepared to make minor repairs himself – repairs that would normally have been made by harness-makers, carpenters, roofers, masons, and weavers – for in an emergency he had no time to call in those artisans, even if he had the means to. In short, he was doomed to doing odd jobs.

Following this line of reasoning, then, country children strictly speaking had no toys, nor even amused themselves playing, for they were always learning.[15]

Growing up among other boys in a gang was tough going. Physical strength and courage were highly valued, requiring such activities as wrestling, tree climbing, stealing fruit, stone-throwing and endless 'dares'. Even Chateaubriand, mixing with the local street children in Saint-Malo during the 1780s, found himself drawn into such risky ventures. Most dangerous of all for him was daring to cross a narrow, sloping parapet 20 metres above the base of a tower on a chateau by the sea. The feat required perfect timing in the interval between two sets of waves crashing against the tower.[16] The teacher and writer Louis Pergaud

---

[15] Hélias, *Horse of Pride*, ch. 5. See also Yann Brékilien, *La Vie quotidienne des paysans bretons, au XIXe siècle* (Paris: Hachette, 1966), ch. VI.
[16] Chateaubriand, *Mémoires d'outre-tombe*, p. 58.

may well have exaggerated the violence for dramatic effect in his fictional account of battles between children: *La Guerre des boutons: roman de ma douzième année* (*The War of the Buttons: Novel of my Twelfth Year*, 1912). He depicted a world entirely free from the supervision of parents, schoolmasters and priests, where the boys from Longeverne and Velrans followed an ancient tradition in battling it out on a common between the two villages. However, there was surely some basis for his emphasis on the cruel, 'Dionysian' side of children left to their own devices.[17] The gangs dealt harshly with prisoners, threatening to mutilate one with a knife, before systematically cutting all the hooks, buttons, buttonholes, braces, pockets, garters and shoelaces of his clothing.[18] Gang-members who betrayed their comrades to the opposition faced dire retribution. Thus the traitorous Bacaillé, who revealed the hiding place of the Longeverne gang, with all its treasures, returned to the village after the gang had finished with him howling pitifully and trembling like a leaf, with his buttocks bleeding profusely, spit all over his thighs and his eyes rolling.[19] The 'tribe' of country children was also frequently cruel in its treatment of animals. Existence, writing during the 1930s of her childhood in a Limousin village, recalled what happened when a group of children got their hands on a fox caught by her father. They beat the animal on the head, and then stood it up again. Next they hurled logs at it, oblivious to its howls of pain and the blood flowing from its muzzle, eyes and paws. They only gave up when it began to cry hysterically as its entrails poured out. Children had no pity for animals in the 'wild and unsociable' Limousin, she observed: their 'education in compassion' had not yet begun.[20]

For all the rough edges to gang life among children, observers note that they generally enjoyed themselves, laughing and joking as they played their games. This sociability surely had many advantages for children compared to the more solitary existence eventually imposed on their counterparts further up the social scale. Under the *ancien régime*, only children of the nobility remained entirely aloof from the games in the fields. In eighteenth-century Languedoc, for example, the son of the notary, the surgeon and the country bourgeois mingled from time to time with those of sharecroppers, farm labourers and handloom weavers. They spent a little more time studying than their plebeian counterparts, but until they went off to their *collège*, they were by no means strangers to them.[21] However, to follow the line taken by the historian Maurice Crubellier, in the nineteenth century the 'bourgeois family' grasped that

---

[17] See above, pp. 45–51.   [18] Pergaud, *Guerre des boutons*, pp. 36–9.
[19] Ibid., p. 269.   [20] Existence, 'Village', *Les Oeuvres libres*, 221 (1939), 283–5.
[21] Castan, *Honnêteté*, p. 227.

its educational aims would not be realizable if its offspring became steeped in the ways of the traditional *société enfantine*. It therefore made strenuous efforts, from the time of the Second Empire in particular, to isolate, control and inspire its children. That is to say, parents closely monitored the friends children could play with, keeping them away from the riff-raff. They paid close attention to the daily routines of their children, as recommended by the likes of Ernest Legouvé, thereby supplementing the efforts of the school system. And they worked on the conscience of their young, seeking to implant individual aspirations to succeed.[22] On the one hand, this provided a suitable framework for academic achievement and the values associated with a 'respectable' upbringing. Careers in eminently 'bourgeois' occupations such as the law, medicine and letters required long years of study and a rather different sensibility to that of the gang. It also suited those children, like the future writers Francis Jammes and Clara Malraux, who disliked the coarseness and philistinism of the children around them. On the other hand, the new approach represented a heavy intrusion of adult influences on the world of the child. Stendhal was an early victim, at the end of the eighteenth century, lamenting that 'the whole of my unhappiness can be summed up in two words: I was never allowed to talk to a child of my own age'.[23] A century later Jules Vallès exposed the wily campaign by his mother to detach him from his friends among the neighbourhood children, whose parents were 'peasants, cobblers and weighers of sugar [grocers]'. The mother of the narrator 'Pierre' in the *Livre de mon ami* (1885) by Anatole France solemnly explained why he could not join the street urchin playing freely in the courtyard below his window: 'Alphonse is badly brought up; it is not his fault, it is his misfortune; but well brought-up children should not associate with those who are not.'[24] Charles Nicolle (b. 1866) made no mention of such overt snobbery in his medical background in Rouen, but he did labour under the austere regime imposed by his mother. He recalled that he suffered from a lack of friends during his childhood, not least because he did not dare bring them home to threaten the carefully ordered and rather joyless routines she had established.[25]

In any case, the modern period saw the gradual transformation of the untrammelled *société enfantine* of the villages and the slums. The primary schools brought a finer age grading of children and more supervision

---

[22] Crubellier, *L'Enfance et la jeunesse*, ch. 2. See also Vassigh, 'Relations adultes–enfants', vol. I, pp. 45–96.

[23] Stendhal, *Henry Brulard*, p. 105.

[24] Vallès, *L'Enfant*, ch. 10; and Anatole France, *Le Livre de mon ami*, in *Oeuvres complètes*, vol. III (Paris: Calmann-Lévy, 1925), p. 221.

[25] Nicolle, 'Mémoires', pp. 43–4.

from adults. *Colonies de vacances* allowed adult leaders in the twentieth century to take hundreds of thousands of working-class children off to summer camps for six to eight weeks of wholesome activity for the body and the soul, be it under a Catholic, republican, socialist or communist banner.[26] Moreover, authorities in the cities were less prepared to tolerate rampaging children than those in the villages. A boy with a catapult was not particularly welcome in the countryside, but on the streets of a town he was potentially a real menace: witness Jules Vallès/Jacques Vingtras firing off stones into the houses around him during a battle between two streets in Saint-Etienne.[27]

La jeunesse

Youth in the villages

Village youth in its turn struggled, by no means unsuccessfully, to maintain its autonomy from adults during the modern period. Its early formal organizations, such as the famous *abbés de jeunesse* and *bachelleries* of the late Middle Ages, struggled to survive in the modern period. The festivals that it helped organize dwindled in number and gradually lost their original meaning in a more secularized and urbanized society. Some of the rituals, such as going round the farms on a *quête* for food at Mardi gras or wearing masks at Carnival, were left to children. And its role in supervising the morals of the local community slowly became unacceptable.[28] However, change came slowly to the villages, so that even in the twentieth century *la jeunesse* or youth stood out as a recognizable age group. It could therefore continue its role in immersing adolescents and youths in a more sexualized and outward-looking world than that of childhood. The group in question, we might recall, consisted of adolescents and youths between the ages of around fifteen and their late twenties or even thirties, those who had achieved 'social puberty' but had not yet married.

Vestiges of the ancient *abbé de jeunesse* continued into the nineteenth and twentieth centuries. In the commune of Lantosque, near Nice, the municipal council followed '*usage immémorial*' during the first half of

---

[26] See the fine study by Downs, *Childhood in the Promised Land*.

[27] Vallès, *L'Enfant*, pp. 92–3.

[28] See, for example, Natalie Zemon Davis, 'The Reasons of Misrule', in *Society and Culture in Early Modern France* (Stanford: Stanford University Press, 1965), pp. 97–123; Yves-Marie Bercé, *Fête et révolte: des mentalités populaires du XVIe au XVIIIe siècles* (Paris: Hachette, 1976), passim; Michel Vovelle, *Les Métamorphoses de la fête en Provence de 1750 à 1820* (Paris: Aubier-Flammarion, 1976); Robert Muchembled, *Popular Culture and Elite Culture in France, 1400–1750*, transl. Lydia Cochrane (Baton Rouge: Louisiana State University Press, 1985), ch. 3.

the nineteenth century in naming two leaders of *la jeunesse* each year. Their role was to maintain tranquillity and order during festivals.[29] The anthropologist Lucienne Roubin tracked down an *Abbaye* still active in the hinterland of Grasse until 1914, another near Aix-en-Provence that functioned until 1940. Otherwise, there were in Provence *chambrées* to help fill the gap from the early nineteenth century onwards. These began as small groups of males, separating those under and over thirty-five in the larger villages, which met to amuse themselves and discuss topical matters.[30] In the north of France, some of the villages continued to elect a *capitaine* of youth, with male *officiers d'ducasse* and female *filles de fête* to run their festivals. The informal group of young people that prevailed elsewhere continued to take on the traditional task of playing a part in the running of festivals such as Carnival, May Day, St John's Eve and the *fête patronale* (when the village celebrated its patron saint's day). In the Bas-Vivarais, for example, Carnival did not die out entirely until the 1930s. In the nineteenth and early twentieth centuries, as a prelude to Lent, the small towns and villages had disguises and a grand parade on Mardi gras, followed by a burning of the mannequin on the Wednesday. Groups of young people brought laughter to the streets as they went round on a *quête* for eggs and sausages. In the Beauce region, near Chartres, Ephraïm Grenadou recounted that as an adolescent around the time of the First World War he and other boys were still happy to wear a mask and dress up in their mother's or their sister's skirt so that their dancing partner would not recognize them. Another custom in various regions saw the young men on the eve of May Day put a *mai* in front of the houses of young women. In the Bas-Vivarais, a poplar plant under the window was good news for the girl, but a fruit tree such as a cherry or fig was not welcome, since it indicated a girl with loose morals.[31] There was in addition across northern France a celebration of St Catherine's Day on 25 November for young women, and St Nicholas's Day on 6 December for boys. At Château-Chinon, in the Nivernais, the girls announced their festival by shouting in the streets '*Saint' Cath'rine, fête des gamines*', and inviting the young men to a ball. Similarly, the boys shouted '*Saint Nicolas, fête des gars!*' and organized a banquet followed by a ball.[32] Groups of young

---

[29] AD Alpes-Maritimes, E 078/01 1003, Archives communales de Lantosque, fêtes et cérémonies, abbés de la jeunesse (Abati), 1814–54. The Comté of Nice did not become part of France until 1860.

[30] Lucienne Roubin, *Chambrettes des provençaux* (Paris: Plon, 1970), p. 171; and Maurice Agulhon, *The Republic in the Village: The People of the Var from the French Revolution to the Second Republic*, transl. Janet Lloyd (Cambridge: Cambridge University Press, 1982), pp. 141–4.

[31] Charrié, *Bas-Vivarais*, ch. 6; Grenadou and Prévost, *Grenadou*, p. 40.

[32] Drouillet, *Folklore du Nivernais*, I, p. 217.

people also continued to censor behaviour that they found objectionable, such as widowers remarrying, especially to younger women, by means of a charivari or 'rough music'. In the Haut-Vivarais, for example, the local authorities tried to curb such raucous behaviour, but without much success in the nineteenth century.[33] Antoine Sylvère recounted his single experience of joining a charivari, in the Auvergne during the 1890s. While walking in the woods, he and his uncle heard shouting, and the sound of trumpets, accordions and pots being violently rattled. It turned out that a woman in a nearby village had given birth to a child two years after the death of her husband. Every evening the local youth of both sexes serenaded her with this infernal racket while she cowered behind the shutters in her closed-up cottage. The young 'Toinou' knew that it was his duty to join in with his toy trumpet. Many years later he reflected:

And, without knowing it, in this way I increased, with my lungs bursting, the sorrows of a poor woman humiliated by the whole area. No doubt, in the most remote corner of her cottage, she was crying in distress, helpless in the face of people's spitefulness.[34]

Such remorse was indicative of the changing attitudes in the twentieth century to youth appropriating to itself the role of bearer of the public conscience.

Besides the occasional festival, there were only a few opportunities for adolescents in the countryside to come together on their own. Village youths did continue the tradition of battling with their counterparts in rival parishes. Fighting often broke out at festivals or dances, as local youths resented outsiders dancing with local girls. In the Morvan, for example, *l'empoignade* or brawl remained a scourge of the festivals into the twentieth century.[35] Dances, nonetheless, provided youth with its best chance of a break from the long working hours on the land, and of mingling with young males and females of a similar age. Eugène Bougeâtre gave an unflattering description of a rustic *salle de danse* in his folklore collection for the Mantois at the end of the nineteenth century. It would be part of a café, and situated either on the first floor or above a stable. It invariably had a rough pine floor, and walls that needed flags or foliage to hide the cracks and the damp patches. Oil lamps provided a smoky, yellowish light. At around 8.00 p.m. the musicians would arrive, normally with a violin and a wind instrument. The girls came dressed in their Sunday best, sometimes with a mother or neighbour to keep an eye on them. The boys were also smartly dressed, and eventually some

---

[33] Pierre Charrié, *Le Folklore du Haut-Vivarais* (Paris: FERN, 1968), pp. 56–7.
[34] Sylvère, *Toinou*, p. 77.   [35] Drouillet, *Folklore du Nivernais*, I, p. 98.

of them would invite a girl to dance. The quadrille would start, 'heavy, confused, not always in time, but what did it matter because people were enjoying themselves'. All the dancers came together for the quadrilles, the couples holding each other by the hand as they went around the room. Besides dancing quadrilles, polkas, mazurkas and 'schottisches', little groups went off for a drink and some intimacy away from prying eyes. At midnight the dance finished abruptly, and the dancers took their partners home. Those girls left on the sidelines dreaded snide comments from their friends over the following week about 'wiping the benches' or 'not selling their butter'.[36]

Ephraïm Grenadou was one such peasant lad at this type of dance, in the Beauce at the beginning of the twentieth century. He described a similar orchestra of violin, flute and trumpet, playing the same mixture of traditional group dances, such as the quadrille, and dances for couples, such as the polka, the mazurka and the 'Scottish'.[37] Again, boys came on their own, while girls were accompanied by their mothers. The boys danced with all of the girls, as they had known each other 'like brothers and sisters' from school.[38] Grenadou remained a peasant all his life, but not surprisingly many young people during the nineteenth and twentieth centuries were eager to leave their villages for the relative independence of a town or a city. Besides a better job, the latter offered the prospect of a more varied cultural and social life.

Youth in the cities

Street battles between youths of different neighbourhoods were a feature of urban as well as rural society. If adults in the villages gave some support to their young men in these brawls, because they defended the honour of their parish, the threat to public order was less acceptable to the authorities in the towns. To take one example, the archives in Lyon hold a report on a huge pitched battle between young men from the Croix-Rousse and Chartreux districts of the town in April 1818. A local official reported that about 600 people took part. At the heart of the battle were two gangs of youths aged between twelve and eighteen years of age, but older people joined them as well. One group had a black flag, the other a white one, and they used the customary weapons of stones

---

[36] Bougeâtre, *Vie rurale dans le Mantois*, pp. 226–7.
[37] Michael R. Marrus, 'Modernization and Dancing in Rural France: From "La Borrée" to "Le Fox-Trot", in Jacques Beauroy, Marc Bertrand and Edward T. Gargan (eds.), *The Wolf and the Lamb: Popular Culture in France from the Old Regime to the Twentieth Century* (Saratoga, CA: Anma Libri, 1977), pp. 141–59.
[38] Grenadou and Prévost, *Grenadou*, pp. 37–9.

and staves. A detachment of soldiers broke up the fighting, but the two gangs managed to meet again on 1 May. A sheaf of letters from local merchants and traders protesting the arrest of their sons indicates that the participants were well-established members of the local community. Antoine Rollin, for example, was a tulle manufacturer who claimed that his fourteen-year-old son was merely curious to see the arrests when he was himself arrested.[39]

More worrying for the urban elites was the criminal activity of gangs of children and youths, again revealing a group of young people exerting its independence from adult authority. Juvenile delinquency emerged as a contentious social issue early in the nineteenth century, as penal reformers campaigned for the separation of child offenders from old lags. Initiatives such as the Petite Roquette, which opened in 1836, and various agricultural colonies, set out to incarcerate and reform offenders less than sixteen years of age. A law of 1850 on 'the education and support of young prisoners' confirmed government approval of these new approaches. Commentators routinely reported that the scale of juvenile delinquency was on the increase, as they continue to do today.[40] Evidence from detention registers for boys in Paris in the middle of the nineteenth century indicated that most of the crimes committed by juveniles were no great threat to persons or property. Over half of those locked up were vagrants or beggars, and most of the rest were involved in petty theft.[41] However, during the 1900s reports of gangs of *Apaches* terrorizing the Parisian *faubourgs* gave a boost to existing fears of an extreme form of what one might call 'tribal' youth. The *Apaches* were represented as a type of bandit, combining crime with a certain questioning of the existing social order. The fearsome image of the gangs was disturbing, with its head-on challenge to the virtues of honesty and hard work associated with respectable adults, but it was easily romanticized in the press, and later in novels, plays and films. According to popular mythology at least, the *Apache* preferred to live on the proceeds of theft and prostitution rather than take a job. He scorned work in favour of a life of leisure, centred on alcohol, tobacco and women. In some ways, the gangs appeared as an alternative society, with their own hierarchies, fashions, slang and tattoos. Madeleine Henry revealed the mixture of anxiety and fascination exerted by the gangs in her working-class neighbourhood with a description of *Apaches* in Montmartre around 1914:

---

[39] AD Rhône, 4 J 176, Police judiciaire; Rixes d'enfants et de jeunes gens, 1818. See also Faure, 'Enfance ouvrière', 18–19.
[40] Roumajon, *Enfants perdus*, passim.
[41] Lenard R. Berlanstein, 'Vagrants, Beggars, and Thieves: Delinquent Boys in Mid-Nineteenth Century Paris', *Journal of Social History*, 12 (1979), 531–52 (534–5); and Michelle Perrot, 'Les Enfants de la Petite Roquette', *L'Histoire*, 100 (1987), 30–8.

Every evening we saw youths moving swiftly, silently, over the uneven ground in linen shoes, their long trousers tight over the hips, wide at the bottom, a red kerchief round their necks, a cap with squares or of black satinette, their long white fingers juggling with the blade of a knife. They had the art of flattening themselves against a wall, stickily, like slugs, darting out of a hiding-place to run swiftly after some man walking home alone, late, perhaps a trifle drunk. They were not killers yet, learning the business till they were of age to move into Paris, but as they were many, without being brave they were insolent. To look in their direction was enough to bring insults on one's head. They were vulgar but often witty.[42]

However, they were not simply delinquents, for, as Michelle Perrot argues, their way of life inspired in young working people dreams of escape from the monotonous life of the *faubourgs*.[43]

It must be said that for most of the nineteenth century the consensus among judges, lawyers, philanthropists and anyone else eager to pontificate, was that juvenile delinquency was caused by a crisis among working-class families. They alleged that children from poor backgrounds were deprived of love, authority and moral direction from their parents. However, in the early twentieth century experts began to see a more complex set of collective and individual influences at work.[44] This takes us closer to the present-day view that it is how people experience their environment that matters on the path to delinquency, rather than any single determining factor such as poverty or a broken home. Part of that environment was the youth gang. Emile Nouguier, the leader of a gang of youths that battered and strangled a woman running a bar in Lyon, produced one such account in 1899. Following the promptings of Alexandre Lacassagne, a medical professor specializing in the study of crime, he agreed 'to retrace his life according to the events that came to his mind'. One might question the assumption in medical circles during the late nineteenth century that, when writing, the individual cannot lie. This memoir was after all written by a young convict awaiting the guillotine.[45] Nonetheless, his testimony did make interesting points about various influences on his slide into criminality. He certainly recorded a turbulent family background. He accused his father of violently abusing him, of neglecting him after the death of his mother and of impregnating his sister. He claimed that he excelled at primary school, being top of his

[42] Henry, *Little Madeleine*, p. 92.
[43] This section relies on Michelle Perrot, 'Dans la France de la Belle Epoque: les "Apaches", premières bandes de jeunes', in *Les Marginaux et les exclus dans l'histoire*, special edition of *Les Cahiers Jussieu* (Paris: Union générale d'éditions, 1979), pp. 387–407.
[44] Faure, 'Enfance ouvrière', 13–16.
[45] Artières (ed.), *Livre des vies coupables*, 'Présentation'. See also Philippe Lejeune, 'Crime et testament: les autobiographies de criminels au XIXe siècle', *Cahiers de sémiotique textuelle*, 8–9 (1986), 73–98.

class at the age of eight, though he also admitted that, finding school-work easy, he was a troublemaker for his teachers. As noted above, his father's indifference prevented him going to a *lycée*, which meant he lost his ambition to succeed in a conventional sense. He evidently formed part of his local 'gang' of children, enjoying battles with rivals from the neighbouring canton, and also sledging in the winter. He left home early, and for a while managed to combine work as a clerk with a 'disordered life' of pleasure with other young people in Lyon. However, he abruptly gave up his job when the firm agreed to send his salary to his father rather than him. There followed a rootless existence, moving between various towns, combining casual jobs such as circus performer and agricultural labourer with pimping and theft, and a succession of casual relationships with young women. He attributed his mistakes and faults as an adolescent to a spell in Paris during the 1890s, when he allowed himself to be led astray by young men and women involved in theft and prostitution. They boasted a life 'without any fears or worries in the arms of beautiful girls and always with money in your pocket'. In 1898, when he was twenty, it all came to an end when he was arrested for murder.[46]

Young unmarried men and women in the towns and cities were as prominent as their rural counterparts in asserting what Van Gennep called the 'right to entertainment' of their age group. The nineteenth century brought a surge of innovations in the cultural life of Paris and, to a lesser extent, other towns, resulting in a huge choice of commercial entertain-ments for those with some leisure and money in their pockets. After the Revolution, there was a certain infiltration of the traditional *bals popu-laires* by 'bourgeois' elements in society. Students from the Latin Quarter came to dominate certain dance halls, for example, imposing the chosen dances and dress codes of their 'tribe'. During the 1820s and 1830s the Chaumière attracted the *jeunesse des écoles*, on account of its varied dances and attractions such as *montagnes russes* (switchbacks). After 1838 the Closerie des Lilas took over during the summer months. Its reputa-tion for eccentricity included bizarre festivals and posters advertising a '*quadrille déchirancochicandard*' or '*exhilarandéliranchocrosophe*'.[47] By the end of the nineteenth century, there were cafés, *café-concerts*, cabarets, dance halls, cinemas, theatres, opera houses and occasional spectac-ular Great Exhibitions.[48] These gave young people as a group some

[46] 'Emile Nouguier', in Artières (ed.), *Livre des vies coupables*, pp. 81–124.
[47] Jean-Claude Caron, *Générations romantiques: les étudiants de Paris et le quartier latin (1814–51)* (Paris: Armand Colin, 1991), pp. 153–9.
[48] Georges Duby (ed.), *Histoire de la France urbaine*, vol. IV, *La Ville de l'âge industriel: le cycle haussmannien* (Paris: Seuil, 1983), ch. 5; Charles Rearick, *Pleasures of the Belle Epoque: Entertainment and Festivity in Turn-of-the-Century France* (New Haven: Yale University

opportunity to escape the clutches of employers, parents, priests and other such adults wielding power over them. They were generally stratified according to social class. By the early twentieth century, working-class youths made certain dance halls, cafés and theatres very much their own territory. Young people from the 'popular classes' of Lille, for example, had *guingettes* such as La Nouvelle Aventure in which to amuse themselves. According to Desrousseaux, there was a bar and games such as billiards on the first floor. On Sundays and Mondays there were dances, and in winter there were comedies, vaudevilles and comic operas.[49] In Paris, young men trying to launch a career in commerce were in a good position to take advantage of the entertainments on offer. Part of their life story, when written in old age, was a period working their way up the scale as a shop assistant in a wholesaler or retailer. The job involved long working hours, relieved only by evenings out with friends. Under the Second Empire, Xavier-Edouard Lejeune (b. 1845) worked as a *calicot*, so called because of the big sales of calico in a drapery store. He explained that the dance halls sent free tickets to the shop assistants in these stores because they livened up the dance floor. With their close attention to their appearance and pretentious manners, they liked to try to pass themselves off as scions of a good family. At the Château-Rouge, he recalled, there were illuminated gardens, a lake with swans and an orchestra. On Saturday nights there was an alluring crowd of coquettish young working girls, fast women from the *demi-monde*, and young men from the middle and even the upper classes. Gustave-Emmanuel Roy (b. 1823) had an easier time than most, since he started in his uncle's firm. He could savour the more refined *spectacles* during the 1840s, balancing work with visits to the theatre: to be precise, the Opéra, the Opéra-Comique, the Théatre-Italien, the Théatre-Français, the Théatre du Gymnase and the Palais-Royal. In the winter, he went out dancing, or to fancy-dress balls given by his friends.[50]

For a young woman from a 'respectable' bourgeois family there was no possibility of venturing into such louche establishments. She had to be

Press, 1985); Eugen Weber, *France, Fin de Siècle* (Cambridge, MA: Belknap, 1986); W. Scott Haine, *The World of the Paris Café: Sociability among the French Working Class, 1789–1914* (Baltimore: Johns Hopkins University Press, 1996); W. Scott Haine, 'The Development of Leisure and the Transformation of Working-Class Adolescence, Paris 1830–1940', *Journal of Family History*, 17 (1992), 451–76; and Vannessa R. Schwartz, *Spectacular Realities: Early Mass Culture in Fin-de-Siècle France* (Berkeley: California University Press, 1998).

[49] Desrousseaux, *Flandre française*, II, pp. 226–9.
[50] Lejeune, *Calicot*, pp. 191–7; and Roy, *Souvenirs*, pp. 59–61. See also Paul Amiel, *Souvenirs, 1844–1911* (Angoulème: Imprimerie ouvrière, 1914), pp. 8–9; and Romain Lhopiteau, *Soixante-deux années de ma vie: récits intimes et commerciaux, 1828–1890* (Paris: Michel et fils, n.d.), pp. 73–4.

chaperoned everywhere, and mix in a narrow social circle carefully vetted by adults. Caroline Brame is a case in point, as a *fille de bonne société* from the Faubourg Saint-Germain during the Second Empire. She had a busy social whirl, but with adults breathing down her neck much of the time. She admitted to feeling strange when, at the age of seventeen, she and her cousin Marie found themselves on the street without a chaperone: 'We laughed, Marie and I, thinking that nobody was behind us, and it seemed that everyone was looking in our direction.'[51] To begin with, friends she had met at her catechism class loomed large in her diary, often under the watchful eye of a priest. They laughed and joked a great deal, as well as being 'very reasonable and serious', but at this stage in her late teens the overall impression remains one of childish innocence. She also had close friends from the *faubourg*, company for ultra-respectable activities such as *bals de jeunes filles* (for girls alone) and society balls. A priest recommended that she restrain herself when dancing on a Sunday, and 'above all no waltzes'.[52] She was notably at ease playing games and dancing with friends at the age of eighteen in the safe environment of La Cave, a chateau near Nevers: 'there I am free, I can find all the pleasures I like; there I am really loved: from morning to night everyone seeks to make life pleasurable'.[53] The diary of a very pious Catholic girl 'Clotilde', published with the approval of the Bishop of Nancy, went as far as to proclaim herself bored in her teens with the conversation of her 'worldly friends'.[54] At the other extreme, the very worldly Marie Bashkirtseff champed at the bit when chaperoned everywhere, complaining in 1879 that as a woman she had no hope of becoming a serious artist if she could not roam freely in the streets, parks and galleries of Paris.[55]

Conclusion

The modern period in France brought various changes in the framework for youth activities. The introduction of military conscription during the 1790s, and the emergence of cohorts of young men focused on the drawing of lots or call-up at the age of twenty, disrupted the broad sweep of *la jeunesse* as an age group on the male side. As with children, the steady inroads made by secondary schools and eventually universities in the twentieth century encouraged the young of both sexes to mix with their

---

[51] Brame, *Journal intime*, entry for 25 November 1865. This section is also indebted to the 'Enquête' by Michelle Perrot preceding the diary.
[52] Ibid., entry for 15 February 1865.   [53] Ibid., entry for 1 December 1865.
[54] *Journal de Clotilde* (Paris: Lefort, 1896), p. 189 (no specific dates are given).
[55] Bashkirtseff, *Journal* entry for 2 January 1879.

particular year. Commercial leisure activities associated with the towns took over from the traditional festivals. Sports such as cycle racing and football came to provide an alternative channel for aggression and rivalry between neighbours. No less importantly, institutions such as *patronages*, sports clubs, boy scouts and girl guides attempted to channel youth away from the streets and into wholesome activities. There was an element of 'spontaneous' sociability from the young themselves in all this, notably when they joined sports clubs. In Lyon, for example, clubs with a predominantly youthful membership included the Le Football-Club de Lyon (1895), the Club sportif de Lyon (1896), Le Fleuret lyonnais (for fencing, 1898) and the Association sportive des étudiants lyonnais (1901). Yet the police recommended that clubs in which minors played a leading role be refused authorization. Thus the Cercle des sports de Lyon, proposing 'practical athletic sports' such as *foot-baal*, running, cycling and fencing, fell foul of authority in 1895. Most of the petitioners were aged seventeen and eighteen, 'and so do not appear to me to present sufficient guarantees of responsibility', as the Commissaire de Police put it. Associations encouraging a combination of leisure and education were also in vogue. In Reims the 1920s and 1930s brought boy scout troops, a youth hostels association, *colonies de vacances*, L'Amicale de la jeunesse rémoise (for popular education), and the Société d'éducation familiale et sociale de Clarmarais, which aimed 'to prepare, reinforce and continue the moral education given at school in raising young people in the practice and love of work and temperance, of Justice and Solidarity'.[56] Such efforts to corral youth under adult supervision came up against resistance from the very start. Gangs of working-class and unemployed youths continued to disturb older generations down to the present. During the late 1950s and early 1960s, there was a phenomenon of gangs of 'blousons noirs' in France as elsewhere in the West, such as those that regularly battled it out with sailors on the streets of Toulon.[57] There were also opportunities for the young to meet after school, in cafés and bars for example, allowing a certain autonomy to continue the age group.

---

[56] AD Rhône, 4 M 603, Associations sportives: sport, gymnastique, 1880–1901; AD Marne, 87 M 71, Associations. Dépôts de statuts, autorisations, déclarations. Reims. Associations d'éducation populaire, loisirs, scoutisme, syndicats d'initiative.

[57] Claude Seignolle, *Le Folklore de la Provence* (Paris: Maisonneuve et Larose, 1963), p. 105. A press report in the *Independent* by John Lichfield, on 30 November 2004, revealed fights between gangs of youths in the suburbs spilling on to the Champs Elysées in Paris, especially on Friday and Saturday nights. One such street battle led to the death of an eighteen-year-old youth, as 'one group of young men from a poor outer suburb west of Paris attacked another group of young men, just like themselves, who came from another poor suburb a couple of miles away'.

Conclusion

Growing up sooner or later involves growing away from parents towards an independent existence. An important part of this process involves mixing with other youngsters and absorbing their view of the world. The 'tribal child' (and youth) emerged in varying circumstances in modern France, according to numerous influences, including gender, socio-economic background and habitat. The gangs of children who roamed the countryside, and the traditional group of youths recognized in the oral record, appeared a relatively 'pure' variety, barely tainted by adult influence. Compared to Britain in particular, the gradual pace of industrialization and urbanization meant that the customs and beliefs surrounding these groups survived for a long time. At the opposite extreme were those children marooned in, say, isolated farmsteads or families determined to preserve them from 'vulgar' influences, who were deprived of sociability with others of a similar age. In between were those young people, notably girls from the middling classes, whose daily routine was more closely supervised by adults, and whose friends were carefully vetted. The general direction of change in modern France was towards a 'long' childhood. An increased emphasis on formal education in the elementary schools, the *collèges* and the *lycées* meant delaying entry into the world of adults, and hence an extended period studying and playing with other children and adolescents. At the same time, young people came to spend more time with authority figures such as parents, teachers and youth leaders. With hindsight, this had many advantages for them. The *société enfantine* and the *jeunesse* of the villages formed part of a culture that flourished in a stable, agrarian society, but appeared outmoded and faintly ridiculous in an industrial one. The 'civilizing mission' of the schools brought wider horizons for the young. In time, a flourishing youth culture would bolster commercial leisure activities in favour of the young. Yet such advantages came at a cost: a certain 'colonization' of childhood and youth by adults, and less opportunity to learn what they needed to know from those of their own age.

Part III

Moving towards adulthood

10 School, apprenticeship and work

The nineteenth century may well stand out as 'the century *par excellence* of the school'.[1] It certainly started with many in the French elite having high hopes of what mass education could achieve. The revolutionaries of the 1790s gave impetus to this movement with a number of ambitious plans. Condorcet in particular championed the notion of instruction as the foundation for equality among all citizens. Although these projects eventually came to nothing, politicians and reformers in the nineteenth century continued the campaign with a more gradualist approach to reform, hoping to promote a prosperous and 'civilized' nation. They passed a series of laws from the *loi Guizot* of 1833 onwards to provide support from the central state. They built up an infrastructure of school buildings, encouraged a trained teaching profession, and gradually extended the curriculum from the basics of reading, writing and arithmetic to such subjects as history and geography. Meanwhile, parents proved increasingly willing to send their children to school, even where it involved fees, perceiving the benefits of education in a more commercial and democratic society. In the words of Françoise Mayeur, schooling had become a habit even before it was made compulsory during the 1880s. By the end of the century, nearly all of the population had reached a basic level of literacy.

Yet the school was only gradually able to assert itself as the main channel for education, supplanting older, informal methods in the family and the local community. The main challenge for campaigners supporting popular education was to integrate the schools into the rural way of life: no mean task when three quarters of the population were still living in the countryside during the 1850s. Large sections of the peasantry remained too poor or insufficiently convinced of the benefits of education to send their children to school regularly. Hence their children grew up spending more time at work on the land than in the classroom. Absenteeism

---

[1] Parias (ed.), *Histoire générale de l'enseignement*, vol. III, p. 12. Other useful surveys of the education system, on which this section relies, are: Prost, *Histoire de l'enseignement*; Françoise Mayeur, *L'Education des filles en France au XIXe siècle* (Paris: Hachette, 1979); and Furet and Ozouf, *Reading and Writing*.

continued to disrupt the education of farm children in isolated areas until the 1930s. Even members of the commercial and industrial bourgeoisie frequently left school early to learn their trade on the shop floor, finding the traditional emphasis on classical humanities of little use to them in their careers. The education system was slow to shake off the heritage of an elementary school for the people on the one hand, which provided only the most basic instruction, and emphasized the need for morality and obedience, and a school for the *notables* on the other, which steeped its pupils in classical or scientific civilization. Thus the working-class leader Anthimé Corbon wrote in 1859 of a typical product of the elementary schools, a thirteen-year-old boy about to seek a trade:

He has attended school regularly since his seventh year. He reads well, and generally understands what he reads; his writing is good, his spelling passable. Of history, he hardly knows anything; but he is a little less ignorant of geography; he has, in addition, a few notions of geometry and geometrical drawing. He is, for us in the working class, an educated fellow; for his father and mother he is a scholar.[2]

Numbers in the secondary schools remained modest until the interwar period of the twentieth century. There was also the well-known reluctance to take seriously the education of girls until around 1850. From the time of the French Revolution, reformers followed established practice in church schools by insisting on separating boys from girls. During the first half of the century in particular most parents were happy to send girls to school for a year or two only, in preparation for their first communion. The content of the education of girls was also different, with the emphasis on religious and moral instruction, and manual skills useful around the home. It follows that the long transition to an extended schooling in the lives of young people was not necessarily experienced as the emancipation from ignorance and superstition that republican reformers had hoped for in the heady days of the Revolution or the early Third Republic.

Work versus school: in the countryside[3]

Child workers in the villages

Growing up on a small farm involved lending a hand with the numerous tasks facing the peasant household. Farm children slowly immersed

---

[2] Anthimé Corbon, *De l'enseignement professionel* (Paris: Dubuisson, 1859), p. 9.
[3] For a fuller treatment of the issues raised in this section and the next one, see my *Childhood in Nineteenth-Century France*. See also the wide-ranging survey, Marjatta Rahikainen, *Centuries of Child Labour: European Experience from the Seventeenth to the Twentieth Century* (Aldershot: Ashgate, 2004).

themselves in the world of work, rather than starting at a set age. From somewhere around the age of six or seven, children could manage little jobs such as looking after younger siblings, fetching water, scaring birds from the crops, collecting animal droppings from the roads, assisting an adult with a team of plough animals and, above all, *la garde des bestiaux*: minding poultry, pigs, sheep, goats or cattle when they were out to pasture. Emilie Carles depicted children being caught up in the intensive labour routines of an isolated mountain village that even during the 1900s had barely escaped from the Middle Ages: 'by the time they were six, children had to do their share of the work in this primitive economy: they had no choice'.[4] Child-labour reformers never paid much attention to the activities of young people employed in agriculture, partly because of the family environment for such work, and partly because of a certain idealization of the peasant way of life among the urban elite. For similar reasons they were slow to pick up on the onerous conditions of employment in the workshops of numerous 'proto-industries' in the villages. Children themselves were generally pleased to be able to help their parents, often recalling their early working life on a farm without rancour. Indeed, they sometimes revealed a pride in mastering the numerous skills of the peasant. The long years learning *sur le tas* (on-the-job), watching and helping adults, served as an informal 'apprenticeship' in the ways of farming. Agricol Perdiguier (b. 1805) reeled off the assorted tasks he performed with his brothers and sisters, as they tended vines, hoed the soil, harvested grapes, picked olives and collected mulberry leaves for silk worms. He boasted in particular of his prowess in the production of manure, contrasting its value to the peasantry with the revulsion shown in the towns:

I would wander the streets, the main roads, the places most heavily used by horses, mules, and other animals, carrying a large basket made of unfinished willow under my arm. That which gentlemen and well-dressed ladies fled in disgust, holding their noses, pleasantly caressed my nostrils, attracting me and arousing my cupidity. I would gather it up with a passion.[5]

The young Antoine Sylvère threatened to leave a miserable home and school life around 1900 with the thought that one of the villagers would take him in. He could after all mind animals, spread manure and pick potatoes.[6] Several authors recalled shepherding as an agreeable occupation. Children could amuse themselves alone, robbing birds' nests and

---

[4] Carles, *Wild Herb Soup*, p. 15.
[5] Agricol Perdiguier, *Mémoires d'un compagnon* (Paris: Maspero, 1977), pp. 46–7 and 50–5; English transl. from Traugott (ed.), *The French Worker*, p. 120.
[6] Sylvère, *Toinou*, p. 156.

carving little pieces of wood, for example, or in company, playing games with other young shepherds out in the fields. In the eighteenth century Rétif de la Bretonne had his Monsieur Nicolas volunteer to look after the family's flock of sheep, even though he was from a wealthy enough background to spare him such tasks. He looked forward to it as a way of mixing with the boys and girls of the village. Similarly, during the early twentieth century, Angélina Bardin started work 'in service' on being released from care by the Assistance publique. Watching over cows in a meadow around the age of thirteen she had a dog for company, and could read old almanacs or sing to herself.[7]

Yet in reality farm work for children was gruelling in its own way. Those who had experienced it recalled the rigours of having to get up early and spend all day in the fields with their animals. Tiennon of *La Vie d'un simple* (*The Life of a Simple Man*, 1904), a character largely based on the experiences of the author's grandfather, admitted that he sometimes found the hours very long. His instructions were to return between eight and nine o'clock in the evening: 'if I returned too early I was scolded and even beaten by my mother, who never laughed, and gave a slap more readily than a caress'.[8] Keeping control of the flocks was not always easy. 'Marie-Claire' in the eponymous novel by Marguerite Audoux (1910) failed as a shepherdess, losing some of her lambs and allowing her sheep to wander into a field of oats. Tiennon left his sheep to their own devices for a while and returned to find them perilously bloated after they had broken into a field of clover.[9] Wolves, snakes and passing strangers presented a threat to a child alone in the fields. Learning to be a farmer was a rough-and-ready process: Frédéric Mistral recalled in 1912 that his education began with the practical jokes played on him by older workers. 'They played all kinds of tricks on me. That's how they teach children on farms not to be stupid,' he wrote.[10] No less importantly, going to school *au cul des vaches* (up a cow's arse, in other words, minding animals) was liable to disrupt a more orthodox education in a primary school. The combination of industrial and agricultural employment characteristic of 'proto-industrial' areas also made heavy demands on child workers. Best documented is the case of Marie-Catherine Gardez (b. 1891), who passed the winters at home in Flanders weaving linen handkerchiefs beside her father and two sisters, and the summers as a farm labourer with her family in Normandy. To begin with, from the age of six, she spent time on her

---

[7] Rétif de la Bretonne, *Monsieur Nicolas*, pp. 45–8; and Bardin, *Angélina*, pp. 93–5. See also Pitaud, *Le Pain de la terre*, ch. 6.
[8] Guillaumin, *Life of a Simple Man*, p. 9.
[9] Ibid., pp. 12–17; and Audoux, *Marie-Claire*, pp. 105–7, 140 and 156.
[10] Mistral, *Memoirs*, pp. 18–19.

handloom after school. At this stage she was so small that she needed special wooden blocks under her feet to allow her to work the pedals. Later she worked fifteen-hour days on the loom. Not surprisingly, by the end of the winter she and her sisters struggled to find enough stamina for this laborious job. Work in the fields came as a blessed relief.[11]

The school in the village

'Schooling' the mass of the French population was a long-drawn-out process. It started with the rather limited opportunities offered by the *petites écoles* ('little schools') of the *ancien régime*, and ended with both the principle and the practice of compulsory schooling by the end of the Third Republic. The measurement of school attendance rates during the nineteenth century has proved notoriously difficult. Official statistics for a long time missed various types of makeshift school, rested on an inadequate system for registering attendance and had to cope with many pupils above or below the conventional school age of six to thirteen. For what it is worth, a recent quantitative study by Grew, Harrigan and Whitney has argued that by the time 50 per cent of the age group attended school, formal education had become an important experience in life for most children. By 1837 this had happened in half of French Departments, by 1850 in three quarters and by 1876 in all of them. The authors emphasize the precocious start to primary schooling in France, the massive boost it received during the 1850s and the regular increases after that. They conclude that French primary instruction welled up from the base of society, as well as from initiatives by governments.[12] Whatever the drawbacks of its sources, this study at least reinforces the findings of earlier studies in revealing widespread schooling before attendance was made compulsory in 1882. It is also reasonable to assume that the central government could not go far in promoting its school system unless the people themselves wanted education for their children. Writing during the 1940s, Roger Thabault took his own village as a case study to give a good idea of why peasants became increasingly willing to make sacrifices for the schooling of their children over the course of the nineteenth and early twentieth

---

[11] Grafteaux, *Mémé Santerre*, chs. 1–2.
[12] Raymond Grew, Patrick J. Harrigan and James B. Whitney, 'La Scolarisation en France, 1829–1906', *Annales ESC*, 39 (1984), 116–48; and Raymond Grew and Patrick J. Harrigan, *School, State and Society: The Growth of Elementary Schooling in Nineteenth-Century France – A Quantitative Analysis* (Ann Arbor: University of Michigan Press, 1991), passim. See also a critique, Jean-Noël Luc, 'L'Illusion statistique', and reply by Grew and Harrigan, 'L'Offuscation pédantesque: observations sur les préoccupations de J. N. Luc', *Annales ESC*, 41 (1986), 887–911 and 913–22 respectively.

centuries.[13] He demonstrated that until the middle of the nineteenth century the people of Mazières-en-Gâtine, in western France, existed in a semi-closed economy, largely cut off from the outside world. There was no affront to their personal dignity if they remained illiterate, since nearly everyone else was in the same condition, nor did their daily activities on the farm require the skills and knowledge taught by the school. They did not need to keep accounts, speak French or use the metric system. The establishment of a school in response to the Guizot law of 1833 was therefore premature.[14] However, from the 1860s an exchange economy began to open the village to the outside world; national politics came to interest the peasantry; and education eventually provided an escape route from rural poverty into secure jobs such as postman or railway worker. At last the peasant could see that it was 'a good and useful thing' to be educated. However, Thabault also pointed out that the first pupils to attend the village school regularly were from families that were the least involved in rural life, notably those of artisans and shopkeepers. As a member of the educational establishment himself, he was surely right to describe the school as an essentially urban institution. It was not designed to adapt its pupils to village life, but rather to open their minds to the broader society.[15]

Everywhere in France, small peasant farmers and agricultural labourers were among the last groups in society to send their children to school or to insist on regular attendance. Even when they did send children to class, they often insisted on farm work before and after. Schoolteachers and administrators in the nineteenth and early twentieth centuries regularly accused country folk of 'apathy' and 'ignorance' where formal education was concerned. During the 1830s, for example, Paul Lorain asserted that they followed the old adage that 'our children will be as our fathers were: the sun rises equally for the ignorant and for the learned'.[16] However, the peasants also faced serious material obstacles. Much depended on such influences as the extent of commercial farming, ease of communication with the cities and access to schools during winter. A study of schooling in the Doubs Department during the late nineteenth and early twentieth centuries by Jacques Gavoille indicates the varying impact of socio-economic and cultural influences. In the urban and industrial zones, various trades offered a few little jobs that took children out of the schools. At the same time, children often started school early in the towns, and pursued it assiduously for a while. By contrast, in the rural

[13] Roger Thabault, *Education and Change in a Village Community: Mazières-en-Gâtine, 1848–1914*, transl. Peter Tregear (New York: Schocken Books, 1971).
[14] Ibid., pp. 65–70.   [15] Ibid., pp. 229–33.
[16] Paul Lorain, *Tableau de l'instruction primaire en France* (Paris: Hachette, 1837), p. 15.

Haut-Doubs, children deserted the schools in droves during the summer months and were often absent at other times, particularly in the more mountainous parts of the Department. The main influence here was the need to employ farm children as shepherds in an area where labour was in short supply. At least the young could prolong their education into adolescence during the long winters. Finally, a lower-lying rural area was the most favourable terrain for schooling. Proximity to the towns and good communications helped open minds to new ideas, access to schools was relatively straightforward and poverty was a spur to academic success.[17] Everywhere, as the historian Laura Strumingher has observed, 'book learning gradually became part of the many unconnected and uncritically examined aspects of rural life'.[18] Yet the case of Mazière-en-Gâtine suggests that peasants were generally unimpressed with efforts by teachers to introduce improved agricultural techniques through schooling, preferring to learn by experience. Hence parents would send children to school to learn little more than the basics of literacy. Asking old farmers in his village during the 1940s if they gained anything useful from the 'Practical Course in Agriculture' at the local school, Thabault found that most remembered nothing.[19] In the Alps during the early twentieth century, according to Emilie Carles, the peasants had a 'morbid mistrust' of the school, fearing that it would deprive them of their farmhands. Such attitudes to schooling were surprisingly tenacious. A study of life in a Norman village in 1949–50 contrasted attitudes to education among industrial workers and farmers. The workers expected a great deal from education, hoping it would strengthen their hand against their employers. Farmers, by contrast, remained suspicious of it. They did not want to be seen as 'donkeys', but feared that their children would become disaffected with agriculture.[20]

Peasant reminiscences of schooling

Childhood reminiscences allow us to pursue in detail these divergences between socio-economic groups, and these ambiguities in attitudes to

---

[17] Jacques Gavoille, 'Les Types de scolarité: plaidoyer pour la synthèse en histoire de l'éducation', *Annales ESC*, 41 (1986), 923–45 (938–40).

[18] Laura S. Strumingher, *What Were Little Girls and Boys Made of? Primary Education in Rural France, 1830–1880* (Albany: State University of New York Press, 1983), p. 11.

[19] Thabault, *Mazières-en-Gâtine*, pp. 128, 200–2, 216–18. For a more positive interpretation of teachers' efforts in this sphere, see Barnett Singer, *Village Notables in Nineteenth-Century France: Priests, Mayors, Schoolmasters* (Albany: State University of New York Press, 1985), ch. 6.

[20] Carles, *Wild Herb Soup*, p. 37; and Lucien Bernot and René Blancard, *Nouville: un village français* (Paris: Institut d'ethnologie, 1953), passim. See also Guenhaël Jégouzo and Jean-Louis Brangeon, *Le Paysan et l'école* (Paris: Editions Cujas, 1976), for the emergence of changing attitudes to schooling among the peasantry in the late twentieth century.

education among the villagers. A boy from a family of well-off peasant farmers, like Rétif de la Bretonne's Monsieur Nicolas in the eighteenth century or Frédéric Mistral's in the nineteenth, would attend school without question. Conversely, for a poor boy like Jean-Marie Déguignet (b. 1834), who had to beg for his meals in his Breton village, it was almost unthinkable. He ended up teaching himself to read and write, using materials left lying around by students on the model farm where he was the cowherd. Agricol Perdiguier spent two or three years at school, but admitted that at the end he still not could read, write and cipher very well: the need to work took precedence. His sisters only managed to attend school because his mother overrode the father's resistance and paid their monthly fees out of her own earnings.[21] Some of the authors describe a family argument to dramatize the case for and against the schools. Oft cited is the debate in the Nadaud family, in the Creuse during the early nineteenth century, over the fate of the narrator Léonard. His mother and grandfather opposed spending money on education, but in the end his father won the day with the assertion that the boy needed some instruction if he was to earn money as a stonemason in the capital. The grandfather and uncle of Antoine Sylvère clashed when the former took pride in the learning of the young boy, while the latter was dismissive, claiming that a man knew enough when he could dig a hole big enough to bury a donkey. In the same period, the late nineteenth century, Jules Reboul used his autobiographical novel to express the limited demands made on the school system by many among the peasantry. His central character, Jacques Baudet, fared well in class, and his father was prepared to make sacrifices to allow him to go further. But his mother was adamantly opposed to such a strategy, considering a little reading, writing and arithmetic quite sufficient. To the line that a *certificat d'études* (primary school certificate) would allow him to secure a better job, she countered that 'positions where one lives with a cane in hand are not for the likes of us . . . His place is here. We only have to leave him a little more land, but you hardly think of this. He will earn a little money and that will help us to set him up with a good position.'[22]

For some village children, success at school made possible an escape from the peasant way of life. In the early twentieth century, Emilie Carles enjoyed her studies, passed her *certificat d'études* and was able to continue

---

[21] Rétif de la Bretonne, *Monsieur Nicolas*, p. 27; Mistral, *Memoirs*, passim; Déguignet, *Mémoires d'un paysan*, pp. 96–109; and Perdiguier, *Mémoires d'un compagnon*, pp. 119–20.

[22] Nadaud, *Léonard*, pp. 27–8; English transl. in Traugott (ed.), *The French Worker*, pp. 183–249 (pp. 186–7); Sylvère, *Toinou*, p. 52; and Jules Reboul, *La Vie de Jacques Baudet, 1870–1930: roman d'une petite existence* (Privas, 1934), pp. 52–3.

her academic career with the aid of a scholarship. Despite some opposition from her family, she eventually achieved her aim of becoming a primary school teacher.[23] Pierre-Jakez Hélias rose to be a *professeur agrégé* in the secondary schools. Others recalled time in class as merely a pleasant interlude in a long, laborious life. Augustine Rouvière, for example, enjoyed her time in school in the Cévennes during the 1890s, grateful for the opportunity to read, sing and act in *saynètes* (short sketches), but went into a factory shortly afterwards. Similarly, Marie-Catherine Gardez described her time in school as the happiest years of her childhood. She learnt a little arithmetic, a little reading and her catechism. Afterwards she went straight to work as a handloom weaver in the family workshop.[24] Georges Dumoulin liked his school in the Pas-de-Calais during the 1880s, and had nothing but praise for his schoolteacher, but added a radical twist by drawing attention to the injustices embedded in the system. On the one hand, as the son of an impoverished agricultural labourer, he was suitably impressed with the school as an institution:

The school, with its big square courtyard, its covered playground, its high walls, seemed to me a vast establishment. Its three classrooms, with their austere equipment, the maps hanging on the walls, the collections of insects, the curious stones and rocks, the globe placed on the master's desk, made me respectful and inspired in me a feeling of pride.

Helped by his teacher with a supply of books, he proved an able pupil. On the other hand, like many peasant children, from the age of eight he had to take time out from school each year between the end of March and November so that he could work in the fields. He therefore struggled to keep up with the pupils whose families could afford to keep them in school full-time. He managed to pass his *certificat d'études*, and even secured a half-scholarship for further study at an *école primaire supérieure*, but his parents could not afford to cover the rest of his expenses. He too went from a promising school career to factory work, in his case in a sugar refinery.[25]

Other children in the villages found school a bruising and humiliating experience, reflecting peasant scepticism on its benefits. Ephraïm Grenadou was doubtless typical of many farm lads who struggled with their studies at school. He recalled the teacher as someone who resorted to a switch all too readily, and was impatient with his mistakes. Grenadou left having failed his primary school certificate. Antoine Sylvère (b. 1888) gave a vivid account of his first day in a convent school at the age of four.

[23] Carles, *Wild Herb Soup*, passim.
[24] Rey, *Augustine Rouvière*, pp. 25–6, 32–3 and 42; and Grafteaux, *Mémé Santerre*.
[25] Dumoulin, *Carnets de route*, pp. 18–26.

He described descending into a hellish place filled with tear-stained children. His teacher, the formidable Sister Saint-Vincent, explained the first three letters of the alphabet to him, but when he failed to pick them out from a page in a book, 'a stinging deluge of blows on the end of my fingers snatched me from my contemplation. It was more painful than any known punishment.' He promptly wet himself. Sylvère acknowledged that the Sister was an effective teacher: all of her pupils, whether lacking in intelligence or not, left her class at the age of seven with a grasp of the three Rs. Even so, he had little good to say about his education at the hands of the nuns. He accused it of relying on fear rather than reason, of failing to make the material interesting and of being more rote learning than real teaching.[26] His time with the Christian Brothers between the ages of six and twelve only fuelled his anti-clerical leanings further. Again he dwelt on the dreadful boredom of the classes and the sadistic pleasure taken by one of the Brothers in chastising him.[27] He described hours studying his school textbook, *Les Devoirs du chrétien* (*The Duties of A Christian*) either half-asleep or reduced to mindless repetition of its contents. The monk teaching him supposedly resembled a local 'idiot', both physically and spiritually. The way out was to forge his mother's signature on letters and play truant.[28]

One might expect that some children in any society would hate school and schoolteachers – and that their testimony would be more dramatic than that of contented pupils. In nineteenth- and twentieth-century France, besides the long hours cooped up in class and the risk of harsh discipline, there was the struggle between Catholics and republicans over control of the schools to stir up hostility against one side or the other. In the north, around 1900, Marie-Catherine Gardez went to school with the nuns, which was in opposition to the state school and its pupils. In Brittany, Pierre-Jakez Hélias was on the other side of the political and religious divide, attending class with the 'Reds' rather than the 'Whites'. More damagingly, as a convinced republican Antoine Sylvère had little good to say about his time in class with the teaching orders.[29] It may be, though, that village children were more impatient with school than others, that they felt more than most that there was much for them to learn outside the school. There were the folktales passed down the generations within the village during the eighteenth and nineteenth centuries

[26] Sylvère, *Toinou*, pp. 29–37.
[27] On the persistence of corporal punishment in schools run by the Jesuits and the Christian Brothers, see Jean-Claude Caron, *A l'école de la violence: châtiments et sévices dans l'institution scolaire au XIXe siècle* (Paris: Aubier, 1999), ch. 2.
[28] Ibid., pp. 89–92, 121–5.
[29] Grafteaux, *Mémé Santerre*, p. 22; Hélias, *Horse of Pride*, ch. 4.

to rival the literate culture of the schools. 'Monsieur Nicolas' liked read-ing, but when he asked a young shepherd boy if he knew any stories, the lad gave a horrible grin and replied:

Oh yes, Monsieur Nicolas! I know some stories, and good ones too! I know ones about sorcerers, ghosts, pacts with the devil, excommunicated people turned into animals and covered with the hide of the devil, which eat everything; and ones about robbers who kill and who carry off young women to their lairs so that they can rape them and cut their throats, and then eat them when the start of pregnancy makes their flesh more tender.

People remembered a combination of wonder and terror on hearing such stories being told at the winter *veillées* or other gatherings in the villages.[30] Frédéric Mistral went further than most in rounding on the 'false and unnatural education' of the schools during the early twentieth century, as part of his campaign to preserve the traditional Provençal culture. Recalling the traditional stories learned on his mother's knee, such as 'The Ship's Boy from Marseille', or the 'The Swine Maiden', he asserted that the harsh and narrow system of the school 'no longer takes into consideration the wings of childhood, the angelic instincts of the budding imagination, or its need for the marvellous'.[31] There was also knowledge of the local countryside, of its numerous plants and their uses, beyond the expertise of an outsider like the schoolteacher, but familiar to the villagers. Antoine Sylvère used time truanting from school to learn from a poacher in the village how to move around noiselessly and locate hiding places known only to the initiated. Pierre-Jakez Hélias noted that school botany never mentioned most of the plants known to him. Above all, Hélias lamented, school was to be shut up five days a week learning things that had nothing to do with daily life, with the real work of men outside. Anything of interest always happened when they were in class: the escape of a bull from the butcher, the making of a cartwheel and the arrival of a circus.[32]

'Apprenticeship' in the villages

To round off their 'apprenticeship' on the land, adolescent males gradu-ally took on the 'real work' of men in the fields. Henri Pitaud wrote that he first learned to work hard at the age of seventeen when employed as a *valet de ferme* (farmhand) with his uncle during the First World War. He

---

[30] For example, Hélias, *Horse of Pride*, ch. 2; Pierre Besson, *Un pâtre du Cantal* (Paris: Delagrave, 1914), pp. 14–16; G. Existence, 'Village, grande nouvelle inédite', *Les Oeuvres libres*, 221 (1939), 245.
[31] Mistral, *Memoirs*, pp. 30–1 and 131.   [32] Hélias, *Horse of Pride*, pp. 158–61.

struggled with the long hours as a harvester, not least because he was less skilled than the older men around him at sharpening his scythe while he worked. Ephraïm Grenadou learned how to plough by watching the men at work in the fields, and having them show him what to do. By the age of fourteen (in 1911), he claimed that he could handle a plough as well as anyone else in the village. In the isolated world of the Limousin forests, Simon Parvery survived as an orphan during the 1870s by learning all the skills of the woodsman, helping with the making of clogs, baskets, bundles of firewood, logs and charcoal. His grandson recorded that at the age of seventeen Parvery became an '*écureuil*' ('squirrel') for a pit-sawyer. This led him into the world of these aristocrats of the forest, their huge strength and stamina required to make long planks from tree trunks.[33] Girls in their turn had to cope with the demanding routines of the women on a farm. Emilie Carles, admittedly coping with 'men's work' as well as women's on a farm during the exceptional circumstances of the First World War, recalled that 'I had no sense of time: a year could have been a day or ten thousand years, it all seemed alike. The only thing that mattered was work and weariness, weariness and work, to the point of exhaustion.'[34]

Girls as well as boys might have to leave home during adolescence to work with another family as a farm servant: vestiges of the 'life-cycle servants' of north-west Europe in the early modern period.[35] Around the age of twelve or thirteen, 'Jacques Baudet' (b. 1870) in the autobiographical novel by Jules Reboul went to work as a shepherd on a small farm in the mountainous area of the Cévennes. '*Le pâtre*' was low in the hierarchy, but he felt pride as a young fellow in charge of his flock, earning some money and sleeping in the straw with other *domestiques*. Others found the experience of moving away from the family home at such an early age more distressing. Jeanne Bouvier (b. 1865) struggled around the age of thirteen as her family started to break up: her mother left her father as money for food and rent ran out. She ended up with a family of market gardeners in Vienne, acting as a maid to two children, helping with the work outside and with anything else that was required. She admitted being lonely when left alone in the house, and crying a great deal.[36] Young people in

[33] Pitaud, *Le Pain de la terre*, p. 218; Grenadou and Prévost, *Grenadou*, pp. 25–32; and Jacques Zanotto, 'Simon Parvery, ouvrier des fours (1865–1945)', *Le Mouvement social*, 125 (1983), 125–46 (128–31).

[34] Carles, *Wild Herb Soup*, p. 61.

[35] See Frans van Poppel, Michel Oris and James Lee (eds.), *The Road to Independence: Leaving Home in Western and Eastern Societies, 16th–20th Centuries* (Bern: Peter Lang, 2004).

[36] Reboul, *Jacques Baudet*, pp. 53–5; and Bouvier, *Mes mémoires*, pp. 61–2 (English transl. in Traugott (ed.), *The French Worker*, pp. 340–70). See also Mary Jo Maynes, 'Leaving

the villages often worked at a number of casual jobs, before leaving for the towns, as the 'rural exodus' gained momentum in the late nineteenth century. Jeanne Bouvier helped on a family farm, started work at eleven in a silk mill, moved on to a series of jobs as a domestic servant and ended up in her twenties as a seamstress. Georges Dumoulin (b. 1877) alternated between school and work on the land beside his father, had a spell in a sugar-refinery and finally left home at fifteen to start life as a coalminer.[37] Such career paths for young people were a combination of parental pressure to earn their keep and individual choices. Jeanne Bouvier, for example, frequently changed jobs as a domestic servant to escape from an oppressive employer or from the embarrassment of her own mistakes.

Work versus school: in the towns

Child labour and education in the towns

Growing up in the popular neighbourhoods of the towns usually meant better access to schools than in the countryside, less pressure to work within the family and a more favourable climate for the literate culture of the schools. Some of the more skilled artisans and workers had a strong appetite for formal education. One outcome was that urbanized Departments delivered proportionately more *certificats d'études* than rural ones, following the diffusion of this qualification during the 1860s and 1870s.[38] However, as the case of the Doubs Department revealed, these relatively favourable conditions for primary schooling did not prevent sections of the urban population remaining untouched by, or alienated from, the system.[39] The very poor, in the town as in the countryside, always struggled with the expense of schooling. Jobs for young children were harder to find in the towns than the villages, but there were possibilities such as running errands, hawking goods or street singing. The spread of factories and 'sweatshops' brought numerous outlets for child labour, which reformers from the 1820s onwards accused of undermining the health, morals and intellectual development of the young. Moreover, the old-established institution of apprenticeship provided a way of bypassing the schools, or of making few demands on them, by preparing a young male or female for work through on-the-job training. Like their rural counterparts, young

Home in Metaphor and Practice: The Roads to Social Mobility and Political Militancy in European Working-Class Autobiography', in von Poppel et al., *Road to Independence*, pp. 315–38.

[37] Bouvier, *Mes mémoires*, pp. 56–81; and Dumoulin, *Carnets de route*, pp. 18–28.

[38] Grew et al., 'La Scolarisation', 137.   [39] See above, pp. 222–3.

people in the towns often turned their hand to more than one job as they sought to carve out their own path through the labour market.

Those brought up in the textile-manufacturing centres prominent during the early stages of French industrialization have left few accounts of their childhood. They formed a small minority of the labour force, and, as noted above, they were generally cut off from the literate culture of the elites.[40] A school inspector in the Haut-Rhin reported during the 1830s that 'the numerous factories that bring honour and prosperity to the department are also fatal to the progress of primary education'.[41] The campaign to reform conditions for children employed in the factories and workshops has left a generally dismal image of industrial life.[42] The celebrated report on the physical and moral state of workers in the textile-manufacturing areas during the mid-1830s by Dr Louis Villermé provides a rich source of quotes for historians eager to write a harrowing account of child labour in the mills. The emotive language used in his oft-cited description of the plight of children employed in the cotton and woollen industries of Alsace, for example, gave a lead that others readily followed:

They remain on their feet for sixteen or seventeen hours a day, at least thirteen in an enclosed space, without changing either their place or their position. This is no longer work, or a task, it is torture; and it is imposed on children of six to eight, badly fed, badly clothed, and obliged to cover, at five in the morning, the long distance which separates them from the workshops, and which finally exhausts them in the evening when they return home.[43]

The riposte from employers that mechanization was reducing the physical burden of work generally receives short shrift from historians. There is plenty of evidence that the early phase of expansion in the manufacturing sector, during the late eighteenth and nineteenth centuries, did bear down heavily on child workers. They might start work at an early age, face long working hours, and suffer from an intensity of work unknown on the land and in the traditional artisan trades. At the same time, it may well be that it was the small, unmechanized workshops that imposed the most gruelling conditions for child labour. Either way, the autobiographical material gives a hint of how young people coped with these trying conditions.

[40] See above, p. 187.
[41] Cited in Heywood, *Childhood in Nineteenth-Century France*, p. 205.
[42] See Katherine Lynch, *Family, Class and Ideology in Early Industrial France: Social Policy and the Working-Class Family, 1825–1848* (Madison: University of Wisconsin Press, 1988): and Weissbach, *Child Labor Reform in Nineteenth-Century France*.
[43] Dr Louis R. Villermé, *Tableau de l'état physique et moral des ouvriers employés dans les manufactures de coton, de laine et de soie* (2 vols., Paris: Renouard, 1840), I, p. 91.

Norbert Truquin (b. 1833) wrote an early example of a worker's autobiography, much cited by labour historians, whose story was one of extreme hardship in the early years. His aim was to use his experiences to bring out the evils of an 'old world' ripe for a socialist revolution. At the end of the book he proclaimed the right of individuals to amuse themselves during childhood and to self-improvement.[44] These were both rights that he was denied, as he struggled to keep body and soul together, and never attended school. His account provides an interesting contrast between employment in a small workshop and in a large mill. He preferred the latter, though one should bear in mind the peculiar circumstances of his career. His time in the workshop began at the age of seven, when his father abandoned him to a wool comber in Reims. He then had to endure the harsh conditions of a 'sweated' trade, without the support of a family behind him. While his master straightened the wool with a heated comb, he held a strand of drawn wool taut between his two hands and picked out any impurities with his teeth. He worked from four in the morning until ten at night, sustained by soup made from vegetables and scraps of meat. Not surprisingly, his predominant memory was of trying to work through extreme drowsiness: every time he began to fall asleep, his master hit him across the bridge of his nose and set off a nosebleed. His only solace was to visit the cathedral while delivering the combed wool to the merchant and marvel at the play of light filtering through the stained-glass windows.[45] By the age of thirteen, he had moved on to employment in a wool-spinning mill near Amiens. Again the working day was very long, running from 5.00 a.m. till 9.00 p.m., leaving him with only five hours' sleep a night. However, from his particular experience, he asserted that the situation of the mill workers was more tolerable than that of domestic workers. They benefited from better ventilation, heating and lighting. Life in the mill was also more sociable: 'when the foreman was absent, workers would tell stories or recite plays. The jokers in the group would improvise a pulpit and amuse themselves by preaching. The time passed cheerfully.'[46] Otherwise, what Truquin brought out was the variety of occupations he had during his childhood and youth, stimulated by a combination of desperation and wanderlust. When thrown on to the streets of Reims at the age of ten, for example, he survived by scavenging food at the markets, selling pins and nails found in the gutters, scraping mercury from urinals to sell to a pharmacist, running errands during a fair and petty theft. Later he enrolled in the National Workshops in Paris during the 1848 Revolution, tried his hand as a settler in Algeria,

[44] Truquin, *Mémoires et aventures*, p. 272.   [45] Ibid., pp. 18–25.   [46] Ibid., pp. 48–51.

and, on returning to France in his early twenties, shifted between manual labouring and an apprenticeship as a silk-weaver in Lyon.[47]

Louise Vanderwielen diverged from Truquin in writing her autobiography for personal reasons, to justify her actions before an estranged daughter, and in presenting it in the form of a popular novel.[48] She spent her childhood in Lille at the beginning of the twentieth century, in circumstances more favourable to education. She managed to pass her primary school certificate before entering the labour force.[49] However, like Truquin, she spent her working life switching between various trades. From twelve to fourteen she was an *apprentie* in a mill, carrying bobbins to the machines. On Sunday mornings she worked selling perfume in a shop, learning to speak and act like a member of the local bourgeoisie. Between fourteen and eighteen she stayed with an aunt in Brussels, employed as a salesgirl in a department store and then in a shoe shop. At eighteen she returned to Lille and a further five years in the mill, marrying at the age of twenty in the middle of it all. Like Truquin, she struggled in the mill with the lack of sleep, as she had to rise at three o'clock every morning. Her escape, and not a particularly helpful one as it kept her up late, was reading popular novels.[50]

The atmosphere in the communities clustering around overtly 'masculine' industries such as coalmining or iron and steel production was in its own way barely compatible with schooling. The novel *Jack* (1876) by Alphonse Daudet was the first to dramatize the plight of young apprentices in industry. This fictional account presented a lurid picture of the Fonderie d'Indret (Loire-Inférieure), depicting it as a temple dedicated to a wild and demanding idol. Dominating the main workshop was a massive, 30,000 kilogramme steam-hammer, like Baal admired and respected by everyone. The foundry men were a rough, tough bunch who had little in common with the delicate and intelligent Jack. As a thirteen-year-old apprentice, he was thrown into the deep end with a huge vice to operate.[51] Some of the real-life denizens of the mines and ironworks emerged as a similar breed in the working-class autobiographies. They too put a premium on physical strength and aggression. After a bruising night shift as a puddler's assistant in a small Parisian foundry around 1860, Jean-Baptiste Dumay concluded that 'workers in certain trades are beasts unworthy of being called human'. Georges Navel began his life in the autobiographical novel *Travaux* (1945) as the son of a labourer in the Pont-à-Mousson ironworks, and recalled a happy childhood except

---

[47] Ibid., passim; English transl. in Traugott (ed.), *The French Worker*, ch. 5.
[48] 'Postface' by Françoise Cribier to Vanderwielen, *Lise du plat pays*, p. 308.
[49] Ibid., p. 35.   [50] Ibid., p. 55.   [51] Daudet, *Jack*, pp. 289–315.

for his sufferings at school. He spent four years in class, and was beaten regularly in a vain effort to turn him into a good pupil, but emerged only with the ability to add up, to read easily and to write with some difficulty. He did not deny the value of his basic literacy, but regretted being pulled from the fields and gardens, where he could develop his physique, to shrivel in utter boredom on a school bench. He only began to flourish during the First World War, when he could develop his strength and his skill in a metalworking shop. Similarly, the coalminer Louis Lengrand (b. 1921) admitted that he had never been interested in learning when at school, thinking only about reaching the age of thirteen so that he could go down the pit. He was, he confessed, '*un voyou, un ours*' ('a hooligan, a boor'), beyond the control of his teacher and eager to cut school for farm work. The teaching of the school was far removed from life at the coalface, where what counted were a number of manual skills and an awareness of the dangers underground. All this was learned working beside an experienced miner. Lengrand followed the usual path of working his way through a series of jobs, first at the pithead and then underground. Thus he started in his mine near Valenciennes as a *trieur*, sorting coal on the surface, moved into the pit as a *galibot*, shoring up galleys with wood and shifting coal, became a *herscheur* pushing wagons to and from the coalface and, finally, at the age of seventeen, made the grade as a face worker. He also learned how to look after himself, not sitting down to eat, for example, because the dangerous gases sank to the floor.[52]

A crisis of apprenticeship

Finally, apprenticeships offered a system of vocational training that partly complemented the knowledge and skills acquired in the schools, partly rivalled them. Apprenticeships were usually undertaken during adolescence, since they required a certain amount of physical strength, leaving ample time for children to attend school first. At the same time, their eminently practical orientation, leading directly to a career in a particular trade, made some young people impatient with the 'book learning' and general education offered by the schools. Increasingly over the course of the nineteenth century, contemporaries perceived the traditional apprenticeship system to be in crisis. The breakdown of the guild system under the *ancien régime* had left it open to abuse. Masters were tempted to treat their charges as servants or cheap labour, so that the

---

[52] Dumay, *Mémoires*, pp. 84–94 (English transl. in Traugott (ed.), *The French Worker*, ch. 6); Navel, *Travaux*, chs. 2–3; and Lengrand and Craipeau, *Louis Lengrand*, pp. 18–19 and 31–48. See also Visieux, *Mineur de fond*, pp. 88–90.

young left with little overall knowledge of the trade. Apprentices for their part exploited the arrangement by breaking their contracts prematurely, leaving the master without adequate compensation for his outlays on training them. The general drift in industry to an increasing division of labour, and the reduced possibilities for apprentices and journeymen to become independent workshop masters, served to undermine the system. Various initiatives by Catholic teaching orders tried to prop up the system, by finding and supervising 'good bosses', but they proved out of touch with economic reality. More promising were apprenticeship schools for manual workers, appearing from the 1820s and 1830s onwards, which combined theoretical studies and time in a workshop. However, the numbers involved were relatively small. By mid-century, apprentices had all but disappeared from the textile mills, mines and ironworks – though, as Yves Lequin has argued, the factories still trained their skilled labour by a similar system of having the young gradually learn their trade by watching and helping established workers. Critics, like Anthimé Corbon in the 1850s, warned that even in small workshops the division of labour meant that male and female workers were only half-trained for their jobs. The survival of the *compagnonnages* beyond the 1789 Revolution meant that the practice of tramping on the Tour de France to learn the manufacturing procedures of each province survived for a while in certain artisan trades. Nonetheless, the *compagnonnages* dwindled in importance from the middle of the nineteenth century onwards, overtaken by a more class-conscious and forward-looking labour movement. Under the Third Republic, a number of municipal administrations established schools for particular trades, notably the dozen or so in Paris running three-year courses in such areas as cabinet making, printing and ceramics. Again, though, the schools could cater for only a tiny proportion of the labour force. The autobiographies suggest that young workers had to take the initiative themselves to secure a thorough vocational training.

Surviving an apprenticeship was likely to require considerable resilience. Masters with the time and the patience to train a young lad were a rarity. The apprentice was younger, weaker and lower in status than those around him. Alphonse Fouquet (b. 1828), looking back on a successful career in the Parisian jewellery trade, emphasized the long hours and rough treatment he endured during five-and-a-half years as an apprentice. 'My boss', he recalled, 'an uncouth, thickset man, strong as a wrestler, with only the most rudimentary instruction and education, trained his apprentices like the inmates of a kennel. They were not spared slaps, boxes on the ear, and kicks; the workers imitated the boss; it was customary at the time.' Similarly, the locksmith Gaston Lucas explained to his interviewer that during the 1920s his *patron* never explained anything: the only way he knew how to teach his trade was to show how he did things him-self. Lucas was content with this method, but suffered from the violent temper of the old man: the slightest mistake provoked a flurry of blows to the head with a cap, while a failure in the welding led to uncontrolled anger.[53] Both Jacques-Louis Ménétra and Agricol Perdiguier followed a common path in learning a trade beside their father and other members of the family. Although this made it easier for them to become a master compared to an outsider, neither found the experience agreeable. The former in particular suffered from the violent character of his father, who 'couldn't control himself and hit me all the time'.[54] By contrast, he and Perdiguier found the long period on the road for their Tour de France very rewarding. Ménétra wrote a boisterous account of his time tramping around the provinces during the 1750s and 1760s, including numerous sexual conquests, brawls and violent deaths. Nonetheless, as the historian Daniel Roche has shown, it played an important part in his transition from adolescence to a responsible adulthood.[55] In the first place, time spent working in a succession of towns allowed him to enhance his skills as a glazier, a trade that involved demanding tasks such as work-ing with leaded and stained-glass windows as well as more routine ones. Second, it gave him the opportunity to display his talents as an orga-nizer and leader. He was elected *premier compagnon* (first companion) in Rochefort, Bordeaux and Lyon, taking charge of administrative matters such as corresponding with other cities on the tour and organizing cere-monies. He was involved in a boycott of masters in Nantes and negotia-tions with the local authorities in Bordeaux over rules for recruitment to the militia. Finally, tramping helped to immerse him in the community of glaziers, as he worked, fought and drank with his fellow *compagnons*. He also nearly found himself a wife, a poor widow in Nîmes.[56] Writing in 1852, Perdiguier reflected the changing attitudes of the time by criti-cizing the ferocious battles that set worker against worker. His tone was more sober than that of Ménétra, with none of the relish for fighting or promiscuous sexual liaisons so evident in the latter's account. Yet he too detailed the new skills he had learned as he moved from town to town during the 1820s, and his administrative experience as First Fellow in Lyon. He noted that masters everywhere preferred to employ men who were on or who had completed their Tour de France. Their experience of

---

[53] Blasquez, *Gaston Lucas*, pp. 40–4; and Alphonse Fouquet, *Histoire de ma vie industrielle* (Paris: Michel, 1899), p. 9.
[54] Ménétra, *Journal of My Life*, p. 25.
[55] Daniel Roche, 'Jacques-Louis Ménétra: An Eighteenth-Century Way of Life', in ibid., pp. 241–358 (section 3).
[56] Ibid., pp. 31–110.

the hazards of life on the road, he suggested, made them less likely than native workers to drift into idleness.[57]

Later generations of workers often found it more difficult to secure what they considered a proper training in their trade. Jean-Baptiste Dumay felt short-changed by his 'absolutely disastrous' apprenticeship at the Le Creusot ironworks during the 1850s. Typical of the training on offer in a large factory, it set him up only for a narrow specialization, in his case making bolts. He claimed that such 'an apprenticeship that was really nothing of the kind' left him knowing as much after six months as he did after three years. He admitted that the constant repetition of a single task made the 'apprentices' highly productive. But rather than settle into the routines and hierarchy of Le Creusot, he resolved to set out on his own Tour de France. By this time, however, the network of workers prepared to support those on the tramp was fast disappearing. In Paris he had to take a job as a general labourer in the big Cail metal works; in other towns, he failed to find work at all. A 'bad number' at the Conseil de révision in his twentieth year led to seven years of military service and an end to this stage in his life. René Michaud in his turn needed considerable staying power to fulfil his aim of becoming a fully trained boot and shoemaker. He began in his early teens, watching specialists in the various stages of production of children's shoes to 'initiate and perfect' his skills. During the First World War he worked on the manufacture of military boots, but this left him with insufficient skill for civilian shoes. During the 1920s he therefore regularly moved jobs to perfect himself as a worker. Shoemaking still retained an artisanal element that needed to be learned on-the-job. Each firm had its own methods and style, but it was up to the individual to take the initiative to concoct his own 'Tour de France'. He further pursued his quest to be a 'complete craftsman' in Lyon, while lying low as an anarchist and deserter from military service. Returning to Paris and work in a factory in Belleville, he concluded that by his early twenties his 'peregrinations' had brought him real skill in his trade.[58] Jeanne Bouvier had an early career that pointed to the limited opportunities for women workers. She began with the cursory training sufficient for work as an eleven-year-old in a silk-throwing mill, feeling confident after a few hours on her first day. Her years as a domestic servant took her into the most common occupation for a young woman, though she managed to move on after a while. She became proficient in the quintessentially female skill of needlework, first in hat making, later in dressmaking.[59]

---

[57] Perdiguier, *Mémoires d'un compagnon*, passim.

[58] Michaud, *J'avais vingt ans*, passim.

[59] Bouvier, *Mes mémoires*, passim. On the limited opportunities for apprenticeships for girls, see Sohn, *Chrysalides*, I, pp. 355–6.

Going into trade

Various middle-class occupations in trade and industry required an apprenticeship that might be started relatively young. Businessmen writing their life stories for the edification of their children sometimes included an account of a gruelling work regime at this stage in their lives. Romain Lhopiteau (b. 1828), for example, gave an account of his private and commercial life to demonstrate what work, perseverance and an unshakeable will could achieve. He took a common path for ambitious young men born in the provinces but anxious to succeed in the capital. He started life on a farm in the Beauce region, with the usual basic schooling and work in the fields. Two years at a boarding school in Chartres to round off his primary education gave him the edge over most of his peers, and the chance to exercise his preference for a career in trade rather than farming. He began an apprenticeship as a draper in the town at the age of fifteen. There he learned the names, prices and qualities of all the materials, and gained experience of selling clothing to the countrywomen. His next step around the age of eighteen was to try his luck in Paris. A first attempt to find a job there came to nought. He was still too much the provincial, and to prove the point, he admitted making a fool of himself by ordering peasant dishes such as vegetable soup and stew in the posh Grand Véfour restaurant. Better prepared later in 1847, he established himself in the capital by moving around wholesale and retail houses as a *calicot*.[60] He recalled a regime of poor food, hard work and only being let out on Sunday evenings.[61] Paul Amiel (b. 1844) took a less 'exemplary' path, though his rapid shifts between trades was common enough. At twelve, his parents placed him as a clerk with a wine merchant. Soon afterwards they moved to Paris and set him up with an apprenticeship in setting precious stones, but he withdrew after suffering problems with his eyes. His next position was in a surgical goods company, learning both the accountancy and the sales side. This time he fell out with one of his superiors. Finally, at fourteen he began a ten-year stint as an *employé* in a men's outfitter, keeping the books and cleaning up the workshops.[62]

Conclusion: schooling the people

In the twentieth century the balance between work and school slowly shifted in favour of the latter during childhood and even adolescence. The gradual drift into work of an agrarian society yielded to the set age for leaving school and starting work that was characteristic of a bureaucratic state.

---

[60] See above, p. 211.
[61] Lhopiteau, *Soixante-deux années*, chs. 1–6. See also Lejeune, *Calicot*, passim.
[62] Amiel, *Souvenirs*, chs. 1–8.

In the late nineteenth century this age was twelve or thirteen, depending on whether one had passed the *certificat d'études* or not, and after 1936 it was fourteen. The time when young people had to sacrifice their primary education to the pressing needs of the family budget, depend on scholarships for secondary education and perhaps undergo the rough-and-tumble of life as an individual apprentice in a workshop would gradually pass. The cost was a withdrawal from the mainstream of the adult world, and subordination to a schools regime that not everyone appreciated. Moreover, for all the talk of the 'democratization' of education under the Republic, equality of access was far from evident in the middle of the twentieth century. A study of the village of Chanzeaux, in Anjou, found that in 1963 only 13 per cent of adolescents were attending a secondary school. Nearly all of them were drawn from the local 'bourgeoisie'. The rest of the youth started a career at fourteen, with the sons of artisans almost invariably becoming artisans, the sons of farmers becoming farmers, and girls helping around the family home, shop or farm. They did so without much enthusiasm, girls in particular expressing a wish to train for another job or to marry a non-farmer. The researchers concluded that in most cases it was a pipe dream.[63] A study by demographers at the Institut national des ètudes démographiques (INED) during the 1960s confirmed such persisting social inequalities at the national level. The child of a worker was twenty-five times less likely to attend university than the offspring of parents in the professions or higher management. The divergences set in early: already around the age of eleven or twelve children from modest backgrounds were on average registering lower marks at school than those from the middle classes.[64]

---

[63] Laurence Wylie, *Chanzeaux: A Village in Anjou* (Cambridge, MA: Harvard University Press, 1966), pp. 301–4.

[64] Alfred Sauvy and Alain Girard, 'Les Diverses Classes sociales devant l'enseignement', *Population*, 20 (1965), 205–32.

11   A 'long' childhood in the secondary schools

While children from the 'popular classes' generally left school at thirteen, those from the elite experienced a prolonged childhood in the secondary schools. The *collège* perfected by the Jesuits in the sixteenth and seventeenth centuries proved a remarkably durable institution. The historian Marie-Madeleine Compère argued that, together with the Napoleonic *lycée*, it provided the dominant model for secondary education over a good four centuries.[1] Only in the 1880s did it face a series of crises, as it struggled to adapt to a democratic and industrial type of society. Its success was based on its role in perpetuating the languages, literature and values of classical civilization. The prestige of 'classical humanities' in the educational sphere remained largely intact among the elite, both lay and clerical, throughout this period.[2] During the Second Empire, for example, even a dynamic group like the bourgeoisie of Mulhouse plumped firmly for an education in the humanities rather than the sciences.[3] The *collège*, we may recall, presented itself as a haven of scholarship for boys in a supposedly corrupt and materialistic world. The practice of sending pupils to be boarders rather than day boys, minimizing contact with the family and other outside influences, reached its peak in the middle of the nineteenth century. Starting with a minority of wealthy aristocrats in the seventeenth century, the *internats* became increasingly popular during the eighteenth century, and accounted for over half of the pupils by the 1840s. The curriculum in classical humanities had certain key characteristics. It preferred Latin to Greek, relied on selections of the more uplifting passages for the young rather than whole works

---

[1] Compère, *Du collège au lycée*, p. 265. Besides this work, the following paragraphs rely on Paul Gerbod, *La Vie quotidienne dans les lycées et collèges au XIXe siècle* (Paris: Hachette, 1968); Prost, *Histoire de l'enseignement*; Crubellier, *L'Enfance et la jeunesse*; and Françoise Mayeur, *De la Révolution à l'école républicaine*, vol. III of *Histoire générale de l'enseignement et de l'éducation en France*, ed. Louis-Henri Parias (Paris: G.-V. Labat, 1981).

[2] See, for example, R. D. Anderson, *Education in France, 1848–1870* (Oxford: Clarendon Press, 1975), ch. 4.

[3] Prost, *Histoire de l'enseignement*, p. 59.

and concentrated on rhetoric at the expense of logic. The *discours* in Latin or French, for example, required the pupil to put noble words in the mouth of a great man, such as a king or an emperor. The aim was to give a moral as well as an intellectual education, preparing the young man for public life. The sciences were by no means ignored, for some of the pupils needed these subjects to enter the *grandes écoles*. However, as a rule in the nineteenth century, these pupils were taught separately in special courses. The rest of the class squeezed in a little science towards the end of their studies. Teaching involved a type of 'apprenticeship' in classical civilization, with pupils spending much of their time working on their own. During the 1870s, for example, of the seven-and-a-half hours a *lycéen* devoted to his studies each day, only four were spent in class.[4]

These institutions were unashamedly elitist. As with the primary schools, measuring the numbers attending them is a hazardous business. Nonetheless, it is clear that until the 1930s their long and costly programme of studies excluded all but a wealthy minority, plus a small number of scholarship boys. In 1900, for example, there were 6.25 million pupils in the primary schools, but only 100,000 in state-run secondary schools.[5] Compère has warned that any assumption of rising numbers in line with the growth of the population and the middle classes will prove unfounded. If there were approximately 65,000 *collégiens* during the early seventeenth century, their total had declined to around 45,000 during the 1780s. She asserts a likely fall in numbers between 1680 and 1740, followed by a long period of stability over the next century. The period from the 1840s to the 1880s brought considerable expansion, but another period of stability followed. In 1881, there were 73,200 boys in the public system of *lycées* and *collèges*, equivalent to 2.35 per cent of the age group concerned. By 1930, this had risen to only 77,100, 3.58 per cent of the age group. The historian Antoine Prost concludes that even if one takes into account the private secondary schools, there remained 'an almost perfect stability' in the numbers of boys in secondary education during these fifty years of a republican regime.[6] The *lycée* in particular was a quintessentially 'bourgeois' institution. The *lycées* recruited above all from the professional classes, the industrial and commercial bourgeoisie, and the upper reaches of officialdom. From the time of the Restoration early in the nineteenth century, the provincial aristocracy in particular preferred to send its sons to the *petits séminaires* of the Catholic Church. The Catholic wing of the middle classes followed suit during the second

---

[4] Ibid., p. 50.   [5] Gerbod, *Lycées et collèges*, p. 97.
[6] Compère, *Du collège au lycée*, pp. 156–67; Prost, *Histoire de l'enseignement*, p. 259.

half of the century.[7] Meanwhile the cheaper and less demanding courses of the minor provincial *collèges* attracted families from the medium and lesser bourgeoisie: lower civil servants, small traders, and even artisans and peasants.

The French were proud of their secondary schools, and with good reason. The Jesuits, Oratorians and other religious congregations allowed their members to pursue their vocations as specialized teachers. The *régents* and *professeurs* of the *lycées* and *collèges* followed a similar path, insofar as they were often devoted to their task but poorly paid. Compère is persuasive in arguing that the initiation into the grammar and style of the classical humanities was as intellectually rigorous as any teaching of the sciences today.[8] Yet the secondary schools were not without their critics. For much of the nineteenth century there were accusations of cramming for exams at the expense of education proper. There was the claim that their curricula overloaded the pupils with work, notably during the 1880s and the 1920s. The system certainly tended to develop the mind rather than the body. The Minister of Education attempted to introduce gymnastics into the curriculum in 1869, but the initiative soon petered out. And there was the long battle between defenders of a classical education and those eager to adapt the schools to the needs of the 'industrial, commercial and agricultural classes'.[9] Finally there was the criticism that the barriers between the elite *collèges* and *lycées* on the one hand, and the primary schools and various intermediary institutions 'hovering in the uncertain regions between primary and secondary education',[10] such as Guizot's higher primary schools and private *pensionnats*, on the other, were out of place in a democratic society. The very persistence of a seventeenth-century model of a college in the post-revolutionary world suggests a certain inertia. There was plenty of tinkering with the system from the late eighteenth century onwards. All the same, the conservatism of the teaching profession, rivalry between Catholic schools and those run by the state, and perhaps also a reluctance to undermine a beacon of stability in the turbulent world of French politics, hindered fundamental change.

'Prisons' for children and adolescents?

Jules Vallès dedicated *L'Enfant* (1879) 'To all those who died of boredom at school or were reduced to tears in their family, who, during their

---

[7] Mension-Rigau, *L'Enfance au château*, p. 3.
[8] Compère, *Du collège au lycée*, p. 266.   [9] Anderson, *Education in France*, p. 65.
[10] Robert Gildea, *Education in Provincial France: A Study of Three Departments* (Oxford: Clarendon Press, 1983), p. 190.

childhood, were tyrannized by their schoolmasters or beaten by their parents.' Vallès was among the minority when he denounced his abusive parents, but was clearly hunting with the pack when he attacked school-masters. A comparative survey of childhood reminiscences by Richard N. Coe revealed that 'there are no children in the world who appear to loathe their schools and to despise their teachers as much as the inmates of the typical French *lycée*'. Coe argued that the French *lycée* could boast high academic standards, but that 'as a means of transmuting the average childhood into a more-than-Dantesque inferno of boredom, dreariness and frustration, it still awaits a rival'.[11] It was easy for hostile commenta-tors to depict *collèges* and above all the larger *lycèes* as prisons or barracks for the young. Their buildings were often forbidding, with high walls and barred windows. Inside they were no better, many being former monas-teries with dark corridors, bare classrooms and notoriously chilly dormi-tories. During the 1870s, Jules Vallès, the most ferocious of the critics, contrasted the lively atmosphere on the streets of Le Puy with the mourn-ful one of his *collège*. On the main square, drinkers shouted, swore and laughed as they sold their pigs and cattle; bars were full of noise and smoke. Two minutes away, the *collège* reeked of boredom and stank of ink: 'people entering and leaving deadened their gaze, their voice, their step, so as not to undermine the discipline, disturb the silence, interfere with the study'.[12]

The heavily academic curriculum was intellectually challenging, but there was little time for play or for sport. Julian Green, an American boy brought up and educated in Paris during the 1900s, brought the critical eye of an outsider to his experiences. Looking back on the austere way of life in a *lycée*, he wrote:

When I think of French youth in those days, I invariably see a boy bent over a desk stacked with books. How carefully he writes his *devoir*, his Latin themes and Greek exercises! At the age of fourteen he can read a page of Herodotus and find his way in the horrible chaos of the Hundred Years War. He can explain Newton's theory of colors and knows the population of distant Russian cities; he is greatly in advance of most European boys, but I wonder if he is happy.

Gymnastics lessons once a week, not taken too seriously by anyone, did little to develop physical strength.[13] The monastic-cum-military disci-pline was also potentially oppressive, particularly for boarders. The daily routine of the boys was minutely regulated, as they moved between the dormitory, the refectory, the study and the classroom. The original Napoleonic *lycée* ordered their movements with a drum. The boys spent

[11] Coe, 'Reminiscences of Childhood', 233–5.
[12] Vallès, *L'Enfant*, pp. 37–8.   [13] Green, *Memories of Happy Days*, p. 107.

long hours studying each day, ate in silence and, if boarding, rarely left the school. They were subject to constant supervision by *maîtres d'étude*. The *internes* rose at 5.30 in the morning and had lights-out early in the evening.[14] The merchant Gustave-Emmanuel Roy recalled a Spartan regime in the Collège Charlemagne between 1836 and 1844, admitting that he found it hard to get up at 5.30 each morning, wash at a tap on the staircase and survive on a stodgy diet. Maxime du Camp also lingered on his dreadful memories of nine years in the Collège Louis-le-Grand during the 1830s, because of the unbearable discipline. He lamented the suppression of all tenderness at a time when children needed it. Even Ernest Lavisse, writing as a famous historian and educational reformer, admitted that he could not face any more time in an *internat* as he reached the end of his school career during the 1850s. The constant jostling with other bodies, the twenty out of twenty-four hours a day without movement, the stale atmosphere, the walls, the rules and the 'ignorance of the laws which regulate the sensitive human plant' were too much for him.[15]

The disciplinary system was less harsh than in the primary schools (or in the English public schools), insofar as corporal punishment was banned at the beginning of the nineteenth century. However, the punishments available took a heavy toll on the free time of pupils. The *maîtres d'étude* or, in schoolboy slang, *pions* who supervised them outside class in secular schools were also generally reviled. The older ones suffered from their uncertain status between master and servant. Maxime du Camp remembered one of his comrades taunting a *maître d'étude* with 'You do well to stay in the college, because it is not in my family that you would be accepted as a *domestique*.'[16] The most common sanction was a *pensum* (lines), followed by temporary or permanent exclusion. Imprisonment in a cell was also an option until 1863. Jules Vallès/Jacques Vingtras, it might be noted, preferred the *cachot* to lines, on the grounds that he was free within its four walls to whistle, draw and play marbles.[17] Balancing the punishments was a system of rewards to stimulate competition among the pupils: good points, 'benches of honour' and prizes at the end of the year. Critics argued that the impersonal system of rewards and punishments in the larger schools pushed the pupils towards revolt. Certainly a number of former pupils bore witness to long-held resentment at their treatment in the schools. Jules Vallès depicted himself in *L'Enfant* (1879)

---

[14] Gerbod, *Lycées et collèges*, pp. 100–1.
[15] Roy, *Souvenirs*, p. 42; Maxime du Camp, *Souvenirs littéraires* (Paris: Aubier, 1994 (1892)), pp. 113–14; and Lavisse, *Souvenirs*, p. 265. See also Gustave Flaubert, *Diary of a Madman* (1838), in *Early Writings*, transl. Robert Griffin (Lincoln: University of Nebraska Press, 1991), p. 170; and Genevoix, *Trente mille jours*, pp. 71–95.
[16] Du Camp, *Souvenirs littéraires*, p. 120.   [17] Vallès, *L'Enfant*, p. 138.

rarely seeing the light of day for the *pensums* that rained down on him: a hundred lines for knocking over his ink-well, a hundred more for dropping his books, five pages of Greek grammar for questioning the imposition. The writer Henry Bataille (b. 1872), son of a Parisian lawyer, recalled the same petty tyranny of a *pion* during his time as a boarder (and recent orphan) at the Lycée Henri IV:

'Monsieur Bataille, five hours of detention . . .'
'But . . .'
'Ten hours.'
'I didn't . . .'
'Fifteen hours.'

He claimed that his 'moral torturer' knew the superiority of this method over corporal punishment, because the latter did not always leave the imprint of 'indelible sadness' on the flesh of the victim. He at least had his revenge when he exposed the *pion* in question as a paedophile. On the other side of the coin, pupils might let off steam by ragging a weak and ineffectual supervisor. In *Le Petit Chose* (1868), Alphonse Daudet revived dreadful memories of waging war as a very young *pion* with a group of fifty well-off sharecroppers' sons from the mountainous parts of the Cévennes – and losing.[18]

Régents and *professeurs* received a mixed press, as might be expected from those who had been subject to their authority. It was easy to pillory the odd eccentric or unpleasant character. Vallès singled out Turfin, *professeur* in the fourth class, who 'holds the *pions* in contempt, the poor in contempt, ill-treats the scholarship boys, and mocks the badly dressed'. During the 1890s Maurice Barrès singled out a philosophy teacher at Nancy as 'a product of pedagogy, a son of reason, foreign to our family, local or traditional customs, entirely abstract and in truth suspended in the void'.[19] Frédéric Mistral railed more generally at the 'grim old gray-beards' in his college in Avignon during the 1840s, Henry Bataille at the 'intellectual stupidity' of the teaching profession, contrasting its 'dogmatic pedagogy' with the 'sovereign fantasy of the mind'.[20] The odd disgruntled soul went as far as to express disenchantment with the content of their education. From an eighteenth-century aristocratic perspective, Jean de Norvins complained that nine years of study in a *collège* and two in a law school, bathed in the 'pale and tired rays of an antique sun', he was

---

[18] Ibid., pp. 138–9; Henry Bataille, 'L'Enfance éternelle', *Les Oeuvres libres*, 7 (1921), 5–60 (38–50); and Daudet, *Petit Chose*, pp. 67–8.
[19] Vallès, *L'Enfant*, pp. 137–8; Barrès, *Les Déracinés*, cited in Gerbod, *Lycées et collèges*, p. 112.
[20] Mistral, *Memoirs*, p. 73; and Bataille, 'L'Enfance éternelle', 19–21.

completely unprepared for the modern world, and had to start a whole new education to adapt. With some justification, Jules Vallès highlighted the emphasis on imitating ancient authorities, rather than on any creativity in the Latin or French language. He had a master tell him that he was at college to chew and rechew what had already been chewed before. The future poet Francis Jammes indulged himself in a long diatribe against the specialized knowledge of teachers. He scoffed at fifty-year-old scholars who burst out laughing because he thought that Virgil was the author of the *Metamorphoses*, or historians who claimed to excite pupils with the clauses of the Pyrenees Treaties. Ernest Lavisse was more measured in his criticisms. He acknowledged the love of Latin and Greek inspired by his teachers, but regretted that the classical authors he studied were never placed in their social context. He also noted his ignorance of the French classics, modern languages and the sciences – a reproach, it is important to add, that served to justify his later educational reforms.[21]

Yet for all the temptation to put down the school system, some writers were prepared to acknowledge the benefits it conferred on them. Those on its margins, who had to leave early for example, certainly showed an awareness of its privileges. André Chamson retained bitter memories from around 1910 of breaking up for the summer at his *lycée* in Alès with the fear that he would never return. As his father teetered on the brink of bankruptcy, he felt only shame and despair. The *professeur* had explained that the following year they would start Latin, the route to being an *honnête homme* and to noble careers in the professions. In similar vein, Jean Guéhenno (b. 1890) lingered on the humiliation of having to leave his *collège* in Fougères at the age of fourteen when his father fell ill. He failed the examination for a scholarship: 'I was excluded, apparently according to the rules and through lack of merit. I was condemned by my own stupidity and rendered up to it.' Yet he could hardly avoid feeling a sense of injustice. His classmates, wealthier than him but no more shrewd, were able to carry on, even if they were not particularly interested in their studies. This 'crisis of his childhood', he reflected, determined the rest of his life. Henceforth, on the rebound, he confessed to overestimating the value of that 'elixir distilled in the colleges and the universities' culture. He eventually became a writer.[22]

It is possible that day boys were more likely than former boarders to harbour positive feelings about their school days. Certainly Anatole

---

[21] Jean de Norvins, *Mémorial de Jean de N.*, pp. 24–5, cited by Bély, 'L'Elève et le monde', 12; Vallès, *L'Enfant*, pp. 227 and 245; Jammes, *De l'âge divin*, pp. 96–7; and Lavisse, *Souvenirs*, pp. 212–29. See also Nora, 'Ernest Lavisse', 75.

[22] Chamson, *Chiffre de nos jours*, pp. 229–34 and 246; and Guéhenno, *Changer la vie*, pp. 129–30.

France was convinced that had he been a *pensionnaire* in a *lycée* his memories of his studies would have been 'cruel'. He made the case that, in avoiding the slave-like existence of the so-called *bagne* (prison), he grew up without hatred. Free to enjoy the bustle of the Parisian streets each day, he could satisfy his curiosity about the world around him and understand the 'social machine'. Moreover, if the school taught him the sciences, the 'domestic school' brought the gentler stimulus of family conversation.[23] The comradeship of the school was important to those who were without close siblings or who had struggled to mix with other children when young. Jules Michelet (b. 1798) admitted that the 'great event of his adolescence' was finding a true friend in his class at the age of thirteen. In Rouen, Charles Nicolle (b. 1866) found, as he put it, comrades, if not friends, hampered by his shyness, his tendency to throw a ball like a girl, and later deafness. Sartre fared better: 'Finally, I had school-friends! Me, the excluded child in the public park, they adopted me on the first day and in the most natural way in the world: I never looked back.'[24] The figure of the '*bon maître*' also appeared beside the bad one. Michelet acknowledged the efforts of one of his teachers at the Lycée Charlemagne, M. Andrieux d'Alba, a man of good heart and of God, who did all he could for a mediocre pupil. Maxime du Camp reserved his venom for the *pions*, contrasting them with the generally knowledgeable and benevolent *professeurs*. Ernest Lavisse took a similar line, hating the *pions* at his *collège* in Laon and his *lycée* in Paris, but praising most of the masters.[25]

Education for girls

Girls were traditionally educated 'on the Church's knees'.[26] This might mean going to a convent school, or simply a thoroughly religious education beside one's mother. Even among clerics, there was a current of opinion favouring the raising of girls safely in the bosom of the family. It received a boost in the early nineteenth century in response to Enlightenment critiques of the cloistering of girls in convents. However, it was also a demanding business, and not all mothers felt that they had the time or the

---

[23] France, *Livre de mon ami*, pp. 311–16.
[24] Michelet, *Ma jeunesse*, p. 53; Nicolle, 'Mémoires', pp. 43–50; and Sartre, *Les Mots*, pp. 180–1.
[25] Michelet, *Ma jeunesse*, p. 95; du Camp, *Souvenirs littéraires*, p. 119; and Lavisse, *Souvenirs*, pp. 145 and 204–5.
[26] The most important study of girls' education remains Mayeur, *L'Education des filles*. This section also relies on Martin-Fugier, *La Bourgeoise*; and, more popular in approach, Isabelle Bricard, *Saintes ou pouliches: l'éducation des jeunes filles au XIXe siècle* (Paris: Albin Michel, 1985).

ability to undertake it. The alternative of sending daughters to a school rested on the same foundations in the Catholic Reformation that had inspired *collèges* for boys. The boarding school found increasing favour with aristocratic and bourgeois parents, particularly during the nineteenth century. To avoid the danger of daughters being led into a religious vocation, they usually sought a short period of a year or two away from home to prepare for first communion. Before 1867, and the innovation of 'special classes' to complement the primary schools, the Catholic Church had a virtual monopoly on the education of girls. Private *pensionnats* provided some competition before then, but it was only late in the nineteenth century that the state took real steps to provide secondary education for girls. Leaders of the Third Republic entered the arena at this point as part of their campaign to snatch education from the hands of the Church. The *loi Camille Sée* of 1880 was an important turning point, insofar as it provided the opportunity for girls from relatively wealthy backgrounds to attend a *lycée* or *collège*. In contrast to boys at this period, the number of girls in secondary education rose considerably, from a few hundred during the 1880s to around 30,000 during the 1930s.[27]

There was a certain logic and coherence to the system of girls' education, though not one that appeals to the twenty-first-century mind. The assumption among leading republicans as much as leading Catholics was that girls had a different vocation in life to men: different in their view, but not necessarily inferior. The ideal was 'la Femme au Foyer', the woman who dedicated her life to her husband and her children. The historian Anne Martin-Fugier has argued that the nineteenth century brought a certain 'colonization' of established aristocratic models for women by a 'bourgeois' model, keen to emphasize women's role as mother and philanthropist. Hence the gradual evolution of a set of ideals for wealthy women who did not need to work, justifying their existence by setting them up as wife, mother, mistress of the house and educator.[28] It followed that they did not need the long immersion in the classical humanities that prepared their menfolk for public life. The appropriate education for them was instead one that developed supposedly eternal 'feminine' values such as compassion, modesty and submissiveness.

Education for girls long revolved around the interests of men. During the 1760s, Rousseau in *Emile* famously designed the education of Sophie so that she would make a suitable companion for Emile. In order to please him, and to be a 'natural woman' as he was shaping up as a 'natural man', she needed practical studies rather than 'principles and

---

[27] Mayeur, *L'Education des filles*, pp. 167–8.   [28] Martin-Fugier, *La Bourgeoise*, pp. 13–14.

axioms' in the sciences. He proposed subjects related to 'the labours of her own sex', notably needlework, lace making and governing the house-hold.[29] Sophie remained the ideal woman for several prominent thinkers on the left during the nineteenth century, from Michelet to Proudhon. Condorcet appeared more radical with his plans during the Revolution to give equal instruction to males and females. Yet again, though, he assumed that women would have a domestic rather than a public role. If they had the same right to education as men, it was so that they could supervise children, maintain equality in the family and help men keep up the knowledge they acquired during their youth. As Françoise Mayeur has observed, the republican legislators of the 1880s appeared to have been raised on Condorcet.[30] Their *lycées* for girls were designed to produce good republican wives and mothers for the elite, not career women. The ideal of the *mère-éducatrice* was as important for republicans as Catholics in the nineteenth century, as both sides perceived the importance of moth-ers as educators in the long battle for the soul of France. Auguste Moll desired that they be 'ni bas-bleu ni pot-au-feu': neither a bluestocking who could not cook, nor a housewife with no intellectual charms.[31] The curriculum in these *lycées* was reasonably progressive, including studies of the classics (in translation), French and other modern languages and the history of civilization. At the same time the girls studied domestic science and hygiene. Yet it led not to the *baccalauréat* and entry into a career, but to the dead-end of a finishing certificate, the *diplôme de fin d'études secondaires*. This whole approach to the education of girls, or rather girls among the elite, began to lose its ascendancy during the late nineteenth and early twentieth centuries. Families pressed for teaching qualifications or the *baccalauréat* for their daughters, and feminists criti-cized the denial of opportunities to prepare for an existence independent of men. As a symptom of changing attitudes, in 1924 the Minister of Instruction decreed that girls should have the option of taking the same course of studies as boys in preparation for the *baccalauréat*.[32]

The girls themselves often accepted, for a while at least, the religious orientation expected of them in many middle-class circles. In 1765, aged about twelve, Manon Phlipon (later Madame Roland) asked to be able to prepare for her first communion in a convent, following a crisis when a pupil of her father tried to seduce her. Ten years later she had lapsed from the Catholic faith. Aurore Dupin (George Sand) experienced a similar

---

[29] Rousseau, *Emile*, pp. 386–7 and 394.   [30] Mayeur, *L'Education des filles*, p. 29.
[31] Cited by Martin-Fugier, *La Bourgeoise*, p. 263.
[32] Karen Offen, 'The Second Sex and the Baccalauréat in Republican France, 1880–1924', *French Historical Studies*, 13 (1983), 252–86.

religious phase during her three years at the Couvent des dames anglaises between 1818 and 1820. At the age of fifteen, she later wrote, she experienced a religious conversion, inspired by the heroic tales of confessors and martyrs. She spent the summer after her first communion in a state of 'complete beatitude', and contemplated entering a religious order. Her Mother Superior, aware that her mother and grandmother would hardly tolerate such a move, and wary of accusations of leading her on, counselled patience. Soon afterwards, the young Aurore became disillusioned with the nuns and their faith.[33] Girls also welcomed the opportunity to make friends among their classmates, though, like their male counterparts, future writers and intellectuals affected to despise most of those around them. On the eve of the First World War, Clara Goldschmidt (the future Clara Malraux) and her friend Lisbeth were harsh in their judgement of the girls at their private school in Paris, the Cours Sainte-Clotilde. Both having Jewish and foreign backgrounds, they adopted the sceptical view of the outsider when judging good Catholic girls. What Malraux found dispiriting above all was the submissiveness of the other pupils: 'you told them that Louis XVI was a saintly man, they accepted it, that the Pope was infallible, they accepted it, that the Chinese fed their children to pigs, they accepted it'. Similarly, Simone de Beauvoir (b. 1908), together with her friend 'Zaza', scorned the 'helpless resignation' of her fellow pupils at the prestigious Cours Désir in Paris. Not for her the acquisition of some feminine accomplishments such as decorating china, occasional visits to the opera and marriage to a suitable young man, for she planned to earn her own living as a teacher.[34]

Girls naturally suffered as much as boys from the dingy surroundings of the typical convent school, the burdens of rules and regulations at every turn, and the occasional vindictive teacher. The notorious Marie Lafarge (b. 1816) recalled from her prison cell in 1841 the contrast between the liberty of her early years before school and the detailed timetable for each day in her *pension*. She struggled to remember all the irksome rules, such as the need to curtsey every time she opened and closed a door, to wear a hat in the refectory and to speak quietly.[35] What stood out above all else in the education of upper- and middle-class girls was its haphazard nature. Boys in this milieu were not always well served by their families, but the higher priority given to their education over that of girls meant that it tended to follow some sort of plan according to their

---

[33] Roland, *Mémoires de Madame Roland*, p. 10; Sand, *Histoire de ma vie*, pp. 393–4 and 405–13.

[34] Malraux, *Apprendre à vivre*, pp. 161–2; and de Beauvoir, *Memoirs of a Dutiful Daughter*, pp. 151–2.

[35] Lafarge, *Mémoires de Marie Capelle*, I, pp. 36–40.

needs. Girls, by contrast, often had to meander around the periphery of the educational system. George Sand, to take an aristocratic example from the beginning of the nineteenth century, began her studies at the age of seven in her home. She learned French grammar from her brother's *précepteur* (tutor), music from her grandmother, and reading and writing from her mother. She started to learn Latin with the tutor, but soon dropped it, and felt in retrospect that she had spent insufficient time on grammar to master her own language during her childhood. Private lessons in dancing, handwriting and drawing for her and her brother she considered so superficial as to be a waste of money. She acquired knowledge for its own sake:

It was not a question of being educated to become better, happier or wiser. I learned so that I would be able to converse with educated people, to read the books in my bookcase, and to kill time in the countryside or elsewhere.

Adolescence with the nuns of the Couvent des Anglaises in Paris brought only a little Italian, a little music, a little drawing, a fair amount of English – and a desire to write.[36] Pauline de Broglie fared no better under a series of private tutors in Paris during the 1890s. 'A little history, a little literature, a little Latin, a little Greek (why not?). When you have no curriculum and are not preparing for any exams, you can do every-thing, and what importance does it have for girls?' When during her teens she visited a school founded by her parents in Anjou, she was ashamed to discover that she could not solve a problem on the board designed for peasant girls aged seven or eight.[37]

Among the upper bourgeoisie, generally more committed to academic achievement than the nobility, girls were still severely disadvantaged com-pared to boys in the early twentieth century. Around the time of the First World War, Clara Goldschmidt moved from the Cours Sainte-Clotilde to a short spell at the Lycée Molière, time in a private school and indi-vidual tutoring in Latin and English. She still failed her *baccalauréat*.[38] Simone de Beauvoir famously challenged the expectations of society at large on what a 'feminine' education should involve. She began with the entirely useless 'Adéline Désir Diploma' awarded by her private school. She envied her cousin Jacques his education at the prestigious Collège Stanislas, feeling like an outcast as she walked past the building. She con-trasted his extensive knowledge of literature and his 'brilliantly clever' teachers with her own 'expurgated, insipid, faded' version of knowledge

---

[36] Sand, *Histoire de ma vie*, pp. 254–69, 309–11 and 387.
[37] Pange, *1900*, I, pp. 216–17, and II, p. 65.
[38] Malraux, *Apprendre à vivre*, pp. 216–17 and 237.

passed on by old schoolmarms. Eventually she succeeded in passing her *baccalauréat*, though some mediocre teaching at the Cours Désir meant that she only scraped a pass in the dissertation section.[39]

Conclusion

The growing intrusion of the school system into childhood and adolescence was one of the major changes affecting the experience of growing up in modern France. The expansion of the secondary schools in particular had the effect of 'prolonging' childhood. It is easy to adopt a triumphalist tone in this sphere. The extensive 'schooling' of the population appears part and parcel of the emergence of a characteristically 'modern' childhood. In the French case, mass education is associated by the majority with a truly republican and democratic society. Yet, as the historian Antoine Prost shrewdly observed, if one asks whether the school system influences society, or society the schools, it is likely to be the latter that is most in evidence.[40] In a highly unequal society like modern France, it is hardly surprising to find differences in access and achievement according to various influences, notably socio-economic background and gender, evident throughout the period under consideration here. Certainly, the emergence of a more 'middle-class' society evened out some of the disparities, and the educational system itself spawned a series of innovations, from higher primary schools to vocational qualifications, in order to bridge the gap between the school of the *notables* and that of the people. The fact remains that it was only in the middle of the twentieth century that the secondary schools began to recruit beyond a narrow social and intellectual elite. Before then, sons and eventually daughters benefited from the exclusion of the vast majority of the population from higher 'civilization' and a career in the liberal professions. In a way, though, they had to earn it. The long years under the austere regime of the typical *collège* or *lycée* were a long way from the voyage of discovery dreamed of by Rousseau in the eighteenth century for his Emile.

[39] De Beauvoir, *Memoirs of a Dutiful Daughter*, pp. 103, 121–2 and 150–60.
[40] Prost, *Histoire de l'enseignement*, p. 345.

The 'modern' vision of childhood that gradually emerged in France and elsewhere in the West from the eighteenth century onwards tends to hold back young people from adult responsibilities for as long as possible. It keeps them away from the world of work, denies them the vote (until they are eighteen) and tries to shelter them from their own sexuality. Its emphasis on the innocence and vulnerability of children certainly brought many benefits to the population. It eventually encouraged nearly everyone in a country like France to think of childhood as a period when the individual would have time to mature physically, morally and intellectually, spared from the burden of having to earn a living. All the same, childhood and adolescence are transition periods, between the complete dependence of infancy and the supposed independence of adulthood. There was an inevitable tension between the desire to stay cocooned within the family and the ambition to make one's way in a wider world. Educators like Rousseau might call for a slowing of the process of maturity, to allow the young person to prepare adequately for the harsh realities of adult life, while the young themselves have often been eager to hurry along the path to the higher status associated with growing up.

The pressure in the modern period to move to a 'long' childhood brought its own peculiar forms of conflict between the generations. In the French case under consideration here, one can find evidence of parents unwilling to discuss sexual matters with their children, notably where girls were concerned. One can also document efforts by various figures of authority to come to terms with the willingness of young people to devote themselves to religious or political causes: part of the 'crisis of originality' associated with adolescence around 1900. In a country tormented by periodic extremes of revolution and counter-revolution, not to mention difficult relations between Church and state, this was not to be treated lightly. What the young had to do in a modern society, where people were less and less likely to live in a meaningful local community, was to form (and re-form) their own individual identity. Sooner or later they also had to move out from the family home and set up their own household.

Establishing identities

Historians have now generally moved on from a Marxist-inspired preoccupation with class and its links to social structures. They have become wary of assuming that, for example, the living and working conditions of nineteenth- and twentieth-century proletarians led inexorably to mobilization under a socialist banner, or that after 1830 the landowning, financial and industrial interests of the *grande bourgeoisie* in France determined a commitment to Orleanism. It was not difficult to demonstrate that the orientation of certain regions to the political left or right was rarely explicable in terms of class backgrounds. Some traditionally left-wing areas of France had large concentrations of workers, but most were heavily rural or service-based.[1] In other words, historians have 'unhooked' political from socio-economic change. They now place more emphasis on autonomous developments within the political and cultural sphere. The result is a widespread abandonment in the recent historiography of relatively fixed and stable notions of class and social structure in favour of 'mobile, fractured and contradictory' identities. These identities are the product of particular historical circumstances. People might consider themselves part of, say, a working class, but they might also identify with a local community, a church or their gender. All such identities emerge as temporary and unstable, since they cannot be tied to a material base in society. Hence, young people inherit certain forms of identity from their parents, acquire others in the school system, might throw themselves into the world of the convent or the socialist movement during a spell of youthful idealism, and continue to adjust to the influences of family, friends, the printed word and historical events throughout their lives.[2]

Local, regional and national identities

The obvious starting point here was the identification of a young peasant with a *pays* or a young worker with the popular *quartier* of a town. One thinks of Frédéric Mistral and the 'Lou Caiéu' plain near Arles, Pierre-Jakez Hélias and the pays Bigouden of Brittany, Emilie Carles and her valley high in the Alps, Jean Giono and the small town of Manosque, René Michaud and the Thirteenth Arrondissement of Paris, or Jean-Baptiste Dumay and the company town of Le Creusot. Antoine Sylvère

---

[1] The case is persuasively made in Hervé le Bras and Emmanuel Todd, *L'Invention de la France* (Paris: Livre de poche, 1981), passim.

[2] See, for example, the Introduction to Nicholas B. Dirks, Geoff Eley and Sherry B. Ortner (eds.), *Culture/Power/History: A Reader in Contemporary Social Theory* (Princeton: Princeton University Press, 1994), pp. 3–45.

admitted that, as late as 1897, his universe was limited to the four cardinal points of the Vallée de la Dore, near Ambert in the Auvergne. The rest of the world, as far as he and his friends were concerned, had nothing to do with them. René Michaud described his street, the passage Charles Berthau, as his Parisian hamlet, similar to a *pays*, with families, friends and workmates sharing their sorrows and their joys in the midst of extreme poverty.[3] Admittedly, not all children from the 'popular classes' were rooted to a particular spot. Some had parents who moved frequently, others preferred to emphasize their poverty and class allegiances over any local identity. Nonetheless, some former peasants pursued their links to a locality by framing their life story in terms of a fierce attachment to a regional identity. Frédéric Mistral famously made a pitch for the defence of the Provençal language and culture as they faced an onslaught from French nationalism during the nineteenth and twentieth centuries. Besides highlighting his early education in Provençal, and time spent in the company of ploughmen, harvesters and shepherds, he revelled in the 'land of Cockaigne' surrounding his village of Maillane. He described how he and his classmates regularly charged out from their boarding school, located in an abandoned monastery high in the hills, and became 'intoxicated by the fragrance of the mountains':

The surrounding hills were covered with thyme, rosemary, asphodel, boxwood, and lavender. There were several small vineyards, which as a matter of fact produced a renowned vintage, the wine of Frigolet; several patches of olive trees planted in the bottom of the valleys; several rows of crooked, blackened almond trees, stunted by the rocky soil; several wild fig trees growing in the clefts of the rock. That was all the cultivated land scattered about that mass of hills. The rest was nothing but wasteland and rubble, but how good it smelled![4]

In similar vein, Pierre-Jakez Hélias used his childhood reminiscences to celebrate the landscape, the village community and the traditional oral culture of his native Brittany, even as they were in the process of being transformed by modernization during the late twentieth century.[5]

Some people noted a commitment to the wider, 'imagined' community of the French nation during their youth, particularly under the Third Republic. Aristocrats claimed that their families had a long tradition of nurturing patriotic feeling for France. A male born in 1911, replying to a questionnaire on his upbringing in this milieu, wrote of his image of France that it was 'The foremost country in the world, the only civilized and civilizing one.' André Chamson waxed even more lyrical, in his case from the perspective of a small-town, middle-class family. Writing

---

[3] Sylvère, *Toinou*, p. 170; and Michaud, *J'avais vingt ans*, p. 16.
[4] Mistral, *Memoirs*, p. 51.   [5] Hélias, *Horse of Pride*, passim.

during the 1950s, he was aware that it was easy to mock such sentiments, but admitted becoming caught up in them during the 1900s. He too proclaimed France the foremost country in the world, learning at his *lycée* that her people were at the forefront of inventiveness, with the aeroplane, the motorcar and the cinema to their credit. Visiting Paris in 1913, he watched assorted infantry, cavalry and artillery regiments march by during the annual Bastille Day parade. He later wrote, 'I was French, and, what I saw, was the French army, the army of the leading country in the world, an army which nobody could beat!' Even a budding socialist worker like René Michaud found himself swept up in the wave of patriotic feeling at the outbreak of war with Germany in 1914.[6] As a foreigner, the American-born Julian Green confessed that he too found the attractions of French nationalism hard to resist on the eve of this war. Filled with stories of 'our ancestors the Gauls', around the age of eight 'I became French the moment I crossed the threshold of our schoolroom and put on my black alpaca apron.' Given that he was writing in the aftermath of the fall of France in 1940, it was doubtless tempting to show solidarity by recalling his immersion in an earlier defeat of the French by their neighbours from across the Rhine. In any case, it was his history teacher who reduced him to tears with stories of the horrors of 1870 and the humiliation of Sedan. He was aware that it was absurd for a young boy to be crying over military defeats that occurred forty years before he was born, but as he put it that was 'part of what we are pleased to call education'. Clara Goldschmidt (later Clara Malraux) found her dual national identity harder to cope with at the same period, since her family background straddled the two rival nations. She recalled her shock at discovering old school exercise books belonging to her German uncle that described military victory in 1870 over those she considered 'us'. She bristled at a German poem with the line 'Spank the beautiful red breeches, of those fine French gentlemen.' The influence of her school, her reading and her friends ensured that her potentially divided loyalties veered towards the French side, even before 1914.[7]

A religious identity

The large majority of French people considered themselves Roman Catholics during the nineteenth and twentieth centuries, but increasingly this meant little more than outward conformity to the rituals of

---

[6] Mension-Rigau, *L'Enfance au château*, pp. 238–40; Chamson, *Chiffre de nos jours*, pp. 37 and 386–8; and Michaud, *J'avais vingt ans*, p. 77.
[7] Green, *Memories of Happy Days*, pp. 28 and 40; and Malraux, *Apprendre à vivre*, pp. 101–5.

baptism, marriage and burial. Membership of the Catholic Church was not an important part of their sense of who they were.[8] Like the villagers, most autobiographers from the towns recorded their first communion as an important event. They might also have a youthful period of religious fervour, as already noted in the cases of Mme Roland and George Sand.[9] Yet if they came from a region of advanced 'dechristianization', or involved themselves in radical politics, they were likely to fall away from the Church soon enough. At the age of sixteen, for example, the worker Louise Vanderwielen (b. 1906) became bored with the Church, not finding that it offered a supportive system for life.[10] At a similar age in Paris, Simone de Beauvoir suddenly withdrew from confession and stopped believing in God. Differences between her pious, Catholic mother and her sceptical father paved the way. 'This imbalance,' she added, 'which made my life a kind of endless disputation, is the main reason why I became an intellectual.'[11]

The young readily followed the strong current of anti-clericalism in French society, particularly after 1789. René Michaud was aware of good and bad priests in Paris during the 1900s: those living close to the poor, and those who gave themselves aristocratic airs, preaching a message of resignation and acceptance. At the same period, Georges Navel, son of a worker in the Pont-à-Mousson steelworks, recounted taking exception to the local priest cuffing him and insulting him. He soon stopped going to Mass.[12] Bizarrely enough, some children found confession an ordeal, because they were not sure of what sins to raise with the priest. Anatole France wrote that at the age of ten he was by no means ready to explore his conscience, not least because he had difficulty in finding any sins to confess. A book of sins was no great help, since there were so many to choose from, including obscure ones such as simony, fornication and concupiscence. François Mauriac evidently solved the problem as an adolescent by running through a set menu every time: 'having been greedy, a liar, disobedient, idle, having said his prayers badly, heard mass poorly, having been proud, a scandal-monger . . .'.[13]

All this should not lead one to ignore the core of devout Catholics in modern France. They may have accounted for only around 10 per cent

[8] For overviews of Catholicism in modern France, see Gérard Cholvy and Yves-Marie Hilaire, *Histoire religieuse de la France contemporaine* (3 vols., Toulouse: Privat, 1985–8); and Ralph Gibson, *A Social History of French Catholicism, 1789–1914* (London: Routledge, 1989).
[9] See above, pp. 248–9.   [10] Vanderwielen, *Louise du plat pays*, pp. 85–6.
[11] De Beauvoir, *Memoirs of a Dutiful Daughter*, pp. 41 and 133–8.
[12] Michaud, *J'avais vingt ans*, pp. 29–33; and Navel, *Travaux*, p. 25.
[13] France, *Livre de mon ami*, pp. 299–300; and François Mauriac, *Un adolescent d'autrefois* (Paris: Flammarion, 1969), p. 24. See also Pange, *1900*, p. 189.

of the population by the early twentieth century. Nonetheless, the long period of repression under the early Third Republic meant that those remaining in the fold had proved the depth of their commitment. There was a gender dimension here, with observance of Catholic rituals such as attendance at Mass associated with women (and children) rather than adult males. The historian Paul Seeley noted the ordeal faced by the odd adolescent boy among the bourgeoisie of Lyon who during the 1860s and 1870s chose to remain a devout Catholic, in the face of scorn and malevolence from his peers at school.[14] There was also a social and political dimension to such a religious allegiance, insofar as the infamous alliance between the 'throne and the altar' under the Bourbon Restoration persisted through the nineteenth and early twentieth centuries. That is to say, aristocratic families, and later wealthy bourgeois ones also, held out against the growing forces of republicanism and democracy by loyalty to those twin bastions of conservatism in France: monarchism and the Catholic faith.[15] This is not to dispute the sincerity of fervent Catholics from this milieu. The 'spiritual diaries' of some of the young women bear witness to their struggle to become worthy Christians. Philippe Lejeune was surely right to note the lack of inventiveness in this type of adolescent diary. To him they all sounded much the same, as the girls set about assimilating the attitudes and discourses of others.[16] They may be a 'pain to read' nowadays, but they at least give some insight into the acquisition of a Catholic identity during the second half of the nineteenth century.

To begin with, they all treated their first communion as a pivotal event in their spiritual life: the day they first received God. In August 1888, Marie Lenéru wrote:

When I examine my memories and seek the passages of my life that I would like most of all to relive, there is a delicious moment, which I cannot think about without my heart beating faster, that moment after my first communion – Ah! My poor dear first communion, you are far away in time but near in my heart – has been the sweetest in my life.[17]

Second, in this 'ultramontane and clerical' form of Catholicism in nineteenth-century France, the young women enjoyed the company of priests, and the liturgy of their 'dear church'.[18] They wrote appreciatively of the sermons they heard, time passed on retreats and the confessional.

---

[14] Paul Seeley, 'O Sainte Mère: Liberalism and the Socialization of Catholic Men in Nineteenth-Century France', *Journal of Modern History*, 70 (1998), 862–91 (883–6).

[15] Mension-Rigau, *L'Enfance au château*, ch. 10.

[16] Lejeune, *Le Moi des demoiselles*, pp. 26 and 39.

[17] Lenéru, *Journal*, 17 October 1888. See also Brame, *Journal intime*, 26 May 1865; and Jeanne G., *Journal*, 18 June 1900.

[18] Perrot, 'Enquête', in Brame, *Journal intime*, p. 200.

Caroline Brame, brought up in the Faubourg Saint-Germain during the Second Empire, recorded a dinner in 1865 with M. De L'Escaille, the parish priest of Sainte-Clotilde, as 'very lively, full of laughter and very mordant; I must say that I teased him a lot'.[19] Finally, they reflected endlessly on their sins, and on their efforts to care for others. Their sins were in truth not very exciting, and their concern for the poor often heavy on the rhetoric. The young girl 'Clotilde' wrote in her diary that she felt guilty at having a nice house when the poor did not. All the same, she stood apart from the society around her during the 1880s and 1890s. She recognized that the labourers on a farm owned by her father 'pass their whole life in work and poverty to provide us with superfluity' and found the conversation of her more worldly friends boring. She eventually found a purpose in life looking after her brother's children when they were orphaned young.[20]

For minority creeds in a nominally Catholic country, a religious identity of some form was difficult to avoid. Protestants were brought up with the heritage of disastrous religious wars and repression in past centuries, plus a suspicion in Catholic circles after the 1789 Revolution that they were associated with liberalism and republicanism. During the 1860s, Pierre Loti gradually lost his early enthusiasm for a vocation as a pastor or a missionary as his faith weakened, yet he revered books and letters passed down within the family from his exiled Huguenot ancestors. Augustine Rouvière (b. 1883) grew up with the blood-soaked religious history of the Cévennes in mind, as Catholics and Protestants still kept to their own in her day.[21] Other young people were conscious of conflicting religious identities within their own family background. Francis Jammes remembered Bastille Day celebrations in Bordeaux in 1880, with his father, influenced by his Huguenot background and Jean-Jacques Rousseau, being careful not to offend his Catholic mother.[22] For the even smaller minority of Jews in France, less than 1 per cent of the population during the late nineteenth century, one can assume a similar consciousness of difference, though there are naturally few childhood reminiscences to draw from. Certainly, Clara Goldschmidt drew attention to her position as the only Jewish pupil in a Catholic school for girls in Paris during the early twentieth century. Although her family was lax in observing the customs of her faith, as a Jewish person in a Catholic country, not to mention a

---

[19] Brame, *Journal intime*, 7 June 1865.   [20] *Journal de Clotilde*, passim.
[21] Loti, *Le Roman d'un enfant*, pp. 126–30 and 138–9; and Rey, *Augustine Rouvière*, pp. 17–18.
[22] Jammes, *De l'âge divin*, pp. 196–9.

part-German one in France, she pronounced herself familiar with 'ambiguity, duality and multiplicity'.[23]

Class identities and political allegiances

Children began by assuming, almost without question, the social attitudes and political beliefs of their families. Parents considered it a duty to pass on their values to their offspring, and the very young were hardly in a position to resist. In the French case, the schools they sent them to emphatically reinforced such values, given the long struggle between Catholic and secular institutions. There was also a generational influence, as young people experienced the shock waves generated by momentous events such as the French Revolution or the Commune of 1871. Finally, adolescents in particular might begin to carve out their own independent identity through their reading, their contacts with other young people and their involvement in various types of political organization. Adults generally adopted a patronizing attitude to youthful forays into politics, assuming them to be naive or misguided.[24] The French political system was generally more democratic than most after 1789, but it was hardly encouraging for the young. During the 1790s, and again after 1848, the constitution laid down twenty-one as the inevitably rather arbitrary minimum voting age. Conversely, the term 'youth' itself took on a political dimension during the late nineteenth century, implying dynamism and greater inclusiveness. Both the Left and the Right made efforts to drum up support among young people with specialized youth organizations.

The social elite of aristocrats and upper bourgeoisie was remarkably effective in immersing its young in a hermetically sealed world of family and friends. By this means it imposed a particular view of the world, barely contaminated by outside influences.[25] As already noted, this *bain culturel* ('cultural bath') included a firm commitment to Catholicism and some form of right-wing politics, at least until the post-1945 period. Aristocratic families had a palpable sense of their own history, being surrounded in their chateaux by books, paintings, furniture and archives from past centuries. They also had their own heroes and villains: Joan of Arc and Bourbon monarchs among the former, *philosophes* like Voltaire and Rousseau, held responsible for 1789, among the latter. The historian

---

[23] Malraux, *Apprendre à vivre*, pp. 19, 109 and 171.

[24] On attempts in contemporary French society to maintain the 'political innocence' of children, see Annick Percheron, *Le Socialisation politique* (Paris: Armand Colin, 1993), ch. 1.

[25] This section is indebted to Mension-Rigau, *L'Enfance au château*, passim.

Eric Mension-Rigau made the point that the French aristocracy was the first of its kind to be 'martyrized'. During the nineteenth and twentieth centuries, nearly every family had its stories of arrests, exile and guillotinings among its ancestors. So vividly were the memories preserved that aristocrats recalled a feeling that it was as if the Revolution had only just occurred. Pauline de Broglie (b. 1888) claimed to know the history of 1789 well before the Scriptures or the catechism.[26] The enquiry into aristocratic upbringings by Mension-Rigau cited a male born in 1902 who wrote that 'my grandfather said more or less humorously that the Revolution had guillotined three of his grandparents and deprived him of his birthright' (the Revolution having abolished primogeniture).[27]

No less important for these aristocratic and upper bourgeois families was the process of instilling into their young what was done and what was not done in polite society. Even in a democratic age, they could not shake off the presumption that they had 'breeding' from birth that *hoi polloi* could never hope to emulate. Childhood emerged as a period of constant harassment from parents, aunts, nurses and teachers in the quest for good manners. The young had to acquire countless signs of distinction: how to walk across a room, how to step down from a carriage, when to speak and when to remain silent. Behaviour at table was particularly important, including French as opposed to English usage: keeping one's hands on the table rather than the knees, and not leaving food on the plate rather than leaving a little.[28]

Whether or not the aspiring 'middle classes' had any hope of learning this *savoir-vivre* of *la vieille France* by reading advice books on the subject is an open question. Either way, they certainly made efforts in their own way to distance their sons and daughters from those of the 'popular classes' milling around them. As already shown, parents from this broad spectrum of society made strenuous efforts to prevent their children mixing with 'unsuitable' friends. The emphasis was all on hard work, self-discipline and academic success.[29] Where this strategy was successful it could produce outstanding examples of social mobility like Ernest Lavisse, whose dedicated parents helped him rise under the Second Empire from being the son of a shopkeeper to the top of the academic hierarchy in Paris.[30] 'Middle-class' parents also made efforts to keep their offspring on what they considered the straight-and-narrow of their political values. Once again, this might prove difficult when families were divided politically. The writer Juliette Adam recalled that during her childhood in the 1830s and 1840s, 'my grandmother supported the Orleanist government, my

[26] Pange, *1900*, p. 30.   [27] Mension-Rigau, *L'Enfance au château*, p. 130.
[28] Ibid., p. 166.   [29] See above, pp. 202–3.   [30] Lavisse, *Souvenirs*, passim.

grandfather was passionately in favour of the Empire, and you had to hear him roll his Rs saying: the Emperor! My father declared himself a Jacobin.'[31] By the 1870s the 'two Frances' had crystallized into one camp bound by republican, freethinking and liberal ideologies, the other by Catholicism and conservatism.[32] School textbooks gave an indication of the divergent values in play. The Catholic ones picked out as their heroes the monarchs of the *ancien régime*, saints, churchmen, and royal ministers drawn from the clergy, for example the Cardinal d'Amboise (minister under Louis XII). Their secular counterparts preferred republican politicians from the nineteenth century, famous soldiers and sailors, scientists, historians and eminent literary figures. The former celebrated the Middle Ages and the *ancien régime*, the latter, the Revolution and the nineteenth century.[33] Hence Georges Bataille at the Lycée Henri IV had the day off for the funeral of Victor Hugo in 1885 and Julian Green knew all about the 'lost provinces' of Alsace and Lorraine from his history teacher at the Lycée Janson de Sailly. Meanwhile at the Cours Désir the young Simone de Beauvoir struggled with her 'sectarian education' and its focus on matters such as Popes and Lateran Councils.[34]

First-hand accounts of wars and revolutions from members of the family served to reinforce these political orientations in a vivid fashion. Gustave-Emmanuel Roy (b. 1823) recalled that as a child he 'almost lived under the Empire' from stories of his parents' youth. His parents recounted the victories and especially the defeats of the Napoleonic armies: with foreign troops at the gates, for example, his grandmother sewed gold and diamonds into clothing in case she had to flee. Such tales evidently helped to fashion his conservative political orientation during the 1830s and 1840s. From a later generation, Xavier-Edouard Lejeune (b. 1845) admitted to a prod towards the left from his firebrand uncle Jules, a shoemaker from the Parisian Faubourg Saint-Antoine. Stories from the barricades during the blood-spattered *journées* of the 1848 Revolution held the young lad spellbound, 'a course in contemporary history that I had not learned at school'.[35]

At the very bottom of the social scale, and proudly so in some cases, were peasants and manual workers. Children from peasant backgrounds

---

[31] Adam, *Mon enfance*, p. 89.
[32] Jean-Marie Mayeur and Françoise Rebérioux, *The Third Republic from its Origins to the Great War* (Cambridge: Cambridge University Press, 1984), p. 7.
[33] Christian Amalvi, 'Les Personnages exemplaires du passé proposés à l'admiration de la jeunesse dans les livres de lecture et de prix de 1814 à 1914', in Glénisson and Le Men (eds.), *Livre d'enfance*, pp. 248–50.
[34] Bataille, 'L'Enfance éternelle', 45; Green, *Memories of Happy Days*, p. 40; and de Beauvoir, *Memoirs of a Dutiful Daughter*, p. 127.
[35] Roy, *Souvenirs*, p. 15; and Lejeune, *Calicot*, p. 104.

were likely to discover the general contempt in which the rest of the population held them. Henri Pitaud (b. 1899) noted this when venturing with the rest of his family in the unfamiliar territory of a long-distance train journey. Pierre-Jakez Hélias became aware in his turn during the 1920s when attending his *lycée* in Quimper: 'I learned once and for all that the seediest bourgeois considered himself far above the most subtle peasant.' It is all too easy to associate the peasantry with conservative political convictions, but this was not necessarily so. The young Henri Pitaud certainly grew up in the Catholic and Legitimist atmosphere of his father's family in the Vendée, an outcome of the bitter memories of repression by revolutionary armies during the 1790s in that region. But the family of Pierre-Jakez in Brittany adhered to the Reds rather than the Whites.[36] As for urban workers, Georges Dumoulin depicted himself as a dyed-in-the-wool militant, absorbing hatred of the rich and anti-clericalism from the cradle.[37] However, most future activists mentioned the material difficulties their families faced during their childhood, leaving the way open for a 'conversion' to socialism during their teens.

Of the generations that emerged from successive periods in French history, the one that experienced the Revolution and Empire stood out most conspicuously, not least for the numerous memoirs it published afterwards. With political radicalism, religious conflict, a mass emigration of opponents of the Revolution, civil war in the Vendée, the Terror and a prolonged period of warfare, the period could hardly fail to have a dramatic impact on many young lives and polarize political allegiances. Right-wing commentators tended to claim that their families supported the principles of the Revolution but recoiled from its excesses. Hence their memories lingered on the threats of violence from unruly mobs, and the arbitrary arrests of close relatives. The future Comtesse de Boigne recalled from October 1789 the streets of Versailles flooded with fearsome-looking crowds, the people shrieking horribly, firing their guns and making outrageous demands. The Duc de Broglie in his turn recalled from his childhood the shouting of the people and the crash of furniture as they pillaged the Hôtel de Castries during the early part of the Revolution, and the consternation on the face of his writing master as he announced the disastrous flight to Varennes by the King in 1792. In his case, his father died in prison in 1794, while his mother managed to escape from imprisonment in Vesoul with the help of an old family servant.

[36] Pitaud, *Le Pain de la terre*, pp. 35–8; and Hélias, *Horse of Pride*, pp. 133–4 and 305.
[37] Dumoulin, *Carnets de route*, pp. 16–18.

The doctor Poumiès de la Siboutie was in retrospect more ambivalent on the turn of events after 1789. As a member of what he called 'that elevated and honourable bourgeoisie, held for centuries in an inferior position by the prerogatives of the aristocracy', he admitted some enthusiasm for the Revolution. He recalled that as a child he danced with his neighbours around bonfires of documents from chateaux, churches and convents, and enjoyed the songs at revolutionary assemblies. However, he also wrote of honest people trembling before a few miserable characters who had the town at their mercy. 'One thing that affected me a great deal,' he wrote, 'and which my reasoning as a child could not explain, was to see badly dressed men, with coarse language and common manners, come to the home of my grandfather in the Périgueux, speak with authority, and make threats against my parents.' He dwelt on threats to his grandmother from unruly *sans-culottes*, hiding a priest in their house and a tip-off that his grandfather was about to be arrested.[38] Stendhal came out in favour of the Revolution at various points in his childhood reminiscences, welcoming the execution of Louis XVI when he was ten, and supporting the Terror in Grenoble (even if it only involved two guillotinings). However, after a visit to the Jacobin Club, he admitted he was inclined to agree with his aristocratic grandfather that the Jacobins were badly dressed and unfashionable: 'I found these people that I should like to have loved horribly vulgar.'[39] Finally, after 1815, when nearly all the men seemed to be war veterans, there were the memories of old soldiers to demonize, or more likely idolize, Napoleon. Eugène Courmeaux (b. 1817) recalled his early veneration of Napoleon, as the son of a vine-grower in the Champagne with thirteen years of service in the revolutionary and Napoleonic armies behind him. Although Courmeaux later came round to the view that Napoleon was a 'modern Attila', he began by feeding off the heroic legends of the French armies and the revolutionary image of their leader. All of the children of former soldiers he knew around Reims considered the prisoner on Sainte-Hélène a glorious martyr for France, and so subscribed to the enduring 'cult of Napoleon', which helped Bonapartism lose its association with oppression and hardship.[40]

[38] Boigne, *Mémoires*, p. 76; Duc de Broglie, *Souvenirs, 1785–1850* (4 vols., Paris: Calmann-Lévy, 1886), I, pp. 8–16; and Poumiès de la Siboutie, *Souvenirs*, p. 1 and ch. 2.

[39] Stendhal, *Henry Brulard*, pp. 138 and 172. See also Lamartine, *Les Confidences*, livre deuxième, describing his noble family's support for the Revolution, until his grandfather was imprisoned at Mâcon.

[40] Eugène Courmeaux, *Notes, souvenirs et impressions d'un vieux rémois* (Reims: Imprimerie Nouvelle, 1891), pp. 70–4. See also Frédéric Bluche, *Le Bonapartisme* (Paris: Presses Universitaires de France, 1981), ch. 2; and Bertholet, *Les Français par eux-mêmes*, pp. 79–89.

The nineteenth and twentieth centuries brought new generations inspired or horrified by successive revolutions.[41] At the age of seven, Gustave-Emmanuel Roy witnessed street fighting during the 1830 Revolution in Paris, with troops firing their guns around him, cannon fire and the evacuation of a barricade. He wrote in his memoirs that 'these three days, known afterwards as the *trois glorieuses*, stayed in my mind with a feeling of dread; it was the first revolution that I had seen'. His second, when he was in his mid-twenties in 1848, brought further bad memories, notably of cowering in his house with the rest of the family while armed gangs banged on doors demanding weapons. Victorine Brocher (1838–1921), daughter of a shoemaker in Paris, recalled dreadful memories of seeing the dead and wounded during the revolutionary *journées* of February 1848. Such was the trauma involved that she claimed to have lost the power of speech for a year. Henry Bataille revealed that his birth in 1872 caused him to be brought up with lurid tales of the Communards. Having seen houses that had been burnt-out by the infamous *pétroleuses* and the 'carcass' of the Tuileries palace, he learned to hate revolution. However, a chance sighting of the Communard heroine Louise Michel while on a visit with his father to the Chamber of Deputies led him to question these received ideas. She seemed to him to have a saintly air to her; he felt that he had been in the presence of 'undeniable moral beauty'.[42]

Young people often found themselves excluded from politics during the nineteenth and even twentieth centuries, particularly before the coming of a liberal democracy during the 1870s. A streak of youthful idealism often led them into subversive territory, yet various forms of authority readily stamped on them. It was easy to create stirring representations of young revolutionaries, notably in the form of the *gamin de Paris*, the Parisian street-urchin. Delacroix placed him at the forefront of his painting *Liberty Leading the People* (1830), charging into the fray with a pair of pistols and an ammunition pouch hanging down incongruously to his knees. Similarly, in *Les Misérables* (1862), Victor Hugo had the young Gavroche jauntily singing subversive songs during the 1832 revolt, and dying heroically on the barricades.[43] However, the fourteen-year-old Marie Capelle found herself banned from politics when she enthusiastically welcomed the 1830 Revolution. Her landowning family was prepared to indulge

---

[41] For an early venture into history focused on a generation, see Anthony Esler, 'Youth in Revolt: The French Generation of 1830', in Robert J. Bezucha (ed.), *Modern European Social History* (Lexington, MA: D. C. Heath, 1972), pp. 301–34.

[42] Roy, *Souvenirs*, pp. 31–3 and 68; Victorine B., *Souvenirs d'une morte vivante* (Paris: La Découverte, 2002 (1909)), pp. 19–29; and Bataille, 'L'Enfance éternelle', 23–5.

[43] Hugo, *Les Misérables*, pp. 984 and 1027–8.

her in activities such as horse riding, she observed later, but would not tolerate any independent thinking.[44] Juliette Adam was expelled from school for her support for the Republic in 1848.[45] Ernest Lavisse failed to make links with the working people of the *faubourgs* when he joined a little coterie of republicans opposed to the Empire in his Parisian *lycée* during the 1850s. A century later the historian Pierre Nora suggested that his 'puerile' efforts formed part of a self-serving attempt in his old age to shore up his reputation as a great republican reformer. The more obvious conclusion was that the early part of his career flourished through his long devotion to the Empire and the Imperial family.[46]

With the consolidation of the Third Republic, the gradual emergence of parties and a vigorous civil society provided a more stable framework for adolescents and youths to participate in political life. In particular, the politicization of the term *jeunesse* (youth) opened up a number of outlets for activists during the 1880s and 1890s, whether Catholic, royalist, nationalist, republican, socialist or communist. However, the police still kept a close eye on organizations associated with youthful revolt.[47] In the Bouches-du-Rhône, for example, the police reported on the activities of extremists on both the left and the right. Among the latter, they reported on a meeting of over six hundred members of the Jeunesse catholique et royaliste, held at Chateaurenard in 1896. The programme was eminently respectable, with a great Mass in the morning, a banquet, political meetings in the afternoon and a ball in the evening, all presided over by the Comte de Régis. However, the 'violent speeches' of the leaders, and the display of white flags, the *fleur de lis* and the slogan 'God, the Fatherland and the King' were provocative for the republican regime. At the other end of the political spectrum was the local branch of the Jeunesse syndicaliste revolutionnaire, founded in Marseille in 1911 by young workers linked to trade unions in the building trades. The local police noted that the twenty or so members were all aged between eighteen and twenty-five, and active in spreading revolutionary propaganda among strikers.[48]

The fate of the *lycéen* Gabriel Peri during an anti-militarist campaign in Marseille during the aftermath of the First World War revealed that youthful idealism was not without its hazards. The police arrested him

---

[44] Lafarge, *Mémoires de Marie Capelle*, I, pp. 98–100.

[45] Adam, *Mon enfance*, pp. 274–318.

[46] Lavisse, *Souvenirs*, ch. 7; and Nora, 'Ernest Lavisse', 76.

[47] See Yolande Cohen, *Les Jeunes, le socialisme et la guerre: histoire des mouvements de jeunesse en France* (Paris: Editions l'Harmattan, 1989), passim.

[48] AD Bouches-du-Rhône, 1 M 845, Report of Commissaire de Police, Chateaurenard, 5 October 1896; and 1M 808, police dossier on the Jeunesse syndicaliste révolutionnaire, 1911–12.

in the street, carrying tracts inciting conscripts to resist military activity in the colonies, Germany and above all Russia. According to their report, he panicked and admitted having 'compromising papers concerning communist propaganda against the security of the state'. Besides extensive police enquiries, he suffered the humiliation of a house search: presumably embarrassing for the son of an accountant in the Marseille Chamber of Commerce. The police investigated fourteen members of the Marseille branch of the Jeunesse communiste, all except one aged between seventeen and twenty-six. It emerged that they had distributed tracts and posters during the 1921 session of the Conseil de révision organizing military conscription. A speaker at the Fédération communiste des Bouches-du-Rhône proclaimed that 'these young people have done what many old militants have not managed, they did not fear braving the forces of the police'. However, it also became clear that the five *lycéens* were model pupils, and that all of the workers associated with them were well respected by their employers and their neighbours. In the end the authorities proved indulgent, with the local military commander sending the leaflets to Paris but declining to press charges.[49]

The interwar period brought further efforts to mobilize the young around an assortment of political banners. In the Seine-Inférieure, for example, the Jeunesse communiste, the Jeunesses laïques et républicaines, the Jeunesse catholique and the Jeunesses patriotes all battled it out for the soul of French youth during the 1920s and 1930s. The communists urged the young to desert from the colonial war in Morocco and to revolt against the slavery imposed by 'Anglo-Saxon plutocrats', while right-wing nationalists, recruited from among students and *employés* (clerks), called for order in place of communist anarchy. The Catholics in their turn pushed for moral discipline and fearless displays of Catholic faith, while republicans countered with secular values and warnings of the danger from extreme nationalist movements under Mussolini and Hitler.[50]

At the same time, it was possible for a young militant to structure his or her life almost entirely around the varied political, social and cultural activities laid on by a party. René Michaud gave a detailed account of his own youthful phase as a member of the Jeunesse anarchiste after the First World War. Experience in Paris of preaching revolt in various workshops of the shoe trade marked him out as an activist: 'that was the end of my

---

[49] AD Bouches-du-Rhône, 1 M 811, dossier on the Jeunesse communiste de Marseille; the reports on Peri and his colleagues are from February 1921.

[50] AD Seine-Maritime, 1 M 273, Jeunesses patriotes, 1934; 1 M 315, Jeunesses communistes, 1923–37; 1 M 321, Jeunesses laïques et républicaines, 1934–5.

existence as an ordinary worker, uniquely preoccupied with earning my crust, eating and joking a little'. He read brochures by libertarian authors such as Peter Kropotkin and Elisée Reclus, and joined earnest discussions with his group in Belleville on anarchist theory and progressive issues such as contraception, vegetarianism and the fight against alcoholism. He admitted that he preferred action to words, battling with police on the streets during the 1st of May demonstrations in 1919, and bringing a 'rowdy, disordered ardour' to political meetings. During the summer, he spent his weekends on excursions with his colleagues, singing anarchist songs on the train home. In winter, there were *fêtes artistiques* featuring anarchist poets and songwriters and shows at the Maison des coopératives in the rue de Bretagne. There were socialist plays to see, socialist songs to sing with workmates and dances with other workers. In 1921, he deserted from the army while doing his military service, and had to lie low in Lyon and Romans. There he read widely in the library of the Bourse du travail and joined his fellow socialists at work and during their leisure activities. Returning to Paris at the age of twenty-two, he continued his efforts as a trade union leader in Belleville. Eventually he lost faith in anarchism, later reflecting that his experience of life made him aware of its limitations as a doctrine. Excused his military desertion, on the grounds that his father's suicide made him paranoiac, he took his 'place in society'.[51] Such a path, as Michaud himself was well aware, was the exception rather than the rule. More typical, bearing in mind the low percentage of French workers who were even unionized in the early twentieth century, was the case of Louis Lengrand. He was born and bred in a coalmining community, had a socialist father and soon after leaving school at thirteen began work underground. He also married the daughter of a communist during the 1930s, herself a member of the Jeunesse communiste. However, both he and his wife soon drifted away from involvement in socialist politics.[52]

Gender relations

It should by now be obvious that the learning of masculine and feminine behaviour pervaded all aspects of life during childhood and adolescence in modern France. Until the late twentieth century, and a recent tendency to play down differences between men and women, the conventional approach was a polarization between the two: women were often associated with nature and emotion, for example, and men with culture

---

[51] Michaud, *J'avais vingt ans*, passim.
[52] Lengrand and Craipeau, *Louis Lengrand*, p. 45.

and reason. Child-rearing practices, educational policy, sociability patterns among children and adolescents, and the sex typing of jobs in the workplace, all had the effect of leading males and females on different paths.[53] The acquisition of a masculine or feminine identity was therefore of more fundamental importance to the formation of a self than, say, the choice of a political party or even a set of religious beliefs. It might be that an individual rebelled against the prevailing customs, indeed tomboyish behaviour might be accepted among girls for a while,[54] and an outstanding character like George Sand could carve out a successful career that challenged convention. Nonetheless there were key institutions that served to mould most people in the desired direction. Convent schools and private schools for girls stood out during the nineteenth century as sites for the grooming of future wives and mothers. Simone de Beauvoir wrote that she was brought up on 'convent morals'. Her exclusive Cours Désir, in contrast to a boy's school, refused to award prizes at the end of the year for scholastic success, on the grounds that they would encourage worldly rivalry among the pupils. She recalled that during her teens she anticipated taking up a profession, but wanted a husband who would be superior to her: 'my education, my culture, and the present state of society all conspired to convince me that women belong to an inferior caste'.[55] For boys, as the historian Odile Roynette demonstrated, military service took on an increasingly important role as an institution for the construction of masculinity. Under the Restoration, and the lottery system, one in ten French males spent time in uniform; under the Second Empire, one in three; and after the republican reforms of the 1880s, six out of ten. From 1870, a series of novels evoked the separation of the recruit from his family, and the harsh physical and moral ordeals he faced in the barrackroom. In particular, the new recruit suffered from humiliating or violent *brimades* (ragging) at the hands of old sweats, even though these were officially banned in 1887, and exercises to 'break him in' such as marching, standing straight and manoeuvring on a battlefield.[56] The world of manual work imposed similar initiation rites and gruelling routines to toughen up the young in the fields or on the shop floor. René Michaud mentioned tricks in the shoe factories such as pulling away stools when someone was about to sit down or poking a brush covered in glue through

---

[53] See Colin Heywood, 'On Learning Gender Roles during Childhood in Nineteenth-Century France', *French History*, 5 (1991), 451–66.

[54] See, for example, Olga Varni, in Germain and de Panafieu, *Mémoire des femmes*, p. 47.

[55] De Beauvoir, *Memoirs of a Dutiful Daughter*, pp. 123 and 143–5.

[56] Odile Roynette, *'Bons pour le service': l'expérience de la caserne en France à la fin du XIXe siècle* (Paris: Belin, 2000), Introduction and ch. 5.

someone's trouser flies.[57] The ultimate aim was to encourage the young male to be independent in an unforgiving adult world.

Conclusion

Thinking about one's identity became an increasingly complex matter in the modern period in France. This was the period when the industrial and democratic revolutions slowly broadened the horizons of the masses beyond their local community. Face-to-face relations in a village or urban neighbourhood were rivalled by national and class allegiances; outward conformity to the Catholic Church turned into a more personalized form of religion, and traditional gender relations were undermined by various social changes, not to mention feminist critiques. The mere act of writing a diary or an autobiography reveals the authors grappling with the desire to establish a personal or collective identity in a way that was unthinkable for all but a few exceptional individuals before the eighteenth century. There were more choices on offer than in the past, but more scope for angst over getting them right. All the same, the young showed plenty of appetite for various causes, fired up by such influences as the revolutionary tradition launched in 1789, militant Catholicism or republicanism, and a desire to preserve local cultures against invasion from Paris.

Sex and marriage[58]

First love

People in the nineteenth and even twentieth centuries were generally reticent when it came to discussing their bodies. The historian Eric Mension-Rigau asserted that, in aristocratic and upper bourgeois circles, the nineteenth century brought a moral reaction against the frivolity of the *ancien régime*. This included a demonization of the body, and attempts by families to draw a veil over the mysteries of procreation for as long as possible. The early twentieth century, he suggested, was a high point for stories about babies being born under a cabbage-patch leaf or brought by a stork. Adults closely supervised any mixing of the sexes in this milieu. One of the respondents to Mension-Rigau's enquiry wrote: 'Religious instruction harmed me in the sense that it judged all relations with a

---

[57] Michaud, *J'avais vingt ans*, pp. 83–4.
[58] For further exploration of this topic, focusd on the sexual experiences of the young, see Colin Heywood, 'Innocence and Experience: Sexuality among Young People in Modern France, c. 1750–1950', *French History* (forthcoming).

young woman as wicked. Hence my stupid marriage.'[59] Women at various levels of society often complained that their mothers failed to warn them about periods, and were too prim to discuss sexual matters with them. Simone de Beauvoir recalled learning never to look at her naked body, to the extent that she had to change her underwear without uncovering herself completely. She needed her cousin Madeleine to hint at what to expect with periods and pregnancy, but neither the cousin nor her mother would elaborate. Even at sixteen, she admitted that for all her reading she was still a novice where sexual matters were concerned.[60] An oral history project with a small sample of women of an advanced age during the 1980s revealed a more nuanced picture. Olga Varni followed the conventional wealthy bourgeois path in claiming that she knew nothing of how babies were born until her marriage. Moreover, Charlotte Poulet (b. 1903), a woman with a Parisian working-class background, would also testify that: 'we knew nothing of our bodies. When I gave birth, I did not know what was going to happen to me, the same as when I slept with my husband. We were told nothing, nothing at all.' By contrast, there was also a down-to-earth, rustic approach to matters, which we have already noted in French literature.[61] Farm children were likely to sleep in the same bed as their parents or among servants in the stables.[62] Madeleine Dissais remembered from her upbringing on a farm near Bordeaux early in the twentieth century that, from an early age, she watched cocks mounting hens and dogs with bitches. People did not hide things from children, she observed. Similarly, a rural upbringing in the Sarthe for Aline Lucas meant that by the age of twelve she knew the facts of life, though not very clearly, since she did not dare question her mother on the subject.[63]

Fortunately for our purposes, an account of the first sexual experience became an accepted part of childhood reminiscences during the modern period. Predictably the degree of indulgence during the early years varied from the impregnable virginity of a well-brought-up young woman in elite circles to boasts of precocious sexual conquests from rogue males. Most authors in fact tried to convey something in between these extremes:

---

[59] Mension-Rigau, *L'Enfance au château*, pp. 251–2.
[60] De Beauvoir, *Memoirs of a Dutiful Daughter*, pp. 57, 85–8 and 161. On similar attempts during the first half of the nineteenth century to preserve the innocence of young people in sexual matters, above all in the case of girls, see Houbre, *Discipline de l'amour*, ch. 4. For the Third Republic, and the widespread ignorance that followed a 'negative' sexual education, see Sohn, *Chrysalides*, I, pp. 371–7.
[61] See above, p. 49.
[62] See, for example, Claverie and Lamaison, *L'Impossible Mariage*, p. 218.
[63] Germain and de Panafieu, *Mémoire des femmes*, passim.

the first, rather 'innocent' stirrings of interest in the opposite sex (or, in some cases, the same sex) during childhood or adolescence. How these modern experiences compare with those of earlier centuries is open to conjecture. It may be that the low level of illegitimacy during the seventeenth and eighteenth centuries is evidence of 'sexual austerity' outside marriage. The historian André Burguière speculated that although people in Western Europe at this early modern period had an exceptionally long wait between puberty and a relatively late marriage, they managed to sublimate their libido into other activities such as religious fervour or hard work. Jean-Louis Flandrin, for his part, refused to believe that the mass of young people could hold out for these ten to fifteen years after puberty, throughout the seventeenth, eighteenth and nineteenth centuries, without some sort of sexual outlet.[64] Unfortunately, the activities he had in mind, such as bestiality and masturbation, were not the sort of thing that writers of childhood reminiscences in the nineteenth century were likely to write about. Antoine Sylvère put forward the sordid image of his classmates masturbating while their teacher, a Christian Brother, worked his way through equations on the blackboard, but denied having a hand in the matter himself.[65] A surge in illegitimate births during the late eighteenth and early nineteenth centuries in Europe might be taken to indicate a 'sexual revolution' among the lower orders. Edward Shorter argued for 'an enormous increase in sexual activity before marriage' from around 1800 onwards. However, his critics counter that it was more likely a matter of traditional sexual behaviour having unfortunate consequences during a period of rapid social change. In particular, the increased movement of population played havoc with the assumption by young women that a partner they agreed to sleep with would marry them if they became pregnant. Shorter also asserted that the resort to contraceptive techniques caused the decline in illegitimacy rates after 1850 by unmarried couples, though he was aware that it might equally be attributed to the effects of repressive 'Victorian' attitudes. Either way, a second 'sexual revolution' allowing young people free rein in their erotic impulses would not occur until the 1950s and 1960s.[66] The inclination here is to follow Anne-Marie Sohn in assuming that modesty was the watchword influencing most behaviour between the sexes during the nineteenth and twentieth

---

[64] André Burguière, 'De Malthus à Max Weber: le mariage tardif et l'esprit d'entreprise', *Annales ESC*, 27 (1972), 1128–38; Jean-Louis Flandrin, 'Mariage tardif et vie sexuelle: discussions et hypothèses de recherche', *Annales ESC*, 27 (1972), 1351–78; and Jean-Louis Flandrin, 'Repression and Change in the Sexual Life of Young People in Medieval and Early Modern Times', *Journal of Family History*, 2 (1977), 196–210.
[65] Sylvère, *Toinou*, p. 269.   [66] Shorter, *Modern Family*, ch. 3.

centuries, at least until the 1950s.[67] What the autobiographical sources reveal is something lost in the quantitative evidence: the slow arousal of interest in the opposite sex at a time when it was still seen as something of a mystery by the young.

The odd eighteenth-century account of childhood and youth provides evidence of the erosion of traditional restraints on sexual relations among peasants and artisans, and doubtless also a public appetite for racy tales at that period.[68] In *Monsieur Nicolas* (1796), Rétif de la Bretonne depicted the eponymous hero managing an early sexual initiation, at the age of ten, with a woman working on the harvest. Sexual adventures also pervade the account provided by Jacques Louis Ménétra of his youthful years during the 1750s and 1760s. The historian Daniel Roche counted fifty-two sexual relationships before Ménétra's marriage, plus casual encounters with innkeepers' daughters and prostitutes. Ménétra started in his early teens when the chambermaid of a 'woman of quality' received his first blushes, moved on to a number of encounters with Parisian prostitutes and had an early encounter with the pox. As Daniel Roche noted, there was little sensuality in any of his encounters, simply a compulsion to boast of numerous conquests.[69]

The nineteenth and twentieth centuries brought a more sober tone to descriptions of sexual activity among the young of the 'popular classes'. The peasant novelist Emile Guillaumin pointed out in *La Vie d'un simple* (*The Life of a Simple Man*, 1904) that there were too many people around for lovers to sneak off on their own at village dances. He had the hero of the novel (born in 1823) snatch a first kiss during his late teens, while walking a girl home from a *veillée*. He emphasized that timidity, modesty and fear of the consequences meant that while courting her he never went beyond 'innocent hugs and long, long kisses'. Jean-Marie Déguignet drew attention to the various sexual games that surrounded Breton children while they were working in the fields during the 1830s, such as groups of women holding down a young man and stuffing earth or cowpats into his trousers, but left himself out of the proceedings.[70] Some peasant memoirs make no mention of sexuality, or, like Antoine Sylvère, assert that they

---

[67] Anne-Marie Sohn, *Du premier baiser à l'alcove: la sexualité des français au quotidien* (Paris: Aubier, 1996), p. 80.

[68] See Daniel Roche, 'Jacques-Louis Ménétra: An Eighteenth-Century Way of Life', in Ménétra, *Journal of My Life*, pp. 263–80.

[69] Rétif de la Bretonne, *Monsieur Nicolas*, p. 33; Ménétra, *Journal of My Life*, p. 26; and Roche, 'Jacques-Louis Ménétra', pp. 276–8.

[70] Guillaumin, *Life of a Simple Man*, pp. 41–4; and Déguignet, *Mémoires d'un paysan*, pp. 33–5.

were indifferent to it. As for the devoutly Protestant Augustine Rouvière (b. 1883), she claimed a 'hard-working and pure' youth in her village in the Cévennes. Marriage at the late age of thirty thrust her fearfully into the unknown.[71]

Urban workers in the towns also often belied in their autobiographies the debauched image bestowed on them by commentators on 'the social question'. Georges Navel harnessed his description of his first sexual encounter to his grim evocation of working-class conditions during the early twentieth century. He described furtive kisses with his landlady's daughter, when he was eleven, in resolutely unromantic terms. The staircase in the cellar where they met stank of cat's piss, coal and damp winter vegetables. Water dripped on their heads from wet laundry. Moreover, he claimed his pleasure was spoiled by the unpleasant, indeed offensive thought that the young Angèle would soon have as much of a beard as her mother. This episode contrasted with a later one, around the age of eighteen, when he fell for another member of the Jeunesse libertaire while on an excursion to the countryside. In the event, a brief kiss proved to be both the beginning and the end of the relationship, plunging him into adolescent despair. René Michaud depicted his first sexual experience at the age of fifteen as a squalid, commercial operation. Being gauche with the opposite sex, an uncle took him to a brothel where, he admitted, a 'granny' of a prostitute needed all her professional skill to relieve him of his virginity. He described it as a 'laborious and humiliating deliverance'. More satisfying was a brief interlude living with fellow anarchist Lili when he was in his late teens. On a different tack, drawn from a female working-class background in Lille, Louise Vanderwielen (b. 1906) launched her tortuous romantic life with a kiss at a dance when aged sixteen. This was a chaste affair, with lips closed, starting a brief relationship centred on the dance floor.[72]

The notorious double standards in sexual matters meant that the daily activities of girls were more restricted than those of boys, especially in middle- and upper-class families. Young women in these circles moved in a largely feminine world, confined to the home much of the time, or on afternoon visits to other families at a similar social level.[73] The diary of the very devout Caroline Brame revealed a young woman in the middle of the nineteenth century nervous about the thorns and sacrifices

[71] Sylvère, *Toinou*, p. 269; and Rey, *Augustine Rouvière*, pp. 85–7.
[72] Navel, *Travaux*, pp. 40–1 and 55–8; Michaud, *J'avais vingt ans*, pp. 139–41; Vanderwielen, *Lise du plat rays*, pp. 90–1.
[73] Perrot, 'Enquête', p. 194.

of marriage, and contemplating a black rather than a white veil later in life. She conspicuously refrained from any mention of physical attraction to a male. Yet she did not emerge entirely uninterested, evidently feeling something for one of the friends she met on holiday at a chateau. She went no further than to write of frantic dances with Albert when they were both eighteen, of missing him when she returned to Paris, and of the puppy he gave her as a present.[74] Dancing lessons might bring some contact with boys for a middle-class girl. Simone de Beauvoir confessed to being so awkward and self-conscious that she found the physical contact with boys overpowering:

I began to detest those dancing lessons, but for another reason. When my partner held me in his arms and held me to his chest, I felt a funny sensation that was rather like having butterflies in the stomach, but which I didn't find quite so easy to forget. When I got back home, I would throw myself in the leather armchair, overpowered by a curious languor that I couldn't put a name to and that made me want to burst into tears. On the pretext that I had too much work, I gave up going to the dancing class.[75]

If sexuality frightened the young Simone, other well-brought-up young ladies avoided the subject altogether in their reminiscences. Whatever they thought about or did with the opposite sex in their youth they kept to themselves.

On the male side, Jean-Jacques Rousseau first risked venturing into the hitherto forbidden territory of intimate confessions on his sexuality during the 1760s. This began as a child, with the famous admission of his bewildered reaction to a spanking from Mlle Lambercier: 'I had discovered in the shame and pain of the punishment an admixture of sensuality which had left me rather eager than otherwise for a repetition by the same hand.' Continuing with the understanding that 'nothing about me must remain hidden or obscure', he later mentioned unwelcome homosexual advances from a 'cut-throat' in Turin, a 'foretaste of the sweetest and purest pleasures of love' in the form of a bashful relationship with a young married woman, near catastrophe when exposing himself to women on the street, and being able to 'dispose, so to speak, of the whole female sex' at will, through masturbation.[76] It was a hard act to follow. Stendhal, writing during the 1830s, went no further than to admit a childish crush on an actress, Mlle Kubly, and, at the age of thirteen, an unsettled feeling in the presence of the sister of one of his friends. At this point in

---

[74] Ibid., p. 212; and Brame, *Journal intime*, 6 June, 18 October, 1 and 3 December 1865.
[75] De Beauvoir, *Memoirs of a Dutiful Daughter*, p. 162.
[76] Rousseau, *Confessions*, pp. 25–6, 71, 76–9, 90–1 and 108–9.

his adolescence he felt the need to talk openly about his difficult relations with his family:

> I shall admit, however, that I much preferred having these very simple conversations with Victorine than with her brothers. Today I can see what my feeling was then, I found it incredible to be seeing that terrifying creature, a woman, from so close to; a woman moreover with magnificent hair, an arm exquisitely shaped, if on the thin side, and lastly a charming bosom often partly exposed because of the excessive heat.[77]

His fellow novelist Gustave Flaubert (1821–80) in his turn began with his 'sweet and strange' feelings at the age of fifteen for an older, married woman, encountered while on holiday in Picardy. He soon followed the bewildered emotions of first love with the guilt of a desperate bid to lose his virginity:

> A woman offered herself; I took her. And I left her embrace, filled with disgust and bitterness to me. But then I could play the part of a Lovelace in the tavern, cursing as much as anyone else standing around the grog punch. *Then* I was a man; as if out of duty I set about committing vice and bragged about it.[78]

Other authors also wrote knowingly as adults about their first sense of a sensual world only dimly perceived in childhood. Henry Bataille (b. 1872) felt that an innocent morning kiss from a young Italian woman sitting as a model for his sisters plunged him into a kind of ecstasy. It was, in retrospect, what he highlighted as his 'first desire', experienced at the age of seven. André Chamson recalled a night at the same age when he was sent to sleep between two servants, Anna and Julienne, and became caught up in their sexual activity. He remembered his feet on their naked thighs and an 'unknown odour from under the sheets', which he slipped closer towards. One of the women uttered a little cry, and the bed shook. Suddenly aware that he was awake, the servants moved him to a bed on his own. He wrote that he was listening to a new discovery, 'a moan without suffering, the sighing of a still incomprehensible joy, of an unknown gaiety'.[79] Pierre Loti maintained the theme of his destiny as a sailor by hinting at the 'savage' nature of the girls who first attracted him. To begin with, at the age of seven, there was Véronique, one of a breed of 'wild creatures' among the fishermen of the Ile d'Oleron. Later, at the age of sixteen, he claimed to have made love for the first time in a shady ravine with a gypsy girl. She was dark-skinned, the colour of 'Etrurian terra

---

[77] Stendhal, *Henry Brulard*, p. 287.
[78] Flaubert, *Diary of a Madman*, pp. 176–91. For further discussion of forms of sexual initiation in aristocratic and bourgeois circles during the first half of the nineteenth century, see Houbre, *Discipline de l'amour*, ch. 3.
[79] Bataille, 'L'Enfance éternelle', 15–16; and Chamson, *Chiffre de nos jours*, pp. 48–55.

cotta', and had thick black hair and dark eyes that appeared to hide all the 'sensual mysticism of India'. That was his initiation into what he called the great secret of life and love.[80] During the early twentieth century it became acceptable to write about the first stirrings of homosexuality – unlike England, it was not a crime in France until 1942. André Gide volunteered the first published account in *Si le grain ne meurt* (1926), recalling his confusion at falling in love with another young boy at a fancy-dress ball. Jean Cocteau wrote of his long-standing love for boys in *Le Livre blanc* (1928). He identified three decisive incidents in his child-hood that revealed his sexual preferences to him: spying a farm lad naked in some water in the grounds of a chateau, seeing some naked gypsies in a wood, and his feelings for a servant and his laugh.[81]

One can hardly avoid wondering how often the first sexual experience was a matter of abuse within the family. It must be admitted that autobio-graphical evidence from the nineteenth century and most of the twentieth century will not help answer such a question. A book such as *Viol d'inceste, auteur obligatoirement anonyme* (*Incestuous Rape, Author Necessarily Anony-mous*), published in 1992, was simply unthinkable in the more prudish atmosphere of the earlier period.[82] It may be that with everyone keeping an eye on each other in small communities, such behaviour was for long discouraged; alternatively, there was a reluctance to intervene in family affairs. The judicial records for the nineteenth and twentieth centuries consulted by Anne-Marie Sohn brought to light a number of cases of rape of young girls by fathers, uncles and grandfathers. In general, after 1870 the population became increasingly willing to report sexual crimes affecting children, such as rapes and paedophilia. However, it usually required public notoriety such as the prostitution of the mother or vis-ible violence for neighbours to denounce incest. The courts punished such cases severely: acquittals were rare, and hard labour for life was common.[83]

Finding a marriage partner

Observing a Christmas dance in a village in the Béarn as late as 1960, the sociologist Pierre Bourdieu noted a sombre group of older men on

---

[80] Loti, *Le Roman d'un enfant*, pp. 103–7, and *Prime jeunesse*, pp. 339–41. See also Jean Giono, *Jean le bleu* (Paris: Grasset, 1932), pp. 114–16 and 205.

[81] Gide, *Si le grain ne meurt*, p. 87; and Jean Cocteau, *Le Livre blanc*, transl. Margaret Crosland (London: Peter Owen, 1969), pp. 21–3. For the medical and legal context, see Philippe Lejeune, 'Autobiographie et homosexualité en France au XIXe siècle', *Romantisme*, 56 (1987), 79–100.

[82] Georges Vigarello, *Histoire du viol, XVIe–XXe siècle* (Paris: Seuil, 1998), p. 241.

[83] Ibid., p. 201; and Sohn, *La Sexualité des français*, ch. 2.

the edge, watching the dancers but never participating themselves. These were the 'unmarriables', for the most part younger sons of poorer peasant families who were more reluctant to leave the village than their female counterparts. Gradually the modern civilization of the towns, with its new fashions, dances and sports, was leaving them behind.[84] The fate of the bachelor or spinster in an agrarian society was indeed not a happy one. In order to achieve adult status one needed to marry, given that the organization of work on a farm or artisan workshop was based on complementary roles for males and females. Most people in modern France therefore attempted to avoid celibacy, unless they had a military or religious vocation, or were younger brothers and sisters expected to remain unmarried so that the oldest could inherit the patrimony intact.[85] The marriage rate remained stable for most of the eighteenth, nineteenth and twentieth centuries at around 16 per 1,000 of population. Permanent bachelors or spinsters, identified at the age of fifty, were a minority of the population, and a declining one at that. Forming no more than 10 to 15 per cent of the total during the nineteenth and early twentieth centuries, they declined to 7 or 8 per cent from the late 1930s. Only during the 1970s did this pattern change, as young people became less and less inclined to marry their partners.[86]

Choosing a marriage partner involved a strategic decision of huge importance for a young person. Yet how much choice did young people have in the matter? The historical anthropologist Martine Segalen warned of the general misconception that 'nowadays we marry for love, whereas in the past people married for pecuniary or other advantages, and that now we choose a spouse ourselves, whereas in the past marriages were arranged by parents'.[87] For the medieval Church, marriage was an indissoluble sacrament formed solely by the consent of the two spouses. However, in the French case, this was not to the taste of the nobility. They could hardly stand by and leave to the whim of their young a choice that affected, in the words of André Armengaud, 'the dignity, the prestige and the wealth of their families'. Hence, during the sixteenth century they put pressure on the King to require parental consent to marriage of children while they were 'minors'. In the event, a royal edict of 1556 required males under thirty and females under twenty-five to obtain parental consent for

---

[84] Pierre Bourdieu, 'Célibat et condition paysanne', *Etudes rurales*, 5–6 (1962), 33–135 (97–8).

[85] See Jean-Louis Flandrin, *Les Amours paysannes* (Paris: Gallimard/Julliard, 1975), pp. 66–9.

[86] INED, 'Septième rapport sur la situation démographique de la France', *Population*, 33 (1978), 279–48; and Segalen, *Historical Anthropology*, ch. 4.

[87] Segalen, *Historical Anthropology*, p. 107.

their marriage. During the seventeenth and eighteenth centuries the civil authorities intervened further, as marriage came to be seen as a contract as well as a sacrament. During the Revolution the Constitution of 1791 proclaimed that, in the eyes of the law, marriage was a civil contract. King and Parlements also reinforced paternal authority over marriages. The Parlements in particular declared invalid secret marriages that went ahead without the consent of parents.[88] Within this framework, according to Martine Segalen, one can discern a number of models for marriage in France, with variations according to the age of first marriage, the conditions influencing the choice of partner and the content of the institution. Only in the twentieth century did these patterns unravel as parents became either unwilling or unable to intervene in marriages.[89]

Members of the aristocracy tended to marry early, while most young people had to wait until their mid- to late twenties before they were in a position to marry. However, the average age at first marriage slowly declined over the long term, from 28.7 years for a man and 26.1 years for a woman in 1821–5 to 25.2 and 22.8 years respectively in 1941–5.[90] The general rule at all levels of society was to marry a partner with a similar social and occupational background to oneself. Peasants tended to look for a spouse in their own village, with up to 80 per cent of unions endogamous, while the wealthy tended to search further afield. The villagers were likely to know each other before they married, and they may even have fallen in love in their own way when courting. They had their own 'codes' for expressing their feelings, alien to observers from the educated elite, which might involve squeezing hands tightly or thumps on the back. Workers in the towns often met their future partners at a dance: the historian Anne-Marie Sohn found that half of her sample of workers' marriages under the Third Republic began this way. Middle- or upper-class fiancés, by contrast, might barely be acquainted.[91] When Sabine Odoard, the daughter of a wealthy landowner in the Drôme, married at the age of nineteen in 1835 she had met her husband only three or four times, and then always in company.[92]

Marriage was always something more than a union of two individuals: it was also an alliance of two patrimonies. Even the poor might think in

---

[88] This section relies on André Armengaud, *La Famille et l'enfant en France et en Angleterre du XVIe au XVIIIe siècle: aspects démographiques* (Paris: Société d'Edition d'Enseignement Supérieur, 1975), pp. 22–8.

[89] Segalen, *Historical Anthropology*, p. 109.   [90] INED, 'Septième rapport', 310, table 15.

[91] Flandrin, *Amours paysannes*, pp. 79–129; Segalen, *Love and Power*, ch. 1; Segalen, *Historical Anthropology*, ch. 4; Sohn, *Chrysalides*, p. 469.

[92] Rambert George, *Chronique intime d'une famille de notables au XIXe siècle: les Odoard de Mercurol* (Lyon: Presses Universitaires de Lyon, 1981), pp. 25–7.

terms of defending the good name of a family and the honour of their women. Historians have plotted the marriage strategies pursued by families in a number of regions, with variations according to local rules of inheritance and social structure.[93] To ensure that they did not squander their wealth and reputation, families among the *notables* invested a huge amount of time in investigating the background of potential spouses for their sons and daughters. To minimize the risk of giving offence, they often conducted their enquiries through an intermediary. In 1895, a priest in Grasse sent a detailed report on a prospective husband for a young woman from the provincial nobility – albeit one in disgrace after she had given birth to an illegitimate child. He described in methodical fashion the suitor's age, health, character, intelligence, religion, habits, wealth and family background. Although the young man was not a practising Catholic and had no working capital, he at least owned three properties and was 'discreet, serious and capable of being the head of a family'. A similar enquiry concerning a young woman included questions on her religion, her temperament, how she hunted, how many horses she had, the character of her mother and the social life of her region.[94] Besides disparities in wealth, suitors might be put off by political differences, or a hint of sexual scandal in the family. According to Eric Mension-Rigau, such enquiries continued into the early twentieth century in aristocratic and *haute bourgeoisie* circles, with questions on the past as well as the present, on morality and wealth, and on health and education. A woman from this milieu, born in 1920, reported that most marriages were arranged:

It was as if there was an immense spider's web presided over by aunts, female cousins and old friends who all had ideas! Kaleidoscope in hand, they put together combinations. If these did not work, they shook the kaleidoscope and tried others.[95]

The traditional patriarch might arrange a marriage without consulting his son or daughter. The case of Pierre Rétif de la Bretonne in *La Vie de mon père* (1779) is well known. He brooked no argument from his son Edmonde when introducing him without warning to his prospective wife, Marie Dondaine. The young woman was no beauty, being described as stout and 'manlike', but she was the daughter of another wealthy local landowner.[96] The more common approach in the modern period, as

---

[93] See, for example, Bourdieu, 'Célibat', 33–58; and Alain Collomp, 'Alliance et filiation en Haute Provence au XVIIIe siècle', *Annales ESC*, 3 (1977), 445–77.

[94] *Marthe*; information on M. Robert d'Aillot, his family and his property, by the Abbé Bosset, Chaplain at the Hôpital de Grasse, May 1895; and Roger d'Amécourt, *Le Mariage de Mademoiselle de la Verne: les avatars de la vertu* (Paris: Perrin, 1987), p. 28.

[95] Mension-Rigau, *L'Enfance au château*, pp. 80–1.

[96] Rétif de la Bretonne, *Vie de mon père*, pp. 52–3.

paternal power waned, was to proceed only with the consent of the two partners. Whether the young were in much of a position to resist pressure from families eager to make an advantageous match remains an open question. When Marie Capelle (b. 1816) hesitated over an advantageous match, her family pointed out that 'without beauty and without a dowry' she could hardly hope for a better prospect. She eventually married a wealthy industrialist whom she found ugly and uncommunicative, but agreed to this marriage of convenience.[97] However, there were examples of other young women successfully refusing a suitor who was too old or too obnoxious for them.[98] Fathers wielded most influence when their offspring depended on them for a start in life, with a dowry in the form of land or a business. At the opposite pole, young wage earners in agriculture and industry could marry relatively early if they wished, since they could set up home in a modest way with their own resources.

Many young people, perhaps the majority during the eighteenth and nineteenth centuries, sooner or later slid into an arranged marriage of some sort. It was only with the coming of the Third Republic, especially after the First World War, that arranged marriages steadily gave way to love matches.[99] The evidence of the 'ego documents' reveals that the degree of initiative left to the young varied considerably during the earlier period. Caroline Duméril, aged twenty-one and from an academic background in Paris, evidently felt that her fate was largely beyond her control. Writing to a friend in 1858, she explained that her family had made extensive enquiries about a prospective suitor, and that she was soon to meet him. 'All this is terrible, I assure you,' she recounted, 'do you understand what it is to see for the first time someone who you will perhaps belong to, someone you are given to, and will have all possible rights over you?' The marriage went ahead, when she was twenty-two and her husband, an Alsatian industrialist, was thirty-eight. Shortly afterwards her tone was more reassuring, as she wrote that 'M. Mertzdorff of whom I was speaking is now my husband and my dear husband.' In similar fashion, Caroline Brame wrote in her diary at the age of nineteen about meeting a stranger deemed suitable for her by an aunt and her Father Confessor. The first meeting took place on 22 February 1866 in the Louvre: a common practice, since the two young people could meet or go their separate ways without drawing

---

[97] See Dauphin et al., *Ces bonnes lettres*, p. 32; George, *Les Odoard*, p. 27; and Lafarge, *Mémoires de Marie Capelle*, II, pp. 68–75.

[98] See, for example, Genlis, *Mémoires*, I, pp. 180–1; Suzanne Voilquin, *Souvenirs d'une fille du peuple* (Paris: François Maspero, 1978), p. 113.

[99] Sohn, *Chrysalides*, ch. 7.

attention to themselves.[100] It was a success, with Caroline recording that she wanted to know the young man better. They met again three days later in the Luxembourg Museum, where she found him amiable and charming, and the day after that she met his parents. On 1 March he proposed to her in the greenhouse in the Bois de Boulogne, and on 19 April they married. The next month she wrote that she felt loved, and love for him. Even young women from relatively poor backgrounds might allow others to take the initiative in arranging a partner. Augustine Rouvière, the daughter of a carpenter, recalled that she 'remained at home, almost an old maid, because I was thirty-one when they thought it was time for me to find a husband'. In the end it was an uncle who introduced her to her future husband, whom she married in 1914.[101]

The businessman Gustave-Emmanuel Roy described the elaborate process of bringing him together with his future spouse around 1850 in a way that suggested he exercised a fair amount of control. The wife of the head of his old boarding school alerted his mother to a potential match in the form of the sister of one of the current pupils. Both came from 'good families', and both were Protestants. Roy asked to see the young woman in question, and sat incognito in the background when she visited her brother. He formed a good impression of the slim young woman, with an 'agreeable and intelligent face'. After discussing the matter with his mother, he gave permission for his name to be mentioned to the family and for notes on his position to be presented. The Berger family welcomed the overtures, leading to a meeting between the two families after they rented adjacent boxes at the Opéra-Comique. Roy subsequently visited Dieppe to meet the young woman, on the understanding that they could both withdraw. The meeting began rather awkwardly, he recalled, but soon he and Mlle Berger were at ease with each other. He summoned his family to Dieppe, and then proposed to her. He returned to Paris for business reasons, but a fortnight later finalized the arrangements: a substantial dowry of 100,000 francs on her side, and 80,000 francs from his parents. On a slightly different tack, Paul Amiel

---

[100] In 1928, an aristocratic mother was warned that a prospective wife for her son would be at a Monet exhibition in the Orangerie, together with her mother, and was given a description of what they would be wearing. The correspondent pointed out that they could then be passed by or approached, and in the latter case they would not be shocked. Amécourt, *Mademoiselle de la Verne*, letter signed Louise (a neighbour of the family) to the Vicomtesse Paul de Gaucourt, 10 February 1928.

[101] Dauphin et al., *Ces bonnes lettres*, Introduction, pp. 40–1 and letter from Caroline to Isabelle Latham, 18 April 1858; Brame, *Journal intime*, entries for 22, 25 and 26 February, 1 March, 19 April and 24 May 1866, and Perrot, 'Enquête', pp. 209–13; and Rey, *Augustine Rouvière*, pp. 85–6.

(b. 1844) almost accepted on the spot when offered the hand of a young woman from Mâcon. Her guardians, an uncle and an aunt, had already investigated his circumstances, and they arranged a meeting through a mutual friend. Amiel claimed to be enchanted with the young woman, not to mention the dowry that he put into his tailoring business. The case of Madeleine Boileau, from a family of affluent landowners in Anjou, highlights the influence of personal feelings as well as material interests in a marriage. According to her family lore, she insisted during the early twentieth century that she wanted to marry a handsome young man she had seen on the streets of Tours. Her family agreed to make enquiries, and happily discovered that the man she had fallen for was unmarried, the son of an industrialist and about to take over the family firm. The couple became engaged two months after their first meeting and married a month later.[102]

Judicial records indicate that throughout the early modern period there were always young people who wanted to follow their own desires and marry an 'unsuitable' character in the eyes of their family. The 'ego documents' of the modern period in their turn provide odd case studies of young people who flouted the wishes of their parents when choosing a mate. The petty provincial nobility has left a scattering of documents concerned with such family conflicts. Aurore Dupin (George Sand) derailed attempts by her mother in 1820 to push her along the conventional path for an upper-class girl that ran straight from the convent to an arranged marriage. She rejected out of hand anyone put before her.[103] During the 1830s, the Pomereu family in Normandy hit a crisis when a daughter persisted in wanting to marry the second son of the famous politician and diplomat Talleyrand (1754–1838). Although the name of the family was illustrious enough, Talleyrand *père* had seriously depleted the family funds during his diplomatic career. This was not the 'brilliant marriage' her mother had hoped for, but after three years of 'struggle and cruel affliction' the family yielded. In 1839 the Marquise de Pomereu wrote that the quarrel had taken its toll on her daughter's health and she did not want to lose her.[104] This was a minor setback compared to the disastrous outcome for the family when a well-born young woman known only as Marthe wanted to marry a penniless local worker in 1892. Her family refused outright, but had to cope with her pregnancy. To

[102] Roy, *Souvenirs*, pp. 84–8; Amiel, *Souvenirs*, pp. 33–5; and Chotard-Lioret, 'Société familiale', pp. 257–60.
[103] Sand, *Histoire de ma vie*, pp. 428–9.
[104] AD Seine-Maritime, 37 J 17, Fonds Pomereu, letters from the Marquise de Pomereu (born Etiennette Marie Caroline d'Aligne) to her mother, 21 and 25 May and 15 July 1839.

cover their shame, her mother promptly sold their chateau in Normandy and spent the next ten years moving around the country with her other daughter. Marthe meanwhile wrote of her struggle with life in a charitable institution, and with the pressure to put her baby up for adoption. Reduced to the lower end of the marriage market, the family rejected a number of suitors, considered too poor, too humble or too dissolute for her. Her sister's tutor described her as 'almost bestial', and thought it desirable for the family to be rid of such a 'dangerous and compromising individual'.[105]

Marriage: the end of the story?

Marriage divides a life into two parts, separating the 'growing-up' phase from full adulthood. Conventionally, it ends happily, with family and friends steering the couple safely into dock, or individuals finding a mate on their own terms. Fifty years after the event, Gustave-Emmanuel Roy looked back on the day he became engaged, and pronounced it the happiest day in his life.[106] However, other authors used marriage to make various points about their lives. Charlotte Poulet (b. 1903) emphasized her poverty, recalling how she married a fellow worker whom she had met on the street in Paris at the age of nineteen. They had a simple wedding at the Town Hall, went back to work the next day and had to work for all of their own furniture. Similarly, Paul Chabot used the rushed wedding ceremonies of his parents in Paris in 1895 to demonstrate the exorbitant demands made by employers on domestic servants. They took an afternoon off for the civil ceremony in the Town Hall, but had to hire witnesses from the street since none of their friends could take time off for them. The church ceremony was equally 'derisory and ridiculous in its simplicity'. The couple simply received the blessing of the priest in a side chapel, exchanged rings and then retired to a nearby café. Then it was back to making dinner for the masters: 'A day like any other that would not tolerate any slackening; their stomachs could not put up with these extravagant ideas and caprices from the servants.' Louise Vanderwielen (b. 1906) in Lille concentrated on the squalid side of a hasty marriage, all too obviously escaping from an abusive father and stepmother. In her story, true romance would come later in life. Her first experience of making love a little before marriage was a disappointment. Borrowing from the language of the popular novel, she described her lover taking her in his arms, undoing her corsage and kissing her breasts – but then

---

[105] *Marthe*, letter from M. de Saint-René to Charles de Cerilley, 7 February 1894.
[106] Roy, *Souvenirs*, p. 86.

he forced himself on her brutally. The wedding night was also a fiasco as her husband passed out drunk.[107] And then there was Xavier-Edouard Lejeune, who swiftly passed over the period when he married, presumably to avoid any reference to an illegitimate birth.

Among those who never married, some appear to have drifted into bachelorhood or spinsterhood, but others consciously decided to reject the conventional path into maturity. Women in particular risked a precarious existence if they remained single, and so faced advice from all sides to find a partner. The diaries written by young women that Philippe Lejeune managed to unearth included the odd example of an author confronting the realities of avoiding marriage. Aline de Lens was twenty-six and a student at the prestigious Ecole des Beaux-Arts in Paris when she did so at the beginning of the twentieth century. On the one hand, she noted that most of her friends were married, and apparently happy, and that she had been warned that one day she would regret her decision. On the other, she expressed her distaste for the conventional existence of a woman of her class, revolving around the home and society. She was proud that she had renounced her old life and committed herself to art, a jealous lover if ever there was one. All she could hope was that love, especially a passionate affair, would pass her by and leave her to her work.[108]

Conclusion

Young people growing up in modern France must have experienced a certain *frisson* venturing into various areas of experience for much of the period covered here, as religion retained its mystical power, politics their revolutionary or counter-revolutionary tinge, and sexuality its series of taboos. The steady emergence of a more secular society and a stable Republic in the nineteenth century, and greater openness in sexual matters in the twentieth, changed the nature of what was exciting for the young. One might emphasize the submissiveness and modesty of the young during the period in the face of various forms of temptation from the adult world. They did after all bear a heavy weight of repression in their unequal relations with parents, schoolteachers, priests and police. Yet there were signs of resistance, be it the subversive political activity of youth under the Third Republic, the willingness of some young women to

---

[107] Charlotte Poulet, in Germain and de Panafieu, *Mémoire des femmes*, p. 188; Paul Chabot, *Jean et Yvonne, domestiques en 1900* (Paris: Tema, 1977), pp. 132–5; and Vanderwielen, *Lise du plat rays*, pp. 100–9.
[108] Lejeune, *Le Moi des demoiselles*, Aline de Lens, pp. 411–14; see also Catherine Pozzi, pp. 265–375.

seek an independent career, or the odd character prepared to allow sexual desire to override social convention. Increasingly in the modern period, children and especially adolescents had to make choices for themselves. It mattered whether they remained with the Church or not (if they retained at least a residual belief in the possibility of eternal salvation); it mattered for their path through life which political 'camp' they opted for; and it mattered whether they chose a compatible partner for themselves.

Conclusion

The Swedish feminist Ellen Key predicted in 1900 that the twentieth century would be the century of the child. She pinned her faith on a regime of improved child rearing within the family. In the event, her vision of institutions such as *écoles maternelles* playing second fiddle to full-time mothers, and schools becoming unnecessary, was hardly realized in the West.[1] Nonetheless, her work reflected a growing interest in the young during the modern period. Members of the educated elite in France joined their European counterparts in re-evaluating the early stages of life, and in establishing institutions to promote the welfare of the young. Already by 1800 the Enlightenment had gone a long way towards undermining common images of the child as at worst vicious and at best uninteresting. Victor Hugo, George Sand and other Romantics in France rivalled their European neighbours during the early nineteenth century in elevating the 'innocent' child on to a rather strange pinnacle of virtue. In similar vein, artists like Géricault and Gros discerned a vitality and even a certain mystique in the child figure. Later, from the 1830s, writers including Stendhal and Pierre Loti helped pioneer the new genre of childhood reminiscences. At the same time, a series of well-known laws bore witness to a newfound interest in child welfare. These included the 1833 *loi Guizot* to encourage primary education, the 1841 law on child labour and the 1889 law to protect 'child martyrs' from abusive parents. This is not to deny an ambivalence in attitudes to the child in France, as elsewhere. There was the continuing influence of a strand of Catholic thinking emphasizing the taint of original sin in the newborn child, and the temptation to equate the child with the savage of 'primitive' races. However, these darker attitudes did not stop further efforts during the twentieth century to understand how the child grew up, and to provide it with a secure framework in the family and the school. As for adolescence and youth, neither was exactly new around 1900, given the long-standing interest in the Ages of Man. Nonetheless, the gradual

---

[1] See Cunningham, *Children and Childhood*, pp. 163–4.

move towards a 'long' childhood in the West logically provoked interest in the years following puberty. Witness the flurry of French-language scientific and literary works featuring adolescence during the early twentieth century, the organizations dedicated to working with adolescents and the expansion of secondary education from the 1930s – and of course the explosion of youth culture in the late twentieth century.

There was a peculiarly French twist to these developments. The French state revealed a persistent obsession with the relatively slow growth of the population, which was what in part motivated its efforts to try to improve the health and education of the young. One can point to efforts under the *ancien régime* to improve standards of midwifery, and the campaign to catch up with the new rival across the Rhine after defeat in the Franco-Prussian War of 1870 with such measures as the regulation of the wet-nursing business in 1874 and the boosting of primary education during the 1880s. The turbulent political history of France also affected the young. They too went to the extremes, being shocked or fired up by the revolutions, and moved to dramatic 'conversions' to a life of devotion to, say, Christian or socialist ideals. There was also the French perception of themselves as bearers of a civilizing mission in the world. This began at home with the education of its people. There was a particular intensity to the study of the classics in French schools for the elite, and, particularly after 1870, a sustained effort to promote the French language and a French national identity in the primary schools of the Republic. All this might suggest a slightly bumpy ride, but that overall there was a story of fairly steady improvement in the condition of young people growing up in modern France. From the middle of the eighteenth century onwards, reformers put in place the framework for a 'modern' childhood, spared the afflictions of high mortality rates, manual work and illiteracy. However, these changes in the climate of ideas and the institutional framework were only half of the story. This study has aimed to tell the other half, by finding out what French people born between the eighteenth and early twentieth centuries made of their experiences of growing up in France. What key points emerge from this perspective on childhood and adolescence?

First, they reveal that, although it is tempting to talk in general terms of the experiences of children and adolescents in France in past centuries, the reality has been one of stark divergences according to such influences as socio-economic background and gender. Time and again the study has highlighted different sections of French society, such as the aristocracy and wealthy bourgeoisie, the urban middle classes, the peasantry, and the new working classes of the towns. These are by no means clear-cut divisions, and others such as religious denomination, region and urban–rural differences cut across them. Yet, broadly speaking, one can trace divergences (as well as similarities) in their ideas on childhood and adolescence, their child-rearing practices, their attitudes to other local children and youth, their expectations concerning work, leisure and education, the values they passed down to their children and their marriage strategies. To put it another way, the young were far from immune to the vast inequalities in wealth and status that prevailed in modern France, the tendency to assign men and women to opposing spheres of existence, and the fierce rivalries between political and religious groupings. Such divergences were remarkably persistent. One might expect to be able to contrast the opulent lifestyle of the future Comtesse de Boigne at Versailles in the eighteenth century with the miseries of the young Jean-Roche Coignet on the farms of Burgundy – or the isolation of the young Talleyrand with the sociability of Jacques-Louis Ménétra in Paris. One might even predict similar contrasts in 1900 during the so-called 'Belle Epoque' between the life of Pauline de Broglie, shuttling between a Parisian town house and a chateau in Anjou, and the grim existence of the peasant Henri Pitaud in his 'hole' of a house in the Vendée. However, more surprising is the tight grip of the upper classes on the *lycées* and *collèges* until the 1930s, and beyond, compared to, say, the limited aspirations of so many peasants in the village of 'Peyrane' in 1950, or the evidence from the 1960s of children from modest backgrounds falling behind their peers at school from around the age of eleven or twelve.

Second, the view 'from below' presents in vivid fashion the numerous burdens faced by the young in the recent past, according to their place in society. The record was by no means all gloom and doom for the young. This study has emphasized, for example, the supportive framework of *rites de passage* in the popular culture of the villages, and the freedom to roam and play enjoyed by young children among the 'popular classes'. There were plenty of 'happy' childhoods in the literature, such as that of Pierre-Jakez Hélias in his Breton village or of Jean Giono in Manosque. However, it is hard to avoid the sometimes shocking evidence of accepted practices that would now be considered harmful to the welfare of the child or downright abusive. One thinks of a long list that includes the willingness in some social circles to send newborn infants away to a wet-nurse, the distance that aristocratic parents liked to maintain from their children, the arbitrary exercise of power wielded by traditional patriarchs, the insensitive treatment of orphans in some religious institutions, the violence of corporal punishments at home or in some of the primary schools, the notoriously unhealthy conditions for a few types of child labour, the rough treatment of apprentices and the intensely academic curriculum of the boarding schools. Young people might occasionally revolt against such oppressive treatment, or wait until old age to vent their spleen, but they were more likely to recognize the principle of *autres temps, autres moeurs*. In other words, they accepted that adults generally acted according to the customs of the times, doing what they thought was best for them. Some children at least proved remarkably resilient under pressure.

Finally, adopting the perspective of the young in earlier generations removes some of the sheen from developments that one normally considered progressive. It appears difficult to dispute the benefits of a greater interest in *puériculture* (child rearing), mass schooling and child medicine. Yet a closer look does not always reveal parents, teachers and doctors in a heroic light. At the very least it provides early hints at the human costs as well as the benefits of an increasingly mobile, productive and competitive society. Mothers and fathers gradually moved away from the aloof approach of aristocratic families or the combination of freedom and occasional harshness characteristic of hard-pressed peasant and working-class families towards a more 'child-centred' family. This could bring more expressions of affection for the child, less in the way of corporal punishment and more attention to formal education. Yet the quintessentially 'middle-class' approach, and the widespread quest for social mobility, was not without its drawbacks for young people. Its emphasis on the need for discipline and academic success tended to cut links with all but a few approved friends, and risked tension within the family. The shift from child labour and traditional apprenticeships towards an extended period of schooling would eventually even out some of the extremes of social inequality, not to mention paving the way for a more productive labour force. At the same time, it raised problems for children and adolescents among the 'popular classes' in perceiving the links between the content of the education and the careers they were aiming for later in life. It also proved difficult to achieve the ideal of equality in education, and continues to do so, as the republican schools after 1870 struggled to shake off their established role of reinforcing existing social differences. Teachers might appear beacons of civilization – or sneering, violent characters. Furthermore, during the nineteenth and early twentieth centuries, doctors introduced modern, scientific medicine, giving hope in the face of the numerous diseases that had threatened the lives of so many infants and young children before the twentieth century. Along with the medicine, though, the doctors for a long period during the nineteenth and twentieth centuries brought a rigid and authoritarian regime for child rearing. In this way, the changes affecting young people between the mid-eighteenth and mid-twentieth centuries anticipated some of the paradoxes of modern childhood and youth in France, indeed of modern civilization in the West.

Bibliography

I. MANUSCRIPT SOURCES

ARCHIVES DEPARTEMENTALES (AD)

Alpes-Maritimes

E 078/01 1003 Archives communales de Lantosque, abbés de la jeunesse, 1814–58

97 J 0003 Fonds Loviaguine

4 M 541 Jeunesses patriotes, 1920s

Bouches-du-Rhône

26 J Fonds des familles Surian, Cadenet-Charleval and Jesse-Charleval

    26 J 6–7 Letters from Jean-Baptiste Surian, 1804–17

    26 J 19 Letters from Jean-Baptiste Surian to his wife, and from his children, 1804–24

    26 J 21 Family letters, 1825–48

    26 J 26 Letters from relatives

61 J Fonds Veray

    61 J 13 Letters to Louise Veray from her nephew, Louis Veray, 1907–30

109 J Collection Froissard

    109 J 25–6 Famille Colla de Pradine, family correspondence

    109 J 32 Famille De Bruny. Letters to Roux family in Marseille, 1729–52

1 M 808 Jeunesse syndicaliste révolutionnaire; jeunesse anti-religieux Ferrer, 1911–12

1 M 811 Jeunesse communiste, 1921

1 M 845 Tracts et affichettes royalistes, 1890–1902

Ille-et-Vilaine

105 J 3 Fonds Adolphe Orain (1834–1918): 'Mes souvenirs', unpublished MS, 1905–6

Marne

1 E 140 Deu de Marson. Family correspondence

30 M 65 Police politique

87 M 54 Sports

87 M 71 Associations. Dépôts de statuts, autorisations, déclarations

Rhône
4 M 176 Police judiciaire. Rixes d'enfants et de jeunes gens, 1817–18
4 M 482 Police administrative: fêtes. Bals d'étudiants
4 M 603–5 Sports gymnastiques, 1880–1920

Seine-Maritime
37 J Fonds Pomereu
   37 J 12 Family documents, 1612–1868
   37 J 17 Family documents, 1835–40
   37 J 19 Family documents, 1869–1937
146 J Fonds Charles Nicolle
   146 J 13 Mémoires et souvenirs de Charles Nicolle, dictated 1935–6 in Tunis
188 J Fonds Delahaye-Le Bouis et Feray
   188 J 1 Family documents
1 M 273–4 Jeunesses patriotes, 1920s and 1930s
1 M 315 Jeunesses communistes, 1923–37
1 M 321 Jeunesses laïques et républicaines, 1930s
1 M 643 Jeunesse catholique, 1934–5

II. PUBLISHED PRIMARY SOURCES

1. CHILDHOOD REMINISCENCES

Adam, Juliette. *Le Roman de mon enfance*, Paris: Alphonse Lemerre, 1902
Bardin, Angélina. *Angélina: une fille des champs*, Paris: André Bonne, 1956
Bataille, Henry. 'L'Enfance éternelle', *Les Oeuvres libres*, 7 (1921), 5–60
Bazin, Hervé. *Vipère au poing* (1948), Paris: Livre de poche, 1976
Beauvoir, Simone de. *Memoirs of a Dutiful Daughter* (1958), transl. James Kirkup, Harmondsworth: Penguin, 1963
Bernard, Marc. *As Little Children* (1942), London: Dobson, 1949
Bonnet, Batisto. *Vido d'enfant* (*Vie d'enfant*) (1894), transl. from the Provençal by Alphonse Daudet, Nîmes: Tourmagne, 1968
Chamson, André. *Le Chiffre de nos jours: roman*, Paris: Gallimard, 1954
Cocteau, Jean. *Le Livre blanc* (1928), transl. Margaret Crosland, London: Peter Owen, 1969
Colette, *La Maison de Claudine* (1922), in *Oeuvres complètes*, vol. VII, Paris: Le Fleuron, 1949
Flaubert, Gustave. *Diary of a Madman* (1838), in *Early Writings*, transl. Robert Griffin, Lincoln and London: University of Nebraska Press, 1991, pp. 161–203
France, Anatole. *Le Livre de mon ami* (1885), in *Oeuvres complètes*, vol. III, Paris: Calmann-Lévy, 1925
   La Vie en fleur, Paris: Calmann Lévy, 1922
Gide, André. *Si le grain ne meurt* (1926), Paris: Gallimard, 1955
Giono, Jean. *Jean le bleu*, Paris: Grasset, 1932
Green, Julian. *Memories of Happy Days*, New York: Harper, 1942
Guéhenno, Jean. *Changer la vie: mon enfance et ma jeunesse*, Paris: Grasset, 1961

Guillaumin, Emile. *The Life of a Simple Man* (1904), transl. Margaret Crosland, Hanover, NH: University Press of New England, 1983

Hélias, Pierre-Jakez. *The Horse of Pride: Life in a Breton Village* (1975), transl. June Guicharnaud, New Haven, Yale University Press, 1978

Henry, Mrs Robert. *The Little Madeleine*, London: Dent, 1951

Jammes, Francis. *De l'âge divin à l'âge ingrat: mémoires*, Paris: Plon, 1921

Loti, Pierre. *Le Roman d'un enfant* (1890), *suivi de Prime jeunesse* (1919), Paris: Gallimard, 1999

Malraux, Clara. *Apprendre à vivre*, Paris: Bernard Grasset, 1963

Michelet, Jules. *Ma jeunesse* (written c. 1820, first published 1884), Paris: Flammarion, 1913

Pagnol, Marcel. *Le Château de ma mère: souvenirs d'enfance II* (1958), Paris: Fallois, 1988

La Gloire de mon père: souvenirs d'enfance II (1957), London: Nelson, 1962

Pange, Comtesse Jean de. *Comment j'ai vu 1900*, 2 vols., Paris: Grasset, 1962

Proust, Marcel. *In Search of Lost Time*, vol. I, *The Way by Swann's* (1913), transl. Lydia Davis, London: Penguin, 2003

Renan, Ernest. *Souvenirs d'enfance et de jeunesse* (1883), Paris: Gallimard, 1983

Sand, George. *Histoire de ma vie* (1854–5), Paris: Livre de poche, 2004

Sarraute, Nathalie. *Enfance*, Paris: Gallimard, 1983

Sartre, Jean-Paul. *Les Mots*, Paris: Gallimard, 1964

Stendhal. *The Life of Henry Brulard* (written 1835–6, first published 1890), transl. John Sturrock, New York: New York Review of Books, 2002

Sylvère, Antoine. *Toinou: le cri d'un enfant auvergnat*, Paris: Plon, 1980

Vallès, Jules. *Jacques Vingtras I: l'enfant* (1879), Paris: Livre de poche, 1985

Jacques Vingtras II: le bachelier (1881), Paris: Gallimard, 1974

2. AUTOBIOGRAPHIES, AUTOBIOGRAPHICAL NOVELS AND MEMOIRS

Amiel, Paul. *Souvenirs, 1844–1911*, Angoulême: Imprimerie ouvrière, 1914

Artières, Philippe, ed. *Le Livre des vies coupables: autobiographies de criminels (1896–1909)*, Paris: Albin Michel, 2000

Audoux, Marguerite. *Marie-Claire*, Paris: Charpentier, 1910

Barrié, Marie-Juliette. *Quand les bananes donnent la fièvre*, Paris: La Pensée universelle, 1973

Benoit, Joseph. *Confessions d'un prolétaire, Lyon 1871*, Paris: Editions sociales, 1968

Besson, Pierre. *Un pâtre du Cantal*, Paris: Delagrave, 1914

Blanc, Julien. *Seule, la vie: 1, Confusion des peines*, Paris: Editions du Pré-aux-Clercs, 1943

Blasquez, Adélaïde. *Gaston Lucas, serrurier: chronique de l'anti-héros*, Paris: Plon, 1976

Boigne, Comtesse de. *Récits d'une tante: mémoires de la comtesse de Boigne, née d'Osmond*, Paris: Emile-Paul, 1921

Bouvier, Jeanne. *Mes mémoires* (1936), Paris: Maspero, 1983

B(rocher), Victorine. *Souvenirs d'une morte vivante*, Paris: La Découverte, 2002 (1909)

Broglie, Duc de. *Souvenirs, 1785–1870*, 4 vols., Paris: Calmann Lévy, 1886

Camp, Maxime du. *Souvenirs littéraires*, Paris: Aubier, 1994

Carles, Emilie, as told to Robert Destanque. *A Wild Herb Soup: The Life of a French Countrywoman* (1977), transl. Avriel H. Goldberger, London: Victor Gollancz, 1992

Caroux-Destray, Jacques, *Un couple ouvrier traditionnel: la vieille garde autogestionnaire*, Paris: Anthropos, 1974

Chabot, Paul. *Jean et Yvonne, domestiques en 1900*, Paris: Tema, 1977

Chateaubriand, François-René, Vicomte de. *Mémoires d'outre-tombe* (1849–50), vol. I, Paris: Flammarion, 1948

Coignet, Jean-Roch. *The Narrative of Captain Coignet, Soldier of the Empire, 1776–1850*, transl. Mrs M. Carey, London: Chatto and Windus, 1897

Déguignet, Jean-Marie. *Mémoires d'un paysan bas-breton*, Ar Releg-Kerhuon, Brittany: An Here, 1998

Dumay, Jean-Baptiste. *Mémoires d'un militant ouvrier du Creusot (1841–1905)*, Grenoble: Presses Universitaires de Grenoble, 1976

Dumoulin, Georges. *Carnets de route: quarante années de vie militante*, Lille: Editions de 'L'Avenir', 1937

Existence, G. 'Village, grande nouvelle inédite', *Les Oeuvres libres*, 221 (1939)

Fouquet, Alphonse. *Histoire de ma vie industrielle*, Paris: Michel, 1899

Genevoix, Maurice. *Trente mille jours*, Paris: Seuil, 1980

Genlis, Stéphanie-Félicité Du Crest, Comtesse de, *Mémoires inédits sur le XVIIIe siècle et la Révolution française depuis 1756 jusqu'à nos jours*, 2 vols., Paris: Ladvocat, 1825

Gossez, Rémi, ed. *Un ouvrier en 1820: manuscrit inédit de Jacques Etienne Bédé*, Paris: Presses Universitaires de France, 1984

Grafteaux, Serge. *Mémé Santerre*, Paris: Delarge, 1975

Grenadou, Ephraïm and Prévost, Alain. *Grenadou: paysan français*, Paris: Seuil, 1966

Guicheteau, Gérard and Namur, Gisèle. *Mémoires des pères*, Paris: Editions de la Martinière, 1993

Hamot, A. *La Vie d'un travailleur*, Paris: Chez l'auteur, 1891

Jamerey-Duval, Valentin. *Mémoires: enfance et éducation d'un paysan au XVIIIe siècle*, Paris: Le Sycomore, 1981

Lafarge, Marie. *Mémoires de Marie Capelle, veuve Lafarge, écrits par elle-même*, 4 vols., Paris: A. René, 1841–2

Lamartine, Alphonse de. *Les Confidences*, Paris: Hachette, 1879

Lavisse, Ernest. *Souvenirs* (1912), Paris: Calmann-Lévy, 1988

Léautaud, Paul. *In Memoriam* (1905), Paris: Mercure de France, 1987

Lejeune, Xavier-Edouard. *Calicot: enquête de Michel et Philippe Lejeune*, Paris: Montalba, 1984

Lengrand, Louis and Craipeau, Maria. *Louis Lengrand, mineur du Nord*, Paris: Seuil, 1974

Léonard, E.-G. *Mon village sous Louis XV, d'après les mémoires d'un paysan*, Paris: Presses Universitaires de France, 1941

Lepage, Constant. *Soixante ans de la vie d'un prolétaire*, Paris: L. Vanier, 1900

Lhopiteau, Romain. *Soixante-deux années de ma vie: récits intimes et commerciaux, 1828–1890*, Paris: L Michel et fils, n.d.

Marmontel, Jean-François. *Mémoires*, Paris: Mercure de France, 1999

Ménétra, Jacques-Louis. *Journal of My Life*, transl. Arthur Goldhammer, New York: Columbia University Press, 1986

Michaud, René. *J'avais vingt ans: un jeune ouvrier au début du siècle*, Paris: Editions syndicalistes, 1967

Mirabeau, Comte de. *Mémoires biographiques, littéraires et politiques de Mirabeau, écrits par lui-même, par son père, son oncle et son fils adoptif*, 3 vols., Paris: Auffray, 1834

Mistral, Frédéric. *The Memoirs of Frédéric Mistral*, transl. George Wickes, Paris/London: Alyscamps Press, 1994

Morieux, Henri. *Autobiographie: les mémoires d'un gogo*, Lille: Camille Robbe, 1903

Nadaud, Martin. *Léonard, maçon de la Creuse*, Paris: François Maspero, 1977

Navel, Georges. *Travaux*, Paris: Stock, 1945

Ozouf, Jacques, ed. *Nous les maîtres d'école: autobiographies d'instituteurs de la Belle Epoque*, Paris: Collection Archives, 1967

Perdiguier, Agricol. *Mémoires d'un compagnon*, Paris: Denoel, 1943

Pitaud, Henri. *Le Pain de la terre: mémoires d'un paysan vendéen du début du siècle*, Paris: J.-C. Lattès, 1982

Poumiès de la Siboutie, Dr F.-L. *Souvenirs d'un médecin de Paris*, Paris: Plon, 1910

Rey, Raymonde Anna. *Augustine Rouvière, cévenole*, Paris: Delarge, 1977

Roland de la Platière, Jeanne-Marie. *Mémoires de Madame Roland*, ed. Paul de Roux, Paris: Mercure de France, 1986

Rousseau, Jean-Jacques. *The Confessions* (written 1764–70, first published 1781), transl. J. M. Cohen, London: Penguin, 1953

Roy, Gustave-Emmanuel, *Souvenirs, 1823–1906*, Nancy: Berger-Levrault, 1906

Shaw, Mathilde. *Illustres et inconnus: souvenirs de ma vie*, Paris: Charpentier, 1906

Talleyrand, Prince de. *Memoirs of the Prince de Talleyrand*, transl. Raphaël Ledos de Beaufort, 2 vols., London: Griffith Farran Okeden and Welsh, 1891

Traugott, Mark, ed. *The French Worker: Autobiographies from the Early Industrial Era*, Berkeley: University of California Press, 1993

Truquin, Norbert. *Mémoires et aventures d'un prolétaire à travers la révolution*, Paris: Maspero, 1977

Vanderwielen, Louise. *Lise du plat pays*, Lille: Presses Universitaires de Lille, 1983

Visieux, Augustin. *Mineur de fond: fosses de Lens: soixante ans de combat et de solidarité*, Paris: Plon, 1991

3. PERSONAL DIARIES, FAMILY CORRESPONDENCE AND ORAL HISTORY COLLECTIONS

Amécourt, Roger d'. *Le Mariage de Mademoiselle de la Verne: les avatars de la vertu*, Paris: Perrin, 1987

Bashkirtseff, Marie. *Journal de Marie Bashkirtseff, extraits*, ed. Verena von der Heyden-Rynsch, Paris: Mercure de France, 2000

Brame, Caroline. *Le Journal intime de Caroline B.*, ed. Michelle Perrot and Georges Ribeill, Paris: Montalba, 1985

Dauphin, Cécile, Lebrun-Pézerat, Pierrette and Poublan, Danièle. *Ces bonnes lettres: une correspondance familiale au XIXe siècle*, Paris: Albin Michel, 1995

Desmoulins, Lucile. *Journal, 1788–1793*, ed. Philippe Lejeune, Paris: Cendres, 1995

Emilie, Paris: Seuil, 1985

G., Jeanne. *Journal et correspondance de Jeanne G., recueillis et publiés après sa mort*, Marseille: Verdot, 1906

George, Rambert. *Chronique intime d'une famille de notables au XIXe siècle: les Odoard de Mercurol*, Lyon: Presses Universitaires de Lyon, 1989

Germain, Christiane and Panafieu, Christine de. *La Mémoire des femmes: sept témoignages de femmes nées avec le siècle*, Paris: Sylvie Messinger, 1982

Journal de Clotilde, pages sérieuses commencées à son retour de pension par Mlle S. W., Paris: Lefort, 1896

Lenéru, Marie. *Journal, précédé du Journal d'enfance*, Paris: Grasset, 1945

Leseur, Elisabeth. *Journal d'enfant*, Paris: J. de Gigord, 1934

Marthe, Paris: Seuil, 1982

Roche, Anne and Taranger, Marie-Claude. *Celles qui n'ont pas écrit: récits de femmes dans la région Marseillaise, 1914–1945*, Aix-en-Provence: Edisud, 1995

4. TREATISES ON CHILDHOOD AND ADOLESCENCE

Binet, Alfred. *Les Idées modernes sur les enfants*, Paris: Flammarion, 1909

Braunschvig, Marcel. 'L'Enfant au XIXe siècle', *Pages libres*, 139 (29 August 1903), 169–84

Brereton, Cloudesley. 'L'Enfant français dans la famille et à l'école', *Revue pédagogique*, 22 (1918), 237–49

Compayré, Gabriel. *L'Evolution intellectuelle et morale de l'enfant*, Paris: Hachette, 1893

Debesse, Maurice. *La Crise d'originalité juvénile*, 3rd edn, Paris: Presses Universitaires de France, 1948

Droz, Gustave. *L'Enfant*, Paris: Victor-Havard, 1885

Monsieur, madame et bébé (1866), Paris: Victor-Havard, 1882

Dupanloup, Félix-Antoine-Philibert, évêque d'Orléans. *L'Enfant*, Paris: Charles Douniol, 1869

Franklin, Alfred. *La Vie privée d'autrefois: l'enfant*, Paris: Plon, 1896

Hément, Félix. *Petit traité des punitions et des récompenses à l'usage des maîtres et des parents*, Paris: Georges Carré, 1890

Henri, Victor and Henri, Catherine. 'Enquête sur les premiers souvenirs de l'enfance (1897)', *Cahiers de sémiotique textuelle*, 12 (1988), 237–48

Legouvé, Ernest. *Les Pères et les enfants au XIXe siècle: enfance et adolescence*, Paris: Hetzel, 1907

Les Pères et les enfants au XIXe siècle: la jeunesse (1869), 5th edn, Paris: Hetzel, n.d.

Mendousse, Pierre. *L'Ame de l'adolescent*, 5th edn, Paris: Presses Universitaires de France, 1947

Rousseau, Jean-Jacques. *Emile, or On Education* (1762), transl. Allan Bloom, London: Penguin, 1991

5. NOVELS AND POETRY CONCERNED WITH CHILDHOOD
AND ADOLESCENCE

Alain-Fournier, *Le Grand Meaulnes* (1913), transl. Frank Davison, Oxford: Oxford University Press, 1959

Bernardin de Saint-Pierre, J. H. *Paul and Virginia*, transl. Helen Marie Williams (1796), Oxford: Woodstock Books, 1989

Bernanos, Georges. *The Diary of a Country Priest*, transl. Pamela Morris (2nd edn, New York: Carroll and Graf, 2002

Cocteau, Jean. *Les Enfants terribles* (1929), transl. Rosamond Lehmann, Harmondsworth: Penguin, 1961

Daudet, Alphonse. *Jack* (1876), Paris: Flammarion, 1973
    Le Petit Chose: histoire d'un enfant (1868), Paris: Panthéon, 1946

Deschanel, Emile. *Le Bien et le mal qu'on a dit des enfants*, Paris: Michel Lévy, 1857

Gide, André. *Les Faux-monnayeurs*, Paris: Gallimard, 1925

Hugo, Victor. *Les Feuilles d'automne*, Paris: Gallimard, 1964
    Les Misérables, transl. Norman Denny, London: Penguin, 1976

Lautréamont, Comte de. *Maldoror*, transl. Alexis Lykiard, London: Allison and Busby, 1970

Le Roy, Eugène. *Jacqou le croquant*, Paris: Mornay, 1925

Marguerite, Paul and Marguerite, Victor. *Poum, aventures d'un petit garçon* (1897), Paris: Plon, 1948

Maupassant, Guy de. 'Le Papa de Simon', in *La Maison Tellier*, Paris: Albin Michel, 1969, pp. 167–82

Mauriac, François. *Un adolescent d'autrefois*, Paris: Flammarion, 1969

Pergaud, Louis. *La Guerre des boutons* (1912), Paris: Mercure de France, 1963

Philippe, Charles-Louis. *Charles Blanchard*, Paris: Nouvelle revue française, 1913

Queneau, Raymond. *Zazie in the Metro* (1959), transl. Barbara Wright, London: John Calder, 1982

Radiguet, Raymond. *Le Diable au corps*, Paris: Grasset, 1923

Reboul, Jules. *La Vie de Jacques Baudet, 1870–1930: roman d'une petite existence*, Privas, 1934

Rétif de la Bretonne, Nicolas-Edme. *Monsieur Nicolas* (1796), Paris: Trianon, 1932
    La Vie de mon père (1779), Paris: Garnier, 1970

Rimbaud, Arthur. *Illuminations: Coloured Plates*, ed. Nick Osmond, London: Athlone Press, 1976

Saint-Exupéry, Antoine de. *Le Petit Prince* (1943), Paris: Gallimard, 1997

Sand, George. *François le champi* (1850), Paris: Garnier, 1962
    La Mare au diable (1846), Paris: Garnier, 1962
    The Master Pipers (1852), transl. Rosemary Lloyd (Oxford: Oxford University Press, 1994
    La Petite Fadette (1849), Paris: Garnier, 1958

Ségur, Comtesse de. *Les Malheurs de Sophie* (1864), Paris: Babel, 1997

Zola, Emile. *Germinal*, transl. L. W. Tancock, Harmondsworth: Penguin, 1954

III. SECONDARY SOURCES (SELECTED)

I. PUBLISHED WORKS

Abbadie d'Arrast, Mme Charles d'. *Causeries sur le pays Basque: la femme et l'enfant*, Paris: Rudeval, 1909

Anderson, R. D. *Education in France, 1848–1870*, Oxford: Clarendon Press, 1975

Ariès, Philippe and Duby, Georges, eds. *A History of Private Life*, vol. IV, *From the Fires of Revolution to the Great War*, ed. Michelle Perrot, Cambridge, MA: Harvard University Press, 1990

Armengaud, André. 'L'Attitude de la société à l'égard de l'enfant au XIXe siècle', *Annales de démographie historique* (1973), 303–12

  La Famille et l'enfant en France et en Angleterre du XVIe au XVIIIe siècle: aspects démographiques, Paris: Société d'Edition d'Enseignement Supérieur, 1975

  'Les Nourrices du Morvan au XIXe siècle', *Etudes et chroniques de démographie historique* (1964), 131–9

Badinter, Elisabeth. *The Myth of Motherhood: An Historical View of the Maternal 'Instinct'*, transl. Roger DeGaris, London: Souvenir Press, 1981

Balcou, Jean, ed. *Ernest Renan et les souvenirs d'enfance et de jeunesse: la conquête de soi*, Paris: Honoré Champion, 1992

Bardet, Jean-Pierre, Luc, Jean-Noël, Robin-Romero, Isabelle and Rollet, Catherine, eds. *Lorsque l'enfant grandit: entre dépendance et autonomie*, Paris: Presses de l'Université de Paris-Sorbonne, 2003

Bély, Lucien. 'L'Elève et le monde: essai sur l'éducation des lumières d'après les mémoires autobiographiques du temps', *Revue d'histoire moderne et contemporaine*, 28 (1981), 3–35

Benrekassa, Georges. 'Le Typique et le fabuleux: histoire et roman dans la *Vie de mon père*', *Revue des sciences humaines*, 172 (1978), 31–56

Berlanstein, Lenard R. 'Vagrants, Beggars, and Thieves: Delinquent Boys in Mid-Nineteenth Century Paris', *Journal of Social History*, 12 (1979), 531–52

Berriot-Salvadore, Evelyne and Pebay-Clottes, Isabelle, eds. *Autour de l'enfance*, Biarritz: Atlantica, 1999

Bertholet, Denis. *Les Français par eux-mêmes, 1815–1885*, Paris: Olivier Orban, 1991

Bethlenfalvay, Marina. *Les Visages de l'enfant dans la littérature française du XIXe siècle: esquisse d'une typologie*, Geneva: Droz, 1979

Bideau, Alain. 'L'Envoi des jeunes enfants en nourrice: l'exemple d'une petite ville: Thoissey-en-Dombes, 1740–1840', in *Hommage à Marcel Reinhard: sur la population française au XVIIIe et au XIXe siècles*, Paris: Société de démographie historique, 1973, pp. 49–58

Boltanski, Luc. *Prime éducation et morale de classe*, Paris: Mouton, 1969

Bougeâtre, Eugène. *La Vie rurale dans le Mantois et le Vexin au XIXe siècle*, Meudon: Collection de travaux et de documents pour servir à l'histoire du Mantois et du Vexin, 1971

Bourdieu, Pierre. 'Célibat et condition paysanne', *Etudes rurales*, 5–6 (1962), 33–135

Bowlby, John. *Attachment and Loss*, vol. I, *Attachment*, London: Hogarth Press, 1970

Bricard, Isabelle. *Saintes ou pouliches: l'éducation des jeunes filles au XIXe siècle*, Paris: Albin Michel, 1985

Burguière, André et al., eds. *A History of the Family*, vol. II, *The Impact of Modernity*, transl. Sarah Hanbury Tenison, Cambridge: Polity, 1996

Calvet, J. *L'Enfant dans la littérature française*, 2 vols., Paris: Lanore, 1930

Caron, Jean-Claude. *A l'école de la violence: châtiments et sévices dans l'institution scolaire au XIXe siècle*, Paris: Aubier, 1999

   Générations romantiques: les étudiants de Paris et le quartier latin (1814–51), Paris: Armand Colin, 1991

Cassidy, Jude and Shaver, Phillip R., eds. *Handbook of Attachment: Theory, Research and Clinical Applications*, New York and London: Guilford Press, 1999

Castan, Yves. *Honnêteté et relations sociales en Languedoc, 1715–1780*, Paris: Plon, 1974

Chartier, Roger, Boureau, Alain and Dauphin, Cécile. *Correspondence: Models of Letter-Writing from the Middle Ages to the Nineteenth Century*, transl. Christopher Woodall, Cambridge: Polity Press, 1997

Chartier, Roger, Compère, Marie-Madeleine and Julia, Dominique. *L'Education en France du XVIe au XVIIIe siècle*, Paris: Société d'édition d'enseignement supérieur, 1976

Chassagne, Serge. *Une Femme d'affaires au XVIIIe siècle: la correspondance de Madame de Maraise, collaboratrice d'Oberkampf*, Toulouse: Privat, 1981

Chombart de Lauwe, Marie-José. *Un monde autre: l'enfance*, Paris: Payot, 1971

Chotard-Lioret, Caroline. 'Correspondre en 1900: le plus public des actes privés ou la manière de gérer un réseau de parenté', *Ethnologie française*, 15 (1985), 63–71

Clarke, Ann and Clarke, Alan. *Early Experience and the Life Path*, London: Jessica Kingsley, 2000

Claverie, Elizabeth and Lamaison, Pierre. *L'Impossible Mariage: violence et parenté en Gevaudan, 17e, 18e et 19e siècles*, Paris: Hachette, 1982

Coe, Richard N. 'Reminiscences of Childhood: An Approach to a Comparative Mythology', *Proceedings of the Leeds Philosophical and Literary Society*, 19 (1984), 223–321

   'Stendhal, Rousseau and the Search for Self', *Australian Journal of French Studies*, 16 (1979), 27–47

   When the Grass was Taller: Autobiography and the Experience of Childhood, New Haven: Yale University Press, 1984

Cohen, Yolande. *Les Jeunes, le socialisme et la guerre: histoire des mouvements de jeunesse en France*, Paris: Editions l'Harmattan, 1989

Collomp, Alain. 'Alliance et filiation en Haute Provence au XVIIIe siècle', *Annales ESC*, 3 (1977), 445–77

   'Famille nucléaire et famille élargie en Haute Provence au XVIIIe siècle (1703–1734)', *Annales ESC*, 27 (1972), 969–75

La Maison du père: famille et village en Haute-Provence aux XVIIe et XVIIIe siècles, Paris: Presses Universitaires de France, 1983

'Ménage et famille: études comparatives sur la dimension et la structure du groupe domestique', *Annales ESC*, 29 (1976), 777–86

Compère, Marie-Madeleine. *Du collège au lycée (1500–1850): généalogie de l'enseignement français*, Paris: Gallimard/Julliard, 1985

Corijn, Martine and Klijzing, Erik, eds. *Transitions to Adulthood in Europe*, Dordrecht: Kluwer, 2001

Crubellier, Maurice. *L'Enfance et la jeunesse dans la société française, 1800–1950*, Paris: Armand Colin, 1979

Cunningham, Hugh. *Children and Childhood in Western Society since 1500*, London: Longman, 1995

Darnton, Robert. 'Readers Respond to Rousseau: The Fabrication of Romantic Sensitivity', in *The Great Cat Massacre and other Episodes in French Cultural History*, Harmondsworth: Penguin, 1985, pp. 209–49

Delaisi de Parseval, Geneviève and Hurstel, Françoise. 'La Paternité "à la française"', *Les Temps modernes*, 42 (1986), 51–93

Delay, Jean. *The Youth of André Gide*, transl. June Guicharnaud, Chicago: University of Chicago Press, 1963

Delumeau, Jean, ed. *La Première Communion: quatre siècles d'histoire*, Paris: Desclée de Brouwer, 1987

Delumeau, Jean and Roche, Daniel, eds., *Histoire des pères et de la paternité*, Paris: Larousse, 1990

Doroszczuk, Catherine. 'Le Récit impudique: réception du récit d'enfance à la fin du XVIIIe siècle', *Cahiers de sémiotique textuelle*, 12 (1988), 9–20

Downs, Laura Lee. *Childhood in the Promised Land: Working-Class Movements and the Colonies de Vacances in France, 1880–1960*, Durham: Duke University Press, 2002

Drouillet, Jean. *Folklore du Nivernais et du Morvan*, 5 vols., La Charité-sur-Loire: Thoreau, 1959

Dugast, Francine. *L'Image de l'enfance dans la prose littéraire de 1918 à 1930*, 2 vols., Lille: Presses Universitaires de Lille, 1981

Dupuy, Aimé. *Un personnage nouveau du roman français: l'enfant*, Paris: Hachette, 1931

Esler, Anthony. 'Youth in Revolt: The French Generation of 1830', in Robert J. Bezucha, ed., *Modern European Social History* Lexington, MA: D. C. Heath, 1972, pp. 301–34

Farge, Arlette and Foucault, Michel, eds. *Le Désordre des familles: lettres de cachet des Archives de la Bastille*, Paris: Gallimard/Julliard, 1982

Faure, Alain. 'Enfance ouvrière, enfance coupable', *Les Révoltes logiques*, 13 (1981), 13–35

Fay-Sallois, Fanny. *Les Nourrices à Paris au XIXe siècle*, Paris: Payot, 1980

Fildes, Valerie A. *Breasts, Bottles and Babies*, Edinburgh: Edinburgh University Press, 1986

Fine-Souriac, Agnès. 'La Famille-souche pyrénéenne au XIXe siècle: quelques réflexions de méthode', *Annales ESC*, 32 (1977), 478–87

Flandrin, Jean-Louis. *Les Amours paysannes*, Paris: Gallimard/Julliard, 1975

Families in Former Times: Kinship, Household and Sexuality, transl. Richard Southern, Cambridge: Cambridge University Press, 1979

Fonagy, Peter. *Attachment Theory and Psychoanalysis*, New York: Other Press, 2001.

Fuchs, Rachel Ginnis. *Abandoned Children: Foundlings and Child Welfare in Nineteenth-Century France*, Albany: State University of New York Press, 1984
  'Crimes Against Children in Nineteenth-Century France', *Law and Human Behaviour*, 6 (1982), 237–59

Furet, François and Ozouf, Jacques. *Reading and Writing: Literacy in France from Calvin to Jules Ferry*, Cambridge: Cambridge University Press, 1982

Gaignebet, Claude. *Le Folklore obscène d'enfants*, Paris: G.-P. Maisonneuve et Larose, 1974

Garden, Maurice. *Lyon et les Lyonnais au XVIIIe siècle*, Paris: Les Belles-Lettres, 1970

Gavoille, Jacques. 'Les Types de scolarité: plaidoyer pour la synthèse en histoire de l'éducation', *Annales ESC*, 41 (1986), 923–45

Gélis, J., Laget, M. and Morel, M.-F. *Entrer dans la vie: naissances et enfances dans la France traditionnelle*, Paris: Gallimard/Julliard, 1978

Gerbod, Paul. *La Vie quotidienne dans les lycées et collèges au XIXe siècle*, Paris: Hachette, 1968

Germer, Stefan. 'Pleasurable Fear: Géricault and Uncanny Trends at the Opening of the Nineteenth Century', *Art History*, 22 (1999), 159–83

Gibson, Robert. *Alain-Fournier: Le Grand Meaulnes*, London: Grant and Cutler, 1986

Gildea, Robert. *Education in Provincial France: A Study of Three Departments*, Oxford: Clarendon Press, 1983

Glénisson, Jean. 'Le Livre pour la jeunesse', in *Histoire de l'édition française*, vol. III, *Le Temps des éditeurs*, Paris: Promodis, 1985, pp. 417–43

Glénisson, Jean and Le Men, Ségolène, eds. *Le Livre d'enfance et de jeunesse en France* (Bordeaux: Société des bibliophiles de Guyenne, 1994)

Grew, Raymond and Harrigan, Patrick J. 'L'Offuscation pédantesque: observations sur les préoccupations de J. N. Luc', *Annales ESC*, 41 (1986), 913–22
  School, State and Society: The Growth of Elementary Schooling in Nineteenth-Century France – A Quantitative Analysis, Ann Arbor: University of Michigan Press, 1991

Grew, Raymond, Harrigan, Patrick J. and Whitney, James B. 'La Scolarisation en France, 1829–1906', *Annales ESC*, 39 (1984), 116–48

Harris, Judith Rich. 'Where is the Child's Environment? A Group Socialization Theory of Development', *Psychological Review*, 102 (1995), 458–89

Hawes, Joseph M. and Hiner, N. Ray, eds. *Children in Historical and Comparative Perspective: An International Handbook and Research Guide*, New York: Greenwood Press, 1991

Hellerstein, Erna Olafson, Hume, Leslie Parker and Offen, Karen M., eds. *Victorian Women*, Stanford: Stanford University Press, 1981

Henry, Louis and Houdaille, Jacques. 'Célibat et âge au mariage aux XVIIIe et XIXe siècles en France. II. Age au premier mariage', *Population*, 34 (1979), 403–42

Hewitt, Leah D. *Autobiographical Tightropes*, Lincoln and London: University of Nebraska Press, 1990

Heywood, Colin. *Childhood in Nineteenth-Century France: Work, Health and Education among the Classes Populaires*, Cambridge: Cambridge University Press, 1988

'Innocence and Experience: Sexuality among Young People in Modern France, c. 1750–1950', *French History* (forthcoming)

'On Learning Gender Roles during Childhood in Nineteenth-Century France', *French History*, 5 (1991), 451–66

Holmes, Jeremy. *John Bowlby and Attachment Theory*, Hove: Brunner-Routledge, 1993

Houbre, Gabrielle. *La Discipline de l'amour: l'éducation sentimentale des filles et des garçons à l'âge du romantisme*, Paris: Plon, 1997

Hufton, Olwen. *The Prospect Before Her: A History of Women in Western Europe*, vol. I, *1500–1800*, London: Fontana, 1997

Hwang, C. Philip, Lamb, Michael E. and Sigel, Irving E. eds. *Images of Childhood*, Mahwah, NJ: Lawrence Erlbaum, 1996

James, Allison and Prout, Alan, eds. *Constructing and Reconstructing Childhood: Contemporary Issues in the Sociological Study of Childhood*, London: Falmer Press, 1990

James, Allison, Jenks, Chris and Prout, Alan *Theorizing Childhood*, Cambridge: Polity, 1998

Jenks, Chris. *Childhood*, London: Routledge, 1996

Jonge, Alex de. *Nightmare Culture: Lautréamont and Les Chants de Maldoror*, London: Secker and Warburg, 1973

Kessel, Frank S. and Siegel, Alexander W., eds. *The Child and Other Cultural Inventions*, New York: Praeger, 1983

Kessen, William. 'The American Child and Other Cultural Inventions', *American Psychologist*, 34 (1973), 815–20

The Child, New York: John Wiley, 1965

'Rousseau's Children', *Daedalus*, 107 (1978), 155–66

Klein, Josephine. *Our Need for Others and its Roots in Infancy*, London and New York: Tavistock Publications, 1987

Knibiehler, Yvonne. *Les Pères aussi ont une histoire*, Paris: Hachette, 1987

Knibiehler, Yvonne and Fouquet, Catherine. *L'Histoire des mères du moyen âge à nos jours*, Paris: Editions Montalba, 1980

Lane, Harlan. *The Wild Boy of Aveyron*, London: George Allen and Unwin, 1977

Lebrun, François. *La Vie conjugale sous l'ancien régime*, Paris: Armand Colin, 1975

Lehning, James R. 'Family Life and Wetnursing in a French Village', *Journal of Interdisciplinary History*, 12 (1982), 645–56

Lejeune, Philippe. *Brouillons de soi*, Paris: Seuil, 1998

'Crime et testament: les autobiographies de criminels au XIXe siècle', *Cahiers de semiotique textuelle*, 8–9 (1986), 73–98

Je est un autre: l'autobiographie de la littérature aux médias, Paris: Seuil, 1980

Moi aussi, Paris: Seuil, 1986

Le Moi des demoiselles: enquête sur le journal de jeune fille, Paris: Seuil, 1993

On Autobiography, transl. Katherine Leary, Minneapolis: University of Minnesota Press, 1989

Pour l'autobiographie: Chroniques, Paris: Seuil, 1998

Lejeune, Philippe and Leroy, Claude, eds. 'Le Tournant d'une vie', special issue of *Recherches interdisciplinaires sur les textes modernes*, 10 (1995)

Lejeune, Philippe and Viollet, Catherine. *Genèses du 'Je': manuscrits et autobiographie*, Paris: CNRS, 2000

Lévy, Marie-Françoise. *De mères en filles: l'éducation des françaises, 1850–1880*, Paris: Calmann-Lévy, 1984

Lévy, Marie-Françoise, ed. *L'Enfant, la famille et la Révolution française*, Paris: Olivier Orban, 1990

Lloyd, Rosemary. *The Land of Lost Content: Children and Childhood in Nineteenth-Century French Literature*, Oxford: Clarendon Press, 1992

Luc, Jean-Noël. '"A trois ans, l'enfant devient intéressant . . .": la découverte médicale de la seconde enfance (1750–1900)', *Revue d'histoire moderne et contemporaine*, 36 (1989), 83–112

'L'Illusion statistique', *Annales ESC*, 41 (1986), 887–911

L'Invention du jeune enfant au XIXe siècle: de la salle d'asile à l'école maternelle, Paris: Belin, 1997

Lynch, Katherine. *Family, Class and Ideology in Early Industrial France: Social Policy and the Working-Class Family, 1825–1848*, Madison: University of Wisconsin Press, 1988

Lyons, Martyn. *Readers and Society in Nineteenth-Century France: Workers, Women, Peasants*, London: Palgrave, 2001)

Martin-Fugier, Anne. *La Bourgeoise: femme au temps de Paul Bourget*, Paris: Bernard Grasset, 1983

Mayeur, Françoise. *L'Education des filles en France au XIXe siècle*, Paris: Hachette, 1979

Maynes, Mary Jo. 'Autobiography and Class Formation in Nineteenth-Century Europe: Methodological Considerations', *Social Science History*, 16 (1992), 517–37

'The Contours of Childhood: Demography, Strategy, and Mythology of Childhood in French and German Lower-Class Autobiographies', in *The European Experience of Declining Fertility, 1850–1970*, ed. John R. Gillis, Louise A. Tilly and David Levine, Oxford: Blackwell, 1992

'Leaving Home in Metaphor and Practice: The Roads to Social Mobility and Political Militancy in European Working-Class Autobiography', in Frans van Poppel, Michel Oris and James Lee (eds.), *The Road to Independence: Leaving Home in Western and Eastern Societies, 16th–20th Centuries*, Bern: Peter Lang, 2004, pp. 315–38.

Taking the Hard Road: Life Course in French and German Workers' Autobiographies in the Era of Industrialization, Chapel Hill and London: University of North Carolina Press, 1995

Mension-Rigau, Eric. *L'Enfance au château: l'éducation familiale des élites françaises au vingtième siècle*, Paris: Rivages, 1990

Mercier, Roger. *L'Enfant dans la société du XVIIIe siècle (avant l'Emile)*, Dakar: Université de Dakar, 1961

Motley, Mark. *Becoming a French Aristocrat: The Education of the Court Nobility, 1580–1715*, Princeton: Princeton University Press, 1990

Newton, Michael. *Savage Girls and Wild Boys: A History of Feral Children*, London: Faber and Faber, 2002

Noesser, Laura. 'Le Livre pour enfants', in *Histoire de l'édition française*, vol. IV, *Le Livre concurrencé, 1900–1950*, ed. H. J. Martin and R. Chartier, with J.-P. Vivet, Paris: Promodis, 1986, pp. 457–67;

Nora, Pierre. 'Ernest Lavisse: son rôle dans la formation du sentiment national', *Revue historique*, 228 (1962), 73–106

Nord, Philip, *The Republican Moment: Struggles for Democracy in Nineteenth-Century France*, Cambridge, MA: Harvard University Press, 1995.

O'Brien, Justin. *The Novel of Adolescence in France: The Study of a Literary Theme*, New York: Columbia University Press, 1937

Offen, Karen. 'The Second Sex and the Baccalauréat in Republican France, 1880–1924', *French Historical Studies*, 13 (1983), 252–86

Panter-Brick, Catherine, ed. *Biosocial Perspectives on Children*, Cambridge: Cambridge University Press, 1998

Parias, Louis-Henri, ed. *Histoire générale de l'enseignement et de l'éducation en France*, vol. III, *De la Révolution à l'Ecole républicaine*, by François Mayeur, Paris: G. V. Labat, 1981

Percheron, Annick. *La Socialisation politique*, Paris: Armand Colin, 1993

Perrot, Michelle. 'Dans la France de la Belle Epoque, les "Apaches", premières bandes de jeunes', in *Les Marginaux et les exclus dans l'histoire*, special issue of *Les Cahiers Jussieu*, Paris: Union générale d'éditions, 1978, pp. 387–407.

'Les Enfants de la Petite Roquette', *L'Histoire*, 100 (1987), 30–8

'Journaux intimes: jeunes filles au miroir de l'âme', *Adolescence*, 4 (1986), 29–36

'Sur la notion d'intérêt de l'enfant et son émergence au XIXe siècle', *Actes: Les Cahiers d'action juridique*, 37 (1982), 40–3

'Sur la ségrégation de l'enfance au XIXe siècle', *Psychiatrie de l'enfance*, 25 (1982), 179–206

Peyronnet, Jean-Claude. 'Famille élargie ou famille nucléaire? L'exemple du Limousin au début du XIXe siècle', *Revue d'histoire moderne et contemporaine*, 22 (1975), 568–82

Pineau, Gaston and Le Grand, Jean-Louis. *Les Histoires de vie*, 3rd edn, Paris: Presses Universitaires de France, 2002

Pomfret, David M. *Young People and the European City: Age Relations in Nottingham and Saint-Etienne, 1890–1914*. Aldershot: Ashgate, 2004

Primault, Max, Lhong, Henry and Malrieu, Jean. *Terres de l'enfance: le mythe de l'enfance dans la littérature contemporaine*, Paris: Presses Universitaires de France, 1961

Prost, Antoine. *Histoire de l'enseignement en France, 1800–1967*, Paris: Colin, 1968

Racault, Jean-Michel, ed. *Etudes sur Paul et Virginie et l'oeuvre de Bernadin de St-Pierre*, Paris: Didier-Erudition, 1986

Rahikainen, Marjatta. *Centuries of Child Labour: European Experience from the Seventeenth to the Twentieth Century*, Aldershot: Ashgate, 2004

Redfern, W. D. *Queneau: Zazie dans le métro*, London: Grant and Cutler, 1980

Riley, Denise. *War in the Nursery: Theories of the Child and Mother*, London: Virago, 1983

Robinson, Philip. *Bernardin de Saint-Pierre: Paul et Virginie*, London: Grant and Cutler, 1986

Rollet, Catherine. *Les Enfants au XIXe siècle*, Paris: Hachette, 2001

Rollet-Echalier, Catherine. *La Politique à l'égard de la petite enfance sous la Troisième République*, Paris: Presses universitaires de France, 1990

Roumajon, Yves. *Enfants perdus, enfants punis: histoire de la jeunesse délinqante en France: huit siècles de controverses*, Paris: Robert Laffont, 1989

Roynette, Odile. *'Bons pour le service': l'expérience de la caserne en France à la fin du XIXe siècle*, Paris: Belin, 2000

Sauvy, Alfred and Girard, Alain. 'Les Diverses Classes sociales devant l'enseignement', *Population*, 20 (1965), 205–32

Schnapper, Bernard. 'La Correction paternelle et le mouvement des idées au dix-neuvième siècle (1789–1935)', *Revue historique*, 263 (1980), 319–49

   'Le Père, le procureur et l'enfant: le mythe des enfants martyrs au XIXe siècle', in *Voies nouvelles en histoire du droit*, Paris: Presses Universitaires de France, 1991), pp. 509–22.

   'Le Temps des poupards (le bébé au XIXe siècle)', in *Voies nouvelles en histoire du droit: la justice, la famille, la répression pénale (XVIe–XXe siècles)*, Paris: Presses Universitaires de France, 1991, pp. 509–22

Scott, Malcolm. *Bernanos: Journal d'un curé de campagne*, London: Grant and Cutler, 1997

Seeley, Paul. 'O Sainte Mère: Liberalism and the Socialization of Catholic Men in Nineteenth-Century France', *Journal of Modern History*, 70 (1998), 862–91

Segalen, Martine. *Historical Anthropology of the Family*, transl. J. C. Whitehouse and Sarah Matthews, Cambridge: Cambridge University Press, 1986

   Love and Power in the Peasant Family, transl. Sarah Matthews, Oxford: Basil Blackwell, 1983

Seignolle, Claude. *Le Folklore de la Provence*, Paris: Maisonneuve et Larose, 1963

Senior, Nancy. 'Aspects of Infant Feeding in Eighteenth-Century France', *Eighteenth-Century Studies*, 16 (1983), 367–88

Shattuck, Roger. *The Forbidden Experiment: The Story of the Wild Boy of Aveyron*, New York: Kodansha International, 1994

Shorter, Edward. *The Making of the Modern Family*, London: Fontana, 1976

Singer, Barnett. *Village Notables in Nineteenth-Century France: Priests, Mayors, Schoolmasters*, Albany: State University of New York Press, 1985

Skolnick, Arlene, ed. *Rethinking Childhood: Perspectives on Development and Society*, Boston and Toronto: Little, Brown and Company, 1976

Snyders, Georges. *La Pédagogie en France aux XVIIe et XVIIIe siècles*, Paris: Presses Universitaires de France, 1965

Sohn, Anne-Marie. *Chrysalides: femmes dans la vie privée (XIXe–XXe siècles)*, 2 vols., Paris: Publications de la Sorbonne, 1996

   Du premier baiser à l'alcove: la sexualité des français au quotidien, Paris: Aubier, 1996

Sroufe, L. Alan. *Emotional Development: The Organization of Emotional Life in the Early Years*, Cambridge: Cambridge University Press, 1996

Strumingher, Laura S. *What Were Little Girls and Boys Made of? Primary Education in Rural France, 1830–1880*, Albany: State University of New York Press, 1983

Sussman, George D. 'Parisian Infants and Norman Wet Nurses in the Early Nineteenth Century: A Statistical Study', *Journal of Interdisciplinary History*, 7 (1977), 637–53

   Selling Mother's Milk: The Wet-Nursing Business in France, 1715–1914, Urbana: University of Illinois Press, 1982

   'The Wet-Nursing Business in Nineteenth-Century France', *French Historical Studies*, 9 (1975), 304–28

Thabault, Roger. *Education and Change in a Village Community: Mazières-en-Gâtine, 1848–1914*, transl. Peter Tregear, New York: Schocken Books, 1971

Thiercé, Agnès. *Histoire de l'adolescence, 1850–1914*, Paris: Belin, 1999

Thiesse, Anne-Marie. 'Mutations et permanences de la culture populaire: la lecture à la Belle Epoque', *Annales ESC*, 39 (1984), 70–91

   Le Roman du quotidien: lecteurs et lectures populaires à la Belle Epoque, Paris: Le Chemin Vert, 1984

Thody, P. M. W. 'Childhood Remembered and Recorded: A Review and Discussion of Three Works by R. N. Coe', *Proceedings of the Leeds Philosophical and Literary Society*, 24 (1993), 3–13

Tilby, Michael. *Gide, les Faux-monnayeurs*, London: Grant and Cutler, 1981

Toursch, Victor. *L'Enfant français à la fin du XIXe siècle, d'après ses principaux romanciers*, Paris: Les Presses modernes, 1939

Tucker, Nicholas. *What is a Child?*, London: Fontana, 1977

Van Gennep, Arnold. *Manuel de folklore français contemporain*, 3 vols., Paris: A. and J. Picard, 1937–58, vols. I.1–I.2, *Du berceau à la tombe*.

   The Rites of Passage (1909), transl. Monika B. Vizedom and Gabrielle L. Caffee, London: Routledge and Kegan Paul, 1960

Vercier, Bruno. 'Le Mythe du premier souvenir: Pierre Loti, Michel Leiris', *Revue d'histoire littéraire de la France*, 75 (1975), 1029–40

Verdier, Yvonne. *Façons de dire, façons de faire: la laveuse, la couturière, la cuisinière*, Paris: Gallimard, 1979

Weissbach, Lee Shai. *Child Labor Reform in Nineteenth-Century France: Assuring the Future Harvest*, Baton Rouge: Louisiana State University Press, 1989

Wood, David, ed. *On Paul Ricoeur: Narrative and Interpretation*, London and New York: Routledge, 1991

Wylie, Laurence. *Chanzeaux: A Village in Anjou*, Cambridge, MA: Harvard University Press, 1966

   Village in the Vaucluse, 2nd edn, Cambridge, MA: Harvard University Press, 1964

Youssef, Nancy. 'Savage or Solitary? The Wild Child and Rousseau's Man of Nature', *Journal of the History of Ideas*, 62 (2001), 245–63

Zanotto, Jacques. 'Simon Parvery, ouvrier des fours (1865–1945)', *Le Mouvement social*, 125 (1983), 125–46

Zeldin, Theodore. *France 1848–1945: Ambition and Love*, Oxford: Oxford University Press, 1979

2. THESES

Chotard-Lioret, Caroline. 'La Société familiale en province: une correspondance privée entre 1870 et 1920', Thèse pour le doctorat, 3e cycle, Université de Paris V, 1983

Vassigh, Darya. 'Les Relations adultes–enfants dans la seconde moitié du XIXe siècle (1850–1914)', 2 vols., Thèse de doctorat en histoire, Université de Paris VII, 1996

Index